D1134975

CHRISTIAN HERITAGE COLLEGE
BY HIM ALL THINGS CONSIST
SAN DIEGO, CALIFORNIA 1970

By John Walton Caughey

HISTORY OF THE PACIFIC COAST

BERNARDO DE GÁLVEZ IN LOUISIANA

MCGILLIVRAY OF THE CREEKS

CALIFORNIA

HUBERT HOWE BANCROFT, HISTORIAN OF THE WEST

◇

Edited by John Walton Caughey

THE EMIGRANTS' GUIDE TO CALIFORNIA
BY JOSEPH E. WARE

HUBERT HOWE BANCROFT

Historian of the West

HUBERT HOWE BANCROFT

HUBERT HOWE BANCROFT

Historian of the West

JOHN WALTON CAUGHEY

UNIVERSITY OF CALIFORNIA PRESS
Berkeley and Los Angeles
1946

UNIVERSITY OF CALIFORNIA PRESS
BERKELEY AND LOS ANGELES
CALIFORNIA

◇

CAMBRIDGE UNIVERSITY PRESS
LONDON, ENGLAND

PRINTED IN THE UNITED STATES OF AMERICA
BY THE UNIVERSITY OF CALIFORNIA PRESS

TO

NANCY AND ARIEL

Preface

IN THE *historiography of western America no name is writ larger than Hubert Howe Bancroft's. He was the first determined collector of the materials on this half continent and the first to undertake to chronicle its history comprehensively and exhaustively. The library that he established is the chief depository of such materials and for a generation has been the area's fountainhead of historical research. Similarly the thirty-nine massive volumes of his* Works *stand today, a full half century after their publication, as the fundamental reference on this vast subject matter and the best reference on a good fraction of the topics which comprise it. Basic to these achievements he had a long career as a businessman reasonably representative of the West in the Gold Rush and post-Gold Rush generations.*

Despite these claims to fame Bancroft has never had a biographer. In a volume entitled Literary Industries, *published in 1890, he put on record a partial narrative of his life, and in* Retrospection *in 1912 he added a few other particulars. There have been fragmentary comments about his collecting, about the launching of his first book, about his method of authorship, but no full-scale treatment. The reason, I believe, is twofold. In common with most of us, Bancroft fell short of perfection. Some of his defects were seized upon, and it came to be the fashion to disparage him not only for these shortcomings but in all that he had done. The result was to becloud his eligibility for biographical attention. An even greater deterrent was the bulk of his published works. These include not only the seven-and-a-half-foot row of* Native Races *and*

History of the Pacific States, *but three other sets, a number of separate books, and a sheaf of pamphlets—in all, some sixty-odd volumes, the majority of them solid and weighty. By their ponderousness they tended to ward off prospective biographers and, it must be admitted, retarded my completing the present effort.*

*In his eighty-five years Bancroft was, among other things, businessman, publisher, collector, historian, essayist, and philosopher. No book of the dimensions of this one could pretend to exhaust such a subject. Its purpose is to perform an introduction; after which, readers who wish to develop the acquaintance further may do so by turning to Bancroft's own volumes and by contemplating the Bancroft Library in its continued functioning. As his biographer, I am tempted to appropriate sentiments expressed by his sales agents in 1882: "It may sound to you, Mr———, something like exaggeration, or at least superabundance of enthusiasm, what I have said about Mr Bancroft and his work. But I can assure you, sir, the half or the tenth has not been told."**

In the prosecution of this study I have had financial assistance, to cover microfilming of certain materials and typing the final draft, from the research funds of the University of California. The staff of the Bancroft Library has been unfailingly helpful: Director Herbert E. Bolton gave counsel and encouragement; the late Herbert I. Priestley supplied much information and constantly facilitated my investigation; and Mrs. Eleanor Bancroft went out of her way to see to it that the library's resources were at my disposal. Mr. and Mrs. Philip Bancroft patiently answered a multitude of questions and made available family papers and mementos. Information essential to the final chapter was supplied by President Robert Gordon Sproul. Lawrence Clark Powell, Lindley Bynum, and the late William B. Rice gave material and friendly

* *Information for Agents to Assist in Selling the Works of Hubert Howe Bancroft* (San Francisco, 1882), p. 8.

assistance. The final manuscript had its cowlicks expertly smoothed by Harold A. Small, to the considerable improvement of its clarity and precision.

I am obliged to a large number of persons—students, friends, and comparative strangers—who in recent years have listened to me talk about Bancroft. Several parts of this book had that sort of tryout. A summarizing paper entitled "Hubert Howe Bancroft, Historian of Western America," was read at the St. Louis meeting of the Mississippi Valley Historical Association in April, 1944, and was published in the American Historical Review *a year later.*

Through all the time that this book has been in process I have become increasingly indebted to my wife and daughters, LaRee, Nancy, and Ariel, for encouragement and endurance. To them my particular thanks.

J. W. C.

Los Angeles, September 2, 1945

Contents

CHAPTER PAGE

1. New England in Ohio 1
2. Introduction to Bookselling 12
3. Off to California 18
4. Teamster and Clerk 30
5. Success Story 41
6. The House of Bancroft 57
7. Diligent Collector 67
8. A Half Continent's History 86
9. The Men on the Fifth Floor 99
10. Excursion into Anthropology 118
11. Managed Reviews 140
12. Spanish Americanist 157
13. Historian of California 182
14. Annals of Neighboring States 201
15. Essayist 231
16. Process of Authorship 253
17. Marketing the Works 278
18. Near Disaster 301
19. Subscription Publisher 313
20. Bitter Harvest 330
21. Time His Ally 349
22. Successful Retirement 366
23. Recognition 382
24. Epilogue: The Bancroft Library 391

Index 409

Illustrations

FACING PAGE

Hubert Howe Bancroft iii
Bancroft as a Young Man 32
Portions of a Letter from Hubert Howe Bancroft to His Father, Mother, and Sister, July 11, 1864 48–49
Henry Lebbeus Oak 96
Second Floor of the Bancroft Library 97
First Floor of the Bancroft Library 97
The Beginning of the Bancroft Collection 112
The Fifth Floor 112
Author's Study in the Bancroft Library 113
The Bancroft Library in 1881 113
Hubert Howe Bancroft in 1879 256
Hubert Howe Bancroft in 1882 257
Bancroft Library Time Book, March, 1883 272
Receipt for Payment by a Subscriber to Bancroft's Works 272
Draft on a Subscriber to Bancroft's Works 273
Letter from Hubert Howe Bancroft to His Granddaughter Lucy, April 16, 1913 368–369
Hubert Howe Bancroft in 1912 384
A Definition of the Province of History 385

[The portraits of Bancroft as a young man and in 1879 and 1882, and the letters of 1864 and 1913, were made available by Mr. and Mrs. Philip Bancroft. The receipt for payment by a subscriber and the draft on a subscriber came from Mr. Fred Oster. The other illustrations are by courtesy of the Bancroft Library.]

1

New England in Ohio

Thus it happened that I was born into an atmosphere of pungent and invigorating puritanism. . . . It may be good to be born into a hotbed of reverential sectarianism; it is surely better, at some later time, to escape it.

Hubert Howe Bancroft, *Literary Industries,* 63–64

BOOKS ARE THE SYMBOL of Hubert Howe Bancroft's career. Throughout the threescore and ten years of his maturity, trafficking in books was his business. He succeeded well; but, fortunately for his enduring fame, this handling of books led to another interest. He became a collector of printed volumes, of lesser breeds of printing such as newspapers and magazines, and of manuscripts, which in a manner of speaking are books unprinted. Developing an active interest in the content of his collection, he next became a creator of books. Using an industrial technique, he brought forth an array of volumes that made him the largest contributor to the history of western North America. Nor was this the end of his bookmaking. In his later years, whenever he had a message which another might have delivered from the lecture platform or in a magazine article, he sat down and wrote at length. Thus, from his first employment in a Buffalo bookstore to his last volume of essays, books were the center of his world.

No less striking was the way in which he became at one with the West. It took less than two years to make him a Californian. A journey back to the States quickly supplied the proof that the West was where he felt at home, and forthwith he returned to the land of his choice. When he took up collecting, it was of western materials, and when he turned to writing, the West was his theme. Had he continued a cramped easterner, there is little likelihood that he would have essayed so large a task as writing the history of half the continent. It was also characteristically western that he was undaunted by his lack of technical preparation for the profession of history. All around him in the West men were doing things they had not been taught how to do. John Marsh was practicing medicine with his Harvard bachelor of arts diploma as a certificate, and Charles Crocker was building the Central Pacific without benefit of any formal training in engineering. To practice history-writing without a license seemed no more presumptuous.

In the patterns of his thought Bancroft was likewise a personification of the West. On the issues of his day, in common with the majority of the Gold Rush and post-Gold Rush generations, he was no placid fence-sitter. He came quickly to an opinion, and, having come to it, was most outspoken in expressing it. Indeed, in voicing an adverse judgment, perchance on John Charles Frémont, Leland Stanford, the backers of Abe Reuf, or the immigrants from eastern Europe, he was occasionally prone to an extravagance of statement that was bad taste, whatever the validity of the judgment. Yet hyperbole, as well as outspokenness, was characteristic of the West in which he lived.

Important though books and the West were to Bancroft, neither was an original element in his make-up. His mother, it is true, extracted his name from a book circulated by the Sunday-School Union, 200 Mulberry Street, New York, *Pierre and His Family: or A Story of the Waldenses,* by the author of *Lily Douglas.*[1] Yet his people were not really bookish, and not until his sixteenth year did he start to become a bookman. He was not a native Californian, and not until he was twenty did he expose himself to the influence of the Far West. All the

[1] The family copy in the possession of Philip Bancroft bears this inscription: "This is where my mother (the best of women) got my name. H. H. B."

years of his childhood and youth were cast in different surroundings. There is, in fact, good reason to believe that the forces of heredity, together with the formative influence of his early environment and upbringing, had determined the major contours of his character before these other influences had a chance to exert their sway.

Bancroft came of sturdy New England stock. His family tree, though boasting no truly illustrious persons, is a respectable regional average. It has standard early American characteristics, such as large crops of children, and is distinctly of New England in the preponderance of its English surnames: White, Spelman, Pratt, Ashley, Phelps, Howe, and the like. Honest, hard-working, competent men and women predominate, with a sprinkling of sprightly or salty characters, in whom, by a moderate exercise of the imagination, one can discern qualities that Bancroft was eventually to demonstrate.[2]

First on the list is John Bancroft, who came from London on the sailing ship "James" in 1632. Of John nothing more is remarked than that he brought the Bancroft name to America and that his coming antedated Hubert Howe Bancroft's birth by exactly two hundred years. Halfway down the line from John to Hubert was great-grandfather Samuel Bancroft, vividly recalled by his grandson as "a tall, thin, voluble old gentleman, fond of company, jokes, and anecdotes. . . . He served in the French and Indian war, and afterward in the Revolutionary war with the rank of Lieutenant. He was paid off in continental money, receiving it in sheets, which he never cut apart. . . . He was very fond of relating incidents of the war, and was never happier than when surrounded by old comrades and neighbors, talking over different campaigns, with a mug of cider warming before the fire."[3]

[2] For an introduction to his forebears consult [Hubert Howe Bancroft], *A Golden Wedding* [San Francisco, 1872]; *Literary Industries* (San Francisco, 1890), 47–63; and *Retrospection* (New York, 1912), 74–77.

[3] A. A. Bancroft, "Recollections of the Bancroft Family," in *A Golden Wedding*, 40–41.

Another great-grandfather, Gerard Pratt, was even more of a character. He had, we are told, "enough peculiarities, which were not affected, to entitle his name to be placed on the roll of great men or men of genius." The eccentricity best remembered smacks but vaguely of genius. "Constantly in season and out of season he wore his hat, a broad-brimmed quakerish-looking affair, although he was no quaker. It was the last article of apparel to be removed at night, when he placed it on the bedpost, the first to be put on in the morning when he arose, and it was removed during the day only when he asked the blessing at the table, which was done standing, and during that time he held it in his hand, replacing it before beginning to eat."[4]

Grandfather Azariah Bancroft was quite eclipsed by these vibrant figures. He is described as a man of good judgment but afflicted with asthma. This last uncomfortable fact is especially worth noting since grandson Hubert had to endure a like susceptibility. Traditive accounts have more to say about Azariah's wife, Tabitha, who "did not possess great physical force, but managed to accomplish no inconsiderable work in rearing a large family, and providing both for their temporal and spiritual wants." Tabitha had eleven children. Two died in infancy. With nine youngsters to feed and clothe, and in a day when clothing meant homespun, made with hand cards, spinning wheel, and loom, and when other household tasks were equally laborious, Tabitha had her hands full. As one of her sons said, "It can be well imagined that my mother was much occupied in her daily duties." He hastened to add, however, that she found time to attend to the instruction of her children.[5]

On his mother's side, Bancroft's American ancestors were less numerous. The fault was mainly John Howe's. Born in

[4] Bancroft, *Literary Industries,* 48.

[5] A. A. Bancroft, "Recollections of the Bancroft Family," in *A Golden Wedding,* 42–45.

London in 1650, John did not come to America until much later. At New Haven, Connecticut, he bought a farm, but not until he was sixty did he marry and not until he was eighty did he beget Ephraim, who, in time, was to be Bancroft's great-grandfather. Curtis Howe, next in descent, upheld the tradition of longevity by reaching the ripe old age of ninety-eight. Thereby, he and John, with incidental assistance from Ephraim, set a record almost unbelievable. Curtis' death in 1870 was 220 years removed from his grandfather's birth.[6]

This Curtis Howe, Bancroft insists, was the best man that ever lived. Deeply religious, he found complete happiness in his absolute faith, which he expressed in a life of benign kindness. His one quirk as an old man was to distrust steam railroads and steamboats. "He was a little doubtful about the newfangled, rattling, screeching, bellowing method of travelling, and he preferred the old sure way, horses and wagons."[7] Nevertheless, for the sake of seeing several of his children and grandchildren he finally, at ninety-four, committed himself to steamer and railroad to travel the Panama route from Kansas to California and back again.

Bancroft's parents, Azariah Ashley Bancroft and Lucy Howe, were about what would be expected of such forebears as these. Though born in Massachusetts and Vermont, as children they were caught up in the westward movement and deposited at sixteen on adjoining farms in Ohio. The Howes had accomplished this in one move; the Bancrofts in two, to Pennsylvania in 1809, and to Ohio in 1814. When Ashley met Lucy, it was a case of love at first sight. But Ashley, besides being bashful, was somewhat of a stammerer. It took him seven years to come out with a proposal (and then it was by writing). Meanwhile, Lucy had become a schoolmarm, following thus the example of her father, her brother, and a whole host of Howes, who, according to Bancroft, had teaching in

[6] Curtis Howe, "Family Sketch Written in 1857," in *A Golden Wedding*, 51–53; Bancroft, *Literary Industries*, 54–55.
[7] Bancroft, *Literary Industries*, 55.

the blood. Shortly after their marriage, Ashley contracted to build a large brick residence at Newark, Ohio. Part of the payment was a hundred-acre farm near Granville. There he built another house, this time of stone quarried from a near-by hill, and this one for his own family.

In 1840 Ashley sold this place and moved with his family to the fertile bottom lands near New Madrid, Missouri. After three years of fine crops and poor markets, and of being shaken by ague and earthquakes, Ashley and Lucy and their children returned to Granville, and tried a new start, but without the house and farm. In 1850 Ashley set off with a Licking County company for the California gold fields. He was back in Ohio by 1852. From 1861 to 1864 he was the Indian agent at Fort Simcoe in Washington, after which San Francisco was his home.[8]

From these scattered glimpses of his antecedents it would appear that Bancroft came honestly by a number of his characteristics. The eighty-six years that he attained were not phenomenal in his family. His father and mother celebrated their golden wedding anniversary and lived on into their eighties. Two of his father's brothers also celebrated golden wedding anniversaries. Two great-grandmothers attained the advanced age of ninety-six, another died of an accident at ninety-five, not to mention Grandfather Howe's ninety-eight years. Bancroft was like his father in having a certain restlessness and more than a little shyness. From almost any of the group he might have inherited the itch to move westward to a new frontier. Brothers, uncles, and cousins, as well as his father and mother, preceded or followed him to the Far West.

Hubert Howe Bancroft was born on May 5, 1832, at Granville, Ohio.[9] The time and place were but a step removed from

---

[8] *Ibid.*, 54–62.

[9] Descriptions of Granville are to be found in Hubert Howe Bancroft, Ohio Yankees: Philip Bancroft, His Book, a manuscript volume in the possession of the son for whom it was written; in Bancroft, *Literary Industries*, 56–71; and in Bancroft, *Retrospection*, 74–89.

actual frontier conditions, yet pioneer characteristics were less conspicuous than what Bancroft labeled "an atmosphere of pungent and invigorating puritanism."[10] Granville owed its existence to a group migration from Granville, Massachusetts, a Puritan swarming that had brought along the name and so much of the thought patterns of the parent community as to make it essentially a bit of New England. In this transplanting to Ohio, Puritanism was but slightly diluted. In the two centuries, however, since it had first been brought to America, it had lost some of its harsher features. Stocks and pillory had disappeared, witches no longer disturbed, and the more forbidding elements of dogma, such as belief in infant damnation, were losing much of their hold. There remained the stern rectitude of Puritan ethics, which in Bancroft's youth was as visible in the Ohio Granville as in New England itself.

Superficially, this ethics was made manifest in a strenuous observance of the Sabbath: sermons morning and afternoon, Sunday School, an evening service, and a generous measure of personal and family devotions. The older members of the community, like their forefathers in New England, found solace and exhilaration in this heroic regimen. The younger generation was almost ready to complain that it was dampening to the spirit. Education likewise was stressed. Throughout the whole Puritan belt of Ohio no town was reckoned complete that did not have its college or academy. Probably more fundamental was the emphasis on the homely virtues, such as thrift and work. Laziness rather than money was regarded as the root of all evil, and children at an early age were taught by precept, example, and experience that the work of the world must go on. Save for an interlude of ten years that is to be credited to his first wife's influence, the churchgoing habit did not take full hold on Bancroft. As to schooling, he stopped short even sooner, after only a brief enrollment in the local academy. The habits of industry, however, he kept.

---

[10] Bancroft, *Literary Industries,* 63.

Several anecdotes of his boyhood have been handed down. It is said that he read the Bible at the age of three years, a feat which the modern psychologist would interpret as indicative of a high I. Q., but which Bancroft dismissed with the remark that it "saved much reading of the book later."[11] In grammar school he was not a happy scholar. On one occasion in particular, when his mother's brother was the schoolmaster, he came to a dead halt over this uncle's text on grammar. His mother, of the schoolteaching Howes, took her young son out of school and gave him grammar lessons at home.

More painful was the episode of the stolen rake teeth. "Stolen" is a hard word, but so was the punishment of the young offender, who made off with three shiny rake teeth from a local factory and, when asked where he got them, fibbed first that he found them and second that a man gave them to him. For the theft and for each of the lies the rod was applied, all to the tune of prayers and exhortations, after which the teeth had to be returned with suitable apology. Bancroft's reminiscent version is that he learned his lessons: first, that one lie would have been better than two; and second, that wickedness did not pay—"at least on so small a scale."[12]

Several years later, at the age of eleven, he performed his most brilliant youthful exploit. One dark night he was dispatched with team and wagon to drive six miles north to Fredonia. In the bed of the wagon were five runaway slaves traveling the Underground Railroad toward Canada. The trip exposed him to no greater danger than a chance of his dozing off and slipping from the seat, but when safely back at dawn he was the triumphant hero.[13] As early as 1836 Bancroft's father had boldly espoused the abolition cause, and incidentally that of freedom of speech. Some speakers came to town to plead for abolition, then of little popularity in New Eng-

[11] Bancroft, *Retrospection*, 79.
[12] *Ibid.*, 79–80.
[13] Bancroft, *Literary Industries*, 71–73; Bancroft, *Retrospection*, 85.

land or Ohio. The use of the church building where Granville's town meetings were held was denied them. Bancroft's father made them welcome in a new barn he had just built, where the meetings were uneventful except for a rotten-egging of the speakers as they were leaving town at the conclusion of the series.[14]

Of this incident, which took place when he was four, Bancroft pretended to no direct recollection. The presidential campaign of 1840, on the contrary, was vivid in his memory. Granville was strongly Whig, the Whig candidate was an Ohioan, and the log-cabin-and-hard-cider motif had particular appeal to these frontier-conscious folk. An eight-year-old boy at the time, Bancroft went with the rest of Granville to a demonstration at Newark, the county seat. There was a jointed liberty pole, 270 feet high; log cabins on wheels, drawn by as many as twenty yoke of oxen; great canoes hollowed out of fifty-foot logs; barbecue, ham, chicken, cakes, gingerbread, pie, cheese, and barrels of hard cider; speeches, songs, cheers, and fist fights. In the years to come Bancroft was to be witness and partisan in many political contests, stretching through the Civil War and Reconstruction periods to the San Francisco graft prosecution and California's Lincoln-Roosevelt League, or Hiram Johnson reform movement. In reminiscence, however, the Granville Whigs of 1840 seemed unsurpassed in the intensity of their approach to politics.[15]

A quarter century later, Bancroft revisited the scene of his youth. He found, of course, that Granville had shrunk, that the Sugarloaf and Alligator hills were much smaller than he had thought, that the stone house his family had lost in the move to Missouri was not the mansion of his recollection, and that the brook where he had fished for minnows was the merest rivulet. As he went the rounds of his boyhood haunts, a

---

[14] Bancroft, *Retrospection,* 84–85. The principal of these abolitionist speakers was the well-known James G. Birney.

[15] *Ibid.,* 87–89.

pleasant melancholia came over him. He recalled a few joys: the golden sweet apples of a certain tree; Sunday-night nut-cracking, as a reward for "keeping" Saturday night; the barnyard where he used to try to ride unbroken colts. Yet for the most part his memories were of a sadder cast and led him to the conclusion that his youth had been unhappy. He remembered how he had hated the chores about the house and barn. He remembered the stubble in the hayfield that had hurt his bare feet. He remembered, as a lad of six or seven, bursting into tears after several hours of riding the plowhorse in the hot cornfield. He remembered the persistent feeling of frustration that had afflicted him after they had lost the stone house. At the school he recalled chiefly the Howe grammar and other experiences painful or humiliating. Most of all, he remembered being a timid and retiring boy, into whom it had been dinged that, no matter what the provocation, he must not strike back. Although Bancroft recognized a certain validity to this principle as an adult way of life, he was equally convinced that it had brought bitter suffering to his sensitive childhood nature.[16]

Doubtless there is a degree of exaggeration in these recollections of the infelicities of his childhood. His parents had been unfailingly kind, and several of his complaints are against the time rather than the place of his youth. He was quick to point out the advantages of a Puritan upbringing, and often congratulated himself that as a youngster he had been held under reins too tight rather than too loose. He affirmed that the truest wisdom was to avoid excesses of every kind, but on the whole he thought excess of goodness better than excess of wickedness.

Nevertheless, he was doubly glad that at sixteen he got away from Puritan Granville, that "hotbed of reverential sectarianism." One reason was the manifold restraints in Puritanism itself. Another and more powerful one was the limited future

[16] Bancroft, *Literary Industries,* 73–88.

that the place seemed to hold for him. "Success there," he reflected, "would [have been] a hundred acres of land, a stone house, six children, an interest in a town store or a gristmill, and a deaconship in the church."[17]

From such a fate, respectable though it would have been, Bancroft was rescued by becoming a westerner and a man of books. The process of rescue was assisted, no one can say exactly how much, by the solid traits he had inherited from his New England ancestors and by the habits and ideals that had been ingrained in him as he grew up in this New England in Ohio.

[17] *Ibid.*, 95.

2

Introduction to Bookselling

Into that bookseller's shop I went with all the untempted innocence of a child.

Hubert Howe Bancroft, *Literary Industries,* 115

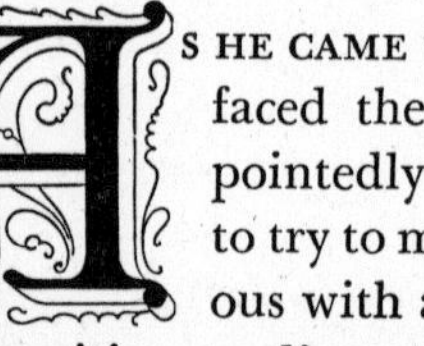

AS HE CAME to the threshold of manhood, Bancroft faced the problem, which comes more or less pointedly to every young man, of deciding what to try to make of himself. His parents were generous with advice and encouragement but had no disposition to dictate the choice. Abetted, however, by the influence of the maternal side of his family, Granville supplied a social compulsion toward further schooling. The prospect of going to college and becoming a professional man, perhaps a lawyer, had its attractions, and in the winter of 1847–1848 he pitched in to prepare himself for college.

As a companion in these studies he had his cousin, Edgar Hillyer, subsequently a federal judge in Nevada. Bancroft describes him as an able and versatile young chap, competent in athletics, nimble on the violin, well read, apt in debate, in age one year his senior but in achievements more advanced. Assisted by this comrade and stimulated by his competition, Bancroft made good progress, in spite of having a heavy load of chores morning and night and occasional interruptions when other work was to be done. Soon, however, Hillyer completed his preparations and went on to college, leaving Bancroft alone. Alone, it became more difficult to keep at his studies. Realizing also what sacrifices his parents would have to make to put him through college, he concluded that it would be wiser to adopt some other course that would lead more quickly to financial independence.[1]

An alternative was at hand. Bancroft, with a fondness for interpreting his personal history in terms of trivial causation, attributed it to a rainstorm and the muddy condition of Granville's streets. His sister, crossing such a street one day on her way to school, had chanced to encounter a sandy-haired young stranger who chivalrously stepped off the plank that she might pass. This meeting soon led to a proposal, and presently to marriage. The brother-in-law thus acquired, a certain George H. Derby, was proprietor of a bookstore in Buffalo. The enthusiasm with which he spoke of the book business kindled Bancroft's interest and led at length to acceptance of the often-repeated suggestion that he come to Buffalo and go to work in Derby's store.[2]

It was in August, 1848, that Bancroft left home and set out to make his own way in the world. His departure was as befitted a country boy going off to the city, or the hero of a standard success story launching his career; from Granville to Cleveland he worked his passage on the canalboat by riding a tow horse. The rest of the journey was made in style on a lake steamer. At Buffalo his sister made him welcome, showed him about the city, took him to visit a political convention then in session, and, most thrilling of all, dropped in with him at the bookstore.

The next Monday he went to work in this, to him, mammoth establishment. His first task was in the bindery, folding and stitching the reports of the above-mentioned convention. He continued in the bindery until October, when that department of the business was sold. For a time his position was undefined and, for that reason, "purgatorial." After it had been made clear that he was not indispensable, he was assigned to the bottom rung of the ladder in the countinghouse.

[1] These matters are related in Bancroft, *Literary Industries,* 89–99.
[2] *Ibid.,* 89, 99–109.

There he tarried for six months, the victim of many jibes and taunts because of his "country angularities," and made further unhappy because his brother-in-law seemed utterly indifferent to his hopes of learning the business and advancing in it. At the time, Bancroft was convinced that Derby disliked him and was persecuting him. Years later, he came round to the opinion that Derby was merely following what he considered the proper way of starting a boy in a business career. Bancroft was also ready to admit that he had been stubborn, headstrong, impatient, and unamiable. At the end of six months, when the head bookkeeper told him he was discharged, it was humiliating, but also a relief.

From this discouragement he rebounded with quick resiliency. He had not been on the payroll and consequently had no money saved up, but he determined to launch out in bookselling on his own account. Derby lent him enough for his fare back to Ohio and gave further evidence of cordiality, and perhaps of confidence, by supplying him several cases of books on credit. Hastening home to Granville, he borrowed a horse and wagon from his father, drove to Mansfield to pick up his books, and then, for the next four months, jogged about over Ohio peddling his wares to whatever country merchants would take them.

He did so well with this first consignment and with additional shipments ordered from Buffalo that by the end of the summer he had squared all his accounts, covered his expenses, and acquired money enough besides to buy a silver watch and a black broadcloth suit. To top it off, he was invited back to Buffalo to a regular clerkship at a salary of $100 a year. His triumphant return to the scene of his earlier discomfiture was more than a vindication; it was a specific that dispelled his former moroseness and kindled his self-confidence. The immediate result, one gathers, was garish to behold. The seventeen-year-old youth bought himself a high hat and a cane, surreptitiously smoked an occasional cigar, and affected gaudy ties and a flashy ring. He thought of himself as the cynosure of all attention, and all the girls, he was sure, were in love with him.[3]

In his reminiscent fifties Bancroft looked back upon the next few years of his life with puritanic remorse. As he paints it, he fell into bad ways, "tramping the streets at night with jovial companions, indulging in midnight suppers, and all-night dancings." Or again, in more extreme terms: "Six years of my young life as good as squandered, in some respects worse, for instead of laying the foundation for health, purity, intellect, I was crushing my God-given faculties, damming the source of high thoughts and ennobling affections, and sowing by Stygian streams the wild seeds of perdition." Like many another oldster, he coveted the chance to relive his youth in the light of the wisdom that maturity and experience had brought him.[4]

The two or three pages in which Bancroft goes on in this vein, if taken literally, convict him of a life of blackest sin. Other circumstances suggest that his self-recrimination is unduly bitter. His impulse toward wickedness seems to have been entirely superficial. When he left Buffalo for California, this whole pattern of conduct was dropped as suddenly as he had picked it up. In spite of his neglect of opportunities, he attended well enough to business; Derby was ready to entrust an important commission to him. Furthermore, the part of his wildness that was not merely the exuberance of youth can be explained in terms of protest against the authoritarianism of his brother-in-law. Derby was an odd mixture of kindliness and cruelty. The peculiarity of his harshness was that he centered it on his relatives and particularly on whatever youth was under his closest guardianship. After Bancroft's return from book peddling in Ohio, the butt of his brother-in-law's nagging was one of Derby's younger brothers. Yet a measure of disciplinary reproof and neglect was left for

---

[3] *Ibid.*, 109–112. [4] *Ibid.*, 114–116.

Bancroft, and it was the chafing under this probably well-meant hazing that impelled him to whatever excesses he did indulge in.

Meanwhile, the cable was being spun that was to draw him to California. In January, 1848, James Marshall discovered gold in the race of the mill he was building for Sutter at Coloma. Almost a full year elapsed before the news of this discovery occasioned any excitement in the eastern part of the United States, but by the early months of 1849 even the placid town of Granville was astir with the gold fever. Among those infected was Bancroft's father, veteran already of several moves westward. A man in his fifties, he was about twice the age of the average forty-niner, and perhaps on that account it took him another year to make up his mind to go. By February, 1850, the die was cast, and a month later he sailed from New York. Bancroft was half of a mind to go along, but did not because he was "more absorbed in flirtations, oyster suppers, and dancing parties than fascinated by the prospect of digging for gold."[5]

Others of his kinsmen emigrated to the Far West, and from one of them in Oregon in January, 1851, came an order for a substantial shipment of books. Besides filling this order, Derby ventured three other shipments to the Pacific Coast. One was lost by fire, and another because the consignee failed in business, but the third yielded a profit of 75 per cent. Set against the aura of fabulous riches which then enhaloed California, these transactions set Derby to thinking about commercial prospects in the golden West. He made it his favorite topic of conversation, he indulged in rhapsodic monologues on the book-publishing and bookselling establishment that he might cause to burgeon on the shores of the Pacific, and at times he seemed perilously near to deserting his Buffalo business so that he might gamble for bigger stakes in California.

In the end, Derby settled on a venture less radical but big

[5] *Ibid.*, 117.

enough to tax his financial resources to the utmost. He would send a shipment of some $5,000 worth of goods to California; and he would put in charge of it his young brother-in-law, whose business ability thus far he had been more in the habit of ridiculing than complimenting.[6]

Though still not smitten with a real case of the gold fever, Bancroft readily agreed to go. His major contribution to the project was to persuade a fellow clerk and boon companion, a gangling and amiable Irishman, George L. Kenny by name, to go along. In the three years that had passed since the first mad rush of gold seekers from the States, travel facilities by Panama had been appreciably regularized. Nevertheless, the journey to California was still a long one, and Bancroft was a lad not yet out of his teens. Under the circumstances, a trip to Granville to bid his mother farewell was more than the appropriate gesture. Upon his return to Buffalo he and Kenny made their way to New York City and by the latter part of February, 1852, were ready to board the steamer.[7]

Bancroft's departure for California was unquestionably a major turning point in his career. In the light of the predestinarianism of his Granville background, there is poetic justice that the decision to go was less his than another's.

---

[6] *Ibid.*, 117–119.
[7] *Ibid.*, 119.

3

Off to California

No young man ever left home for the California mines and arrived at San Francisco the same person.
Hubert Howe Bancroft, *Retrospection,* 135

HAD BANCROFT set off for California from Granville in 1849, the chances are he would have taken an overland route. From New York in that first year of gold madness he might easily have joined one of the companies sailing round Cape Horn. By 1852, emigrants were still using the overland trails and heavy freight was sent round the Horn, but the Panama route had become the choice of discriminating travelers.

Even before the discovery of gold, steamer lines by way of the isthmus had been authorized. Congressional interest was on the assumption that merchant steamers would be convertible into fighting ships and that such vessels would help to introduce naval officers to the mysteries of steam. Reflecting also the relative esteem in which the several parts of the Pacific Coast were held in 1848, the subsidy voted was for carrying mail to Oregon. California's gold changed all this. By the time the first steamer reached Panama for its run to San Francisco, gold seekers were crowding the isthmus. Immediately, the New York capitalists who were the enterprisers in this business saw that in passenger-carrying there was a golden harvest that would exceed even the fat mail contracts. As quickly as possible they put additional ships into service, and when they saw that the business was to continue, they had palatial liners of the walking-beam, side-wheel variety built to order for the California run. From 1852 to 1869, when the transcontinental railroad took over most of the passenger business, a minimum of 15,000 to 20,000 traveled westward each year and some 10,000 journeyed eastward. The Atlantic line encountered ruinous competition from the Vanderbilt steamers, but the Pacific Mail Steamship Company profited by as much as 25 to 30 per cent in dividends annually.[1]

To California throughout the score of years from 1849 to 1869 the Panama steamers were more than a convenience; they were the one reliable link connecting with the United States. Technically, to be sure, California was in the Union. On a map showing the western territories it appeared to be contiguous. But so far as regular passenger travel was concerned, and most of the time so far as mail service was concerned, the state was an overseas possession, distant two ocean voyages and an isthmian transit through the territory of a foreign nation.

Californians might be dependent on this steamship line; through their fares they might render tribute to New York capitalists; but they had a sort of revenge. The passenger lists westward were filled so completely with actual and intended Californians and eastward with actual or disillusioned Californians that sociologically the Panama steamers were annexed to California. It was a common saying that one was in California as soon as he walked up the gangplank in New York. Bancroft did not find this literally true, but the five weeks he spent on the way in the spring of 1852 partly prepared him for the California he was to meet.[2]

On the first night out of New York the "Ohio"[3] ran into

[1] For a discussion of the facilities for travel by way of the isthmus see John Haskell Kemble, *The Panama Route, 1849–1869* (Berkeley and Los Angeles, 1943).

[2] Bancroft describes this journey briefly in *Literary Industries,* 120–121, and in *Retrospection,* 116–123. A more detailed account, offered as representative of the average experience of the forty-niners by Panama, appears in his *California Inter Pocula* (San Francisco, 1888), 121–224.

[3] Bancroft is not consistent in his identification of the steamers in which he traveled. In *California Inter Pocula* (124, 152) he asserts that he sailed

stormy weather, wherefore Bancroft's first and most vivid recollection of this voyage had to do with seasickness. His ruminations on this melancholy but ludicrous affliction are spread over several pages. A modest sample is quoted here.

Sea-sickness is a great leveller. It prostrates pride, purges man of his conceit, makes him humble as a little child; it is specially conducive to repentance and after repentance to resignation. I know of nothing, after the first fear of death has passed away, that makes one so ready to die. A great wave places its back under the ship and lifts you up, up, into the very clouds; then it stands from under and you go down, down, with a tickling sensation within, until you stop your breath waiting for the vessel to strike upon the bottom of the sea. Then comes a mingled pitching and rolling, when the innermost loses cohesion, oscillates, rotates and upheaves, when the foundations of the great deep are broken up within you, when the strong man bows himself as it were a woman grinding at a mill, and the mourners go about the cabin like apocalyptic angels, wailing as they pour their vials out; and by this unrest and the revels of devils within, the image of God is degraded into that of a self-acting hydraulic pump. The mind becomes concerned, the brow overcast; it is like clapping on the head a hope-extinguisher, and squeezing the body at once of every rest and comfort flesh aspires to; as if the inner lining of the man were rolled up and wrung out down to the very dregs of gall and bitterness. Then the body assumes a doubling posture, the spinal column becomes flaccid and limpy, the victim is filled with a desire to sink to the floor or lie prostrate; manhood oozes out at the finger's ends, and Caesar becomes like a sick girl.[4]

Other elements in the behavior of passengers and crew caught Bancroft's attention. He comments on homesickness and table manners; on the swinelike treatment of the steerage passengers; on the dilution of the Sabbath at sea. His observations seem surprisingly mature and mellow for a callow

---

from New York on the "George Law" and at Havana transferred to the "Georgia"; in *Retrospection* (116), that the transfer was from the "Ohio" to the "George Law." Neither of these combinations could be correct, because the "George Law," later renamed the "Central America," was not launched until October, 1852, and did not go into the New York–Aspinwall service until a year later (Kemble, *The Panama Route,* 226). Bancroft evidently traveled on the "Ohio" and the "Georgia."

[4] Bancroft, *California Inter Pocula,* 139.

youth of nineteen. They are, in fact, impressions compounded from a dozen or more voyages that he made by Panama or Nicaragua in the era before the railroad short-circuited the steamer route.

Authentic to this first voyage, however, is his recollection of Havana. They sighted the Island of Cuba a few hours before dawn and, in accordance with the port regulations, hove to off the entrance to Havana harbor until sunrise. Bancroft was on deck drinking in the beauty of the tropical scene, glimpsing the waving fronds of his first palm trees, making out the orange groves nestled against the mountain backdrop, impelled to serious thought by Morro Castle sternly commanding the entrance, and inwardly amused at the pompous customs and health officials, who performed their duties "to their dignified satisfaction" before allowing the steamer to enter the port.

While the mail, baggage, and freight were being transferred to the New Orleans steamer that was to take them on to the isthmus, the passengers trooped ashore. Captivated by the exotic beauty of rose-covered walls, the perfume of orange blossoms, the avenues lined by stately palms or orange trees golden with fruit, Bancroft was also entranced by the narrow streets, the broad promenade, the fountains, the magnificent villas, the ornate opera house, the countinghouse with mosaic mirrors, the gay music, and the dark-eyed, half-veiled señoritas. Occasional elements in this foreign culture were not entirely to his liking; for example, the cruelties imposed upon the scrawny nags harnessed to the *volantes,* the two-wheeled cabs of Havana. There is rebuke also in his description of the customs officer who waived the export duty on a thousand Havana cigars in consideration of a half-dollar bribe, pocketed "amidst vehemently gesticulated protestations" which Bancroft took to be "a sort of mock battle between conscience and duty; or it may be he deemed the bribe insufficient to satisfy virtue so august." Bancroft's total impression of Cuba, however, was that it deserved to be called "the most brilliant jewel in the crown of Spain." This fleeting glimpse of Havana made him mindful of the antiquity of Spanish influence in the New World and drew his attention to the effectiveness with which Spain had implanted her civilization.[5]

Kingston, Jamaica, was the next stop. Bancroft was interested in the mechanics of coaling. Some fifty Negro women and girls, with sixty-pound tubs on their heads, marched unconcernedly up the gangplank, all to the tune of loud jests, song, and laughter. More interesting was the sight of the free Negro come into his own. British humanitarians had brought about the freeing of the slaves and the enfranchisement of the blacks some two decades before Bancroft's visit. In the United States these steps were as yet for the future. As a former conductor on the Underground Railroad, Bancroft might have been expected to applaud. Instead, he points out the ludicrous aspects of this black man's paradise "where a white man was as good as a black one" so long as he behaved himself.[6]

Three days later the "Georgia" dropped anchor off Chagres, which since the beginning of the Gold Rush had been the point of disembarking. Now, however, some seven miles of the Panama Railway had been completed, and the owners of the steamship line, who were also owners of the railway, held that the latter should be encouraged by the patronage of the "Georgia's" passengers. Accordingly, the captain lifted anchor and steamed eastward to the bay formerly and at present known as Colón, after the great discoverer, but then known as Aspinwall, in honor of the New York financier prominent in the directorate of the Panama steamship and railway companies. Bancroft admits that there was a thrill in the five-dollar ride on open flatcars to Gatún on the Chagres, but he points out that *bongos* for ascending the river could have been hired as easily and as cheaply before this railroad journey as afterward.

[5] *Ibid.*, 151–153. [6] *Ibid.*, 153–154.

Life on shipboard had tested the adaptability of the passengers; the hiring of the *bongos* was a test of their ingenuity and initiative. There was no set price for boat hire, and singly or in groups the passengers had to bargain with the native and Negro boatman for passage to Gorgona. The boatmen, having dealt with shipload after shipload of California-bound travelers, were experienced hagglers. Bancroft's fellow travelers proved equally determined. They were, he says, "mild-mannered as belted brigands."[7] At length they were off, four to ten of them to a dugout canoe, and, despite the sweltering heat and the rains that descended without warning, alert to the humor inherent in their experiences. The boatmen propelled their craft by poling, or at times by pulling from the shore or wading through rapids. It was a slow and laborious method of travel; the sustained speed was not much better than a mile an hour. Two days and two nights, with some time consumed in rest periods, were required for the fifty-mile ascent to Gorgona.

At Gorgona the wrangling for boats was reënacted, with the difference that saddle and pack animals were now in demand. This bargaining was overshadowed by an encounter with a group of returning Californians who, in effect, were exchanging steamers with Bancroft and his companions. A few had obviously succeeded in their search for gold. Others, though traveling steerage, were taking a fair amount of treasure back to the States. A larger number had fared ill in California, and not a few of these were loud in their denunciation of the land, its possibilities, and its people. Through variegated scenery the trail wound across the isthmus and down to Panama. Bancroft's journey was uneventful, except that his baggage packer collected in advance and absconded with his belongings.

A week's wait in Panama gave him ample time to poke about the city. The crumbling cathedral caught his fancy, as

[7] *Ibid.*, 162.

did the mingling of racial types and of Indian, Spanish, and European styles of dress. But, for all its historic aroma, Panama made no such appeal as Havana had done. As soon as the steamer was readied for the voyage to San Francisco, he was delighted to go aboard. Because of the combination of big tides and shelving beach the steamer had to anchor some distance out in the bay. A prospective passenger mounted the back of a Negro porter for the trip through the surf to a small boat, which conveyed him to the steamer, in this instance the renowned "Panama."

Like other vessels on the Pacific run, the "Panama" was larger and better designed for passenger accommodation than the Atlantic steamers. She was, furthermore, scrupulously clean, and her officers and crew had an attitude of politeness and consideration for the passengers that was in happy contrast to what had been met with earlier. Besides these creature comforts was the lift of spirits that came with the happy thought that the hardships and difficulties of the journey were over. Baggageless though he was, Bancroft lounged under a deck awning and gratefully relaxed. Idly he gazed back across the warm bay and reflected on the quaint, old, drowsy town of Panama, "wakened once a century by a Pizarro, a Morgan, or an influx of Californian gold-seekers."[8]

When the full contingent of 594 passengers was aboard and the baggage, mail, and fast freight were safely loaded, the "Panama" raised anchor and steamed away. For ninety miles the course was almost due south. Then, when Punta Mala was rounded, the captain put to westward, hugging the shore to gain the protection of the forested mountains that buttress this coast. After rounding the island off Punta Mariato, the course shifted somewhat northerly, though of course the trend of the entire coast from Panama to San Francisco called for an inclination more to the west than to the north. The first night was enlivened by a tropical thunderstorm, which Ban-

[8] *Ibid.*, 194–195.

croft found quite unlike those of his native temperate zone. The next day they skirted the shore of Nicaragua, passing San Juan del Sur, where the rival steamship line had its isthmian terminus. Off the Guatemala coast they saw ahead a cloud of smoke on the horizon, which materialized as the steamer from California. This meeting was a highlight of the trip. The Pacific Mail steamships, though they would be dwarfed by modern liners, were in some respects more impressive. They belched forth great clouds of black smoke, their paddle wheels made a show of power that is denied to the modern submerged propeller, and their walking beams lent an ungainly but purposeful air of majesty that the concealed mechanism of a steam turbine or a Diesel motor cannot challenge.

Other episodes enlivened the voyage out of Panama. A fire drill—apparently there had been none on the Atlantic steamers—took the passengers by surprise. A young man succumbed to Panama fever and was buried at sea with the customary solemnity and dispatch. After the strenuous period of the isthmian crossing, most of the passengers were content to take life easy; but for the relief of tedium two avenues opened. One, of which Bancroft disapproved, was gambling: his fellow passengers wagered not only at cards and on the daily log, but also on such impromptu matters as how long it would take some dignified passenger to put off his shoes and put them on again. The other was viewing the varied prospect which this coastal voyage had to offer. The glory of sunset upon a tropical sea seemed to Bancroft to surpass all gorgeous displays of nature that he had previously witnessed. To starboard a constantly changing shoreline, bedecked in the lush foliage of tropical rain forest, wheeled past, and in the background a series of mountain ranges, peaks, and volcanic cones.

At the time of this first voyage Bancroft had only the faintest inklings of the history of this coast. Later he could reflect that his steamer was retracing the route of the early sixteenth-century Spanish navigators from Balboa to Cabrillo, who had first charted this shore from Panama to California; or again that this voyage of a fortnight rapidly paralleled the northwestward push of Spanish colonization which in two and a half centuries had advanced from Panama and southern Mexico to the province of Alta California. Impressions of the magnitude of this Spanish achievement did not awaken an immediate zest for history, but, stored away in Bancroft's mind, they ultimately yielded a historical dividend.

The "Panama's" first scheduled stop was at historic Acapulco, at one time more famous than New York and busier than any other North American port save only Vera Cruz. Its glory and most of its traffic were now departed, and its population had shrunk from 15,000 to 3,000. Deserted and crumbling buildings gave the whole place an aspect of decadence. Bancroft, however, was well pleased with the neatness of the brightly whitewashed buildings of the occupied quarter; he enjoyed the fruit vendors and divers for coins who paddled out to surround the steamer; and he was ecstatic in his descriptions of the mountain-girt and landlocked harbor so placid as to seem a highland lake.

Acapulco, when they arrived, still had on hand about half the passengers and crew of the Nicaraguan steamer "North America," which had run aground on the beach about fifty miles to the south on February 27. No lives had been lost in the beaching of the steamer, though in the sweltering heat at Acapulco a number had sickened and died. Thirty-eight or so of these stranded wayfarers were taken aboard the "Panama." Most of the 400 remaining had to wait until the line's agent at San Francisco chartered a clipper ship to pick them up. This shipwreck was by no means the worst disaster marring the record of early steamer operation in California,[9] but the detention at Acapulco involved suffering and danger as

[9] Data on founderings, shipwrecks, and lesser disasters on the Panama route are set forth in Kemble, *The Panama Route,* 140–145, and in Hubert Howe Bancroft, *History of California* (7 vols.; San Francisco, 1884–1890), VII, 135–136.

well as exasperation. It reminded Bancroft that the way to California was not without hazard.

For several hundred miles beyond Acapulco the "Panama" continued to skirt a hot and steaming shore line, redundant in vegetation and backed by forested mountains. Opposite Mazatlán they steamed across to Cape San Lucas, suddenly exchanging their tropical landscape for one of barren hills and the sparse growth of a semiarid land. At the same time they were met by a bracing northwest wind, bringing the first taste of California's coastal climate

Normally the "Panama" should have steamed right on to San Francisco, but since the coal supply was almost exhausted the captain thought it wise to put into San Diego to refuel. While cordwood was being loaded—this being the only fuel on hand—Bancroft had a chance to appraise this oldest settlement of Alta California. Not yet acquainted with any of the Spanish accounts of the founding, he was interested to check it against the two most widely circulated descriptions, Dana's in *Two Years before the Mast,* and Bayard Taylor's in *Eldorado.* The Gold Rush had changed San Diego but slightly since Taylor had put in there a little more than three years earlier, on the first voyage of the "Panama." Bancroft noted the incongruity of the frame buildings mixed among the tiled adobes of the town. He praised the excellent and commodious bay and, of course, the climate.

At nightfall the "Panama" steamed out of San Diego Bay into the teeth of a storm that grew steadily worse. With unabated fury it continued through the night and through all the next day. It was impossible to make headway against the storm, but the only safety seemed to be in holding the ship nosed into the oncoming seas. This effort took heavy toll of the scant fuel supply and gave all hands concern lest a slip of the helmsman, a breakdown of the machinery, or exhaustion of the fuel should leave the vessel at the mercy of the waves. The "Panama" was relatively new, but she took such a pounding that her seams spread and the pumps could barely keep the water out.

The following night and day were a little less tumultuous. As they plodded forward on their course, the California coast looked greenly inviting. It was spring, and the coastal plain and adjacent slopes, which most of the year are brown, wore their temporary mantle of green. Scattered over this pasture land, herds of cattle and horses frequently appeared, and once or twice the façade of a Franciscan mission structure could be made out.

At nightfall, once more short of fuel by reason of the storm, the captain was obliged to put in at Monterey. It was morning before Bancroft got a good view of the place. He calls the anchorage "an indentation of the coast, scarcely to be called a harbor," yet affording vessels some protection. With the town and its setting he was more taken. "Rising behind a town of five hundred inhabitants, of spacious well-built tiled adobes, intermixed with dwellings of wood, with government buildings, and a fort on an eminence near the water, is an amphitheatre of wooded hills glowing like an illuminated panorama in the warm hazy air."[10] This description is more graphic than Bayard Taylor's, yet is in agreement with the latter's comment, "The town is larger than I expected to find it, and from the water has the air of a large New England village, barring the adobe houses."[11]

For all its picturesque charm, this former capital of California was not a functioning coaling station. No coal was to be had, and no cordwood either. All hands, consequently, had to go ashore to cut wood and get it aboard. The 31st of March was spent thus. That night they steamed northward, and at dawn they were inside the Farallones and approaching the Golden Gate. To travel-weary passengers impatient to be

[10] Bancroft, *California Inter Pocula,* 222.

[11] Bayard Taylor, *Eldorado, or Adventures in the Path of Empire* (2 vols.; London, 1850), I, 51

ashore after their long voyage the ship now seemed to slacken its pace. At length the hovering outside the entrance was over, the "Panama" churned into the bay, turned aside from Angel and Alcatraz islands, and tied up at the Pacific Mail wharf.

Having no baggage to detain him, Bancroft was doubtless one of the first ashore. A bath, a change of clothes, and breakfast were his first wishes, after which it would be time to look around. First impressions, though fleeting, were favorable. A violet haze shrouded the hills, but on the city itself a golden sun was shining—symbolic, it seemed, of the rich metal that had drawn all these emigrants from afar.[12]

---

[12] Bancroft, *California Inter Pocula,* 224.

4

Teamster and Clerk

It was some time in March, 1852, that I first landed in San Francisco. I was not yet twenty years of age, and too absolutely fresh and inexperienced to be anything but honest. Why my late employer, supposed to be possessed of ordinary bookselling sanity, should have sent me at such an age, to such a place, and for such a purpose as to sell and publish books, I could never imagine.

Hubert Howe Bancroft, *Retrospection,* 114

AT THE TIME of Bancroft's arrival, San Francisco was the unchallenged metropolis of a state approaching the quarter-million mark in population. Of this number somewhat more than a tenth had congregated in the excited city sprawled over the sand dunes on the shore of the bay.

With mission and presidio, Spain had established San Francisco as an outpost of empire in 1776. Through threescore years and ten the tiny settlement led a placid existence, witnessing such changes as the substitution of Mexico's flag for Spain's, the coming of sea-otter hunters, of whalers in search of fresh provisions, and of hide-and-tallow traders eager to barter for by-products of the most successful branch of the province's agriculture. All this modified but slightly the routine and the conventions of Spanish American frontier life. Even the infiltration of resident traders from the United States and from England and, in the 'forties, of a few settlers bent on farming, left the pattern essentially unchanged.

In 1846 the tempo quickened. The Bear Flag Revolt on the north shore of the bay roused the provincial authorities and threatened to create an international incident. This movement in turn was interrupted by news that Mexico and the United States were at war. Captain John B. Montgomery, acting for the hesitant Commodore Sloat, sailed into the bay and, unresisted, took charge of the presidio, the secularized mission, and the village of Yerba Buena, which had begun to take shape some eleven years earlier. Besides additional naval forces, the war brought the New York Volunteers, who were expected to do garrison duty and then remain in the province, and a shipload of Mormon colonists under the leadership of Elder Sam Brannan.

Two of Brannan's enterprises were important to Yerba Buena. One was the opening of a hotel called the Portsmouth House, under the proprietorship of a certain John Brown. The other was the founding of a newspaper, the *California Star,* preceded only by Walter Colton's *Californian* at Monterey. A change of greater ultimate consequence is attributed to Washington Bartlett, the first *alcalde* or mayor. Late in January, 1847, he published an ordinance changing the name of Yerba Buena to San Francisco. The move is sometimes explained as a tribute to St. Francis of Assisi. A more prosaic purpose was to make sure that General Vallejo's projected city, Francisca, later named Benicia, would not be mistaken for the bay's chief city.

Notwithstanding its accretions and its new name, San Francisco continued to drowse until several months after the discovery of gold. The initial burst of the gold excitement drew off most of the 800 inhabitants and threatened to reduce the village to a ghost town. Soon, however, a backwash set in from the mines, larger numbers halted on their way to the diggings, and still others came with the express purpose of doing business in San Francisco. The amazing growth of the city is a familiar story: one has read, times over, about the startling increase in its population, the ways of its cosmopolitan and predominantly male citizenry, its muddy streets, its gambling facilities, its problems of law and order. It has frequently been said that San Francisco was built up without plan, without supervision, and without much use of the customary building materials.

Flimsy construction, together with crowded buildings, high winds, and inadequate policing and fire protection, created a hazard which restless and lawless elements in the population took advantage of. Between Christmas Eve, 1849, and June, 1851, six great fires, several of them purposely set, ravaged the business district. The property loss was immense, and many businesses were ruined, but the city was cleared of its most makeshift structures, and the fires were an object lesson teaching the wisdom of substantial construction. When Bancroft arrived, building was more orthodox, and order was emerging from chaos in the physical appearance of the city.

In the spring of 1852 the most pressing problems related to land ownership. The commission authorized by the United States Land Act of 1851 was scrutinizing the claims to land under Spanish and Mexican grants, all of which had been thrown into jeopardy by the act. Even assuming that some of these titles would be confirmed, there was so much overlapping of pueblo, mission, and private claims that no one could be sure which would prevail. Adding to the confusion were assertions of fraud in the sale of water-front lots which, after assignment by the state, the city had disposed of. Another sizable number of lots had been sold for a song at a sheriff's sale to satisfy the claims of a certain Peter Smith against the city. Furthermore, there were squatters who put no trust in Mexican grants, water-fraud ownership, or Peter Smith titles, but subscribed rather to the American frontier doctrine that possession was nine points of the law.

A nineteen-year-old boy, with two days to spend in San Francisco, could not be expected to devote his time to analyzing this issue of land titles. Bancroft spent the daylight hours wandering about the business district, wading muddy streets, and climbing hills. By night he made the rounds of the gam-

BANCROFT AS A YOUNG MAN

bling houses on Commercial Street and the plaza, "observing the crowds of people come and go, watching the artistic barkeepers in their white coats mixing fancy drinks and serving from gorgeously decorated and mirrored bars fiery potations of every kind, gazing in rapt bewilderment upon the fortune-turning table with its fatal fascinations, marking the piles of money increase and lessen, and the faces behind them broaden and lengthen, and listening to the music that mingled with the clinking of gold, the rattling of glasses, and the voices of rough, loud-laughing men."[1] Nothing suggests that Bancroft advanced beyond the role of spectator; certainly he had not the wherewithal for more than nominal patronage, and Buffalo, the steamship passage, and the isthmus had but slightly eroded his Puritan upbringing.

By steamboat from Long Wharf, Bancroft went to Sacramento, where he consulted with Barton, Reed, and Grimm, commission merchants with whom Derby had had profitable dealings. Their judgment, in which Bancroft concurred, was that Sacramento offered a far better opportunity for a bookstore than San Francisco. A letter was dispatched telling Derby of this decision. In reply a shipment of books was sent by the Cape Horn route, which could be expected to arrive in eight or nine months.

Thus circumstanced, Bancroft took the boat to Marysville and hurried on to Long Bar in search of his father and his eldest brother, Curtis, who had been the first of the Bancroft tribe to come to California. Curtis, after highly profitable operation of a store and hotel at Long Bar, had moved on to Rich Bar on the Feather River. It is said that he intended to put his first $5,000 of profits into San Francisco city lots, but like many another pioneer he passed up the opportunity. His father likewise had acquired a new interest that Bancroft had not heard about. He was on hand, however, to greet his son at Long Bar.

[1] Bancroft, *Literary Industries,* 123.

Their first night together, which they spent at the hotel at Long Bar, was a memorable one. Here Bancroft had his first encounter with a phenomenon recorded in so many of the early narratives—the California flea.[2] He made also his first close acquaintance with the men of the mines, or, as he called them, "the great hairy unwashed," who were "strewed about on bunks, benches, tables, and floor." From their "loud snorings and abominable smells" he at length took flight to sleep rolled in a blanket on a pine-needle couch on the hillside.[3]

In two years in the diggings Bancroft's father had made a respectable pile, with which he was planning to return to Ohio. Doubtless he would have done so, but an opportunity offered "without risk" to multiply his fortune several fold by joining in a quartz-mining venture at Brown Valley, not far from Long Bar. The name of the company may have had something to do with his investment, for it was Plymouth, "always a pleasing name" to his Puritan ear.

Bancroft followed the line of least resistance by going to work with his father in the interest of the Plymouth Company, and it did not take him long to discover how arduous life in the diggings could be. Since he had a good mule team, Bancroft Sr. was employed in hauling firewood and quartz to the eight or ten stamps that had been erected on Dry Creek, about a mile from the ledge in Brown Valley. This may have sounded ordinary enough, but it was not a matter of simple teaming. Axe in hand, they climbed the oak trees dotting the valley, hacked off good-sized branches, loaded these heavy lengths on the wagon, and added them to the mountainous pile at the mill. Or they broke out the hard and sharp quartz at the ledge, loaded it, and unloaded at the stamps. At night they slept heavily in a cloth house near the quartz outcrop.

[2] Representative comments are assembled in "The Flea in California History and Literature, as Revealed by Extracts from Spanish, French, English, German and American Sources between the Years 1769 and 1878," California Historial Society *Quarterly,* XV (1936), 329–337.

[3] Bancroft, *Literary Industries,* 127.

Their meals were of course of their own cooking, and consisted of a monotonous round of beans, pancakes, bread, potatoes, beefsteaks, and coffee, with occasional canned fruit.

Bancroft did not object to the fare or the cooking, though his friend Kenny would have none of it and took his meals at a boardinghouse near by, but he developed a violent dislike for the wood-and-ore hauling. Consequently, he attacked these tasks (and the mules) with an intemperate fury, against which his father protested in vain. Working thus furiously, he hauled prodigious amounts of material to the mill, and, since the pay was by the load, earned as much as twenty-five dollars a day. Payments were in stock in the company rather than in gold dust or cash, and however rich the Plymouth Company might be in future expectations, its immediate operations, because of unexpectedly hard ore, inadequate stamps, imperfections in the recovery process, and other such difficulties, were showing no profit. After two months of toil Bancroft and his father decided to go to Rich Bar. That they still had faith in the Plymouth enterprise is evidenced by the sale of the mule team for additional shares in the company. When, in the end, nothing was realized on this Plymouth stock, Bancroft was moved to resolve that, although he might speculate with his money, never again would he do so with his labor. The unfortunate outcome of the Plymouth venture embittered his soliloquy on the picture of father and son trudging across country to Rich Bar:

> Behold us now! my old father and me, tramping over the plains beneath a broiling sun about the middle of June, each with a bundle and stick, mine containing my sole possessions. In the early morning, fresh from sleep, with gladness of heart at leaving the beautiful valley of hateful occupation behind, we marched away over the hills at a round pace. But as the sun above our heads neared the point from which it poured its perpendicular and most effective wrath, I became excessively fatigued. My feet blistered; my limbs ached; water was to be had only at intervals; the prayed-for breath of air came hot and suffocating, like a sirocco, mingled with incandescent

dust beaten from the parched plain. Thinking over my short experience in the country and my present position, I exclaimed, "If this be California, I hope God will give me little of it." As we trod slowly along, stepping lightly on the ground, I began to think the mules would have been better for our purpose than the shares, but I said nothing.[4]

In his Rich Bar store Curtis made a place for his younger brother as a clerk, and the next six months passed uneventfully. Then, in November, Bancroft went down to Sacramento to meet the shipment of books soon due. As he left Rich Bar, tidings came of the death of a brother-in-law, Harlow Palmer, and at Sacramento was the even more harrowing news that George Derby had died. Realizing full well that no executor of the estate and no other book dealer would make further shipments to an inexperienced boy, Bancroft saw his future thrown into uncertainty. On the other hand, his sister could count on little from Derby's estate beyond the proceeds of the California shipment, and consequently there was special pressure to market it quickly and to advantage.

Sacramento, meanwhile, had been visited by fire and flood. As a "burned-out mud-hole" it offered a poor setting for this crucial venture in book vending, and Bancroft, with wisdom born of necessity, shifted his scene of operations to San Francisco. There, after preliminary discouragements, he finally persuaded a certain William B. Cooke to take over the entire shipment and to pay for it at the rate of not less than $500 on each steamer day. This deal was a happy solution of the problem of disposing of the Derby books. Remittances were made promptly and in full. It also made a place for Bancroft's traveling companion, Kenny, for Cooke gave this amiable Irishman a partnership in his firm.

Young Bancroft, however, was left out in the cold. For a short time he felt it his duty to drop in at the bookshop to make sure that there would be no hitch in the arrangements.

[4] *Ibid.*, 130–131.

As the payments continued without interruption, this responsibility melted away and his sole worry came to be to find himself a job.

Throughout the next six months he trudged the streets of San Francisco in a fruitless search for work. It was the slack season, of course, when the winter rains had driven thousands of miners out of the diggings to seek employment in the towns and cities. Bancroft was candid enough to admit, however, that as a callow, diffident, and awkward youth he was not a likely prospect. In retrospect it seemed that he was never more miserable than in these six months in the army of the unemployed. To find that his services were nowhere wanted dashed his conceit and undermined his self-confidence.

At last, having used up his Rich Bar earnings, he saw that he would have to leave San Francisco. Australia and China loomed as possibilities, but in the end he decided to go to Crescent City. This new town on a curving bay just short of the Oregon line was beginning to attract attention as the supply point for rather extensive mining operations in northwestern California and southwestern Oregon, mines which previously had been supplied from Portland by way of Scottsburg and from the Sacramento Valley by way of Shasta. Lumbering and the tourists who come to marvel at the mighty redwoods keep the town going today, though there still is "much more crescent than city." When Bancroft arrived, he found only a few tents and split-board houses that "stood trembling between the sullen roar of the ocean at the front door and the ofttimes whistling wind in the dense pine forest at the back."[5]

It was in mid-May that Bancroft arrived at this potential metropolis. He came armed with a case of books and stationery obtained on credit in San Francisco. He alighted from the coastal steamer much the worse for wear. The vessel had been crowded, the northward passage had been rough, and sea-

[5] *Ibid.*, 136.

sickness and weariness left Bancroft heart enough merely to crawl to the hotel and tumble into bed.

A day or so later he began to look about the town, and soon he made an arrangement with Crowell and Fairfield, who operated a general store, to attend to their bookkeeping for a stipend of $50 a month, to which would be added the privilege of sleeping in the store and of using a part of the store, rent free, to shelve and sell his stock of books and stationery. How advantageous this arrangement was is indicated by the fact that two years later, when Crowell and Fairfield had gone into bankruptcy. Bancroft had run his personal balance sheet out of the red to show assets of between $6,000 and $8,000. After the failure of Crowell and Fairfield, Bancroft took over a part of their stock and tried operating a general store of his own, but within a few months he disposed of this business and put his money into a one-story brick building, which he rented at $250 a month to a hardware concern.

Bancroft's description of his experiences at Crescent City is gratifyingly clear, considering the interval of almost four decades before it was set down in writing, but it is a generalized description. He comments, quite correctly, that socially and in its intellectual manifestations Crescent City was a counterpart of the mining towns, with "the same element in the community, the same lack of virtuous women, the same species of gambling-houses, drinking-saloons, and dens of prostitution."[6] It was normal that a Mr. Lacy who tried to build a church should have had scant success. An anecdote about Indian relations departs somewhat from the norm. One night a drunken Crescent City man inadvertently set fire to the Indian *ranchería* on the northern horn of the crescent. Throughout the diggings violence against the natives was not usually regarded as calling for punishment. But the citizens of Crescent City forthwith haled this offender before an impromptu court, required him to pay the Indians for the damage done, and

[6] *Ibid.*, 138.

banished him from their city. Herein perhaps is a token of nobility, though Bancroft hints that the real animus was one of humiliation that a citizen of Crescent City had not been able to carry his liquor.

Whether Bancroft participated in this trial is not recorded. One night when a drunken brawl in front of his store ended in murder, he fortunately refrained from rushing out to investigate. Those who were first on the scene lost almost a month's time attending and testifying in the trial at Yreka.

Bancroft's diffidence did not exclude him from all the goings-on in the town. As he describes them: "On Sundays there was horse-racing, or foot-racing, or cock-fighting on the beach; and often a band of rowdies, composed of the most respectable citizens, would start out at any time between midnight and daybreak, and with horns, tin pans, and gongs, make the round of the place, pounding at every door, and compelling the occupant to arise, administer drink to all, and join the jovial company."[7] By preference, however, Bancroft spent his spare time with a kindred spirit, Theodore S. Pomeroy, county clerk and editor of the *Herald* and described by Bancroft with due modesty as "probably the most intelligent man in the place."[8]

In November, 1855, Bancroft yielded to the insistence of his sister Mrs. Derby and set out by the Panama route for the States. Accompanying him was his friend Pomeroy, intent on claiming an Albany bride known to him as yet only through correspondence. At San Francisco, Bancroft found that the firm of Cooke, Kenny and Company had been overtaken by bankruptcy; he thanked the providence that had carried him to Crescent City instead.

The first sensations of homecoming were overwhelmingly pleasant. He writes with rapture of things almost forgotten: frost, snow, young ladies, oysters. He was amused at a young-

[7] *Ibid.*, 139–140.
[8] *Ibid.*, 139.

ster's perplexity that a Californian was not a bear and at the surprise of many others that he was not brown, bearded, and red-shirted. To have come home successful was a distinct advantage, and he noted that even his devoted relatives, who would have welcomed him if empty-handed, lionized him now as a young man who had made good. Through the winter and early spring he luxuriated in these mellow surroundings and nursed an honest intention to settle down near his sisters and his parents. Independent of his will, however, another resolve claimed his attention. Bit by bit he became mindful that the eastern way of life, for all its comforts and refinements and its advantages of companionship, was a little close, a trifle staid, prosy, and old-fashioned, and much too quiet. He was by no means the only exile from California who longed to return. "And so round many a poor pilgrim California has thrown her witcheries, drawing him back to her bright shores whenever he attempted to leave them, like the magnetic mountain in the Arabian story, which drew the nails from any ship that approached it."[9] Yet to him it was a surprise that, although he had never thought of the West as home while he was there, he should now be homesick for California.

---

[9] *Ibid.*, 144.

5

Success Story

I have been prospered in my business & have made money.
Hubert Howe Bancroft to his father, July 11, 1864

It was in April, 1856, that Bancroft determined to return to California. To his surprise, his sisters made no strenuous objection. On the contrary, Mrs. Derby proposed that he help extract her $5,000 from the place where it was unsatisfactorily invested and make it the working capital for his California venture. Inasmuch as this was the principal property of a widow and her three children, it was quite a responsibility to thrust upon a youth of twenty-four. Bancroft was reluctant to assume the responsibility, but Mrs. Derby, entertaining no doubts about her brother's making good, insisted, and in the end it was so arranged. Bancroft took the money, actually some $5,500, and when his sister declined a partnership in the venture, he gave her his personal note in this sum, bearing interest at one per cent a month.[1]

With the money in hand he then went down to New York City. He carried a letter of introduction to an old friend of Derby's, John C. Barnes, of Ames, Herrick, Barnes and Rhoads, one of New York's largest stationery houses. To him Bancroft unfolded his plans and bespoke help in establishing a credit with the leading publishers. He then made the rounds of the publishing houses to ask, not merely for credit, but for long-term credit to compensate for the six months or more that his goods would be in transit, and for rock-bottom prices

[1] Bancroft, *Literary Industries,* 144–145.

so that his markup would not have to exceed what the uncertain California market would bear.

Almost every man he talked to had lost money on California shipments, some of them heavily. California was notorious for fires and floods, and also for failures, some due to misfortune, others to dishonesty. The publishers consequently did not warm to the idea of extending credit to a prospective San Francisco book dealer, and some of them were choleric in their refusal ever to send a dollar's worth of goods to California without first receiving the dollar. Bancroft, notwithstanding, put up a brave front. He spoke of his honest intentions, of the advantages that would be his through starting fresh, and of the asset of his experience in the West and his knowledge of California conditions. Finally, he referred them to John Barnes. When he made the rounds again, he found most of the publishers ready to sell to him on his terms—no mean achievement, considering the current low rating of California credit.[2]

Using his newly established credit conservatively, Bancroft bought some $10,000 worth of books and stationery. These were dispatched by the Cape Horn route to California, and Bancroft, choosing to do his waiting in New York rather than in California, went back to his sister's until October and then took the Panama steamer for San Francisco.

Arrived there, he had little difficulty in persuading his friend Kenny to join forces with him. From Naglee the brandy maker they rented a storeroom on Montgomery Street near Merchant, and there, about the first of December, 1856, the firm of H. H. Bancroft and Company opened for business. The beginning was modest enough. To reduce the $250 rent one-third, offices were let to a broker named Woods and to an insurance agent, Jonathan Hunt. In the first weeks of operation, business was done on an open-air basis. The front of the building was being remodeled, and each night a barricade

---

[2] *Ibid.*, 145–147.

of packing cases was erected to close the shop. Kenny and Bancroft were the entire staff. Kenny was the salesman—a better one, Bancroft insists, than his employer. Bancroft attended to almost everything else. Sleeping on a cot behind the counter, he acted as night watchman. In the morning he removed the barricade, swept out the shop, attended to the bookkeeping, opened cases and restocked the shelves, waited on customers, and made himself generally useful.

Spurred by ambition, and by the responsibility for his sister's investment, Bancroft left no stone unturned to make his business a success. Further stimulation, if that was necessary, was supplied by the hard times then afflicting California. Gold was flowing from the mines in about the same quantity as before, but it was not so easily picked up in the diggings, and those who had to struggle harder to get it were less willing to part with it. The decline in spending was a heavy blow to merchants with large stocks on hand, and all too often with an indebtedness hanging over them at California interest of two or three per cent a month. All around the Bancroft house, old firms, firms of five or six years' standing, were going to the wall

In a way, this might seem to signify a most inopportune time for the launching of a business. Near the bottom of the business cycle, however, there was little incentive for overreaching or extravagance. Hard times suggested thrift, economy, careful trading, and conservative management. The Bancroft shop had the advantage of a fresh stock, carefully selected and well bought; an expert salesman, who had already built up a good personal following; and a hardworking proprietor. Yet Bancroft ascribed much of its success to the depression in which it began to operate. "Hard times," he insisted, "are the very best of times in which to plant and nourish a permanent business."[3]

Whatever the explanation, H. H. Bancroft and Company flourished. Sales mounted steadily, and before twelve months

[3] *Ibid.*, 147–151.

had passed, Bancroft was envisioning expansion. The handiest way to expand without heavy capital outlay seemed to be through persuading the eastern publishers to send out goods on consignment. Backed by the good record his firm had built up in its short period of operation, Bancroft decided to lay this proposal before them. To help out Kenny, who would otherwise have been left alone, Bancroft persuaded their tenant, Jonathan Hunt, to take a third interest in the firm. This done, in the autumn of 1857 he sailed once more by Panama steamer for New York. His business there came quickly to a happy conclusion. Orders were placed for some $60,000 or $70,000 worth of goods to be shipped on consignment, and, before setting out to receive these shipments in California, Bancroft had time to visit his parents at Granville and his sisters at Auburn and Buffalo.

At the latter place his sister Mrs. Palmer saw that he met a Miss Emily Ketchum. Bancroft says of her that her face was not exactly beautiful, but very refined and very sweet. As to other particulars, she was tall, blond, exquisitely formed, and very graceful. She was an accomplished singer, a bright and witty conversationalist, and withal well endowed with common sense. Finally, "her mind was far above the average female intellect."[4] Such a paragon of attractions immediately captivated him. He determined to marry her—if he could. But the time he could spare from his work in California was not long, and five or six meetings with her was all he could manage. No Victorian youth could blurt out a proposal that suddenly; nor was it seemly to suggest that they write to each other.

Fortunately a way opened to triumph over convention. It so happened that the young lady, though a Christian all her life, had recently undergone an intensification of religious zeal. She took Bancroft to be a heathen of the worst sort, a California heathen, his soul a brand to be snatched from the

[4] *Ibid.*, 151.

burning. Passionately, therefore, she laid siege to him as a likely convert. On his part, he was nothing loath to hear her discourse ardently on the joys of the true religion; he would have listened as attentively had she chosen to demonstrate a problem in Euclid. As he bade her farewell, to be off to California, she agreed to write occasionally in hopes that a reminder now and then would help to keep him on the path of piety and churchgoing. Bancroft thereby was privileged to write in reply, and he did so to such good advantage that when he next went east Emily became his wife.[5]

Convenient and calculating though this interest in godliness was, it was not all simulated. En route to California, Bancroft made a high resolve. Arrived in San Francisco, he "put his brains in his pocket" and "joined the good people of Calvary church in their march heavenward."[6] He attended regularly its Sunday and midweek services, taught a class in the Sabbath school, paid tithes, observed the Sabbath with such scrupulousness that he would not even read a Sunday newspaper, and achieved an absolute orthodoxy of belief. For a decade this continued, and might have gone on much longer had not Emily Ketchum Bancroft died. Thereupon Bancroft's religious zeal vanished as suddenly as it had appeared, his later attitude, as the phrases quoted above indicate, was one of profound skepticism about organized religion, and he was appalled by the thought that he had once subordinated reason so completely to dogma and blind faith.

Meanwhile, his book business had been undergoing sundry changes. The enlarged stock, acquired through the shipments on consignment, necessitated a larger store, which was arranged by renting two Merchant Street rooms which adjoined the original shop at the rear. Before long even this space was not enough and H. H. Bancroft and Company took over the entire building on Merchant Street, a structure three stories high and measuring forty feet by sixty. The staff was of course

[5] *Ibid.*, 151–153. [6] *Ibid.*, 152.

much increased, and Bancroft, though not much more than a boy himself, took special interest in "his boys." He did not inflict upon them quite the paternalism attributed to Collis P. Huntington at his San Francisco establishment, but he was concerned about their conduct after hours as well as at work, and he took special pains to see that each had duties appropriate to his aptitudes. From top to bottom in his organization he was able to develop an excellent esprit de corps.[7]

Changes likewise occurred in the management of the firm. Jonathan Hunt continued only briefly as a partner, and in 1860 a disagreement over opening a branch house to deal in blankbooks and stationery led to dissolution of the partnership with Kenny. The friendship between these two original partners also seemed likely to disintegrate. They differed over the division of the stock, and Kenny took the matter to court, but before the case came to trial Bancroft conceded all that had been demanded and their friendship was recemented. Kenny established a competing house, but the venture did not prosper, and ultimately he came back to Bancroft as an employee.

The place these men might have had thus was opened to Bancroft's younger brother, Albert L. Brought to California in 1858 on Bancroft's return from the East, Albert entered the store as a bookkeeper. Although he was only seventeen, he at once began to manifest "those admirable traits of stern integrity and strict attention to all the details of business." In 1859, when the blankbook and stationery outlet was to be established, he was chosen to operate it, and it was opened at 146 Clay Street, with the two brothers as equal partners, and under the name of A. L. Bancroft and Company. A year later this business was consolidated once more with the Montgomery Street store, in which Albert was assigned a one-fourth interest. This was quick success for a lad of nineteen. He was, all the evidence indicates, mature beyond his years. Less imag-

[7] *Ibid.*, 153.

inative than his brother, he had the cautious temperament to be a conservative balance wheel and "a wholesome check to the more sanguine enthusiasm" of others in the firm.[8]

The next several years witnessed great turmoil in national affairs as North and South finally decided to submit their differences to the arbitrament of arms. California merchants found some of their accustomed ways of doing business disrupted during the war years. One circumstance, however, played directly into their hands. While the rest of the nation was handling its transactions with depreciated paper money, California remained on the gold standard. For anyone who wanted to borrow money—a southern California ranchero, for example—this was most awkward. Likewise to anyone who wanted to sell California goods in the East it was the equivalent of a 25 to 50 per cent reduction in receipts. With Bancroft and many another merchant the shoe was on the other foot. Their California receipts were in gold, but their eastern accounts could be paid off in the depreciated currency. It was a windfall of some magnitude.

This Civil War bonus, augmenting the profits that his business was already showing, enabled Bancroft to enlarge the operations of his firm still further, and to enjoy the pleasures of travel. Thus far, he had made several business trips to New York by way of Panama and Nicaragua. In 1862, however, he advanced beyond business journeys to travel for its own sake. In the summer of that year he set off for London, Paris, New York, and Buffalo, at the last place picking up his wife, who had gone back to visit her parents earlier in the year. A more extensive tour was begun in the summer of 1866. This time, the Bancrofts spent some twelve months in the British Isles and on the Continent, after which they returned to Buffalo for the winter, visited Washington in the spring of 1868, and did not return to San Francisco until the fall of that year.

[8] "A Cosmopolitan Publishing House: History of the Establishment of A. L. Bancroft & Co., San Francisco, Cal.," *The Paper World,* March, 1881.

In harking back to these travels Bancroft makes much of their educational value. In Ohio, New York, and California he had come in contact with diverse habits and customs, and en route to California he had had glimpses of still other mores. Reading had also given him some preparation for what to expect; yet he says that Europe's "antique works and ways" were "at once a romance and a revelation." Beyond the opportunity for seeing and observing, travel conferred an inestimable boon in the stimulation it gave to meditation and planning. "It was then that ambition was fired, and ideas came rushing in faster than I could handle them." Of these ideas none was more arresting than that suggested by what he saw of the European leisure class. Their disdain for work Bancroft thought an unjustifiable affectation, but he glimpsed underlying it a corrective for the prevailing American enslavement to money-making. He came back from Europe seriously questioning whether he should devote the rest of his life to the accumulation of more and more wealth.[9] As later chapters will explain, he worked out a sort of compromise between continuing in business and retiring from it. His European travels, at any rate, had much to do with shaping his determination not to be merely a businessman.

The journey itself is incontestable proof that H. H. Bancroft and Company had flourished. Only a decade earlier, Bancroft had been his own night watchman and janitor. Now, profits were adequate to finance a grand tour of the Continent, and the firm was so far developed that it could carry on successfully for two years and more without active supervision by the proprietor.

A rough idea of the dimensions and proportions of the business may be derived from an advertisement or business card which was inserted in the back pages of a volume published by the firm in 1863.[10] (See page 50.)

[9] Bancroft, *Literary Industries,* 154–157.

[10] *Guide to the Colorado Mines,* published by H. H. Bancroft & Co., San Francisco, 1863.

San Fran^d. July 11. 1864

My dear Father Mother & Sis

You want something consoling and I think I can give it to you. Now I have said it a great many times and I will say it once more. All you have to do when you are through there is to square up every thing and <u>come right here to me</u>. This has always been my idea and I would not have it different. I mean to take your matters in hand. Just what I will do I dont know, but all you have to do is to come here just as soon as you are ready. I am ready for you to day. I have just moved into a larger house at Oakland & I can make you all very comfortable. I have been prospered in my business & have made money & I know of no better use to put it to upon the face of the earth than to minister to your comfort

FROM A LETTER OF BANCROFT'S, 1864

her father & mother and done her
duty. I will take care of them
now and she can go off and
get married if she wants
to. but if she wants to
come down to San Fran° with
them. so much the better,
and she can live with them
and keep house if she
wants to.

About the books and other
things, bring down whatever you
want to keep and is worth
bringing and sell or give
away the balance.

Write and let me know all
about it. and give yourselves
no trouble for the future. for I
shall miss my calculations very
much if you do not have a
heap less trouble here than
you have up there

H H B

FROM A LETTER OF BANCROFT'S, 1864

Testimony less explicit in detail, yet eloquent of the phenomenal success that Bancroft had attained, is recorded in a letter he wrote to his father the next year.[11] It was occasioned by the termination of his father's appointment as Indian agent at Fort Simcoe. The San Francisco store was not yet eight years old, and Bancroft was only thirty-two, yet we find him writing thus:

"My dear Father, Mother & Siss [Siss being Mary, the youngest of his sisters[12]]:

"You want something consoling and I think I can give it to you. Now I have said it a great many times and I will say it once more. All you have to do when you are through there is to square up everything and *come right here to me.* This has always been my idea and I would not have it different. I mean to take your matters in hand."

He went on, then, to assure them that he could easily accommodate them. "I have been prospered in my business & have made money," he wrote, "& I know of no better use to put it to upon the face of the earth than to minister to your comfort." Siss, he continued, had had a long siege at Fort Simcoe and had done her duty by her parents. He would welcome her warmly at San Francisco, but if she preferred to marry the man of her choice, and it developed that she did,[13] he was ready to give her his blessing "good and strong." To his parents he repeated, "give yourselves no trouble about the future, for I shall miss my calculations very much if you do not have a heap less trouble here than you have [had] up there."[14]

Bancroft's toying with the idea of retiring is additional proof, if that be needed, of the flourishing condition of the business. Another bit of evidence is that the Bancrofts were

[11] Hubert Howe Bancroft to his father, mother, and sister, San Francisco, July 11, 1864. MS in the possession of Philip Bancroft.
[12] Bancroft, *Literary Industries,* 154.
[13] *Ibid.*
[14] Bancroft to his father, mother, and sister, July 11, 1864.

H. H. Bancroft & Co.,

Booksellers & Stationers

Keep constantly in store one of the Largest Stocks of

Books and Stationery

in the World

Particular attention is called to

Bancroft's Celebrated Hand-made Writing Papers,

Letter, Note, Legal, Foolscap.

The best and cheapest paper made.

Bancroft's Extra Quality Gold Pens

Photograph Albums, Blank Books,

Law Books, School Books,

Miscellaneous Books, Medical Books.

Books in every department of literature, and staple and fancy stationery, at wholesale and retail at the Lowest Rates. Regular shipments are received direct from London, Paris, New York, Boston and Philadelphia.

The public and dealers are respectfully invited to examine the goods.

H. H. Bancroft & Co.,

No. 609 Montgomery Street, & Nos. 607 & 609 Merchant Street

San Francisco, Cal.

planning a more commodious and sumptuous residence than the one they had been occupying on Harrison Street. While in England and the eastern states, they advanced beyond the planning stage and purchased "hard-wood finish from New York, roofing-slate from Vermont, and tiles and stained glass from England," and much else to be used in the actual construction.[15]

Upon his return to San Francisco in the autumn of 1868 Bancroft faced another building problem. His business had far outgrown its quarters on Montgomery and Merchant streets. Two additional rooms had been rented on Commercial Street, but quantities of goods had to be left in storage in various warehouses. No better place being available for rent, it seemed the obvious solution was to build. Accordingly, Bancroft began a systematic search for an appropriate site. He combed the business district thoroughly and found nothing that would do. The lots that were available were too small, and real-estate prices, in expectation of the boom that the transcontinental railroad was counted on to produce, were inordinately high. But finally, by going out Market Street all the way to the 700 block and thereby running some risk of not being found by prospective customers, he got the space required. To buy it he had to deal with five different owners for seven parcels of land and he had to pay a good stiff price, but he ended with a property running through to Stevenson Street and measuring approximately 75 by 170 feet. "There was a good deal of surprise, and even merriment," runs one contemporary comment, "at the choice of such a location. Bancrofts are going to move their store to the country; was a common joke in the city, and dealers in the southern counties rejoiced that the house was getting so much nearer as to materially diminish freight charges."[16]

---

[15] Bancroft, *Retrospection,* 323–324.

[16] B. E. Lloyd, *Lights and Shades in San Francisco* (San Francisco, 1876), 295; Bancroft, *Literary Industries,* 155–158; Bancroft, *Retrospection,* 320–322.

Plans were drawn for a five-story structure, to be "one of the most elegant and conspicuous in the city," and in 1869 work commenced. At the same time other workmen began erecting the "elegant dwelling" at California and Franklin. He was not unmindful of the heavy outlay that this double building program would entail, but he was confident that the momentum his firm had gathered in its thirteen years of operation would see it and him safely through the undertaking.

In the midst of this preparing for the future—in December, 1869—his wife died. Bancroft had been deeply devoted to her and the loss was a crushing blow. He describes his state of mind as "that of being entirely alone in the universe, that of being on not very good terms with the invisible, and caring little or nothing for the visible." The once cherished house now was unbearable to him and he had the work on it stopped. More than a year later he had the workmen resume, not because he was interested in having the house, but "to save the material." Some relief came in clumsy and none too effectual efforts to comfort his little daughter, Kate. More effective was driving himself relentlessly at the tasks at hand; but it was years before he made even partial conquest over the bitterness thus engendered.[17]

Meanwhile, work on the business block had progressed so rapidly that by April, 1870, it was ready for occupancy. Done in the most approved ornate style of the period, the building is described as "one of the largest and most architecturally attractive in the city."[18] Pictures of its front confirm that statement. Staunchly built, it was equipped with a steam engine in the basement which supplied power for all the machinery; and, more arresting to modern attention, it had an artesian well on the premises which gave the firm its own water supply. Besides the five floors measuring 75 by 170 feet, the build-

[17] The depth of his grief is described with feeling in *Literary Industries,* 158–162.

[18] "A. L. Bancroft & Co.," *Pacific Printer,* June, 1877.

ing had a full basement extended by storage vaults under the sidewalks. It was thus amply capacious for the several departments of the Bancroft enterprise and enabled the firm to take rank as the largest book and stationery house west of Chicago.

Stock and fixtures were carted over and made ready for the opening to the public on April 26. The old departments handling stationery and books were installed on the first and second floors and in the basement. A new department given over to sheet music, pianos, organs, and other musical instruments was added, and other new features were introduced. The most important element in the firm's expansion was the addition of manufacturing facilities. New departments for printing, engraving, lithographing, and bookbinding were equipped, in what was doubtless the most practical and expeditious fashion, by purchasing several smaller establishments and moving their entire equipment to the new site.

One such acquisition was the blankbook and stationery house of William B. Cooke and Company, which for many years had operated in the Montgomery Block on Montgomery Street, and through which Bancroft had disposed of the Derby consignment in 1852. The trade of this house was absorbed, and its machinery, installed on the fourth floor, enabled the Bancroft Company to manufacture "a full line of blankbooks from the smallest memorandum book to the largest and most expensively bound ledger or county assessment-roll," at prices and quality, furthermore, to compete with those of any eastern manufacturer.[19]

The other main purchase was the Sacramento Street printing establishment of Turnbull and Smith. Transferring its equipment to the third floor of the new building, Bancroft installed Walter Turnbull as business manager of this department, James H. Smith as foreman in special charge of job work, and W. P. Morrill in charge of book printing.

The entire fifth floor of the new building, as will be related

[19] *Ibid.*

later, was reserved for Bancroft's library and his literary pursuits, and since he intended to devote most of his time to the fifth-floor activities, leaving the day-to-day management of the commercial establishment to others, he decided, coincident to opening for business in the new location, to change the name of his firm to A. L. Bancroft and Company. The brother to whom this honor and responsibility were accorded was at the time only twenty-nine, but he had twelve years' experience in the business, almost all of it in positions of responsibility. Bancroft's own interest and liability in the firm was undiminished, and he intended to go carefully over the monthly reports the several department heads would submit.[20]

As it worked out, he had to do far more than inspect monthly reports. The next five years brought harder times than anyone had expected. First of all, the transcontinental railroad, which had been universally counted on to bring an upsurge of prosperity and which was greeted by the San Franciscans as though it were the millennium, dealt that city a stunning blow. Real estate, which had been expected to boom, went down. Retailers throughout the West decided to save one profit by buying from New York rather than from San Francisco wholesalers. Failures resulted and large stocks were thrown on the market, and the stocks held by retailers and jobbers alike had to compete with those now pouring in from the East. Bancroft's business of bookselling and book publishing was especially vulnerable to these railroad blows. He was dealing in a commodity that sold best when hot off the press and for which the production center was New York.

Concurrently, San Francisco's business, which had been thrown off stride by the completion of the railroad, was slowed almost to a standstill by a series of dry winters. Today, irrigation and industrialization have made California's prosperity measurably independent of rainfall, but in all previous epochs

[20] "A Cosmopolitan Publishing House," *The Paper World*, March, 1881; Bancroft, *Literary Industries*, 162–163.

the activity of commerce was determined chiefly by the welfare of agriculture, and that in turn by the adequacy of the seasonal precipitation. Having tied up its principal assets in an ambitious building program, the Bancroft firm had little with which to combat the depression. And having expanded to something like twice its previous dimensions, it was in poor position to pare expenses to fit the slack times.

Almost every day, therefore, the problems of the market place were carried to the proprietor in his ivory tower on the fifth floor. Still oftener, business worries intruded upon his thoughts whether he would or not, and concentration on his scholarly labors seemed out of the question. Repeatedly his downstairs employees protested against drafts on the meager surplus of the business to support the admittedly noneconomic venture ensconced above.

In time, these doubts and difficulties were overcome. The business struggled through the five lean years and went on to firmer footing. With experience, means were found to make the transcontinental railroad a useful servant instead of a barrier to commerce. A. L. Bancroft and Company substantially increased the total volume of its business. It continued to supply the whole West Coast from Mexico to Alaska and to reach across the Pacific to Hawaii and the Orient. It was one of the largest concerns of its type in the world and quite unrivaled west of Chicago. Thus, despite the serious worries of the early 'seventies, in the long run Bancroft's judgment in deciding to make a large outlay for a building and to double the scope of his business was amply vindicated.[21]

Other comments might be made about Bancroft the businessman. The notion of retiring from business had struck him in the course of his tour of Europe when he was only thirty-five or thirty-six. Thereafter the nonbusiness phases of his career may seem the more significant; but it should be noted that many of these activities were made possible by the finan-

[21] Bancroft, *Literary Industries,* 163–167.

cial success of his business enterprises, that his retirement was only partial since he was called back at intervals to take full charge of the firm, and that he carried the methods of business over into such matters as the collecting and organizing of his library, the study, organization, and writing of history, and the publication and marketing of his historical works. These several considerations lend additional significance to the span of years from 1856 to 1870 when Bancroft as a young man in his late twenties and thirties was achieving a phenomenal and substantial success in business.

6

The House of Bancroft

For thirty years I have had a bookstore in this town, and the first and finest one here, or within two thousand miles of the place. Hubert Howe Bancroft, *Literary Industries,* 775

By the time of the move to Market Street the general pattern of the Bancroft business was well established. The firm was already the West's largest and foremost bookselling concern. It was handling stationery and office supplies as well as books of all types. It was operating at both wholesale and retail. It was active in publishing books and periodicals. Its work, furthermore, was carefully "systematized and divided into departments," each under a responsible, alert, and expert head. Its growth to even larger proportions in the 'seventies and 'eighties resulted in part from the addition of new departments, particularly in the manufacturing branches of printing and bookbinding, but much of the increase, and perhaps most of it, resulted from expansion within the framework previously outlined. The methods whereby this enlarged success was achieved call for more detailed description.

The prime feature of the system employed was complete departmentalization. A twofold theory underlay this method of organizing. A major consideration was "that every class of buyers and dealers in the book, paper and stationery lines may fully realize that their special wants in trade have been especially considered in this mammoth establishment, and that they need not look any farther to find just what they need on the best possible terms and rates of purchase."[1] The other

[1] "A Cosmopolitan Publishing House," *The Paper World,* March, 1881.

main purpose was to achieve efficient conduct of the business, the ramifications of which were so varied that no one man could be attentive to them all. Judging by the vigor and ingenuity with which the work of many of these departments was carried on, the proprietors were particularly expert in choosing the right men to put in charge.[2]

A review of the evolution of the business may be had through a survey of the several departments as they were functioning in 1881, about midway in this latter period. The setup is suggested by the vivisectional view of the Bancroft Building which was used in some of the firm's advertising.[3] The building is displayed with an entire side wall shorn off and the humming activity on the six levels exposed to view. This picture may properly be kept in mind as we proceed through the several departments.

The wholesale department, directed by F. A. Colley, had its offices on the first floor. This department prided itself on its knowledge of the particular wants of western customers and on the completeness of its stock of booksellers' and stationers' goods. It carried a full line of writing papers, envelopes, blankbooks, and school supplies, and stood ready to supply "a stationer with everything in his line, from a wooden toothpick to a printing press, and a book-seller with every trade book published from *Mother Goose* to Audubon's magnificent *Birds of America,* and from a dime novel to the *Encyclopedia Britannica*."[4] For this department it was claimed that it had no equal west of the Alleghanies; certainly the business that it did was large and increasing.

Also on the first-floor front was the retail and library department, headed by H. R. Coleman, who had been with the firm since 1868. The salesroom is described as handsome and commodious, the shelving spacious, and the counter cases

[2] For a tribute to them see Bancroft, *Literary Industries,* 609.
[3] Reproduced also in "A Cosmopolitan Publishing House," *The Paper World,* March, 1881.
[4] *Ibid.*

elegant. The stock included "every variety of book published in the United States and Europe," and also "all that is beautiful, dainty and useful in fancy articles and cutlery, artistic in card and visiting requirements, and everything in the way of fine card engraving that the edict of fashion demands."[5] A subdivision headed by J. A. Hofmann catered to private and public libraries and offered advice on the choice of standard works appropriate for them.

The law department, also situated on the first floor, was one of the most active. Its manager, F. P. Stone, then in his thirty-ninth year, had been fourteen years with the firm and knew this branch of the business thoroughly. His department put out some 1,500 different kinds of legal blanks, carried in stock law books and legal stationery inventoried at $20,000 to $50,000, and could supply any law book wanted.

Under Stone's direction the law department was an active publisher, having put out, since 1866, some 165 volumes. Included among these were the *Supreme Court Reports* for the states of California, Oregon, and Nevada, the *Reports* of the United States Ninth Circuit Court; certain works of national reputation, such as *Freeman on Judgments* and *Estee's Pleadings;* and a number that related particularly to the West, such as Hittell's *Codes* and a four-volume treatise on *Mines and Waters.* A still more ambitious work was in progress, a series of reports entitled *American Decisions,* which was designed to give annotations on the leading cases of the United States and was expected to run to seventy-five volumes.[6] Inclusive of managers, salesmen, writers, and printers, this department gave work to some fifty men. It controlled practically the entire trade of the lawyers in the states of California, Nevada, and Oregon, and the territories of Arizona, Utah, Montana, Idaho, and Washington, as well as a good fraction of such business in New Mexico, Colorado, Wyoming, and the Dakotas.

---

[5] *Ibid.*

[6] Bancroft's law-book publishing is discussed in Ruth Doxsee, Book Publishing in San Francisco, 1848 to 1906 (MS, Berkeley, 1931), 25.

The bank and official department, also on the first floor, was managed by the veteran George L. Kenny. From it, merchants, bankers, brokers, corporations, businessmen of all descriptions, and public officials could get every form of official stationery, blanks, and blankbooks. This department benefited not only from Kenny's long experience with this type of merchandise and from his wide contacts up and down the Coast, but also from the superior facilities for the manufacture of these office supplies which other departments of the Bancroft establishment afforded.

The music department, quartered on the first floor and in the front part of the basement, was under the supervision of Charles E. Bancroft, a nephew of the proprietors. It stocked pianos, organs, and other instruments in all price ranges, and sheet music in endless variety. Noteworthy in this department was its circulating library of some 100,000 pieces. For a nominal monthly fee a subscriber could borrow several pieces of music each week and at the end of the month could have music to the full amount of his subscription. The music department compared favorably with any other such outlets on the Coast.

From offices on the second floor the subscription department put a small army of agents in the field. With pardonable exaggeration it is asserted that its agents and subagents covered the territory from the Missouri River to the Sandwich Islands and Australia, and from Panama to British Columbia, "canvassing every reading individual within those extensive boundaries."[7] A subordinate branch specializing in serials was particularly effective. Under the direction of F. Person it had achieved phenomenal success in getting subscriptions for Stoddart's American reprint of the *Encyclopedia Britannica.*

In quarters toward the rear of the building the educational department offered teachers "everything necessary for their use in the fulfillment of their important and arduous duties

[7] "A Cosmopolitan Publishing House," *The Paper World,* March, 1881.

of training the youthful mind to the development of all the faculties to the highest point of intellectual culture." It carried the most approved textbooks, "all the necessary apparatus for illustrating the new and improved methods of object-teaching," appliances appropriate to instruction by the Kindergarten and Quincy systems, local maps of the Coast directly published by the house, standard maps and historical, geographical, astronomical, and political charts published in the East, and standard and classical works—in short, "everything required for the fitting out of a school, academy, or college." This department was under the supervision of another nephew, Harlow P. Bancroft, who exhibited the family traits of drive and acumen.[8]

A particular effort of the educational department was to promote the Bancroft series of school readers and spellers, which had been designed to meet the special needs of the West. Administered by F. G. Sanborn, this branch of the business had state adoptions in Oregon, general adoptions in Arizona, Utah, and Idaho, and scattered but increasing adoptions throughout the West.

A free placement bureau was maintained in the educational department. Teachers in want of a school were invited to record their names, addresses, and educational standings in a register kept in the department, from which information was supplied on request to trustees or superintendents in search of a teacher.

Still other departments functioned at least for a time, though they are not listed in the description for 1881. On the Bancroft letterhead on the eve of the move to Market Street there is mention of departments of scientific books, of medical books, and of religious books. At that time, also, the house published the *Pacific Medical and Surgical Journal*, the *Occident*, and *Putnam's Magazine*.[9]

---

[8] *Ibid.*

[9] As appears on a letter in the writer's possession, H. H. Bancroft to E. W. Moore, San Francisco, January 9, 1870.

The general offices of the firm were at the rear of the second floor. T. A. C. Dorland, the cashier, was a veteran of fifteen years' standing. He supervised the daily cash receipts and expenditures of the several departments and also the several thousand running accounts of customers of the firm. R. W. Graff was head bookkeeper, and Charles Bachman had charge of the firm's eastern correspondence.

The rear basement, besides housing the power plant, accommodated the receiving, packing, and shipping department, which for a decade had been managed efficiently by Edwin Brown. Some idea of the volume of business transacted is afforded by the statement that postage on books mailed out in a single day had amounted to $800.

The third and fourth floors were given over in their entirety to the manufacturing end of the business, the third floor housing the print shop, and the fourth floor the bookbindery. The print shop, as indicated, was initially equipped with the machinery transferred from the shop of Turnbull and Smith. As the business expanded, much new equipment was added. Several new fonts of type were acquired for the compositors. Since typesetting was done by hand, the installations were less impressive than in the pressroom, where by 1877 some thirty-one pieces of machinery were in operation. These are itemized as:

One large Adams' bed and platen press
One small Adams' bed and platen press
One large Hoe cylinder
One small Hoe cylinder
One large Taylor cylinder
Four large Campbell cylinders
Two half-medium presses
Two quarter-medium presses
Six eighth-medium presses
One forty-inch cutting machine
One routing machine
One dry-pressing machine
Six lithographic hand presses
One lithographic cylinder press
One copper-plate press
One bronzing machine[10]

The bronzing machine, invented in the department and built to order in San Francisco, was an especial object of pride.

[10] "A. L. Bancroft & Co.," *Pacific Printer,* June, 1877.

It could bronze and brush sheets of paper measuring 22 by 29 inches at the rate of 800 an hour.[11]

Personnel in the printing department shifted rapidly in the first few years on Market Street. By 1872, Turnbull, Smith, and Morrill had departed. In March of the following year, W. B. Bancroft, still another nephew of the proprietors, was placed in charge; he continued in this capacity until the late 'eighties.

The fourth-floor bindery, its nucleus the equipment and skilled workmen brought over from William B. Cooke and Company, had as its foreman George W. Cooke, brother of the late head of that firm. It had every facility for bookbinding and was prepared to turn out books of all descriptions, "from the cheap and wire-sewed school book to the elegant full gilt Russia-bound illustrated Doré Bible."[12]

The manufacturing work done by the firm fell into three principal categories, one of them orthodox and well-known, one archaic, and one bizarre. Book publishing, the first of these categories, was and is standard work for a printing concern. The Bancroft Company, as everyone knows, plied this business vigorously, embarked on an ambitious program, and produced an impressive line of books. The earliest had been two duodecimo volumes by the Rev. W. A. Scott, *The Giant Judge; or, The Story of Sampson, the Hebrew Hercules,* and *Esther, the Hebrew-Persian Queen,* issued in 1859, the former illustrated with woodcuts after Charles Nahl's spirited drawings. Published by the firm, though printed elsewhere, these volumes were well designed and executed and represented an auspicious beginning for their publisher. Other important titles included on the firm's early lists were a translation

[11] *Ibid.*

[12] "A Cosmopolitan Publishing House," *The Paper World,* March, 1881. See also a pamphlet entitled *An Essay on Bookbinding as an Art, with Some Suggestions to Collectors on the Care of Books* (A. L. Bancroft and Company, San Francisco, 1886), which was really an advertisement for the "Binding in Leather" branch of the Bancroft house.

of Francisco Velasco's *History of Sonora* (1861), William H. Knight's *Hand-book of the Pacific Coast* (1862), the *Guide to the Colorado Mines* (1863), Franklin Tuthill's *History of California* (1866), Oscar Shuck's *The California Scrapbook, a Repository of Useful Information and Select Reading* (1868), and *The Natural Wealth of California* (1868) by Titus Fey Cronise, "a book so well done typographically that it might be placed first on the list of books which have been produced on the Pacific Coast."[13]

These volumes were followed by a host of others, among them Frederick Hall's *History of San Jose and Surroundings, with Biographical Sketches of Early Settlers* (1871); *Men and Memories of San Francisco in the Spring of '50* (1873), by the courtly saloonkeepers T. A. Barry and B. A. Patten; A. S. Evans' *A la California: Sketch of Life in the Golden State* (1873); the five massive volumes of *Native Races* (1874–1875), printed in the East but from plates prepared in the Bancroft Building; and the two sumptuous tomes of Alonzo Phelps's *Contemporary Biography of California's Representative Men* (1881).[14] There were many others, not to mention various maps, the Pacific Coast School Books, and the several series of law books. The quantity of output is suggested by an estimate that in the first seven years of operations in the Market Street building the number of copies of books and pamphlets printed had passed 350,000.[15] Though phenomenal in quantity, this sort of printing will strike the modern reader as perfectly orthodox and regular.

By contrast, the production of blankbooks seems archaic. Modern office practice calls for the use of a variety of printed forms practically all of which are loose-leaf. In Bancroft's day the preference was for bound volumes to be used as account books, ledgers, daybooks, and the like. Their manufacture

[13] Ruth Doxsee, Book Publishing in San Francisco, 1848–1906, pp. 25–27.
[14] *Ibid.*
[15] "A. L. Bancroft & Co.," *Pacific Printer,* June, 1877.

was not simply a matter of job printing, but required bookbinding facilities on a considerable scale. Revenue from this source was one of the principal elements in the receipts of the Bancroft Company.

The bizarre product was in the firm's lithography. Nowadays, business concerns lean toward severity and dignified simplicity in their letterheads, envelopes, and billheads. In the 'seventies and 'eighties the tendency was to be orchidaceous. After 1881 the Bancroft Company itself affected a billhead decorated with a threefold device: at the left the ornate front of the Market Street building, at the right a reproduction of the Spartan exterior of the library building on Valencia Street, and in the center a draped bookcase in which were ranged the thirty-nine volumes of Bancroft's *Works*. Other firms went in for devices still more elaborate, which meant a good demand for lithography and engraving.

In addition, the lithograph department got orders for vast amounts of colored-label printing. In one season it was called upon by the salmon canners of Oregon and California for 20,000,000 labels.[16] Here alone was work enough to keep the bronzing machine and four of the largest cylinder presses running night and day for three months. In the fruit-canning season the demand was almost as great. Few users of the Bancroft Library or the Bancroft histories are aware that a fair fraction of the financial backing for those scholarly enterprises came out of the manufacture of labels for canned salmon and fruit. It is a fact, nevertheless, which ought to be on record.

Such, in brief, was the nature of the business conducted at 721 Market Street. That it flourished so phenomenally may be explained in part by such elements of luck as the Civil War bonus, the head start over most would-be competitors in the West, and the rapid growth of San Francisco as the metropolis

[16] *Ibid.;* "A Cosmopolitan Publishing House," *The Paper World,* March, 1881.

of the West and much of the Pacific. On the other hand, a major part of the explanation is to be credited to Bancroft's business genius, to the administrative skill of his brother Albert, to the competence of the junior executives, and to the admirable way in which the business was systematized and divided into autonomous departments.

7

Diligent Collector

There were not three men in California, I venture to say, who at that time knew anything either of the intrinsic or marketable value of old books.
Hubert Howe Bancroft, *Literary Industries,* 183

ANYONE WHO DEALS in books runs the risk of becoming a collector. California has had several conspicuous examples; next to Bancroft the most notable was Robert Ernest Cowan, whose prowess is represented in a magnificent store of Californiana (recently transferred to the University of California, Los Angeles) and a three-volume bibliography of the history of California, the standard in its category.[1]

Bancroft's impulse to collect had a practical origin. As an adjunct to his bookselling he published a Pacific Coast handbook. One day in 1859 it occurred to him that it would be a convenience to William H. Knight, the editor of this handbook, if all the books in stock pertinent to the subject were brought together. Accordingly, shelves were cleared in the vicinity of Knight's desk, and books pertaining to California and the West were ranged at his elbow. The shop yielded fifty or seventy-five such titles, which rather surprised Bancroft. He remarked to Knight, "That is doing very well; I did not imagine there were so many."[2] Doubtless he would have been still more astounded had anyone suggested that around this nucleus he was about to build up a collection of 60,000 volumes.

[1] Robert Ernest Cowan, *A Bibliography of the History of California, 1510–1930* (3 vols.; San Francisco, 1933).
[2] Bancroft, *Literary Industries,* 174; see also Bertha Knight Power, *William Henry Knight, California Pioneer* (n. p., 1932), 34–39, 56–74.

Bancroft added nothing to this original assortment until some time later. But one day he dropped in at the Washington Street bookshop of Epes Ellery and by chance noticed a few California pamphlets. They were early California imprints; he calls them old, but in all probability this means merely that they had appeared earlier in the 'fifties. These he promptly bought to add to Knight's reference shelf. Then followed more careful search in the stocks of Ellery, of Carrie and Damon, of the Noisy Carrier, and at lesser stands and bookshops round about town. At auction shops and wherever else he went, Bancroft was on the prowl for more materials for his collection. If, for example, in a lawyer's office he happened to spy a California pamphlet, he had no compunction about trying to buy it.[3]

The actual beginnings of important things are seldom recognized for what they are. The start of the Bancroft Library was no exception; apparently, no inventory of the original fifty or seventy-five titles has been preserved. By all that is logical the bookstore should have yielded the principal works on California published in the late 'fifties, such as Soulé, Gihon, and Nisbet's *The Annals of San Francisco,* Marryat's *Mountains and Molehills,* Parkman's *California and Oregon Trail.* Earlier works may well have been represented by Dana's *Two Years before the Mast,* Frémont's *Report,* Robinson's *Life in California,* Bryant's *What I Saw in California,* Palóu's *Life of Serra,* and Venegas' *Noticias de la California;* but all this is conjectural.

Thus early the philosophy and the practices that were fundamental to Bancroft's ultimate success as a collector were clearly in evidence. He was diligent and ingenious in ferreting out material. He was omnivorous. He seized on every picture, map, manuscript, pamphlet, or book that bore even slightly

[3] Bancroft, *Literary Industries,* 174–175. In his accounts of later activities there is repeated evidence of aggressive and resourceful collecting; *ibid.,* 365–445, 468–561, and 618–649.

on his subject. His policy was, when in doubt, to buy; he thought it cheaper than to waste his time examining an item with extra thoroughness and debating with himself whether it should be included. That many an item thus acquired was practically worthless bothered him not at all, because he was convinced that completeness was the highest desideratum in a collection and that the most insignificant item when made part of a larger family would prove of value, perhaps of sizable value.[4]

Bancroft professed to have a tolerance for the impractical collector, the small boy who was amassing marbles "to see how many kinds he could get," the English gentleman who boasted of an assortment of old china worth £20,000, the book collectors who went in for old bindings, early imprints, or first editions. For his own part, however, book collecting focused on the mere externals had no appeal, and consistently he judged books by their substance, their content. The question he asked was whether a given volume contained information, facts, or statements that would swell the fund of evidence already reposing in his library.[5]

On his next trip east he browsed in the secondhand bookshops of New York, Boston, and Philadelphia. He disclaims going to any special trouble, but it is apparent that he gave hours and days to this searching. So matters went for several years, with the collection growing now by a single pamphlet, now by a box of books, until it had increased to about a thousand volumes.

By this time Bancroft had reached such a point of diminishing returns from the California and eastern book markets that he began to regard his collection as completed. When he visited London, however, in 1862, and saw what quantities

[4] The Bancroft Library itself is the best expression of his theory and technique of collecting. See also the comments in *Literary Industries,* 168–197, and *Retrospection,* 301–318.

[5] Bancroft, *Literary Industries,* 175–177.

of books there were in its hundreds of secondhand bookstores, he realized that his labors were just beginning. He could not tarry at this time to do more than scratch the surface of London's hoard of books. He bought enough to fill a dozen packing cases, but promised himself that he would come back for a longer stay and do justice to the opportunity. Meanwhile, he continued to pick up random items in bookshops here and there, and occasionally he located other materials through scanning dealers' catalogues.

In the interval before his return to London he also determined to broaden the scope of his collecting. He had started with an interest in California. Since only by complete arbitrariness could California be cut off from the adjacent areas of Washington, Oregon, Nevada, Lower California, and Sonora, Bancroft soon found himself collecting for this larger area. The next step was to recognize that California's historical roots went farther down into Mexico and even into Central America, that the rest of the Rocky Mountain West was closely akin to the portion for which he was already collecting, and that there was an essential unity embracing British Columbia and Alaska along with the American Northwest.[6] This willingness to go beyond the posted boundaries was a major contribution toward Bancroft's success as a collector. Had he sat at the feet of the current masters of American history, no such breadth of vision would have been urged upon him. Had he conned the pages of local history, he would have found no such example. Even today, when isolation is under a cloud, when Pan-Americanism is in the ascendant, and when global thinking is in fashion, the regional view is usually far more provincial than Bancroft's was.

Having discovered a larger entity that overlay the political units, he resolved to make his hunting grounds the whole western half of North America, from Panama to Alaska, and with Central America and Mexico included in their entirety.

[6] *Ibid.*, 180–181.

In all, it was a modest one-twelfth of the land surface of the earth. At the time, Bancroft did not consider that he had embarked upon a particularly large undertaking. Later, when he reflected upon it, he was inclined to doubt that any private collector had ever assigned himself so Herculean a task.[7] Certainly no other comes to mind who got as far along toward completeness in collecting materials on the history of any comparable area.

In 1866 opportunity at last offered to carry the quest vigorously to England and the Continent.[8] With the business in San Francisco running smoothly, the Bancrofts set off to do Europe. First stops were in Ireland and Scotland, and then followed London and the Continent. What Mrs. Bancroft thought of this European junket is not recorded. To judge from her husband's account and from the harvest of materials after they got past Ireland and Scotland, it must have been essentially a tour of the bookstores and stalls, with only an occasional day stolen to view cathedrals, art galleries, and the like. Bancroft, at least, reveled in rummaging through cords of dusty tomes.

Although Scotland and Ireland yielded almost nothing for his purpose, London exceeded his fondest expectations. It was not that he found in London any systematized array of western Americana. On the contrary, he seemed to be the first customer in most of these shops who had ever expressed an interest in so outlandish a branch of literature. In shop after shop he would be told that they had nothing on his specialty. But the books were there, and by scanning the shelves, checking catalogues, and rummaging through the storage rooms Bancroft turned them up by the score—large books and small books, books that had been on his want list, and books he had never heard of. With scarcely a doubling

[7] Bancroft, *Retrospection*, 315–316.

[8] Described circumstantially in a manuscript journal of some 240 pages, Hubert Howe Bancroft, Journal While in Europe, 1866–1867, MS in the Bancroft Library. See also his *Literary Industries*, 178–185.

on his tracks Bancroft put in three solid months gathering his harvest from the London bookshops.

To facilitate his search he retained a Mr. Joseph Walden to work on a bibliography of western American history. This Mr. Walden was accredited as a linguist and a scholar, and was recommended by the proprietor of *The Bookseller,* Mr. J. Whitaker, who became Bancroft's London agent. To Walden was assigned the task of going through the British Museum and other principal libraries in London and making a card for every book, pamphlet, article, or manuscript relating to Bancroft's field, the western half of North America. He was to make memoranda concerning subject matter. Most of his notes were brief enough to go on a 4 by 4-inch card. When longer comments were necessary, he used paper of this same width but accordion-folded to provide whatever space was required. Walden did a little more than a thousand dollars' worth of card making at the rate of two guineas a week. Bancroft speaks of his card index as a great convenience in building up the library and a much more practical guide to western American materials in these London libraries than any descriptions published by them. Walden at length was asked to stop, not because he had exhausted the possibilities—he estimated that there was seven years' more of work to do,—but because his guide to printed books was judged adequate for use in conjunction with the Bancroft collection.[9]

While Walden was in the midst of his card making, Bancroft carried his book quest to the Continent. He entered Paris fully expecting to garner as many books as he had in London. He applied the same technique of searching through catalogues, open shelves, and storage piles, but his actual purchases were much smaller. Although this was partly because many of the items he found duplicated his recent purchases, it was chiefly because Paris lagged behind London as a book center.

---

[9] Bancroft, *Literary Industries,* 181–182, 196–197.

From Paris, in January, 1867, he advanced on Spain, the nation that had performed the lion's share of the exploration of the Pacific Coast, had colonized and governed the southern half of his chosen area, and had lost possession thereof only about twoscore years earlier. Naturally, he assumed that Spain would have a wealth of material on the exploits of her own heroes in the opening up of western America. He found precious little. He says that although he had thought the London dealers apathetic, they were sprightly as compared with the Spaniards. On the main plaza at Burgos, "which was filled with some of the most miserable specimens of muffled humanity" he had ever encountered, were two small shops where traps and trinkets, as well as books, were on sale. Here he found "a few pamphlets which spoke of Mexico." Through a "Californian-looking country" they went on to Madrid. The catalogues of the bookstores were a disappointment, the stores themselves still worse. Two weeks of purposeful hunting brought in only books enough to fill two large boxes. At Saragossa and Barcelona books proved equally scarce. In Bancroft's estimation it all pointed a moral: "If book-selling houses are significant of the intelligence of the people—and we in California, who boast the finest establishments of the kind in the world according to our population, claim that they are—then culture in Spain is at a low ebb."[10]

The conclusion may stand as substantially correct, yet in one of his premises Bancroft was fundamentally in error. For all its lack of bookstores, Spain had a wealth of material for the historian of colonial America. It was manuscript material stored in the archives of the government and the church, particularly in the old Casa Longa at Seville, which had housed the Casa de Contratación, the recording agency for Spain's American empire. Bancroft did not get wind of these manuscript materials, nor, to any appreciable degree, did other historians of his generation. It is interesting to speculate on

[10] *Ibid.*, 184.

what Bancroft might have done had he got into the Long House, yet it is not entirely fair to berate him for neglecting a resource which all his contemporaries were equally unmindful of.

From Spain, Bancroft went on through southern France into Italy and Switzerland, then back to Paris, on to Holland, up the Rhine, and across Germany to Vienna. Nowhere on these travels did he find any great quantity of books to add to his collection, but everywhere he went he found something. The Paris and London bookshops were on his return itinerary, and then, as related previously, he visited Buffalo and Washington and at last reached California in the autumn of 1868.

Thanks particularly to his successes in London, his collection now numbered some ten thousand items, times over more than he had dreamed existed when chance had started him on his career of book gathering. His recent experiences had made him doubtful that a collecting job such as his could ever be carried to absolute completion, and yet, having combed the United States, England, and the Continent, he began to think that he had practically reached the end of his journey. His library was builded; as he borrowed a Latin tag for it, "*Finis coronat opus*."[11]

From this incipient complacency he was jolted, late in 1868, by receipt of a catalogue[12] from List and Francke, of Leipzig, announcing a forthcoming auction sale of the José María Andrade library. Bancroft read this catalogue with increasing absorption. It described a collection of some seven thousand

[11] *Ibid.*, 185.

[12] *Catalogue de la riche bibliothèque de D. José María Andrade. Livres manuscrits et imprimés. Littérature française et espagnole. Histoire de l'Afrique, de l'Asie et de l'Amérique. 7000 pièces et volumes ayant rapport au Mexique ou imprimés dans ce pays. Dont la vente se fera lundi 18 janvier 1869 et jours suivants à Leipzig, dans la salle de ventes de MM. List & Francke, 15 Rue de l'Université, par la ministère de M. Hermann Francke, commissaire priseur* (Leipzig, 1868). The Bancroft Library copy of this catalogue has a price list in thalers and neugroschen bound in.

pieces of Mexicana, manuscript and printed, which Andrade, one of the most zealous and intelligent of Mexican collectors, had been years in gathering. When Maximilian came to Mexico, Andrade had been persuaded, on the promise of suitable compensation, to turn his books over to the emperor to become the nucleus of a projected imperial library. This plan, together with many others, came tumbling down with the defeat and execution of the ill-starred ruler. Thereupon, Andrade promptly repossessed his library and, before the Juárez patriots had time to reach Mexico City, boxed it up, loaded it on the backs of two hundred mules, packed it off to Vera Cruz, and in the end got it safely to the auction rooms of List and Francke in Leipzig.

Bancroft had previously acquired a few Mexican imprints. Never before, however, had the idea struck him with full force that Mexico should be a principal source of materials for his collecting. The Andrade catalogue, with its examples of Mexican printing running back into the 1540's, and with item after item obviously fundamental to the history of western America, was convincing on this score. As Bancroft read, he became increasingly aware that here was an opportunity surpassing any that had previously offered and the like of which might not arise again in his lifetime.

The auction, however, was to start on January 18, 1869. It would be held so far from California that he could not get there for the opening. Nor was there time to check the catalogue against his own holdings. He did, therefore, what seemed the next best thing; he telegraphed $5,000 to Whitaker in London and requested him to attend the sale and purchase at discretion. Bancroft admits to some trepidation in issuing this carte blanche. Although Whitaker knew what sort of collection Bancroft was trying to build, and although he knew something of the recent acquisitions, he was not familiar with the collection as a whole, nor was he a specialist on western Americana.

The outcome was favorable beyond all that Bancroft had dared hope. Whitaker missed hardly a catalogued item that Bancroft would have purchased. He bought 3,000 volumes. A very few were duplicates, but these were more than balanced by others which took rank among the most valuable items in the entire collection. Mindful though he was of the irreparable loss to Mexico when Andrade's mule train got away, Bancroft reckoned the Leipzig auction one of the brightest spots in his career as a collector.[13]

In June of that same year, Puttick and Simpson offered another lot of Mexican works known as the Fischer collection. Whitaker again represented Bancroft and bought almost one-third of the 2,962 items offered.[14] Other auctions followed, in England, on the Continent, and in the United States, and Bancroft was an openhanded but discriminating buyer. Particularly momentous was the sale of E. G. Squier's collection in April, 1876. A diplomatic representative of the United States, a man of means, and a man of letters, Squier had been extraordinarily well qualified for collecting. His library was particularly rich in manuscripts, newspapers, pamphlets, and early books on Central America. It also included a generous helping from the library of Alexander von Humboldt, not to mention other materials acquired in Spain through Squier's good friend Buckingham Smith. Of 2,034 numbered items Bancroft bought 210, which yielded him some 600 volumes to add to his library.[15]

In 1880 the library of another Maximilianist exile was offered for dispersal at London. It consisted of some 1,290 numbered items collected by José Fernando Ramírez of Durango,

---

[13] Bancroft, *Literary Industries,* 185–191.

[14] *Biblioteca Mejicana: A Catalogue of an Extraordinary Collection of Books & Manuscripts, almost wholly relating to the History and Literature of North and South America, particularly Mexico. To be sold by auction by Messrs. Puttick & Simpson . . . , London, June 1, 1869 and seven following days.* The Bancroft Library copy indicates purchasers and prices.

[15] *Catalogue of the Library of E. G. Squier,* edited by Joseph Sabin (New York, 1876); Bancroft, *Literary Industries,* 629–631.

a lawyer, a state judge, a federal judge, head of Mexico's national museum, minister of foreign affairs, president of Maximilian's first ministry, and, with the retirement of the French troops, an exile. At this sale Bancroft was represented by the famous London dealer Henry Stevens, who had been supplied with a copy of the catalogue of the sale marked to show Bancroft's wants, but without a specified buying limit. When the bill came in, Bancroft was surprised to find that it amounted to almost $30,000. The sale had been a public one, presumably honest, and there were no auctioneering antics to boost prices artificially. Instead, the principal purchasers, Bernard Quaritch, Count Heredia, and Stevens, who, besides representing Bancroft, had certain commissions for the British Museum, sat round a table and submitted such bids as they chose on the items offered, whereupon the auctioneer recorded the highest. Though he was taken aback by the prices at this sale, which he thought cast doubts on the general sanity of mankind, Bancroft was pleased with the acquisitions he made. He could also console himself by reflecting that if the Ramírez prices reflected actual values as of 1880, his entire collection must be worth at least a million dollars.[16]

These spectacular intakings did not terminate Bancroft's book gathering. From booksellers' catalogues he made frequent purchases. New books, bearing on his chosen subject, were acquired immediately on publication. And agents throughout the book world turned up single items and small lots to add to the mounting total. Through the Smithsonian Institution and through friends in the government of the United States and the western territories and states he was enabled to acquire government publications that made an important addition. As a collector he continued "lying in wait for opportunities."[17] In 1868 he had about 10,000 volumes. A year later, thanks largely to the Andrade auction,

[16] Bancroft, *Literary Industries,* 194–196.
[17] *Ibid.,* 196.

he had 16,000. Ultimately he was to reckon his holdings at not less than 60,000 volumes.[18]

As the library grew in this lusty fashion it required larger quarters. First it had been accommodated on a few shelves round Knight's desk. Then it filled one corner of the second floor of the Merchant Street building occupied by the bookstore. The rapid growth of the library was one of the factors in the crowding of those quarters and in the determination to build. As soon as the new building on Market Street was finished, the library was installed on its fifth floor. It occupied a space the full length of the building, 170 feet, 50 feet wide at the south end and somewhat narrower at the north. The newspapers were put at one end, works of general reference at the other, and in the intervening space the other books were shelved alphabetically by authors.[19]

This location was in most respects satisfactory, but in one particular it gave Bancroft great concern. The building was not fireproof, and although protection of the financial investment was possible through insurance, Bancroft was more concerned about the irreplaceable character of the materials he had assembled and the irreparable loss to himself, to his plans, and to society, should these books and papers be consumed. Several times fire threatened, and once it came near to gutting the whole building. The trouble started in the basement of the furniture store adjoining to the west. This store was practically destroyed, the bookstore suffered heavy damage, and smoke poured into the fifth-floor rooms

[18] There are many descriptions, but see particularly Reuben Gold Thwaites, "Report on the Bancroft Library," *University [of California] Chronicle,* VIII (1905–1906), 126–143; Flora Haines Apponyi, *The Libraries of California* (San Francisco, 1878), 13–60; [Hubert Howe Bancroft], *The Bancroft Historical Library* (San Francisco, 1886), a 38-page pamphlet; [Hubert Howe Bancroft], *Evolution of a Library* (n.p., [1901]), a 28-page pamphlet; Bancroft, *Literary Industries, passim;* Charles Gregory Crampton, The Bancroft Library (Berkeley, 1938), typescript in the Bancroft Library; and Carl L. Cannon, *American Book Collectors and Collecting* (New York, 1941), 96–102.

[19] Bancroft, *Literary Industries,* 198–200.

in such quantity that the library workers had to climb out through a skylight to the roof. The fire was extinguished just in time to save the library—and, incidentally, the people stranded on the roof.[20]

After this experience Bancroft was in a mood to be easily persuaded to house his library more suitably. The persuasion came in a plea from the manager of the manufacturing division that he needed the fifth floor for his department. Accordingly, Bancroft's financial resources now being more than adequate for the purpose, he decided to go ahead.

For some time he had been mulling over in his mind the problem of the ideal location for his library, considering Oakland, San Rafael, San Mateo, and Menlo Park, as well as various parts of San Francisco. General Vallejo, in the same generous fashion in which he had once proffered to the state ample grounds for its capitol, pressed him to accept a site at Sonoma. Another possibility seriously considered was to place the library near the campus of the University of California. Bancroft was positive that a collection such as his would sooner or later make its influence felt in the direction of historical investigation, and he was curious to know what effects it would have on "the graduating members of a great institution of learning." In the light of the ultimate depositing of the library on the Berkeley campus, these thoughts take on added interest. For the time being, however, choice of location was determined, not by such idealistic reasoning, but by more mundane factors. For the prosecution of the work already started in the library a San Francisco location seemed preferable.

At Valencia and Mission streets a lot was found, measuring 120 by 126 feet. Near its center, so as to avoid contact with any other building, a two-story brick structure was erected. As a further safeguard against fire its openings were covered with iron shutters. Notwithstanding the penchant of the ar-

[20] *Ibid.*, 200, 572–573.

chitects of the period for ornateness, the building was severely plain. Forty feet by sixty in size, it was amply capacious for the 35,000 volumes that comprised the collection in 1881, and it had good working space for those who were to use the library.[21]

Long before the Ramírez sale in 1880, Bancroft had begun to make serious use of his collection. The employment of it soon suggested other ways in which it could be enriched as a collection, and in the 'seventies and 'eighties two methods in particular were used to bring in additional materials.

The first of these was through stressing newspapers. Long before John Bach McMaster was to discover that newspapers are a valuable source for general United States history, Bancroft had a high appreciation of their value for local history. They were, he insisted, often the only record for the initial happenings of a given locality, and even when supplemented by formal histories and volumes of reminiscence they continued to provide a more consecutive record than any other source. Therefore, he kept piling in newspapers until he had the equivalent of some five thousand volumes and runs totaling five hundred years.[22]

His other principal addition in the 'seventies and 'eighties was of manuscript materials. He sent copyists and abstracters to the California provincial archives, to the land office to go through its entire body of records, to the mission archives, and the archbishop's archives. Personally and through secretaries he got several hundred old-timers and pioneer settlers to dictate statements of their experiences. In addition, he was able to gather in historical manuscripts held by individuals. Occasionally, this was by purchase, as when he acquired the several hundred volumes of scrapbooks and miscellany assembled by Benjamin Hayes. More often, he was able to convince the possessors of important historical documents that their treasures would be safer in his collection. Still others, especi-

[21] *Ibid.*, 200–204. [22] *Ibid.*, 574–575.

ally in California, became interested in the history-writing project which Bancroft had undertaken, and were happy to place whatever they had in his library so that it would be available for use in his writing. In this spirit the Vallejo papers, for example, one of the richest manuscript files in the entire collection, were made available by General Mariano Guadalupe Vallejo.

Besides swelling the size of the collection, these manuscripts and newspapers turned out to be perhaps the choicest treasures in the library.[23] So far as Bancroft the collector is concerned, they are of special interest because they were afterthoughts. They illustrate him as a self-taught collector, learning by experience, not blindly following a preconceived plan, but developing his methods and objectives in opportunistic fashion.

Many encomiums have been accorded the Bancroft collection and Bancroft the collector. With respect to his writings, his business success, and most else, Bancroft had a measure of modesty, but when it came to his collection he yielded to no one in singing its praises. Thus, for example, he asserted:

> There is no American collection with which this can fairly be compared. There are other large and costly private libraries; but the scope, plan, and purpose of the Bancroft Library place it beyond the possibility of comparison. It is made up exclusively of printed and manuscript matter pertaining to the Pacific States, from Alaska to Panamá. To say that it is superior to any other in its own field goes for little, because there are no others of any great magnitude; but when we can state truthfully that nowhere in the world is there a similar collection equal to it, the assertion means something. And not only does this collection thus excel all others as a whole, but a like excellence is apparent for each of its parts. In it may be found, for instance, a better library of Mexican works, of Central American works, of Pacific United States works, than elsewhere exists. And to

[23] "The great value of the library today consists not in the collection of books but in the wealth of manuscript and printed material which Mr. Bancroft obtained from the old California grandees, and the personal reminiscences of the pioneers which were dictated to some of his agents." Henry Raup Wagner, *Bullion to Books* (Los Angeles, 1942), 251.

go further, it may be said to contain a more perfect collection on Alaska, on New Mexico, on Texas, on Colorado, on Utah, on Costa Rica, and the other individual states or governments than can be found outside its walls. Not only this, but in several cases, notably that of California, this library is regarded as incomparably superior to any state collection existing, or that could at this date be formed in all the United States or Europe.

There is no other state or country whose historic data have been so thoroughly collected at so early a period of its existence, especially none whose existence has been so varied and eventful, and its record so complicated and perishable.[24]

Any cautious person, reading this statement, might be expected to wonder if Bancroft had not made his claims a trifle too far-reaching. At the time of his writing, however, they were incontestably correct. To fit the present, some allowance might have to be made for collections built up within the last half century, at the University of Texas, in New Mexico, and elsewhere, yet the essential assertions would still hold. As a collection of Pacific states materials the Bancroft Library is still without a peer, several of its parts are unsurpassed in their more limited fields, and the California section, particularly for the early and middle nineteenth century, has qualities seldom approached in other state and local collections.

Much of this excellence, to be sure, is attributable to the nature of western American history and to the circumstances in which Bancroft did his collecting. It was his good fortune to be the first to undertake to assemble materials on the western half of the continent. A generation later, scores of collectors, both private and institutional, were at work in this field, and their competitive bidding drove prices skyward. At the time of his collecting, furthermore, he was so close to the period of first American contacts with the West Coast, American acquisition, the Gold Rush, the building of the first railroads, and other stirring events, that he had a superlative opportunity to gather in the personal testimony of partici-

[24] Bancroft, *Literary Industries,* 213–214.

pants still living, and to pick up early newspapers and pamphlets as well as the more obvious grist for a collector's mill, books.

Nevertheless, it was not luck and circumstance alone that brought him his success. His personal contribution was very great. It was advantageous that he was in the book business when he began to collect. It was highly convenient that his affairs so prospered that his collecting was never seriously hampered by budgetary limits. The success of the project also owed much to his zeal and his willingness to give unstinted time and energy to collecting. Agents were employed, to be sure, and often with excellent results, but essentially the library was built around the materials that Bancroft accumulated by personally scanning dealers' catalogues and auction lists and by devoting days on end to ransacking stocks.

Given these three advantages—a professional bookman, ample money, and a diligent searcher—the collection still might not have attained much significance. Had Bancroft veered off, as some collectors have, in the direction of fine bindings, first editions, or some restricted specialty, his library might have had little more than curiosity value. His wisdom in seeing beyond state and national limits and his brashness in taking in the entire western half of North America were basic contributions. Similarly, his policy of collecting everything that bore on western history, whether it was prose or poetry, book or pamphlet, broadside or newspaper, authoritative or partisan, was worth much to the ultimate importance of his library. In fact, the broad scope and the attempted completeness are the particular strengths of the Bancroft Library.

Without being captious, a critic can point out certain flaws in this collecting. Unkind rumor has it that materials borrowed for use in the library were not always returned. Anyone who has borrowed or lent a book will admit this possibility. Bancroft's preserved correspondence points to at least one such instance. On February 20, 1889, D. W. Craig of Salem,

Oregon, wrote to acknowledge receipt of the files of the *Oregon Argus* which he had lent to Bancroft several years earlier. "They are handsomely bound," Craig wrote, "and are in as good condition as when they came from the press. . . . Allow me to thank you for the fine appearance of these files." He went on to say, however, that besides the eight years of the paper that had come back to him, there was another six months, some twenty-four numbers, and he earnestly requested their return, preferably bound.[25] Receiving this letter in San Diego, Bancroft dashed off a note to his office assistant: "David," he wrote, "You need say nothing about prepaying charges to D. W. Craig. Let it go. Here comes another letter for more *Argus*. Will we never get rid of this man & his *Argus*. Please answer it. Tell him I am away. If you can find his papers send them to him, but not bind them. Tell him in my absence you are not authorized to do so."[26] Irritation shows in this note, but along with it is evidence of honest intention to restore materials to the rightful owner.

Doubtless there were other instances of the sort, some of them arising from misunderstanding or clouded recollection of the terms under which some items, usually family papers, were taken to the library. And vindication of a kind is to be found in the fact, as a former librarian of the Bancroft Library has pointed out, that Bancroft was never sued for improper appropriation of materials.

But though that charge may be dismissed as a calumny, other criticisms are valid. Mention has already been made of how it did not occur to Bancroft that there was anything for him in the archives of the Spanish and Mexican governments. Similarly, though assiduous in collecting government publications, he made no effort to examine the manuscript collections in government offices at Washington. A consequence is

[25] D. W. Craig to H. H. Bancroft, Salem, Oregon, February 20, 1889, MS in Bancroft Library.

[26] Hubert Howe Bancroft to David [ ], San Diego, February 28, 1889, MS in Bancroft Library.

that in the archives of these three nations something was left for twentieth-century researchers to exploit, and this has been one of the main ways in which modern study of western America has supplemented Bancroft.

Bancroft had another characteristic all too commonly encountered in local historians. He was less attentive to the recent past than to the more remote. His collection was richer on the Bear Flag Revolt than on the orange industry, more replete on the Gold Rush than on railroad building, more exhaustive on the pioneer settlers than on the migration of the later nineteenth century. True, his major writing project was completed in the 1880's, but he lived until 1918, his library did not pass to the University until 1905, and he might have assembled much on these later aspects of western history. That he did not was primarily because he was not particularly impressed with the history being made in the West after 1870 or 1880. If this neglect is bad, today's historians are equally guilty. They have higher esteem for such things as the rise of the orange industry, the oil industry, and the railroads, but are correspondingly slow to take notice of the automobile and its highways, the new agriculture, and the industries established in the last quarter century.[27]

Notwithstanding these gaps, Bancroft built in his library an enduring monument. It is still first in most of the categories in which he claimed preëminence in 1890. What is more to the point, it has become, especially in the last twenty years, the chief fountainhead of research on the history of western America. This result, one is constrained to believe, would have been highly gratifying to Bancroft, the diligent collector, because his aims were above all utilitarian.

---

[27] See John Walton Caughey, "The Local Historian: His Occupational Hazards and Compensations," *Pacific Historical Review,* XII (1943), 1–9; and John D. Hicks, "California in History," California Historical Society *Quarterly,* XXIV (1945), 7–16.

8

A Half Continent's History

I would strike at once for the highest, brightest mark before me.... History-writing I conceived to be among the highest of human occupations, and this should be my choice.
Hubert Howe Bancroft, *Literary Industries,* 228–229

As Bancroft in retrospect charted his course, he said it was from bibliopolist to bibliophile, and from bibliomania to bibliogenesis[1]—which means that he advanced from bookseller to booklover, and from the collecting of books to the writing of them. That his collecting should have had issue in something tangible seems almost inevitable. From the very outset, when he assembled the western books in stock for the convenience of editor Knight, his collection had had a utilitarian aspect. His collecting technique, furthermore, with its emphasis on content rather than externals, had likewise presaged use of the library. His obvious personal interest in the ingathering, and the zest with which he underwent the drudgery of searching out additional materials, are clues to his rising appreciation of the significance and the possibilities of the great subject on which he was collecting. They foreshadowed the next step when he would undertake to release, through writing, some of the knowledge and wisdom stored up in his collection. The question was merely what and how.

It was shortly before 1870 that the urge to write overtook him. The call was not simple and unmistakable, but multiple and confusing. Perhaps overstimulated by his financial success, by his travels, and by his contact with some ten thousand

[1] Bancroft, *Literary Industries,* 168–176.

volumes of western Americana, his brain supplied him with a host of topics on which he thought he would like to do a book or a series of books. Included among the projects that attracted him were a history of gold, a volume on interoceanic communications, one on the Pacific railways, a condensed voyages and travels, a geography of the Pacific states, an ethnology of western America, a one-volume popular history of the Pacific states. He was also tempted to publish or republish fifty or a hundred of the choicer items in his collection. Years later, Bancroft came back to two of these projects, by that time somewhat modified.[2] One other the present writer had the pleasure of essaying in 1933.[3] Some of the rest still await doing. Bancroft, meanwhile, fretted under the discordant tugging of these various impulses. This ability to see many things to do, he did not interpret as a mark of genius; he did not recognize it as a true mark of the scholar. On the contrary, he assumed that it was common to all who labor under the pressure of *cacoëthes scribendi.*[4]

None of the topics listed above got his first attention. Instead he inclined, or rather allowed himself to be persuaded to lean, toward the preparation of a Pacific states encyclopedia. Although the plan never elicited his full enthusiasm, Bancroft could see that it had its points. Here was his library, packed with information that might be highly valuable to the people of the West. The encyclopedia form appeared the most efficient one for making this information accessible. It was not proposed to supersede all other encyclopedias, but to deal with the Pacific states with far greater thoroughness. A format of fairly small volumes was planned, with the expectation that certain articles, such as those on bibliography, ethnology, and mines and mining, might fill an entire volume and enjoy a separate circulation. So ran the plans.

---

[2] Bancroft, *Native Races* (5 vols.; New York, 1874–1875), and Bancroft, *California Inter Pocula* (San Francisco, 1888).

[3] *History of the Pacific Coast* (Los Angeles, 1933).

[4] Bancroft, *Literary Industries,* 222–226.

Collaborators in plenty, Bancroft was assured, stood ready to contribute. By circulars, through agents, and in person he set out to recruit the necessary writers. Everyone seemed willing. John S. Hittell, author of a much-used handbook on the resources of California, offered his not inconsiderable services. Other San Franciscans, such as Archbishop Alemany, the historian John W. Dwinelle, and Judge Ogden Hoffman, promised to contribute, as did such outlanders as J. J. Warner of southern California, E. G. Squier of New York, and Joaquín García Icazbalceta of Mexico, not to mention several score others. A call on Brigham Young roused his interest and got a promise of help from informants in all parts of Mormondom. From New York came word that William T. Coleman would dictate a statement about the Second Vigilance Committee, which he had headed, and that James W. Simonton would write an article on western journalism, provided Bancroft would supply the data.

The managers of coöperative writing projects have, by repute, an onerous and thankless task. Bancroft began to sense this as he went about among the California literati and the men of vision and experience whom he wished to enlist as contributors. Most of them were sincere enough in their expression of willingness to help, and a few, like Hittell, were filled with genuine enthusiasm. Yet it was obvious that some would never get around to writing, that others would not turn out what was wanted, and that the majority, aware of the superlative collection of materials that Bancroft possessed, would tend to rely on him for the factual framework. Here was the rock on which the project finally foundered. The responsibility of supplying the facts, when superimposed on the burdens of editorship, was more than Bancroft cared to shoulder. After lining up several score contributors, giving much thought to planning the encyclopedia, and issuing a detailed prospectus, he decided to abandon the project.[5]

[5] *Ibid.;* Bancroft, *Retrospection,* 319–320.

This false start toward utilization of his library was made in the spring of 1871. It was a time when the recent loss of his wife preyed heavily on his mind. It was also the period when he was straining every effort to bring his expanded business through the hard times that had accompanied the arrival of the transcontinental railroad. Under these circumstances the encyclopedia project had something less than a fair chance. To top it all, Bancroft's health broke. He mentions no malady and no organic disorder other than nervous exhaustion, but describes himself as despondent, irritable, and indifferent. He resolved, therefore, on a vacation trip to the East. On the way, he interviewed Brigham Young and other leading Mormons on behalf of the encyclopedia, but this was the last flickering of his interest in that project. He passed the summer "lounging about" among his friends in the East, "listless and purposeless."

"From this lethargy," he recites, "I was awakened by the accidental remark of a lady." He describes her as "an earnest, practical woman, cool and calculating." Established social position and the security afforded by more than adequate wealth had augmented her natural egotism. She was, furthermore, a friend of long standing and a person endowed with intellect and judgment well above average. Accordingly, she had little difficulty in seeing that her guest was miserable because he was at loose ends and had no task that challenged his capacities. And having diagnosed his troubles, she had no hesitancy about telling him what was wrong and prodding him to a solution of his problem. Without any beating around the bush she put it up to him: "The next ten years will be the best of your life; what are you going to do with them?"[6]

On the threshold of his forties, Bancroft faced this question. He had pondered it before, but never so directly. Should he return to San Francisco, take charge of his business again, and concentrate on solidifying its financial position? Or should

---

[6] Bancroft, *Literary Industries,* 226–228.

he aspire to a literary career? These seemed to be the alternatives, the first a course of prudence and sanity, the second a hazardous and perhaps presumptuous program for a man so largely self-taught, and experienced only in business. Yet the more he thought about it, the more he was fired with ambition. He resolved "to strike at once for the highest, brightest mark" before him.[7]

Exactly what that should be was a detail to be worked out; yet the choice was soon made. He was drawn irresistibly to history writing, which he "conceived to be among the highest of human occupations," and the branch of history that he should select was virtually predetermined by his collecting of western Americana. As a partial legacy from the late project of a Pacific states encyclopedia came the determination to make this history a thorough presentation of the information contained in his library. Proposal of a comprehensive history was also in accord with his desire to set up a goal that would be a challenge to his best efforts. Thus, at any rate, his plans took shape. He would produce a history of the Pacific states, the western half of North America, and it would, if possible, be a complete and detailed exposition of that subject, utilizing to the full the vast resources of his collection.[8]

Determined on his course, Bancroft in the fall of 1871 returned to San Francisco. There, as he and his librarian began to survey the collection, the magnitude of his self-assigned task became increasingly apparent. Recently enriched by the Andrade purchases, the library now numbered eighteen or twenty thousand volumes. Most of the collection had been alphabetized by authors, but this was only a feeble step toward making it usable or toward assisting the researcher to find what the library contained on any particular topic. Today, given this same collection and some sort of finding list, one could proceed with some assurance toward a comprehensive

---

[7] *Ibid.*, 228.

[8] *Ibid.*, 228–229. See also Bancroft, *Retrospection*, 324–328.

history of the area, because general and specialized bibliographies are available, monographs have been written on a great number of topics scattered through the field, and several syntheses have been attempted for the history of the region or its parts. In Bancroft's day hardly anything of the sort had been done. Aptly describing the plight he and his librarian were in, he appropriated[9] Coleridge's lines,

> We were the first that ever burst
> Into that silent sea.

The expanse of this uncharted sea was enough to give Bancroft pause. Of the books in his library he had not read a half, or a fourth. Indeed, he calculated that at eight hours a day of conscientious application he would be four hundred years in going through them. Yet all these books were pertinent to his grand subject and if he was to cover it thoroughly he could not afford to disregard any item in his library. All this pointed to an inescapable conclusion: he must use readers, copyists, abstracters, clerks—or, as we say now, "research assistants." From the outset his plans were laid accordingly.[10]

Just how to put these helpers to work was a more perplexing problem. The conventional technique of coöperative historical writing was, and is, to break down the larger subject into parts, each of which may be assigned to an individual investigator. For Bancroft's project this method seemed to hold little promise. With his collection in the state in which it was, such a parceling out of topics would have meant that many of the investigators—for example, those studying agriculture, or transportation, or Indian relations, or the San Francisco Bay area—would still have to paw through the entire library. What was needed was a sorting or regimenting

[9] Bancroft, *Literary Industries,* 230.

[10] Bancroft consistently and repeatedly avowed this use of assistants. See his *Literary Industries,* 245–277, 365–376, 513; *Retrospection,* 326–339; *A Brief Account of the Literary Undertakings of Hubert Howe Bancroft* (San Francisco, 1892), 10–11; and many of the other advertising brochures issued to assist the canvassers for the *Works.*

or classifying of the collection so that a researcher on any phase of Pacific states history could find his way quickly to the materials on that particular topic.

As a first move toward classifying his collection, Bancroft set his librarian to cutting up duplicates and severalizing the parts. Bibliophiles may cringe, but this was one way of getting order out of chaos. Not a very good solution, neither was it a complete solution. Only a few books were available in duplicate copies, and some of these were so rare or so costly that it seemed a crime to do violence to them.

The next resort was to a system of extracting. Bancroft and his librarian went through certain volumes marking passages to be copied. A staff of copyists then took these books and with pen and ink scratched out longhand extracts which could be segregated by subject matter. Had typewriters been available, this process could have been much accelerated. It would still, however, have had the fundamental defect of uncertain accuracy. When Bancroft began to use these transcripts, he found that they would not do. The possibility of a copyist's error constantly hovered in the background, and there was a more fundamental defect, which even today's techniques of photocopying would not have overcome. The removal of these extracted passages from their contexts robbed them of much of their meaning and rendered them unsatisfactory. Only after six or eight men had labored thus for several months, filling some twenty-five reams of paper with their writing, did Bancroft conclude that the method was faulty. Thereupon, it was "but the work of a moment" to consign the fruit of their labors "to the waste heap."

This experiment came to its inglorious end in December, 1871. A year later there was another large quantity of manuscript to be thrown out. The idea of a collection of Pacific Coast voyages and travels had long appealed to Bancroft, and now it occurred to him that this might be a suitable introductory venture in letters. Accordingly, Hakluyt, Navarrete,

Humboldt, Edwin Bryant, Bayard Taylor, and the like were parceled out to the several copyists, who were to extract the Pacific Coast portions or to follow "a devised system of condensation." In the end Bancroft realized that these condensed narratives would be a poor substitute for the originals and that the extracted passages tended to wobble when cut loose from their moorings. Happily, therefore, without regard to the time and money that had gone into this further copying, he decided to drop the plan.[11]

Meanwhile, still another program of classifying the collection had been started. It was, simply, to make a subject index to the whole library, much as one might index a single book. On the face of it, this idea seemed foolproof. Surely it would enable one to find his way about in the labyrinth of the library. Forthwith, therefore, the work began, with the librarian indexing the Hakluyt and Navarrete collections of voyages, another doing likewise for the California legislative documents, another for the *Atlantic Monthly* and lesser American periodicals. Anyone with indexing experience could have told Bancroft that on cards an analytical index of almost any history book will bulk larger than the book itself, and consequently that a comparable index to a library would be larger than the library. No one told Bancroft, but he and his assistants soon discovered that the index, as they had originally planned it, would be prohibitive in cost, and cumbersome and unwieldy to the point of uselessness.

Reluctant to abandon the idea of an index, the proprietor, librarian, and staff frequently discussed alterations that might make it feasible, and after much tinkering they contrived a plan for a simplified index. For one thing, they resolved to index only Pacific states history, disregarding all that was irrelevant. Thus at one stroke they were able to eliminate tons of extraneous matter, the "trash," Bancroft calls it, "with

[11] For discussion of these various unsuccessful experiments see Bancroft, *Literary Industries,* 230–238.

which every author seems bound in a greater or less degree to dilute his writings." They would omit, for example, a writer's ideas of religion, his accounts of what he saw or did outside the Pacific area, and his personal affairs, "unless of so striking a character as to command general interest."[12] Here was an appreciable saving and a comparable increase in the efficiency of the index.

Having narrowed the field to the materials actually pertinent to Pacific states history, they next sought a unified plan of attack, simple and direct, so that the cards turned out by all the workers engaged in the project would fit together. If, for example, one worker indexed material on the Indians under "aborigines," another under "natives," another under "redskins," another under "savages," and so on, endless confusion would result. To obviate this difficulty they listed forty or fifty broad subjects which seemed to them to "embrace all real knowledge" with regard to western North America. These included such headings as Agriculture, Antiquities, Architecture, Art, Bibliography, Biography, Botany, Commerce, and so on down the alphabet. Abbreviations for these headings were agreed upon.

The system was further standardized. An indexer examining a given passage would first select whichever of the forty or fifty main headings was most appropriate. In abbreviation this heading was written on a 3 by 5-inch slip of heavy paper, followed on the same line by other entries further refining the analysis of subject matter. A certain flexibility was permitted, but in general the entries followed this pattern: (1) *what* (abbreviation indicating one of the forty or fifty main headings), (2) *where,* (3) if necessary *a particularization of what or where,* and (4) *when.* Line 2 cited the reference by author and title, place and date of publication, volume and page. A third line contained catchwords indicating the nature of the material there to be found. Thus the index card

[12] *Ibid.,* 238–239.

here reproduced informs that the passage indicated has information on the location, character, dress, and manufactures of the Zapotecs of Tehuantepec as of 1847. The cards then were sorted by topic, within the topical groups by place, and within the geographical groups by date.[13]

Ind. Tehuan. Zapotecs. 1847.

Macgregor, J. Progress of America. London, 1847. Vol. I., pp. 848–9.

Location, Character, Dress, Manufactures.

The whole procedure sounds simple enough. It was soon discovered, however, that not every applicant for work could follow the specifications. Librarian Henry L. Oak spent much of his time explaining the method to successive indexers. An indexer was put to work on a book, and the cards he produced were then inspected and checked. If they passed muster, he was allowed to proceed. If not, the work was done over. A surprising number of intelligent and willing workers seemed totally unable to develop the knack that was required—a circumstance most discouraging to those who tried to instruct them. Others, however, proved adept; Bancroft says about one in twenty. By their hands, and Bancroft's pocketbook, the index was fashioned.

[13] For description of the technique developed see *ibid.*, 238–244, and Bancroft, *Retrospection*, 329–330.

Modern office practice would doubtless have suggested that the cards be filed in a battery of drawers and secured by a rod passed through punched holes, as is done universally with library card catalogues. As a dealer in stationery and office supplies Bancroft would have been informed of these devices when they came into general use. His, however, was an era lacking the card file, and consequently he was thrown back upon his own resources to design a receptacle for his index. Carpenters and tinsmiths were summoned and set to work fashioning cupboards about five feet high and four wide, with a depth of six inches or less. Vertical partitions were set in, a card's length apart, and tin shelves were inserted, tilted toward the back so that the cards would not fall out.[14] These open-faced containers, somewhat similar to the contraption used in sorting mail, had a certain convenience for the work of sorting the index slips. But as permanent files they were not well designed. The slips were left loose. In ordinary use, it was inevitable that some would be misplaced. With the cases so shallow in proportion to their height, there was also a good chance that one might topple over, and in an earthquake country, furthermore, it seems reckless to have depended entirely on the tilt of the shelves to hold the slips in these open-faced cases.

There are other respects in which it seems that modern library techniques would have saved Bancroft much time and expense. A card catalogue of his books by author, title, and subject, and a classification putting them in place on the basis of their general subject matter, would have provided a basic framework. Except where special bibliographies have been prepared, these are the devices that most researchers depend upon today to direct them to the books they should use. In his day, however, library cataloguing and classifying were but rudimentary sciences. The Harvard Library was only just

[14] The Bancroft Library has one of these cupboards, long since retired to inactive storage.

HENRY LEBBEUS OAK

SECOND FLOOR OF THE BANCROFT LIBRARY

FIRST FLOOR OF THE BANCROFT LIBRARY

then acquiring the first card catalogue. The spread of this system to other libraries was still to come, and the development of classification, as we know it, was to wait until yet later. Had these devices been available, it is possible that Bancroft would have contented himself with them. Yet perhaps not. His index certainly went much further. It covered his whole collection—periodical material, newspapers, and manuscripts as well as books—and it was thoroughly analytical of subject matter for the history of his chosen area, whereas modern library catalogues are only superficially so.

The index represented the work of a score or more of men, some of whom were engaged on the task for years, and it cost some $35,000. Far from begrudging this sum, Bancroft thought the money well invested, because he regarded the index as of incalculable value. It constituted a guide to the literature on every conceivable phase of Pacific states history, even the most insignificant, such as the texture of an Eskimo's hair or the construction of a Paiute wickiup. Bancroft prized the index as a key unlocking the treasures of his collection, as the magic wand that had produced order in its unrestrained chaos. Describing the magic of the index, he explained:

> A man may seat himself at a bare table and say to a boy, Bring me all that is known about the conquest of Darien, the mines of Nevada, the missions of Lower California, the agriculture of Oregon, the lumber interests of Washington, the state of Sonora, the town of Querétaro, or any other information extant, or any description, regarding any described portion of the western half of North America, and straightway, as at the call of a magician, such knowledge is spread before him with the volumes opened at the page. Aladdin's lamp could produce no such results. That commanded material wealth, but here is a sorcery that conjures up the wealth of mind and places it at the disposition of the seer.[15]

In further praise of his index Bancroft pointed out that the

[15] Bancroft, *Literary Industries,* 241. It should be noted that Henry L. Oak, who for years was Bancroft's right-hand man, put a lower estimate on the cost and the value of the index. *"Literary Industries" in a New Light* (San Francisco, 1893), 27–28.

method could be adapted to any collection; he insisted that only through indexing could there be effective utilization of the contents of a large collection; and he reasoned that the larger the library, the greater the necessity for indexing. Pursuing this line of thought to its ultimate conclusion, he suggested that a universal index, covering the books of the world collectively, would be of incalculable advantage to civilization. It may be questioned whether a universal index, because of its very size, would have been of much practical use. Bancroft was aware that the task of compilation would far surpass the resources of any one person, and he was not optimistic that group action would bring it about. Yet he was confident that the great libraries of the world would adopt his system or something comparable

Finally, Bancroft gave best proof of his high opinion of the index by leaning on it heavily in the preparation of his histories. Without it they obviously would not have been produced. The mark of the index is apparent throughout the thirty-nine volumes, in their organization as well as their content, and in their footnotes a good fraction of it is incorporated.

9

The Men on the Fifth Floor

I had only raw material to put at work on raw material. If ever I was to have assistants, I must make them.
Hubert Howe Bancroft, *Retrospection,* 336

FROM THE MOMENT of his decision to attempt a comprehensive history of the Pacific states, Bancroft had been aware that assistance would be required. As the work progressed and he came to a clearer realization of the magnitude of his self-assigned task, he responded by surrounding himself with a larger staff than he originally contemplated. In all this his attitude was that of an engineer, manufacturer, or businessman planning a venture that would obviously require more than one pair of hands. It all seemed perfectly natural to him, yet his employment of assistance has been remarked as one of the distinguishing features—possibly unique—of his history writing.

The implication is not that no other historians have had help. The practice, though not universal, is by no means peculiar. Coöperative works are numerous and utilization of assistants is a common practice. Nor is it a recognition simply of the number of helpers used. In this respect Bancroft was phenomenal, but more essentially his distinction lay in the type of assistants he employed, in the technique he developed for the division of labor in historical research, and in the mass production he was able to achieve through the application of this technique.

His idea, in brief, was that historical research could be broken down into a number of fairly simple operations, that these need not all be performed by the same person, and that the end result would be attained more rapidly through such a division of labor. The $35,000 index was a long step toward putting this plan into execution and was fundamental to its success. Other ways were soon devised in which assistants could be used in assembling data and in note taking.[1] Bancroft, however, was not ready to stop at this point. He was certain that staff members could render equally valuable assistance in writing up the results of investigation. To some of his helpers, therefore, were assigned tasks of outlining what was to be written on certain subjects and of drawing up first drafts of parts of chapters, whole chapters, or series of chapters.[2]

The theory was that Bancroft, besides taking some part in the earlier stage of the work, would go over the drafts submitted by his assistants and would so far revise and rewrite as to make the writing his own. In practice, especially in the later stages, his revisions were often much more perfunctory. And since the histories were published with only his name attached, there arose some complaint and some criticism, as is discussed below in the chapter entitled "Process of Authorship." Here the point intended is that Bancroft expected to use his assistants not merely for gathering data and taking notes, but also for the subsequent and perhaps higher duties of historical composition.

This fact accounts in part for the size of the staff. First and last, more than six hundred persons were employed in his literary workshop. A number were on the payroll only briefly, but there were occasions when as many as fifty were at work, and in all the twenty years given to the project the minimum seldom fell below half a dozen. Of the six hundred there apparently was not one who was a member of the staff from the

[1] Oak's testimony is that the notes would have cost more than $80,000 to reproduce. *"Literary Industries" in a New Light,* 28.

[2] The plan is set forth and argued in Bancroft, *Literary Industries,* 230–306.

beginning to the end. At least twenty, however, were wheel-horses in the organization, and five or six proved so competent and valuable that they seemed indispensable.[3]

On the surface it may appear that Bancroft's intention to delegate much of the responsibility of writing would have necessitated employment of trained historians. The actual practice was quite the contrary; his staff included no one formally trained for history writing and almost no one with an established reputation as a writer. This relative indistinction of the men on the fifth floor was not because Bancroft purposely sought mediocrity. He actually demonstrated the quality, not always possessed by great men, of preferring to surround himself with the best talent available. Were Bancroft launching the same work today, he doubtless would use a staff of Ph.D.'s in history. But in the 1870's men with such a background were not available, and there was a particular dearth of trained men in the as yet undiscovered field of western American history. Bancroft perforce made use of such men as he could get.

The consequence, that the writing of the history of the Pacific states was entrusted to a group of men inexperienced in scholarly writing, unversed in the science of history, and for the most part innocent of any collegiate training, Bancroft viewed with equanimity. He had a democratic attitude toward this business of history writing that was reminiscent of Andrew Jackson's attitude toward the eligibility of the common man for public office. Special training might help, but the main thing was to find someone endowed with common sense and with a willingness to work. Accordingly, Bancroft went about recruiting his staff by the same method of trial and error that he had used in developing his system of collecting, in selecting his subject, and in devising the index. Likely-looking applicants were put to work, irrespective of their training or lack of training. Those who gave satisfaction were

[3] *Ibid.*, 245.

retained, and those who showed special aptitudes were advanced to tasks of greater responsibility.

The six hundred who were tried, the hundred or more who had protracted employment, the score who made a substantial contribution, and even the half dozen who came to be regarded as indispensable were so heterogeneous that a composite description seems almost impossible.

They hailed from all parts of the earth. England contributed a larger number than the United States, while among the twenty principal helpers were natives of Ireland, Scandinavia, Germany, Russia, Italy, and Cuba, as against only one whose birthplace was California. They had come to San Francisco by way of a still greater variety of places—the West Indies, South America, Central America, Mexico, Oregon, Alaska, Hawaii, and Australia.

The majority had not enjoyed much more of formal schooling than their employer, though various members of the staff had completed courses of study at Dartmouth, Cambridge, Louvain, and elsewhere. A few had had a fling at teaching, but the more common backgrounds involved journalism, hack writing, editorial work, and consular service. The multilingual character of the materials in Bancroft's collection put a premium on proficiency in the languages, and on this point the group deserves a high scoring. A fair number also resembled the proprietor in having read widely and traveled extensively.

Besides the employments listed above, various members of the staff had put in time as sailors, soldiers, miners, interpreters, storekeepers, clerks, and bookkeepers. Several had come to California for their health, others in search of adventure. Measured by their previous attainments, the majority had not made a great mark in the world; the employment Bancroft had to offer and the wages he was ready to pay would not have had attraction for the conspicuously successful. Yet the staff did include Carlos F. Galán, a former governor of Baja California, Arundel Harcourt, who claimed to be a scion of the British nobility, and William Nemos, whose alias cloaked a distinguished Scandinavian name.

Principal among the assistants was Henry Lebbeus Oak.[4] Born at Garland, Maine, on May 13, 1844, Oak was a dozen years Bancroft's junior. His boyhood was spent in a typical New England small-town environment, not unlike what Bancroft had known in Ohio. Having displayed some aptitude for scholarship, he spent the years of the Civil War as a student at Bowdoin and Dartmouth, graduating from the latter institution in 1865. In winter vacations betimes he taught school in various small towns in Maine. The year after his graduation he taught at an academy in Morristown, New Jersey. Then, through the intervention of his roommate, he was offered a job as clerk in McNabb Brothers' grain warehouse in Petaluma, California. Serious illness soon forced him to give up this work. His recovery is attributed to the generous care of Mr. S. F. Barstow and his wife, the latter a sister of the former roommate who had persuaded him to come to California.

Oak was next befriended by that famous and beloved California schoolman, John R. Swett, who procured him a place as principal of the public school at Hayward. After one term he transferred to a Methodist school, the Napa Collegiate Institute, as assistant principal. In the persistent absence of the principal, most of the duties devolved upon him, including the responsibility of conducting school prayers. Since he inclined toward agnosticism, this duty was an unwelcome one. Nor was teaching particularly to his liking, and consequently, after five months, he was glad to resign. A period of idleness was followed by a year's employment as editor of the *Occident*, a Presbyterian journal published by the Bancroft house, and in 1869, when the publication of the *Occident* was transferred

[4] *Ibid.*, 219–224, 246–251; Oak, *"Literary Industries" in a New Light;* Henry L. Oak, *Oak–Oaks–Oakes: Family Register of Nathaniel Oak of Marlborough, Mass. . . . with Sketch of Life of Henry Lebbeus Oak* (Los Angeles, 1906).

elsewhere, Oak was retained as librarian of Bancroft's historical collection. He continued in this capacity for almost a score of years, throughout almost the entire life of the history-writing project.

When Oak took over, the collection had not been put into satisfactory order; in fact, one of his first problems was to devise some system for logical arrangement of the materials. This task was soon complicated, and at the same time made the more necessary, by the arrival of Bancroft's purchases from the Andrade sale. Accessions followed steadily. While these problems were still in process of solution, moving day came. It was Oak's duty to prepare an inventory[5] of Bancroft's holdings and to supervise the transfer from the Merchant Street quarters to the fifth floor of the Market and Stevenson block. Though moving is an ordeal that comes to most librarians once or never in a lifetime, Oak had it to do again in 1881 after the completion of the Valencia Street building.

Adding also to Oak's responsibility was the fact that, throughout the years he was in charge, the Bancroft Library was emphatically a working library. His position was no sinecure. The materials had to be put in order and kept in order so as to be available when called for by Bancroft or any of his assistants.

These tasks, important though they were, constituted by no means the total of Oak's part in the work on the fifth floor. He had a good deal to do with devising the index and with supervising actual work on it. He also became chiefly responsible for investigating the Spanish voyages to California and the Northwest Coast and the history of California as a Spanish and Mexican province. On these topics he was the best-informed man on the staff and, *ipso facto,* as Bancroft might have phrased it, in the world.

---

[5] Henry L. Oak, Catalogue of Books and Pamphlets in the Bancroft Library, a manuscript volume of some 500 pages, Bancroft Library. See also Bancroft, *Literary Industries,* 222.

Librarians are said to have as occupational characteristics "a lean and ascetic look and a cat-like tread." Oak was quiet and reserved. In his relations with others he was pleasant and affable, but he did not go out of his way to seek companionship. To the work in the library he was content to devote his wholehearted attention, and for a long time he was actually domiciled on the fifth floor. He was methodical, patient, a steady worker, and in many other respects the good librarian. He possessed several other qualities which made him particularly valuable in Bancroft's plans for history writing. He was expert in the Spanish and French languages and more or less familiar with several others. He had executive ability of an unusual order and is to be credited with much of the administration of the work done in the library and with a share of the planning of that work. Furthermore, he had a talent for simple, clear, and effective writing, and since he acted rather as editor for the entire output of the writing staff, his contribution was not altogether limited to the portions that were his personal assignment.

William Nemos[6] ranked close to Oak as a key man in the organization. Like him he was quiet and retiring, a tenacious and enthusiastic worker, and possessed of no little executive ability. His background, however, was about as far removed from Oak's as can be imagined. He was born in Sweden in February, 1848. His father was of the nobility, his mother of a prominent family and wealthy. Early in life his parents began introducing him to the languages of northern Europe, and as a child he was bundled off to St. Petersburg for schooling that might lead to a position under the czar. "Wrapped in contraband stuffs, he was passed tremblingly through the hands of the fierce Muscovites into the gentler ones of a lady for whom the goods were intended, and who unrolled him with affectionate care."[7] After a year he returned home and was next enrolled in the gymnasium at Stockholm, prepara-

[6] *Ibid.*, 251–255. [7] *Ibid.*, 252.

tory to entering Upsala University. Reverses in the family fortunes thwarted this intention, and instead the young man went to London to learn the English language and to toil as a clerk in a commission and ship broker's office. Into these workaday surroundings he was unwilling to bring his ancestral name and thenceforth chose to be called William Nemos.

In his spare time Nemos continued his studies, particularly of philosophy. Then followed five years' employment with one of the leading houses trading with India, his summer vacations usually being spent in travels on the Continent. He might have continued indefinitely in this work, at which he was doing well, but when a sister died of consumption he fell to worrying about his own health, which was showing the effects of long hours of study and office work and a minimum of exercise. A letter to the family physician brought suggestion of a long sea voyage. Nemos thereupon resigned his position and early in 1870 took passage on a sailing vessel for Melbourne.

Soon after his arrival, he went up into the Australian gold diggings, where he entered into partnership with an ex-convict and some others who should have been convicts. Too late, Nemos discovered that he was providing the flour, bacon, whisky, and other necessaries, and that his partners were concealing whatever gold the claim yielded. Having discovered the nature of the partnership, he was quick to break it up. As Australia offered no other employment, he sailed away to Hawaii and thence to San Francisco. No work offering in San Francisco, he went on to Oregon, where he took a job as assistant engineer in the construction of a railroad. At the conclusion of this work, in 1873, he returned to San Francisco, intending to go on to New York, where he hoped his talent in languages would earn him a satisfactory job. At this juncture in his career, happening to hear of what was going on in Bancroft's literary workshop, he applied and was put to work.

In the library Nemos' expertness in languages and his

scholarly proclivities found congenial opportunity. His earlier business experience had sharpened a talent for office management, and before long he became Bancroft's right-hand man in the training of workers and the planning of procedure.

Another wheelhorse was Thomas Savage.[8] His ancestry on both sides was of New England for several generations back, but he was born at Havana, on August 27, 1823, and spent all his youth and early manhood in Cuba and Central America. Spanish was his original language, to which French and English were subsequently added. His early schooling was designed to prepare him for the law, but a shortage of funds occasioned by his father's death, together with his own ill health, deterred him from pursuing this study further. His first job was as a bookkeeper. Then he entered the United States consulate at Havana, where he continued for twenty-one years, part of the time acting as deputy or as chief. In these capacities he was called upon to render various unusual services to the California gold seekers, especially to those stranded in Havana on their return from the mines. The López expeditions also made much work for the Havana consulate. When the Civil War broke out and the consul displayed Confederate leanings, the work of the office devolved upon Savage. The principal responsibility was to gather and forward information about blockade runners headed for Southern ports, but Savage also passed on information which helped to frustrate Confederate plots to seize a Pacific Mail steamer at Acapulco and in 1864 to capture the treasure steamer from San Francisco. He also forwarded information about an asserted plan for an uprising of Confederate sympathizers in southern California.

Soon after the end of the war, Savage resigned his position, spent some months in the United States, and then went to Panama, where he edited the Spanish part of the *Star and Herald,* served as consul for Guatemala, and married his sec-

[8] *Ibid.,* 255–259.

ond wife, "a most charming lady, young, beautiful, accomplished, and wealthy, and withal devotedly attached to her husband." When the greater part of his wife's property was destroyed by fire, Savage moved to El Salvador, where he taught, wrote for the newspapers, and served as United States consul. The next stop was Guatemala, with journalism again the employment, and in 1873 the Savages came to San Francisco. Four months later he went to work for Bancroft.

Savage's outstanding qualification was his expert knowledge of Spanish. Several members of the staff were more than reasonably at home in the language, but whenever questions arose they deferred to him as the authority. Valuable also was his knowledge of Caribbean and Central American geography and customs, and his familiarity with Spanish American legal and juridical practices. He supervised most of the copying and abstracting of the several collections of Spanish manuscripts in California: the provincial archives, the mission records, the papers of the land office, and the archives of the archbishop. He likewise was the logical choice for the sections of the histories relating to Central America and Mexico. Bancroft speaks of him as methodical and clearheaded, remarkably well read in general history, a neat penman, a constant sufferer from bodily ailments, but one who never complained and seldom let his ill health interfere with full performance of the duties assigned him.

Next among the chief assistants was Frances Fuller Victor.[9] Though born in the state of New York, on May 23, 1826, she had spent her girlhood in Ohio and had received her schooling in a young ladies' seminary at Wooster, Ohio. When only fourteen, she began to have success in getting her writings into print, first in the county papers, then in the Cleveland *Herald*,

[9] *Ibid.*, 259–261; William Alfred Morris, "The Origin and Authorship of the Bancroft Pacific States Publications," *Oregon Historical Quarterly*, IV (1903), 314–318; William Alfred Morris, "Historian of the Northwest: A Woman Who Loved Oregon," *In Memoriam: Frances Fuller Victor; Born May 23, 1826; Died November 14, 1902* [Portland, 1902].

English journals, and the New York papers. Spending a year in New York, she was encouraged (through what she later characterized as mistaken kindness) to bring out a volume of poems by herself and her sister Metta. Not long thereafter, the death of their father placed on these sisters the responsibility of supporting themselves and their invalid mother. Metta, as the more facile writer of the two, proved the more successful. Also, there was a better market for her stories than for Frances' verses. Oftentimes they collaborated in planning or writing a potboiler.

After a time Frances and Metta both married, and though they married brothers they soon were separated by the width of the continent. Metta's husband took her to New York. Frances' husband, Henry C. Victor, was a naval engineer, and in 1863 he was ordered to San Francisco. Coming thus to California, Mrs. Victor found that navy pay in depreciated greenbacks was not a sufficient income. To supplement it, she began to write editorials and society items for the *Bulletin,* adopting, therefore, two customs of the country: a humorous vein that was much appreciated, and a pen name, Florence Fane, that came to be almost as famous as the previous decade's Dame Shirley.

In 1865, when her husband moved to Oregon, Mrs. Victor followed him and promptly made the Northwest the central theme in her writing. In letters to the *Bulletin,* in articles for the *Overland Monthly,* and in a descriptive volume, *All over Oregon and Washington* (San Francisco, 1872), she extolled the romance and grandeur of this farthest corner of the nation. Another volume, entitled *River of the West* (Hartford, 1870), recited the history of the region in terms of the life of Joseph Meek, fur trapper, guide, and pioneer settler. By 1878, therefore, when Frances Fuller Victor joined Bancroft's staff, she brought with her a wealth of experience in journalism and more serious literary endeavor, together with a well-established reputation as a writer. Bancroft commends not only these qualifications, but also her conscientiousness and faithful enthusiasm.

Among all his assistants Bancroft's particular fondness seems to have been for Enrique Cerruti.[10] This slender and sallow Italian was in his late thirties when he presented himself at the library. He was of a withered and melancholy appearance, yet had about him a jaunty and debonair manner that made one forget the cheap suit in which he was attired, the flatness of his features, and the droop of his mustache. He represented himself to be an expert in Italian, French, and Spanish, which he was, and a former consul-general and an intimate of the leading men of Spanish America, which he was not. "He liked to be called a general, even though he had been but a consul-general, even though he had been but a consul, even though he had slept but a fortnight in a consulate."[11]

Bancroft and the rest of the staff humored the general in this aberration, for he was, all in all, a likable fellow. His chief flaws were a loose-hinged tongue, which he set in motion at the least provocation, and an irresistible tendency to rise above the truth. He was not exactly a liar, even when palming himself off as a general, a former benefactor of Dictator Melgarejo of Bolivia, or a man who had once enjoyed great wealth as well as influence. Rather, he was an embellisher of the truth, an exaggerator. To these traits he joined consummate skill in the art of flattery; Bancroft insists that no one could have been more adept in blandiloquence. He had an unerring perception, furthermore, of individual susceptibilities; he knew whom to cajole, whom to flatter, and with whom to be matter of fact.

At his first assignment, which was to abstract certain Indian

---

[10] Bancroft, *Literary Industries,* 365–376, 383–445. See also Henry [Enrique] Cerruti, Ramblings in California, 1874, a manuscript volume of 213 pages, Bancroft Library. The title page is inscribed, "These ill connected lines are respectfully dedicated to Hubert Howe Bancroft."

[11] Bancroft, *Literary Industries,* 370.

materials, Cerruti was not conspicuously successful. Nor did he shine at other tasks in the library, especially when skill in writing was required, and for a time it appeared that his main usefulness would be as a filing clerk. Before long, however, he was writing long articles in Italian, French, and Spanish about the Bancroft collection, the projected histories, and the first volumes as they were published, and these articles he unfailingly placed in the foreign-language press of San Francisco and New York, and the papers of Mexico, Italy, France, and Spain. This successful publicizing endeared him to Bancroft, as did also another faculty which he soon demonstrated. He began to bring in historical materials, picked up in places where Bancroft had not thought of looking. No one was more adept than he in gaining the confidence of the old-time Californians, and he proved an ideal amanuensis to take down their statements. His crowning achievement was to lay siege to General Mariano Guadalupe Vallejo, from whom Bancroft had been able to get only perfunctory responses, and to win him over to enthusiastic support of the western history project. Vallejo first permitted Cerruti to examine a few documents, then lent him a few to copy, then allowed his entire collection to be taken to the fifth floor for copying, and finally presented them as an outright gift to Bancroft. The acquisition of this body of manuscripts was one of the biggest coups in Bancroft's whole experience as a collector. He willingly accords to Cerruti the entire credit for its accomplishment. Nor was this the end of Vallejo's contribution. Once his interest was aroused in the Bancroft project, he went about among his countrymen urging others to follow his example of placing materials at the historian's disposal. As a further token of his personal interest, Vallejo, in protracted sittings scattered through 1874 and 1875, dictated to Cerruti a long statement of his reminiscences of California affairs, especially valuable for the period 1815–1845. This work was aptly entitled "Historia de California."

Cerruti, who had surpassed all others as a collecting agent in California, continued in Bancroft's employ only until the summer of 1876. At that time he suffered what may best be labeled a nervous breakdown, occasioned by a series of heavy losses on mining stocks which left him in debt to the amount of fifteen or twenty thousand dollars. From these difficulties, which to a high-strung and prideful individual seemed unbearable, Cerruti chose to escape by suicide, and at Sonoma, on October 9, he ended his life by taking strychnine. Lamenting his death Bancroft exclaims:

"Poor, dear Cerruti! If I had him back with me alive, I would not give him up for all Nevada's mines. His ever welcome presence; his ever pleasing speech, racy in its harmless bluster; his ever charming ways, fascinating in their guileful simplicity, the far-reaching round earth does not contain his like. Alas, Cerruti! with another I might say, I could have better lost a better man!"[12]

Concerning others on the staff, shorter comment must suffice. Walter M. Fisher[13] and T. Arundel Harcourt[14] were two young Englishmen who joined the group in 1872. Fisher was born in Ireland in 1849, wherefore he called himself a forty-niner; but he wanted no one to take him for an Irishman. Schooled at Queen's University at Belfast and very widely read, he aspired to a literary career. Bancroft modestly affirms that the world could have provided no better training ground than his library. Later, Fisher and Harcourt took over the editorship of the *Overland Monthly,* already waning from its Bret Hartean glory. Upon his return to London, Fisher published *The Californians* (London, 1876),[15] in which he was acerbic about many things Californian, but not about Bancroft, his project, and his staff. In fact, his volume is inscribed to Bancroft, the "greatest of The Californians."

Harcourt, two years Fisher's junior, was somewhat more

[12] *Ibid.,* 445. [13] *Ibid.,* 261–263. [14] *Ibid.,* 261–265.
[15] The work had appeared in an earlier edition, San Francisco, 1876.

THE BEGINNING OF THE BANCROFT COLLECTION

THE FIFTH FLOOR

AUTHOR'S STUDY IN THE BANCROFT LIBRARY

THE BANCROFT LIBRARY IN 1881

widely traveled but had not been so diligent a reader. He represented himself as of the English nobility. He worked in the library for two or three years, drifted into newspaper work, and died in San Francisco in 1884. Albert Goldschmidt[16] came to the library at about the same time. He was an affable German whose chief contribution was as a translator. His particular delight was Old Dutch.

Another Englishman, J. J. Peatfield,[17] a Cambridge graduate, came to the library by way of gold mining in British Columbia, cacao and cotton planting in Costa Rica, bookkeeping and consular duty in Guatemala, and teaching and bookkeeping in San Francisco and White Pine, Nevada. He joined the staff in 1881. Still another Englishman, Alfred Bates,[18] came to California from New South Wales, spent a year at teaching and two years assisting John S. Hittell on his *Commerce and Industries of the Pacific Coast,* and, recommended by Hittell, joined the Bancroft staff. Edward P. Newkirk[19] of New York had likewise worked for Hittell. He was a veteran of four years' service in the Civil War, in which he was twice wounded and attained the rank of captain. Continuing in the army, he was ordered to California in 1872 and thence to Alaska, where he almost lost his life in a walrus-hunting expedition.

Ivan Petroff[20] had been schooled in St. Petersburg as a military interpreter. An impediment in his speech halted him in this career, and he moved on to Paris and then to New York. Joining the Union army, he saw much action, was twice wounded, and emerged as a lieutenant. After the war, he signed for a five-year turn as correspondent at Sitka for the Russian American Fur Company. En route, he set off on a horseback tour of the Pacific Northwest in the course of which he was wounded in an attack by Shoshone Indians. In Alaska he actually worked as chief trader at the post at Cook's Inlet,

[16] Bancroft, *Literary Industries,* 264.
[17] *Ibid.,* 265–267.
[18] *Ibid.,* 267.
[19] *Ibid.,* 268–269.
[20] *Ibid.,* 270–272.

whence he returned to San Francisco in 1870. For Bancroft his chief value was his command of the Russian language, but he was a capable translator from other languages, a skillful draftsman, and a useful searcher for historical materials in Alaska and Washington.

So the list might go on, with a few men of special schooling but a larger number whose experience was as clerks, bookkeepers, bank tellers, and the like.

Such were the men with whom Bancroft undertook to write up the history of half a continent. They were a miscellaneous group and by certain yardsticks of training and experience they offered little promise. Nevertheless, in the procession of men who applied for work there was latent capacity for the investigation and writing that Bancroft wanted done. It is much to his credit that he so frequently recognized it when it came along and that he was ingenious enough to devise means of utilizing an Oak, a Savage, a Goldschmidt, a Petroff, and a Cerruti for the furtherance of the great task at hand.

In the roll call of the workers on the fifth floor one additional entry must be made—a mention of the proprietor himself. The basic facts about his birth and upbringing, his success in business and in collecting, and his choice of a scholarly objective have already been indicated. Observations recorded by various of his contemporaries afford a basis for a more circumstantial description of his appearance, his personality, and his work habits.

One correspondent, for example, after commenting on Bancroft's vitality and his iron constitution, went on to say: "While he is a man of large proportions, the energy of his character is concealed by a quiet, almost apathetic manner. This simply-dressed and genial gentleman . . . has the appearance of a prosperous merchant."[21] Another thumbnail sketch is dated 1882: "Mr. Bancroft is now 50 years of age, but with a physique indicative of enormous vitality. In ordinary speech

[21] William H. Rideing, in the New York *Post,* July 12, 1879.

he is slow and sometimes hesitating; but with a pen once between his fingers and his theme warm in his heart, sheet after sheet glides silently away with the hours, till morning not unfrequently breaks upon his unwearying toil."[22]

A year earlier, in a series of feature stories on California writers, the San Francisco *Chronicle* had been even more detailed: "Mr. Bancroft is a man about six feet tall, broad shouldered, erect and imposing in figure. His hair is dark brown, slightly sprinkled with gray, and he wears a full beard and heavy mustache. His forehead is broad and high, face full and round, and the general expression of his features one of placid good-nature. The careless observer sees a man of fine physique, with a kindly, gentle expression, noticing nothing remarkable until the gaze falls upon his eye. A clear, dark-brown eye, which meets another quietly and steadily; an eye which is a revelation of the whole intense, untiring inner nature of the man."[23]

Again, in 1887: "Mr. Bancroft is 55 years of age, in vigorous health, and possesses a more than common endurance. He usually writes standing, as does Palmerston. His desk is accordingly made about breast-high, and close beside it is a circular table, about eight feet in diameter, fitted with a revolving top, on which he arranges his authorities, turning the table top round as he requires them. His faculty for work is said to be particularly well developed, and though from the nature of the undertaking fast writing is impossible, yet he applies himself so many hours at a time as to cover almost as much ground as a speculative writer, untrammeled by the constant necessity of consulting authorities, would ordinarily do. He frequently stands at his desk for eleven or twelve hours."[24]

---

[22] Ten Eyck, in the Kansas City *Journal,* August 17, 1882.

[23] "California Writers, Their Lives, Productions, and Characteristics: Bret Harte and H. H. Bancroft, the First of Our Local Story-Tellers—the Historian of the Native Races of the Coast," San Francisco *Chronicle,* January 3, 1881.

[24] William F. Clarke, "Hubert Howe Bancroft," *Golden Era,* July, 1887.

Oak likewise testifies to Bancroft's skill and delight in writing and supplies much incidental detail about the ways in which he participated in the work. In summary he characterizes his employer as "a man who, by his force of character, would have achieved success in almost any direction."[25]

Bancroft's devotion to his literary task was several times demonstrated. In 1875 he declined a Republican nomination for Congress, wryly observing that there were "ten thousand ready to serve their country," but not one to do his work should he abandon it.[26] Earlier he disposed of his fine house on California Street, not merely because it was larger than he as a widower had need of, but also to reduce the social demands that tended to divert him from his main task. For several years also, although he was by nature highly uxorious, he resisted all suggestions that he remarry. What chiefly deterred him, he afterward admitted, was the fear that a wife would interfere with the prosecution of his work. Even the most devoted companion could hardly be expected to have a deep appreciation of his literary undertakings, and more probably would make demands upon his time and his energy to the serious imperilment of the history project. Under these circumstances remarriage did not seem indicated.[27]

On one of his eastern trips, however, he met a young lady of New Haven, Matilda Coley Griffing, and all this discretion and reluctance melted away. He called upon her several times in New Haven, followed her to Bethlehem in the White Mountains, and there persuaded her to become his wife. The marriage, described in the New Haven press as "an event of considerable interest in social life and to literary people both here and abroad," took place at the home of the bride's mother on October 12, 1876. It was a gala occasion. Mrs. Griffing called in a professional caterer and built a spacious addition to her dining room in order to accommodate the wedding

[25] Henry L. Oak, *"Literary Industries" in a New Light,* 35–36.
[26] Bancroft, *Literary Industries,* 577.
[27] *Ibid.,* 447–448.

guests. Among the latter were the governor of the state, a former governor, several judges, the mayor, the president of Yale, several Yale professors, and, from San Francissco, Mrs. A. L. Bancroft and the bridegroom's daughter, Kate.[28]

A better wife, a better historian's wife, Bancroft could hardly have found.[29] She supplied him all the comforts of home, including, ere long, four children, Paul, Griffing, Philip, and Lucy. She did not tempt him to social frivolity, but preferred to see him at his writing, in which occasionally she rendered some direct assistance. On at least one occasion she turned out a description of the library and the history project that was printed *in extenso* in several newspapers. Bancroft reciprocated by making his wife, his children, and his home the center of his life. The histories and the business had a claim upon him. They compelled his interest, and they received his strenuous attention; but, demanding as these activities were, he did not allow them to interfere with his role as husband and father. His family saw a great deal of him, and his children remember him as extremely generous with his time, attentive, and indulgent.

---

[28] Clipping from the New Haven *Journal and Courier,* October 13, 1876, in the possession of Mr. Philip Bancroft.

[29] For his tribute see *Literary Industries,* 456–460.

10

Excursion into Anthropology

I became satisfied that something must be done with the aborigines. Wherever I touched the continent with my Spaniards they were there, a dusky, disgusting subject. I did not fancy them. I would gladly have avoided them. I was no archaeologist, ethnologist, or antiquary, and had no desire to become such. My tastes in the matter, however, did not dispose of the subject. The savages were there, and there was no help for me; I must write them up to get rid of them.

Hubert Howe Bancroft, *Literary Industries,* 295

THERE MAY BE subjects which arrange themselves so inevitably that a historian, having gathered his materials, need only plunge into his writing. Bancroft's experience was somewhat different. Even after he had determined on the history of the Pacific states as his topic, he was uncertain where to begin. First of all, he was irresistibly attracted to the conquest of Mexico. He knew and respected Prescott's classic account, but his collection contained much collateral material that had not been available to Prescott, and besides, the theme seemed to him grand beyond comparison. Here it was, then, that he began. His initial impulse, influenced no doubt by the eloquent style of Prescott, Gómara, and other chroniclers of the Spanish-Aztec contest, was to pay more attention to phrasing than to factual foundation. Laboring hard in this fashion, he turned out several chapters—but saw that they were "sententious nothings." Rewriting only made them worse, and so he tore them up.

The Cortés epic set aside, Bancroft decided to begin at the beginning of Pacific states history. He shifted his attention, therefore, to the Isthmus of Darién and its discovery and conquest, with of course some attention to its antecedents, the Spaniards in the West Indies, the discovery of America, and the background of European, particularly Spanish, institutions and character. To assist in the preparation of a suitable introduction he employed a savant who was "well informed in all medieval knowledge." In these words Bancroft describes how it worked out: "He read, and read, eagerly devouring all he could lay hands on. And he would have continued reading to this day had I been willing to pay him his salary regularly for it. He liked to read. And I said to myself, this is glorious! Surely, as the result of such enthusiasm I shall have a bushel of invaluable notes."[1]

Two months later, when there were but five or six pages of written matter to show for all this reading, Bancroft urged his medievalist to put something on paper, and at the end of the fourteenth week he insisted upon it. A manuscript of some thirty pages was thereupon produced, consisting, however, of the most commonplace statements and equally disappointing to employer and employee.

While this "really talented and intelligent assistant was floundering in a sea of erudition," Bancroft had been applying himself to the same topic. Carefully studying some two hundred volumes, he culled from them a good deal of information, particularly about Spain at the close of the Middle Ages. Ideas also occurred to him that would be a fit core for the introduction, and these he fitted together in a manuscript of three hundred pages. A revision cut its length by half, and a second rewriting brought further reduction. In this form it may be seen in the first sixty-seven pages of his *History of Central America*. Although these are not the most profound words written on the background of Spanish activity in America, they provide a sympathetic and clear picture of Spanish character at the time of the discovery, and they suggest the

[1] Bancroft, *Literary Industries*, 289.

similarities and contrasts of Old World and New World civilizations as the two were about to be brought in contact. The style is straightforward and never lacking in clarity. There is a wealth of literary allusions, and a freshness of diction and phrasing. For all the revising, the impression remains that Bancroft had a facile pen.

Having composed this introduction, and in the same six months, with the aid of various assistants, having compiled a formidable "Summary of Geographical Knowledge and Discovery from the Earliest Records to the Year 1540,"[2] Bancroft went on with the history of the isthmus as he had planned it. In proceeding, however, he became more and more conscious that "something must be done with the aborigines." The early history of his area, as indeed of all America, consisted largely of the interactions of Europeans and the native Americans whom Columbus had named Indians. The Europeans, whether Spanish, French, Russian, British, or Anglo-American, would be reasonably familiar to Bancroft's readers. The Indians, however, were not nearly so well known. To make the region's history understandable, he would have to interrupt his narrative repeatedly to introduce this tribe or that, and to describe its military, religious, and social customs, its material and nonmaterial culture, its language, or physical characteristics. The only alternative appeared to be to deal with the Indians separately as a preliminary to the histories proper. This Bancroft decided to do. In describing his decision to venture thus into the realm of anthropology, he struck the very nadir of unenthusiasm—for his task, and for the Indians.

"Wherever I touched the continent with my Spaniards they were there, a dusky, disgusting subject. I did not fancy them. I would gladly have avoided them. I was no archaeologist, ethnologist, or antiquary, and had no desire to become

[2] Appended in fine print as an 88-page footnote to this introduction; Bancroft, *History of Central America,* I, 67–154.

such. My tastes in the matter, however, did not dispose of the subject. The savages were there, and there was no help for me; I must write them up to get rid of them."[3]

The task, as he envisioned it, was to describe the Indians in their pre-Columbian status "as they were first seen by Europeans along the several paths of discovery." He would describe them "in all their native glory, and before the withering hand of civilization was laid upon them."[4] Everything relating to their subsequent experiences would be reserved for treatment in the historical volumes, where indeed it belonged.

The pre-Columbian subject matter would be large enough, for Bancroft's quarter of the western hemisphere contained somewhat more than a quarter of the aboriginal population and considerably more than a quarter of the cultural diversity which the New World as a whole could offer. The Indians between Alaska and Darién ranged from simple hunters and seed gatherers to sophisticated city dwellers. Politically they were split into hundreds of independent nations and tribes, their languages and dialects were almost as numerous, and their manners and customs were a hodgepodge with many more unlike than common factors.[5]

From the outset he had placed certain limits on his aims. It was never his intention to engage in archaeological investigations or to devote himself to field work among the surviving Indians. At best with these sorts of research he could have covered only a few scattered bits of the vast subject matter with which he proposed to deal. Except that direct study might have sharpened his understanding of the Indians, it was as

[3] Bancroft, *Literary Industries*, 295.

[4] *Ibid.*, 296.

[5] The standard references are *Handbook of the American Indians North of Mexico* (2 vols.; Washington, 1907–1910), edited by F. W. Hodge; Clark Wissler, *The American Indian* (New York, 1917); and A. L. Kroeber, *Cultural and Natural Areas of Native North America* (Berkeley, 1939). For a brief description see John Walton Caughey, *History of the Pacific Coast* (Los Angeles, 1933), 1–45.

well that his continent-long survey should be based simply, as it frankly was, on the written records that had been collected in his library. These he scrutinized with the aid of the index and of his several assistants. His aim, he says, was to gather and arrange in systematic, compact form all that was known about these Indians, and lest that purpose be defeated he preferred to eschew speculation and theorizing and to limit his work to a compilation of facts.

In another connection Bancroft remarks that the purpose of *Native Races* was to provide conveniently what those who were reading the histories would wish to know about the Indians. Professional anthropologists, of course, do not have so limited an objective and see much value in their studies beyond the mere supplying of a background for history. Bancroft, however, was not a professional anthropologist. Nor was there such a person anywhere in the vicinity whom he could call on for advice. Published anthropological literature, furthermore, supplied no obvious pattern that he might have followed. Consequently, as in so many other of his undertakings, he had to draw up his own plan and fabricate his own pattern. He is to be thought of as a self-made anthropologist.

His approach, as those who have read thus far must have grown to suspect, was direct and heavily dependent on common sense. He asked, "What is it we wish to know about these people?" The topics thereby called to mind, running all the way from dietetic habits to belief in a hereafter, and from the care of the young to the power of rulers, suggested a basis for the organization of the work. He would begin with the general topic of manners and customs and would deal with its subtopics in turn. There would be a discussion of housing, a section on dress, another on food habits, another on military equipment, and so on down the entire list.

For a single people or for several tribes whose manners and customs were essentially alike, such a procedure would have worked. But as Bancroft became better acquainted with the Indians of his distended area, he soon realized that the wide diversity of their cultures demanded some other treatment. "In points of intellectual growth and material progress, of relative savagism and civilization, there were such wide differences between the many nations of the vast Pacific seaboard that to bring them all together would make an incongruous mass, and to fit them to one plan would be farfetched and impracticable."[6] Recognition that the Indians were culturally heterogeneous was the first great step toward an intelligent description.

Parenthetically it may be remarked that the Americans of Bancroft's day had this awareness only within limits. Cooper's Leather-Stocking Tales had tended to fix the impression that Indian life was substantially uniform. The United States government operated on the principle that an Indian was an Indian and that a policy which was effective with one tribe ought to work with the rest. American frontiersmen and pioneers, moving westward across the continent, had likewise been inclined to fail to notice the differences among the various Indian groups encountered. Up and down the western coast of the continent the differences were sharper than in any horizontal swath that might have been marked off, yet Bancroft was one of the first to show an awareness of the remarkable heterogeneity in Indian America.

Toward the solution of his Indian problem Bancroft resorted to several devices. One was to increase the space allotted to the description of pre-Columbian America from two volumes to five. This amplification removed much, though not all, of the pressure for condensation of the Indian materials, and thus far simplified the problem of organization. Second, certain topics were noticed which seemed to call for treatment on a continent-long basis. Thus mythology, languages, antiquities, and primitive or pre-Columbian history were docketed

[6] Bancroft, *Literary Industries*, 297–298.

for separate survey. It was equally obvious that the Mayas and Aztecs of southern Mexico and Central America had attained a degree of elaboration in their civilization which set them apart from the rest of the natives from Darién to Alaska. Bancroft resolved upon separate volumes for the "civilized nations" and the "wild tribes."

As finally organized, the five 800-page volumes of *Native Races* were ranged in this order: I, *Wild Tribes,* a description of their manners and customs; II, *Civilized Nations,* a similar treatment of the Mayas and Aztecs; III, *Myths and Languages,* with 500 pages to the former and 300 to the latter; IV, *Antiquities,* perforce confined almost entirely to Central America and southern Mexico; V, *Primitive History,* concerned principally with southern Mexico.

In certain respects Volume I is the most interesting of the set. Since its subject matter covered the widest range, it presented the biggest problem of organization. Having seen that an over-all description of the wild tribes was impossible because of their diversity in manners and customs, and aware also that a tribe-by-tribe description would be interminable, Bancroft sought some compromise of these methods. He found it by devising half a dozen geographical groupings, within each of which a rough uniformity of culture existed. In definition this sounds very much like the culture areas of the modern anthropologists. His reason for resorting to the device was the same as theirs: to obtain a short cut to the presentation of ethnographical data which otherwise would have involved endless repetition.

Beginning at the north, Bancroft designated as Hyperboreans all Indians living north of the 55th parallel. Those between the 55th and 42d, he called Columbians, after the river system draining much of this area. His Californians included the inhabitants of the Great Basin; and the term New Mexicans was also used in broader connotation to include the tribes along the Colorado River, in Lower California, and in northern Mexico. Rounding out the list came the peoples of central and southern Mexico and of Central America, the Mayas and Aztecs omitted.

In the actual descriptions offered, and in the maps illustrating the chapters, some further refinement of the areas is to be noted. Thus, for the Hyperboreans, a line paralleling the coast cuts off the insular and coastal part of Alaska, where lived the Eskimo, from the interior where ranged the Tinneh, or, as the word is now rendered, the Dene. The chapter on the Hyperboreans also makes it abundantly clear that there was a fundamental distinction between the Eskimo and the Tinneh. The same line is extended through the Columbian region, almost precisely where in current practice the Northwest Coast area is marked off from the Plateau area.

Principal credit for authorship and elaboration of the culture area concept for North America is now accorded to Clark Wissler and A. L. Kroeber. Wissler first applied the device in his book, *The American Indian* (1917), while the most recent and thoroughgoing application is in Kroeber's *Cultural and Natural Areas of Native North America* (1939). If the Wissler-Kroeber areas are superimposed on Bancroft's, a striking resemblance appears. These modern scholars make a bit sharper the distinction between Eskimo and Dene, and of course make clear that both cultures stretched on eastward out of the territory with which Bancroft was dealing. They assign the Tlingits (in Bancroft's spelling, "Thlinkeets") of southern Alaska to the Northwest Coast rather than to the Eskimo area. They also point a sharper cleavage between the Northwest Coast and the Plateau. Bancroft's California–Great Basin area has professional sanction, with the minor correction of assigning southern California, along with the Colorado River basin, to the New Mexican area. With this slight enlargement the New Mexican area is accepted as Bancroft marked it, though relabeled Southwestern. Finally, Bancroft's line between Mexican and Central American cultures is erased. Furthermore, the Mayas and Aztecs are reckoned not something apart, but in this area as its central or climactic feature.

This similarity, striking though it is, does not necessarily mean that Wissler and Kroeber are indebted to Bancroft. Rather, it indicates that, in his early effort to systematize the data on the Indians of the western half of North America, Bancroft came to substantially correct conclusions about the logical groupings of the various tribes, and that in so doing he foreshadowed the culture-area concept of today's leading anthropologists.

The term culture area was not in his vocabulary. Yet the charting of his course was in terms that would virtually serve as definition for this more modern expression: "In the groupings which I have adopted, one cluster of nations follows another in geographical succession; the dividing line not being more distinct, perhaps, than that which distinguishes some national divisions, but sufficiently marked, in mental and physical peculiarities, to entitle each group to a separate consideration."[7]

Besides its utilization of what was essentially the culture-area device, the volume on the wild tribes impresses one as being carefully organized. A master outline can be discerned, by which each of the chapters was constructed. In general, Bancroft began by defining the area and describing the conditions of life afforded by its climate, topography, vegetation, and animals. After indicating the main divisions of the people of the area, he described one such group in detail, progressing from physical characteristics and the basic elements of dress, dwellings, food, weapons, and tools, to such matters as government, social organization, amusements, medical practices, and religion. The survey was then extended to the people of other parts of the area, with stress on the variations from the practices just described. Finally, in smaller type, as a sort of

[7] Hubert Howe Bancroft, *Native Races* (5 vols.; New York, 1874–1875), I, 36.

appendix to each chapter, he inserted a discussion of tribal boundaries, in which he set forth all the facts that he had been able to gather about the habitat and range of the several tribes, and cited authorities for his statements.

First drafts of the later chapters of this volume were written by some of his assistants, but the chapter on the Hyperboreans Bancroft took as a personal assignment. One may picture him standing at his writing desk on the fifth floor, with the notes on these northernmost Indians and the principal references upon them spread out on the revolving table at his elbow. In this hundred-page essay on the Hyperboreans one also has a good index to his capacity to handle an anthropological theme.

Certainly he grasped the prime fact about Eskimo life, that it is a constant warfare with nature for an adequate supply of heat-producing food, and that special adaptations in housing and clothing are also requisite. This is the main point of his essay. As to the development of this theme, it is a fair criticism that he was not sufficiently appreciative of Eskimo resourcefulness and inventiveness. He lauds the snow house, quoting Sir John Franklin's tribute in which it is likened to a Grecian temple reared by Phidias, and he mentions such items as the kayak, snow goggles, and the sinew-backed bow. Yet by no means all their inventions are catalogued, and Bancroft's comments on their clothing are mostly on the score of appearance, to the neglect of the most significant element—the fact that these were tailored garments. Explanation is perhaps to be found in the fact that he was not well informed on the attainments of primitive peoples elsewhere in the world. Lacking this broader knowledge, which a trained anthropologist would have as a matter of course, Bancroft was handicapped in measuring and picking out the distinctive elements in Eskimo culture.

Throughout the chapter he shows a hardheaded practicality; for example, in the first footnote, a long discussion of the various names for this region north of the 55th parallel, Alaska, Aliaska, Unalashka, and divers others. Sensibly, he concludes: "As these names are all corruptions from some one original word, whatever that may be, I see no reason for giving the error three different forms. I therefore write Alaska for the mainland and peninsula, and Unalaska for the island."[8] When it came to certain phases of Eskimo life, however, he was not as toughminded as anthropologists usually profess to be. He recoiled visibly from such practices as tattooing and the wearing of labrets, he was sharply critical of Eskimo indifference to sanitation, and he was abashed at their food habits. Longer experience in anthropological science would have made Bancroft less squeamish—not by dulling his sensitivity, but by giving him a different outlook on the customs of an alien people.

On the whole, however, the description of the Hyperboreans stands up well under scrutiny. Discerning what were the essential facts about these far notherners, Bancroft effectively describes the people, their land, and their adaptation to it. As a recital of facts about the daily habits of a primitive folk, his account necessarily has a pedestrian tone, yet here and there it is lighted up with more flowery rhetoric, as when he describes the aurora borealis, or with a striking phrase, often given a humorous turn, as when he writes: "Choice dishes, tempting to the appetite, Arctic epicurean dishes, Eskimo nectar and ambrosia, are daintily prepared, hospitably placed before strangers, and eaten and drunk with avidity. Among them are:"—and there follows a list of the more outlandish and revolting items on the Eskimo menu.[9] Or, to quote a sentence from the next chapter, "The Nootka complexion, so far as grease and paint have allowed travelers to observe it, is decidedly light, but apparently a shade darker than that of the Haidah family."[10] And again, "Water in abo-

[8] *Ibid.*, I, 38.
[9] *Ibid.*, I, 54–55.
[10] *Ibid.*, I, 177–178.

riginal days was the only Nootka drink; it is also used now when whisky is not to be had."[11]

The subsequent chapters round out a good working description of the Pacific Coast natives. For the Northwest Coast area there is a proper highlighting of fish as the basic foodstuff, of woodworking as the foremost handicraft, and of wealth as the one avenue to honor and reputation. Borrowing a phrase from Veblen, one now would make clearer that "conspicuous consumption" of worldly goods was the path to prestige. Also, more stress would have been appropriate for the totemic element in Northwest Coast culture. For the inland tribes of the Plateau area Bancroft correctly selects housing and hunting as the distinctive traits.

In the California area he is in step with all subsequent writing on the aboriginals when he stresses the paradox of favorable environment and cultural backwardness. "From the frozen, wind-swept plains of Alaska to the malaria-haunted swamps of Darien, there is not a fairer land than California; it is the neutral ground, as it were, of the elements, where hyperboreal cold, stripped of its rugged aspect, and equatorial heat, tamed to a genial warmth, meet as friends, inviting, all blusterings laid aside." On every side Indians of higher attainment are encountered. "It is not until we reach the Golden Mean in Central California that we find whole tribes subsisting on roots, herbs, and insects; having no boats, no clothing, no laws, no god. . . . Why . . . California breeds a race inferior to the lowest of their neighbors, save only perhaps the Shoshones on their east, no one can tell."[12]

On the negative and rudimentary elements in California culture he is sufficiently explicit. Nowadays it is the fashion to praise more effusively the basketry of the Pomo and their neighbors. Bancroft also gives unduly short shrift to the ingenious and laborious technique of leaching acorn meal to make it palatable and digestible. He has a salty comment on

[11] *Ibid.*, I, 188. [12] *Ibid.*, I, 399–400.

Revere's remark that acorn bread "looks and tastes like coarse black clay, strongly resembling the soundings in Hampton Roads, and being about as savory and digestible."[13] Bancroft's rejoinder runs thus: "Never having eaten 'coarse black clay,' I cannot say how it tastes, but, according to all other authorities, this bread, were it not for the extreme filthiness of those who prepare it, would be by no means disagreeable food."[14] This is effective repartee, but not an adequate presentation of the acorn-leaching process, which was the fundamental element in the California culture and in a measure explains why these Indians did not stress hunting, fishing, and other such pursuits. In the sentence above quoted, Bancroft is guilty of unprofessional fastidiousness. Unprofessional also is his dictum on the same page, "The bestial laziness of the Central Californian prevents him from following the chase to any extent, or from even inventing efficient game-traps."[15]

Concerning the Southwesterners, Bancroft does better justice to the Apaches and their brethren than to the Pueblos. Research on Pueblo handicrafts, on governmental and social forms, on ceremonial practices, and on chronology has brought out much information that was not available in the 'seventies, and Bancroft's account naturally suffers by comparison. The segregation in another volume of data on mythology also impairs the description of the Pueblos.

As for the wild tribes of Mexico and Central America, a similar criticism of the organization of the *Native Races* is in order. These people are best understood if considered as marginal to the more advanced Mayas and Aztecs—as enjoying in diluted form certain elements of this remarkable southern Mexican civilization. It would be more profitable to read about these surrounding tribesmen after perusing the discussion of the culture leaders, and Bancroft should have

[13] Joseph W. Revere, *A Tour of Duty in California* (New York, 1849), 121.
[14] Bancroft, *Native Races*, I, 373, note.
[15] *Ibid.*

planned it that way. Here, however, the criticism rests on the distributional approach to anthropological phenomena, which, like the culture-area concept, has only recently come into favor. Consequently the criticism, though valid, is not entirely fair.

In organization one pattern runs through all the chapters on the wild tribes. In literary style, however, there is less of uniformity. The Hyperborean chapter is universally admitted to have flowed from Bancroft's pen. The next two, on the Columbians (pp. 150–321) and on the Californians (pp. 322–470), are so consistent in tone and flavor that it seems certain that Bancroft either wrote them or else reworked them so thoroughly as to make them his own. The three chapters on the southernmost tribes (pp. 471–797) have occasional marks of similarity, but on the whole the writing is much more prosaic, or even awkward. There are passages—for example, in telling how the Pueblo girls took the initiative in arranging marriages—where the master would have sparkled. The conclusion is that Bancroft gave this part of the volume only perfunctory attention, and that it is the worse for his neglect.

From his wild tribes Bancroft turned with zest to the civilized nations. Not only did he regard them as intrinsically a more fascinating subject, but also he looked forward to the opportunity, with ample space at his disposal, to spice the description more generously with illustrative anecdotes. Technically the second volume resembles the first. It is a résumé of the existing literature on the Mayas and the Aztecs, a presentation of the culture of these Indians as reported by the earliest Spanish narrators and as elucidated by nineteenth-century scholars. A major problem was to reconcile the variant descriptions and interpretations, and one of the most praiseworthy aspects of the volume is that for doubtful matters—whether the doubt was reasonable or slightly less than reasonable—the alternative testimony and opinion is not suppressed.

As the group preponderant at the time of Cortés' arrival and most extensively treated in the published literature, the Aztecs claimed chief attention. To them was allotted the first three fourths of the volume, after which the decadent Maya culture was taken up. For each of these peoples the description runs the gamut from food, dress, and housing to the more complicated and abstruse matters of government, social organization, and intellectual attainment.

Minor flaws may be cited. In common with Clavigero, Humboldt, Prescott, and other distinguished Mexicanists, Bancroft gave credence to the story of Xochimilco's "floating gardens," which modern realism insists never floated.[16] His description of Nahua military habits gives the impression that the Aztecs were bow-and-arrow Indians, whereas in reality they had a preference for the *atlatl,* or throwing stick.[17] The Aztecs' combined hereditary and elective system of selecting a chief is well described, but there is inadequate understanding of the role in tribal government of the council and the *cihuacoatl,* or snake woman.[18] Similarly, in the analysis of the Aztec calendar, its essential features as a day-count and a permutation system or cycle seem not to have been perfectly grasped, nor is its derivation from the Mayas made as clear as might be.[19] Throughout the description of Aztec ways the counsel of perfection would call for more emphasis on religion as the hub around which the entire culture revolved.

Yet the Bancroft account is an effective introduction to the manners and customs of these most advanced natives of North America. Anyone who reads it will get a clear picture of the economic basis on which southern Mexican society was founded, of the remarkable skills of these Indians in such diverse matters as metallurgy and number notation, of the

[16] *Ibid.,* II, 345–346; consult Norman L. Willey and Carlos García Prada, "El Embrujo de las Chinampas," *Hispanic American Historical Review,* XIX (1939), 83–100.

[17] Bancroft, *Native Races,* II, 350, 410.

[18] *Ibid.,* II, 81 ff.

[19] *Ibid.,* II, 502–522.

complex social patterns in which they lived, and of the elaborate governmental superstructure they had erected. Perusal of the volume will prompt agreement with Bancroft's conclusion that "the Nahuas, the Mayas, and the subordinate and lesser civilizations surrounding these [were] but little lower than the contemporaneous civilizations of Europe and Asia, and not nearly so low as we have hitherto been led to suppose."[20]

Volume III opens with a discussion of mythology in 500 pages. Here a topical segregation was begun, with groupings on the origin and end of things; on explanations of physical realities, the sun, moon, wind, fire, earthquakes, etc.; and on animal fables. At this point, however, the subject of gods, supernatural beings, and worship was reached, which required seven chapters—370 pages. A final chapter grouped myths describing the hereafter. For those whose interest is specifically in mythology this arrangement is satisfactory. For those, on the other hand, whose interest in Indian myths is for the light they might shed on material and social customs and on habits of thought, the segregation and topical organization are not ideal. This section was intended to be only a sampling of the vast store of Indian myths accessible in the Bancroft collection. More recently, by recourse to living informants, the quantity of myths on record has been still further increased.[21]

Doubtless the most technical part of *Native Races* is the section on language. Here some general observations are offered on the significance of speech, on the relatively high achievement of the American Indians in developing their languages, on the surprising diversity of those languages, and on the unscientific endeavors of pseudo-linguists to prove through language similarities a connection between some Indian tribe

[20] *Ibid.*, II, 805.

[21] For example, see E. W. Gifford and G. H. Block, *California Indian Nights Entertainments* (Glendale, 1930), and *California Indian Folklore, as Told to F. F. Latta* (Shafter, California, 1936).

and some Old World group. An effort is made to indicate relationships in western North America, sometimes on the basis of verbal similarities as in the Tinneh (now called Athabascan) family, and again through recurring rules of grammar or pronunciation as in the Aztec (now called the Uto-Aztecan) family. The majority of the tongues of the area, especially the California portion, are not assigned to any family, yet the prediction is made that the developing science of linguistics will increasingly recognize such relationships,[22] as has indeed proved true.

In addition to the effort at classification there is a running description of Indian speech from north to south, with frequent illustration through word lists, specimen conjugations, and translations of such things as the Lord's Prayer or the speech of an American Indian agent. Outstanding features of the various languages are discussed, ranging from the almost insuperable difficulties in voicing Tlingit, Haida, Chinook, and Apache, to the agglutinative tendency in Nez Percé, the eloquence of the Cayuses, the euphonic elisions of the northern Californians, the richness and elegance of the Aztecs. These three hundred pages are not a primer from which one could master "the interminable intermixture of tongues and dialects, spoken, grunted, and gestured between the Arctic Ocean and the Atrato River,"[23] but they do convey a sufficient impression of the variety, the range, and the adequacy of the languages native to the Pacific states.

Volumes IV and V supplement the description of the civilized nations at the time of the Spaniards' arrival. In the volume on antiquities Bancroft has something to say of the Colorado and New Mexico cliff dwellings, of the Ohio Valley mound builders, and hastily of monumental remains in Peru, but his chief concern is naturally with the Central American and Mexican discoveries and descriptions. His customary pro-

[22] Bancroft, *Native Races,* III, 554.
[23] *Ibid.,* III, 795.

cedure of digesting and harmonizing the available literature on the subject had here, perhaps, its least satisfactory result. How useful this volume would have been in the 1870's is a bit hard to determine. Since then, these southern regions have proved a happy hunting ground for archaeologists both scientific and otherwise. Photography and the illustrative arts have made comparable strides. In consequence, this volume is doubly antiquated.

The discourse on primitive history has worn much better. Its first sixth is a review of attempts to prove that the Indians were originally Chinese, Japanese, Scandinavian, Irish, Egyptian, Hebrew, or what not. Modern protagonists for several of these theories have arisen, but the arguments and logic by which Bancroft disposes of all these assertions would avail equally against recent theorizers. Resisting even the impulse to call the Indians autochthones, he takes refuge in a "quien sabe" stand. Modern science, of course, posits derivation from a Mongoloid stock, from which various East Asian peoples are also descended.

By way of introduction Bancroft also stated his credo about the admixture of fable and truth in primitive history.

> I have compared the American past to a dark sea, from the bluff coast line of which projects an occasional cape terminating in precipitous cliffs, quicksands, and sunken rocks, beyond which some faint lights are floated by buoys. The old authors, as Torquemada, Clavigero, and Veytia, had but little difficulty in crossing from the headlands to the tower of Babel beyond the Sea of Darkness; they told the story, fables and all, with little discrimination save here and there the rejection of a tale infringing apparently on orthodoxy, or the expression of a doubt as to the literal acceptation of some marvelous occurrence. Of modern authors, those who, like Wilson, refuse to venture upon the projecting capes of solid rock and earth, who utterly reject the Aztec civilization with all its records, are few, and at this day their writings may be considered as unworthy of serious notice. Other writers, of whom Gallatin is a specimen, venture boldly from the main coast to the extremity of each projecting point, and acknowledge the existence of the rocks, sands, and buoys

beyond, but decline to attempt their passage, doubting their security. These men, in favor of whose method there is much to be said, accept the annals of the latter Aztec periods, but look with distrust upon the traditions of the Chichimec, Toltec, and Olmec epochs; and hardly see in the far distance the twinkling floating lights that shine from Votan's Empire of Xibalba. Then there are writers who are continually dreaming they have found secure footing by routes previously unknown, from rock to rock and through the midst of shifting sands. Such are the advocates of special theories of American history resting on newly discovered authorities or new readings of old ones. They carefully sift out such mythic traditions as fit their theories, converting them into incontrovertible facts, and reject all else as unworthy of notice; these, however, have chiefly to do with the matter of origin. Finally, I may speak of Brasseur de Bourbourg, rather a class by himself, perhaps, than the representative of a class. This author, to speak with a degree of exaggeration, steps out without hesitation from rock to rock over the deep waters; to him the banks of shifting quicksand, if somewhat treacherous about the edges, are firm land in the central parts; to him the faintest buoy-supported stars are a blaze of noonday sun; and only on the floating masses of seaweed far out on the waters lighted up by dim phosphorescent reflections, does he admit that his footing is becoming insecure and light grows faint. In other words, he accepts the facts recorded by preceding authors, arranges them often with great wisdom and discrimination, ingeniously finds a historic record in traditions by others regarded as pure fables, and thus pushes his research far beyond the limits previously reached. He rejects nothing, but transforms everything into historic facts.

In the present sketch I wish to imitate to a certain extent the writers of each class mentioned, except perhaps the specialists, for I have no theory to defend, have found no new bright sun to illumine what has ever been dark. With the Spanish writers I would tell all that the natives told as history, and that without constantly reminding the reader that the sun did not probably stand still in the heavens, that giants did not flourish in America, that the Toltec kings and prophets did not live to the age of several hundred years, and otherwise warning him against what he is in no danger whatever of accepting as truth. With Wilson and his class of antiquarian sceptics I would feel no hesitation in rejecting the shallow theories and fancies evolved by certain writers from their own brain. With Gallatin I wish to discriminate clearly, when such discrimination is called for and possible, between the historic and the probably mythic; to indicate the boundary between firm land and treacherous quicksand; but also like Brasseur, I would pass beyond the firm land, spring from rock to rock, wade through shifting sands, swim to the farthest, faintest light, and catch at straws by the way;—yet not flatter myself while thus employed, as the abbé occasionally seems to do, that I am treading dry-shod on a wide, solid, and well-lighted highway.[24]

His readers thus forewarned, Bancroft, with Brasseur de Bourbourg as his chief reliance, recites the Indian stories which purport to give an account of pre-Cortesian happenings in America. In the earliest of these, Votan's Book, the Popul Vuh, and the Codex Chimalpopoca, he expresses but slight confidence. Reliability gradually increases as the record proceeds through the Toltec, Chichimec, and Aztec periods. Incidental narratives, on the whole of lesser validity, are presented for the Mayan stocks of Central America and Yucatán. Since Bancroft's time, specialists have fixed with somewhat more certainty the chronology of parts of this prehistory. They have not materially enlarged the factual or anecdotal content, which leaves to his summary recital a considerable measure of usefulness for today's scholars.

Such are the five volumes of *Native Races*. Unquestionably they have a miscellaneous cast, which, in conjunction with Bancroft's allocation of special credit to four of his assistants for the final four volumes,[25] has prompted the general assumption that there was little of central supervision or authorship. Actually, however, every section has touches that seem unmistakably Bancroft's. More important, a common purpose runs through the entire set. There is a structural unity throughout, particularly in the reflection of the geographical divisions as worked out for the description of the wild tribes. Each volume, furthermore, is a factual record, a digest or summation of the existing literature on its subject, with theorizing strictly excluded. Thereby Bancroft avoided what is

[24] *Ibid.*, V, 153–155.   [25] *Ibid.*, I, xiii.

probably the most common pitfall of the amateur anthropologist, that of starting with a conjecture and presenting only such evidence as comports with this preconceived notion. The *Native Races* certainly are not vitiated by this error.

There are certain respects in which the set now seems old-fashioned. Modern anthropology not only utilizes the device of the culture area, but also recommends study of a culture in its entirety. Bancroft's topical segregations thus would be frowned upon, and a rearrangement of *Native Races* recommended which should bring together all the material descriptive of the Indians of Central America and southern Mexico, to be followed by integrated descriptions of each of the cultures to the northward. Now regarded as good anthropology, this rearrangement would also provide a more serviceable background for the prospective student of the region's history. No writer or compiler in the 1870's could be expected to forecast or anticipate this development in scientific anthropology. Correspondingly, any work such as *Native Races,* as a review of what had been made known, was bound gradually to go out of date. As intimated above, this aging has not been uniform, because students of the Indian have made more progress along some lines than along others; the section on primitive history, for example, is less superseded than that on antiquities.

In their day these volumes had a great utility for those who were interested in the natives of western North America but lacked the time or the opportunity to go direct to the voluminous source materials. They have a continuing value for students of any phase of Indian affairs in this area, though of course they must be supplemented by whatever information has more recently become available. In still another respect this set of volumes is notable: among the reading public of the United States and the world it attained a circulation seldom if ever achieved by any anthropological work of comparable size, weight, and factuality.

At the risk of anticlimax one further note may be added about Bancroft's qualities as an anthropologist. In 1883, prompted by the appearance in the New York press of two unfavorable reviews of his first volume on Central America, Bancroft took up his pen as a pamphleteer.[26] His comments on the ethics and the intellectual requisites for reviewing need not concern us here. These reviews, however, were by disciples of Lewis H. Morgan, and what Bancroft had to say about standards and methods in anthropology is pertinent. With some asperity he attacks Morgan's arbitrary definition of barbarism, savagism, and civilization, and the insistence of the Morgan school that the Indians of the Central American and southern Mexican tableland were at a lower cultural level than the Iroquois. He particularly objected to the corollary to this latter point, whereby the testimony of the early Spanish chroniclers, from Díaz, Cortés, and the Anonymous Chronicler, to Torquemada and Clavigero, was discountenanced because it was not in accord with the Morgan theory. Bancroft's defense of the chroniclers is convincing, and his criticism of the theorizing rather than the factual approach to the problems of anthropology is decisive. He displays the truly scientific spirit of insisting that the evidence must determine the conclusions, and as an anthropologist he has an awareness that civilization is a relative term, that there are as many cultures or civilizations as there are peoples, and that no two will prove exactly comparable.

[26] Hubert Howe Bancroft, *The Early American Chroniclers* (San Francisco, 1883); 45 + [5] + 13 + [1] pp. The first 38 pages, slightly moderated in wording, were reprinted as Chapter 1 in his *Essays and Miscellany* (San Francisco, 1890).

11

Managed Reviews

Never probably was a book so generally and so favorably reviewed by the best journals in Europe and America. Never was an author more suddenly or more thoroughly brought to the attention of learned and literary men everywhere.

Hubert Howe Bancroft, *Literary Industries*, 361

MEASURING the man-hours that went into the preparation of *Native Races*, Bancroft calculated that the five volumes represented a fifty-year achievement. By utilizing assistants, however, he had been able to expedite the work, and in 1874 the first volume was ready for release and the others were well along toward completion. He faced, therefore, the ordeal that comes to every author—and with greatest poignancy in connection with his first book,—of having the child of his brain run the gantlet of the reviewers.

On occasion, Bancroft professed indifference about the comments the reviewing fraternity might make, realizing full well that a book must stand on its merits. Yet, in common with most authors, he was acutely sensitive, and willing to argue that this was to be desired as well as expected. "The thoroughbred is thinner-skinned than the ass. A man who is not sensitive about his reputation will never make one." And still more personal is his additional comment, that "the results of long labor, involving the best efforts of a new aspirant, are given to the bulls and bears of literature tremblingly."[1]

Unlike the usual author proffering his maiden effort, Bancroft was well experienced in the world of books. As a dealer

[1] Bancroft, *Literary Industries*, 317.

he had witnessed the burgeoning and the bludgeoning of each year's crop. As a publisher he had observed the way in which favorable or adverse criticism could make or break a book, at least so far as its immediate commercial success was concerned. He knew that the established critics were mercurial and that they could be merciless. He was aware that deep-seated prejudice existed against attempts at scholarly writing by men of the market place, and that there was a reluctance to believe that any major contribution to scholarship could come out of California. An example of pillorying by the reviewers on grounds that were trivial or mistaken was fresh in his mind. Franklin Tuthill's *History of California* (San Francisco, 1866), though an honest, capable job, and by all odds the best that had then appeared on its subject, was dismissed flippantly or condescendingly by the late author's brother editors in California. Bancroft was ready to generalize that "a book written, printed, and published at this date on the Pacific coast, no matter how meritorious or by whom sent forth, that is to say if done by any one worth the castigating, would surely be condemned by some and praised coldly and critically by others."[2] For himself least of all did he count on exemption. His success in business had generated envy, and competition had created enemies; indeed, if his words may be taken literally, there were hundreds in California who damned him every day.

Bancroft, furthermore, was not merely an author, laying on the lap of the gods the product of his studies, his meditations, and his scrivenings. His investment in the enterprise far transcended the ordinary. Money without stint had gone into the amassing of his collection, into the preparation of the index, and into the maintenance of the staff on the fifth floor. Time and thought, no less, had been put into the planning of the work as a whole, into projecting the grand design, and into plotting the detailed procedure. The reviewing of the volume

[2] *Ibid.*, 310.

on the wild tribes thus loomed not merely as the proving ground for that opus, and not merely as the first trial for the five volumes of *Native Races,* but also as the baptism in fire for the *Works* as a whole and for the design of his historical and literary method. These several considerations prompted him to prepare carefully for the launching of his first volume.

The initial step seemed obviously to sound out, or rather to prepare, public opinion in the West. There was already, of course, some awareness of what was going on in Bancroft's literary workshop. It was notorious that Bancroft had been collecting Californiana. As long ago as the talk of a Pacific states cyclopedia there had been intimation that something would be done to make available the essential information stored in his library. Occasional comments on the collection and on the work in progress had also appeared in the San Francisco journals, though as yet Bancroft had not luxuriated in any detailed publicity releases. As publication date approached, something more ambitious seemed necessary.

The first overt move was to invite several of the Bay region's most illustrious men of letters to inspect the library, the fifth-floor workshop, and the proof sheets for the first volume and for parts of the second and third. Included were such men as Benjamin P. Avery, editor of the *Overland Monthly* and soon to become minister to China; J. Ross Browne, currently the best-known writer on the coast; Daniel C. Gilman, president of the University of California; Brantz Mayer, author of several books on Mexico; and Frederick Whymper, author of a book on Alaska. With no little relish Bancroft tells how George Davidson, head of the coast survey and president of the California Academy of Sciences, kept callers waiting in his outer office while he pored over the proof sheets of the volume on wild tribes. Davidson, Gilman, and practically all the others obliged with letters of endorsement and praise. The choicest phrases were culled from these letters, and, with other testimonials that soon came in, they provided copy for a sixteen-page pamphlet, appropriate for circulation to prospective purchasers or reviewers.

Concurrently, news items began to appear in the public press. The first of any consequence were two articles by Bancroft's chief of staff, Henry L. Oak. One, a description of collecting and indexing as carried on by Bancroft, appeared in the department of "Literary Notes" in the *Overland Monthly* for March, 1874.[3] The second, "Some Rare Books about California," was a more pretentious piece and dwelt at length upon certain treasures in the collection.[4] Neither piece announced the proximate appearance of *Native Races,* but both intimated that the materials were being worked, and the second mentioned Bancroft's "self-imposed life work of condensing his material into a series of standard works on Spanish North America, with its English and Russian additions in the northwest, a territory which he terms the Pacific States."[5] Local papers copied these articles in whole or in part, and reporters flocked into the library. One from the Sacramento *Record-Union* spent an entire day conferring with Oak in the fifth-floor workshop, and the result was a full-page story in that newspaper. Some of this writing was inspired. Enrique Cerruti, it will be remembered, particularly endeared himself to his employer by placing numerous laudatory descriptions in the foreign-language press of California and the eastern metropolises and in the leading journals of the Latin and Latin American countries. Before the year was over, hardly a newspaper reader throughout the West but had been exposed to the information that Bancroft's library was a remarkable one and that in it a literary project of some magnitude was afoot.

Thus far, western editors had coöperated most generously, and had Bancroft been concerned merely to get a favorable

[3] Pp. 283–284.
[4] *Overland,* XII (June, 1874), 566–572.
[5] *Ibid.,* 566; quoted in Bancroft, *Literary Industries,* 315.

reception on the West Coast, he might have contented himself with these preparations. His ambition, however, was by no means confined to the making of a local reputation, gratifying as that might have been. He craved approbation from the highest critics, the men acclaimed as the best minds of the day, and, naturally enough, wise men of the East rather than of the West. In this wish for approval from the supreme court of scholarly criticism there was an obvious streak of egotism. But, in addition, Bancroft insisted that he was thinking in terms of the broad potentialities and the fundamental significance of the project he had undertaken. Also, he pointed out that in their uniqueness his plan and methods were experimental. Before prosecuting the task further, he felt that he must have an advisory opinion from the scholars most competent to judge whether his work was sound in plan, reliable in execution, and likely to prove of any value in the extension of knowledge. In all this explanation a bit of rationalizing may be seen, but also at least a modicum of reasonableness and propriety.

In August, 1874, accompanied by his daughter Kate, who was to be placed in school in Connecticut, he boarded the train for New York.[6] In his trunks were printed sheets of as much of *Native Races* as was then in type; namely, Volume I entire, 150 pages of Volume II, 400 pages of Volume III, and 100 pages of Volume IV. That he set out in trepidation is indicated by his repeated requests, to President Gilman, to Clarence King, and to other friends, for reassurance that his course was a proper one, and likewise by his restlessness en route, while visiting his sisters at Buffalo, and while tarrying with other friends at Bridgeport.

He hastened on to New Haven, only to find that most of the Yale professors were vacationing. At Hartford the next

[6] Bancroft's invasion of the East is reported in detail in his *Literary Industries*, 326–364; for a modern and unflattering version see Oscar Lewis, "The Launching of Bancroft's 'Native Races,'" *Colophon*, n.s., I (1936), 323–332.

day he had somewhat better luck, because a scientific association was in session. President Gilman introduced him to such men as William H. Brewer, professor of agriculture at Yale, and Asa Gray, professor of botany at Harvard. Brewer had been a participant in the Geological Survey of California, and his letters, published in 1930 under the title *Up and Down California,* form one of the most satisfactory descriptions now extant of the state in the early 'sixties.[7] In Brewer, Bancroft should have found a kindred spirit, and doubtless would have if this book had been circulated earlier. Actually, he has more to say of the botanist, Gray. Gray advised him not to press recipients of advance copies for written comments; and Bancroft, in turn, protested sharply when Gray proposed to deposit the book Bancroft had just given him in the Harvard Library. "This fashion of giving public libraries presented books," Bancroft expostulated, "I do not relish. It is a sort of cheat practised upon the author."[8]

At Hartford, Bancroft effected a temporary alliance with a certain Porter C. Bliss, an ardent genealogist, a professed authority on Mexican antiquities and literature, and a character of no little oddity such as might have stepped out of a Yankee *Pickwick Papers.* The portrait Bancroft sketches of him in several leisurely pages is worthy of Dickens.[9] To Bliss is attributed "the appearance of the Wandering Jew, overtaken by Mexican highwaymen and forced to a partial exchange of apparel." He is likened to "an extract from a vellum-bound Nahua vocabulary, a half-civilized cross between an aboriginal American and an Englishman." He read omnivorously and gluttonously, but, save for genealogy, his knowledge did not extend beneath the surface. Apart from advising whom to see and where, Bliss did not appear likely to be of

---

[7] *Up and Down California in 1860–1864: The Journal of William H. Brewer, Professor of Agriculture in the Sheffield Scientific School from 1864 to 1903,* edited by Francis P. Farquhar (New Haven, 1930).

[8] Bancroft, *Literary Industries,* 334.

[9] *Ibid.,* 328–333, 339, 347.

much help in the pilgrimage among the literati. Yet in their call on Emerson it was Bliss's effusions on genealogy that came nearest to thawing the great man. Similarly, when they invaded the impressive premises of J. G. Palfrey, Bancroft, after one glance at the "weazen face," the "close-fisted features," the "pinched form and muck-worm manner" of this "antiquated genius," sought only an excuse to beat a "respectable retreat." Bliss, however, broke in boldly with a detailed account of what Bancroft had been doing, "and asked if the learned historian of New England would be pleased to look at the unlearned efforts of one who aspired to write the record of the last and mightiest west."[10]

"Then shook the attenuated form with its antiquated apparel, and loud lamentations broke from the learned lips. 'O talk not to me of new fields and new efforts!' he cried. 'I am finished; I am laid upon the topmost library shelf; the results of my life fill a space against a few house-walls hereabout, and that is all. Forgotten am I among men. Ask me to look at nothing, to say nothing, to do nothing.' " This, Bancroft continued, "was exactly what in my heart I was praying he would do—nothing. So we gat ourselves upon the street."[11]

Palfrey's response goes far to justify Bancroft's opinion that, as a companion to the sorrowful figure that he himself cut, Bliss "doubled the dolor without adding much diplomatic ability." Yet to have the irrepressible Bliss at his elbow was fortifying to the spirit in the ordeal of facing the celebrities of New England. Another unassailable reason justified retaining him. Bliss had in New York some three thousand volumes that he had collected in Mexico. If let slip, "he might have his books sold and be in Nova Scotia, where indeed he talked of going on somebody's genealogic business," before Bancroft could return to New York. And on this score, at least, the retaining of Bliss profited Bancroft. When they reached New York the first move was to unpack Bliss's stock of books

[10] *Ibid.*, 331–333. [11] *Ibid.*, 333.

and go over them volume by volume. They found four or five hundred items to add to Bancroft's library, a neat haul for him as a collector.

This book buying had not been a prime purpose of the trip east, but merely represents Bancroft's irresistible urge to round out his holdings. A matter of business was to be transacted. The whole process of manufacturing *Native Races* could have been handled in his own plant in San Francisco. Considerations of propriety and expediency, however, indicated that an established eastern house ought to be brought in as publisher, at least for the first volume. At the Riverside Press of H. O. Houghton and Company, of Boston, Bancroft made arrangements for the printing and binding, he to supply from San Francisco the electrotype plates. At New York he contracted with D. Appleton and Company to act as his publisher for a five-year term. Bancroft was to supply the volumes printed and bound and, as the publisher disposed of them, was to receive half the list price. To the uninitiated this must seem a lopsided bargain; actually it is a more liberal arrangement than most publishers would now offer on a specialized nonfiction title, and even though Appleton did not push *Native Races* vigorously, Bancroft was well satisfied with the bargain. This contract was followed by others on a commission basis to Longmans and Company to act as publisher in England, to Maisonneuve et Cie to act in France, and to F. A. Brockhaus to act in Germany.

As a California printer and publisher, who could if necessary have brought out *Native Races* with no assistance from any other firm, Bancroft faced only a fraction of the problem usually confronting an author. He saw enough of it, however, to brand it "one of the severest trials of an author's life." He felt, he says, "more keenly than ever before what it is to bring one's brains to market. There before the august magnate lies for dissection the author's work, the results of years of patient toil, representing innumerable headaches and heartaches, self-sacrifice, weariness of soul, and ill-afforded money. Author and publisher are in solemn deliberation. One regards this unborn book with that fond enthusiasm by which alone a writer is sustained in his work, the value of which he measures by the pains and sufferings it has cost him. The other eyes it with suspicion, looks upon the author and his work with a cold commercial eye, concerned not a whit for the worth of the man or for the value to mankind. The dollars that are in it, that is all the brain-dealer cares about."[12]

These musings were an outgrowth of the secondary purpose of the trip east—to arrange for a regular publisher. Meanwhile, the interviews with the mighty men of New England continued. Several of those first encountered were as cold and unbending as New Englanders can be. Immediately after Palfrey's rebuff, Bancroft and Bliss met another of "the gods of Harvard," made known their business to him, and were sternly informed that he had no time for such trifles, no knowledge of them, and no interest in them. James Russell Lowell, when Bancroft called on him and began to describe his literary project, sat apparently unresponsive so long that Bancroft feared he had encountered another Palfrey. It turned out, however, that Lowell was listening intently and with interest. Having heard Bancroft through, he asked for further details, advanced several helpful suggestions, and offered warm encouragement.[13]

Others equally famous extended an immediate and hearty welcome. Wendell Phillips saw at once where he could be of assistance and, without interrupting the flow of his animated conversation, dashed off eight or ten letters of introduction. John Greenleaf Whittier proved to be kindliness personified. He lent a sympathetic ear to Bancroft's story and penned introductions to Emerson, Barnard, and Longfellow. That to Longfellow contained these phrases: "I have been so much interested in his vast and splendid plan of a history of the

[12] *Ibid.*, 346–347. [13] *Ibid.*, 337.

western slope of our continent that I take pleasure in giving him a note to thee. What material for poems will be gathered up in his volumes! It seems to me one of the noblest literary enterprises of our day." This letter Bancroft said he would deliver only if permitted to retain it. "We in California," he explained, "do not see a letter from Whittier to Longfellow every day."[14]

Certain other easterners, though not of such lofty reputation, were in better position to measure Bancroft's achievement. These, without exception, gave hearty commendation. Among this number were Charles C. Jones of New York, the antiquarian, who reviewed *Native Races* in several long articles in the *Independent;* Charles Nordhoff, the travel writer, who had just obliged the "Big Four" with a guidebook to California; John W. Draper, who was amassing for the Wisconsin Historical Society an Ohio Valley historical collection in some respects comparable to Bancroft's gathering of Pacific Coast materials; and Francis Parkman, then certainly the brightest luminary among American historians.

Charles Francis Adams having suggested that it would be a "great thing" for *Native Races* if Parkman could be persuaded to review the volumes for the *North American Review,* Bancroft made bold to broach this matter to him. With no mention of his ill health or of the many demands on his time, Parkman agreed, warning only that he would have to review the work on its merits and that he was not sure he was "competent to do the subject justice." On these two points Bancroft expressed, respectively, complete agreement and disagreement.

Elsewhere on his rounds Bancroft took up the matter of reviews, with Thomas Wentworth Higginson of *Scribner's,* George Ripley of the *Tribune,* E. L. Godkin of the *Nation,* Charles Dudley Warner of the Hartford *Courant,* and William Dean Howells of the *Atlantic.* With the last-named it

[14] *Ibid.*, 337–338.

was arranged that Bliss should write a notice of some ten pages. Some weeks later, at Yale, Bancroft encountered Clarence King, whom he regarded as one of the most brilliant of American scientists. King, as buoyant and generous as he was learned, at once inquired what he could do for his old friend, whose library he had often visited in San Francisco. "Review my book," was Bancroft's reply. The *North American Review* or the *Atlantic* would have been Bancroft's choice as the spot for the review by the scintillating author of *Mountaineering in the Sierra Nevada,* but Parkman and Bliss were already slated for these journals. The *Nation* appeared the best alternative. Fortunately, however, the redoubtable Bliss was so overwhelmed by the affluence resulting from Bancroft's purchase of six cases of his Mexican books that he had done nothing on the promised article. He readily agreed to send his manuscript "elsewhere," and thus the columns of the *Atlantic* were opened for King's review.

Bancroft established contact with scores of other notables. Still others, including Bryant, Holmes, Longfellow, Mark Twain, Edward Everett Hale, and Henry Adams, were not reached personally, but were recipients of presentation copies. In England, copies were similarly sent to such men as Herbert Spencer, Sir Arthur Helps, E. B. Tylor, R. G. Latham, W. E. H. Lecky, and Charles Darwin.

Few returned any comments prior to the appearance of the first reviews, and Bancroft wondered whether his pilgrimage or his circulation of advance copies had had appreciable effect on the reviewers. The majority of these men, however, sent handsome acknowledgments and several wrote repeatedly and at length. Bancroft thus had a rich harvest of endorsements which he put to good use in promoting the sale and reception of his subsequent works.

Charles Dudley Warner reported that Mark Twain was in "an unusual state of excitement" over the first volume. "You may have a picture of his getting up at two o'clock this morning and, encased in a fur overcoat, reading it till daylight."[15] Herbert Spencer wrote, "I am finding your collection of facts very valuable for my own more immediate ends in writing the *Principles of Sociology*." Lowell reported, "I have read your first volume with so much interest that I am hungry for those to come," and Oliver Wendell Holmes sent word, "*Robinson Crusoe* never had a more interested reader among the boys, than I have been in following you through your heroic labor." A. R. Spofford characterized the *Native Races* as "truly a monument of literary and historical industry." Darwin's phrase was "magnificent work"; Thomas Carlyle's, "exceedingly interesting and important." John W. Draper predicted, "It will be consulted and read centuries after you are gone." Bryant and Longfellow were amazed, the one at the "extent and minuteness" of Bancroft's researches, the other at his "courage and perseverance" in working his way "through such a chaparral of authorities" as he quoted. The London *Westminster Review* likened his style to "the straightforward simplicity of Herodotus," and Wendell Phillips hailed him as "the Macaulay of the West."

Granted that many of these compliments were given after hasty examination of *Native Races,* they still were excellent ammunition with which to win sales and influence critics. Bancroft had frankly planned his calls and his distribution of advance copies with this latter point in mind, but, as has been mentioned, the majority of these comments were not received until after the reviews had begun to appear. Still, there is little doubt that his interviews with editors and literary celebrities went far to procure a favorable press, both in terms of space accorded and judgments expressed. A question of ethics may seem to obtrude; to which two responses come to mind. First, today's publishers do not hesitate to circulate advance copies or to solicit and use the comments of eminent men. There is no gainsaying that such words—or perchance

[15] *Ibid.,* 363.

the fact of selection by the jury of a nation-wide book club—carry weight with reviewers. Second, the men whom Bancroft approached—Lowell, Holmes, Longfellow, Draper, Spencer, and Darwin, for example—were of unquestioned intellectual integrity.

Biographically, the tour of New England has a further interest. In view of his New England ancestry and his Puritan upbringing, it might well have been a sort of spiritual homecoming for Bancroft. Actually it was anything else. Partly, to be sure, this was because he came as a tradesman, a self-taught scholar, and one of no reputation, attempting to mingle with men who were steeped in tradition, scholarship, schooling, and literary recognition. Yet a measure of his embarrassment was because he came as a Californian to whom many of New England's ways seemed to smack of "clerical cant and conventionalism." Clear indication of the gulf between East and West is afforded in a paragraph of Thomas Wentworth Higginson's in *Scribner's:*

> It is safe to say that there has not occurred in the literary history of the United States a more piquant surprise than when Mr. Hubert Bancroft made his appearance last autumn among the literary men of the Atlantic cities, bearing in his hand the first volume of his great work. That California was to be counted upon to yield wit and poetry was known by all; but the deliberate result of scholarly labor was just the product not reasonably to be expected from a community thirty years old. That kind of toil seemed to belong rather to a society a little maturer, to a region of public libraries and universities. Even the older states had as yet yielded it but sparingly; and was it to be expected from San Francisco? Had Mr. Bancroft presented himself wearing a specimen of the *sequoia gigantea* for a button-hole bouquet it would hardly have seemed more surprising.[16]

Returning from the effete East without such a boutonniere but with an impressive sheaf of testimonials, Bancroft was ready to take up the matter of western notices. Of all the re-

[16] *Scribner's,* X (July, 1875), 386; quoted in Bancroft, *Literary Industries,* 341–342.

viewing media, it seemed to him that the one to start with was the *Overland*, auspiciously launched by Bret Harte a half decade earlier, then the most influential of western literary organs, and still recognized as the most distinguished journal that the West has ever boasted. Bret Harte having migrated eastward and Benjamin P. Avery westward to China, its editors now were two graduates of the Bancroft workshop, Fisher and Harcourt, whose connection with *Native Races* had been close, to say the least. They were ready to coöperate with Bancroft to the fullest extent. They took the initiative, apparently, in urging that a review article be prepared in time for the December holiday number—and they asked Bancroft's advice on the selection of a reviewer.

When Fisher and Harcourt suggested Daniel Coit Gilman, Bancroft was well enough pleased. Gilman had obliged with many introductions in the course of the eastern trip; he had manifested a cordial interest in the work, and a more than cordial interest in getting Bancroft to deposit his library on the University of California campus. At the time of the removal of the University from Oakland to Berkeley, he proposed to erect a fireproof building in which Bancroft could house his collection, with full liberty to remove it at his pleasure. Bancroft did not agree, partly because of the obligation that he would have felt, and partly because he was in the midst of employing his collection as a working library and that work could go on more conveniently in San Francisco.

One November evening, the two young editors, with Bancroft in tow, ferried across to Oakland and waited on the university president to persuade him to undertake the review. He agreed, but with the proviso that, since his time was so much occupied, he be provided with memoranda from Oak, Nemos, Harcourt, and Goldschmidt on the collection, the index, the author, the method, and the book to be reviewed. He visited the fifth floor again, examined materials, index, notes, and so on, and questioned several of the assistants.

In due course the manuscript was submitted. After a hasty perusal, Fisher bounded up the stairs to Bancroft's headquarters on the fifth floor, laid it before him, and, fairly out of breath, exclaimed, "Here's a pretty go!" Bancroft read, and then—in a gesture that must excite the envy of many an author—without ado tore up the manuscript and threw it in the wastebasket. Unfortunately for posterity, President Gilman's opus has not survived. We know it only through Bancroft's description, which is summed up in the one word, "Flabby." More specifically, the trouble seems to have been that Gilman preferred to hide behind Oak, Nemos, and his other informants, and that he was reluctant to come out positively to say that the work was good, bad, or indifferent, in its entirety or in any particular. Bancroft appreciated that Gilman was hesitant to take a stand before the high priests of criticism in the East had committed themselves. Yet he had no patience with such cautious diplomacy, and concluded that Gilman lacked either the stamina of mind to have an opinion, or else the courage to state it. Thereafter, Bancroft had little esteem for him.[17]

Fisher then advanced the helpful suggestion that J. Ross Browne,[18] better known in the East than Gilman, was "the best man on the coast, if we could get him." "I can get him," said Harcourt, and off he went across the bay to Browne's pagoda-like villa in the Oakland hills. Travel writer, novelist, court reporter, Indian agent, and veteran of the American foreign service, Browne had had a diversified career which well fitted him to appreciate Bancroft's contribution in *Native Races*. He entered upon the task willingly, and in the Decem-

[17] Gilman, it should be remarked, was subsequently summoned to Johns Hopkins University to be its first president and there made an important contribution toward establishing the first real graduate school in the United States.

[18] For a discussion of Browne's career and his capacities as a writer see Dorothy O. Johansen, "J. Ross Browne," *Pacific Northwest Quarterly*, XXXII (1941), 385–400; and Francis J. Rock, *J. Ross Browne* (Washington, D.C., 1929).

ber *Overland* a laudatory review, describing the library, the index, and the volume entitled *Wild Tribes,* appeared over his signature.[19]

In the Gilman fashion Browne had been supplied with memoranda by members of Bancroft's staff. To what degree he leaned on these notes, we do not know. Some years later, when he was at outs with Bancroft, Henry L. Oak asserted that in reality he wrote the article for the *Overland,* in his haste "cribbing one or two elegant phrases from President Gilman's previous effusion," and that Browne was good-natured enough to allow his name to be used.[20] The fact that time was pressing makes the assertion plausible; also, the whole procedure with regard to this review had involved an unusual degree of author control. Nevertheless, Browne was universally assumed to be the author, he never denied it, and by signing the review, whether he phrased it or not, he subscribed to the opinions therein expressed. Choicest of Browne's compliments was his characterization of *Native Races,* Volume I, as "California's greatest contribution to the world's literature."[21]

Backed by this endorsement, Bancroft now proceeded fearlessly to issue review copies to the friendly and not-so-friendly California press. He let these editors know that the book would soon be reviewed in eastern and European periodicals and journals. And, after the customary practice of publishers, he enclosed with each review copy a dodger reproducing comments selected from those generated by his summer and fall campaign. Bancroft puts it mildly when he says that "the daily papers of San Francisco spoke well of the *Native Races.*" Actually, these western journals, with oboe and flageolet, gave out in unison the theme of praise, which was soon taken up by the mightier diapason of the eastern organs, after which the chorus swelled and echoed to the ends of the earth.

---

[19] *Overland,* XIII (December, 1874), 551–560.

[20] Oak, *"Literary Industries" in a New Light,* 57.

[21] For a narrative of the whole affair see Bancroft, *Literary Industries,* 319–324.

Bancroft was particularly elated over two columns in the London *Times* and thirty or forty pages in the *Westminster Review,* but he was not unmindful of attention in the *Revue des Deux Mondes, Europa und das Ausland, La Voz del Nuevo Mundo,* the Hongkong *Press,* the Gold Hill *News,* and the Los Angeles *Star*. Clippings of these notices filled two stout quarto scrapbooks and led him to this substantially correct conclusion: "Never probably was a book so generously and so favorably reviewed by the best journals in Europe and America. Never was an author more suddenly or more thoroughly brought to the attention of learned and literary men everywhere."[22]

[22] *Ibid.,* 361; or, as a modern writer has paraphrased it, "No budding historian before or since ever launched his maiden effort with a greater splash." Oscar Lewis, "The Launching of Bancroft's 'Native Races,'" *Colophon,* n.s., I (1936), 327.

12

Spanish Americanist

And now I suppose you feel as Gibbon says he did on completing his "Decline". . . He felt as if the occupation of his life was gone. But you are far more energetic than he. You are only at the beginning of your intellectual life: he was near the close. You will find something more to do.

Letter from John W. Draper to Hubert Howe Bancroft, written upon receipt of the fifth volume of *Native Races*. Quoted in *Literary Industries*, 579

WHILE THE WORK of "disposing of the Indians" was yet going on, Bancroft had begun to direct attention to his larger objective, the histories of the Pacific states. The advisability of beginning at the beginning had already been seen, but some necessity remained of laying out a general plan and apportioning space. This was not a task to be finished at a sitting; in fact, it was not until some time later that the dimensions of the several parts were finally determined. Yet the general plan was chosen early, and, before any of the histories were published, the scope of each of the twenty-eight volumes had been defined.

The plan may be visualized most concretely by surveying the completed histories in their place on the long shelf of Bancroft's *Works*. They follow the five volumes of *Native Races* and stand in this order:

History of Central America, 3 volumes
History of Mexico, 6 volumes
History of the North Mexican States and Texas, 2 volumes
History of Arizona and New Mexico, 1 volume
History of California, 7 volumes

History of Nevada, Colorado, and Wyoming, 1 volume
History of Utah, 1 volume
History of the Northwest Coast, 2 volumes
History of Oregon, 2 volumes
History of Washington, Idaho, and Montana, 1 volume
History of British Columbia, 1 volume
History of Alaska, 1 volume

Obviously, the prime character of the plan is the breaking down of western North America into convenient and conventional geographical units. For one thing, there would be a better market for the set of books if the residents of California, of Utah, of British Columbia, and so on, could clearly see that the history of their particular region was covered.[1] Another reason, equally practical and even more compelling, was that this device reduced Bancroft's vast and sprawling subject matter into workable units. There were defects, to be sure, in this system of compartmentalizing; but other possible approaches would have had their imperfections, too. For example, a strictly chronological treatment would have entailed much jumping about from place to place and would have produced a set of annals almost certain to be confusing and deficient in unity.

By their shelf arrangement one might infer that the histories are to be read from south to north, beginning with Central America and ending with Alaska. They stand in that order, and appropriately, since western American history unfolded approximately thus, with its earliest beginnings at the far south, and penetration of the northwest delayed until many years later. It would be a mistake, however, to assume that the writing was consecutive from the first volume on Central America to the last on Alaska. Actually, work on several parts of the set was carried on concurrently, and the order of appearance of the various volumes related rather to the

[1] This argument was specifically brought to the attention of sales agents: see *Information for Agents to Assist in Selling the Works of Hubert H. Bancroft,* 5–6.

period covered than to the area involved. Thus, the first volumes on the early history of Central America and Mexico appeared in 1882 and 1883, and the corresponding volumes on California and the Pacific Northwest in 1884. Yet the series on these southern areas were not completed until 1887 and 1888; those to the north, by 1890.

Even a casual inspection of these twenty-eight volumes reveals that a good half of them relate to the history of Spanish America. Included would be the nine volumes on Central America and Mexico, most of the two on the North Mexican States and Texas, the greater part of the volume on Arizona and New Mexico, the first four on California, and assorted bits from various others, such as the first on the Northwest Coast. These alone would make Bancroft's contribution as a Spanish Americanist a large one. A later volume in the series, *California Pastoral,* must be taken into the reckoning, and likewise several that appeared separately: a life of Porfirio Díaz, a volume on the resources of Mexico, and a one-volume popular history of Mexico.

This total output of a score of volumes, filling a yard or more of shelving, gives Bancroft a quantitative claim to a place in the first rank of contributors on Spanish American history. The publications of such famous authorities as Prescott, Helps, and Moses do not bulk so large, and few of the present leaders in the field have done as much. Mere quantity, of course, signifies little unless buttressed by the findings of qualitative analysis. On that score, the over-all judgment had best be based on a measurement of the parts. First to be examined are the volumes on Central America.[2]

The three volumes allotted to this part of the Pacific Coast are fairly representative of Bancroft's methods and achievements. Like the earlier volumes on the native races, they are thick books, just short of 800 pages each. Mechanically, they

[2] Hubert Howe Bancroft, *History of Central America* (3 vols.; San Francisco, 1882–1887).

resemble their predecessors in having analytical tables of contents, repetition of these subheadings at the beginning of each chapter, an alphabetical list of authorities in the forepart of the first volume, and an index to round out the set. The bibliographical list fills 48 pages, and the index 30. Again, the notes are voluminous. Perfunctory thumbing of the leaves will bring one to footnotes filling the better part of a page. In each of the volumes, furthermore, Bancroft displayed his virtuosity in a cadenza of fine print. In Volume I it was on pages 67 to 154, with a "Summary of Geographical Knowledge and Discovery from the Earliest Records to the Year 1540"; in Volume II, on pages 735 to 766, with a "Bibliography of Voyage Collections"; and in Volume III, on pages 710 to 746, with a discussion of projects for "Interoceanic Communication."

The time span covered by the three volumes is 1501 to 1530, 1530 to 1800, and 1801 to 1887. Arithmetically, this equalizing of the first 30 years, the next 270, and the final 87, may seem questionable. With respect to historical significance, however, Bancroft maintained that it was justified. The discovery and early conquests called for exhaustive treatment; thereafter, the annals of the several provinces ran "in grooves too nearly parallel long to command the attention of the general reader"; then, in the nineteenth century, the end of Spanish rule, the wars of liberation, and the launching of the nations demanded more extended discussion. These proportions, it may be remarked, are consonant with the almost universal practice in histories of Spanish America, where one finds a detailed narrative of the beginnings, a rapid view of the rest of the colonial period, and a concentration on liberation and early nationalism.

In its further elaboration the plan of these volumes is sound. Volume I opens with the analysis of Spain and her civilization as she came to the threshold of empire building. Shorter chapters follow on Columbus and his discoveries, the first voyages to Darién and the Central American coast, and the early administration of the West Indies. Then comes what is really the heart of the narrative, the story of the unbelievable hardships endured by Alonso de Ojeda, Diego de Nicuesa, and their respective followers, of the genius with which Vasco Núñez de Balboa took charge of the faltering colony and assured its success, and the arrival of Pedrarias Dávila to supplant Balboa and eventually to encompass his execution. Resisting the pull of Peru, which had beckoned Balboa, Pedrarias turned toward the north and west into Central America, where some of his men, such as Andrés Niño and Gil González Dávila, performed prodigies of conquest and conversion, and where others came into conflict with Hernán Cortés and his lieutenants, advancing southeastward after their conquest of the Aztecs. Throughout the latter part of this chronicle, the crafty, heartless, and vindictive Pedrarias is the dominant figure. Bancroft glosses over none of the crimes of this old blackguard, yet accords him due credit for the results accomplished, including the dispatch of hundreds of thousands of natives. No reader can escape the conviction that Balboa was the true hero of Isthmian colonization.

Intended, as it was, as an introduction concerning the Spaniards on the American continent, this first volume is freighted with technical information on a number of elements in the Spanish colonial system. Lest these explanations should distract from the exciting narrative that formed the main body of the book, most of them were relegated to the notes. To Bancroft's notion, the permissible length of a footnote was almost limitless. His definitions and discussions of such terms as *repartimiento* (pp. 262–264), *audiencia* (pp. 270–273), *Consejo de Indias* (pp. 280–283), and *Recopilación de Leyes de los Reynos de las Indias* (pp. 285–288) are unquestionably adequate. Yet they are inconspicuously displayed in fine type, and many a reader of this volume, intent merely on the engrossing story of the adventures of the conquistadores, has doubtless skipped lightly over them.

The second volume has a more miscellaneous cast. It begins with a chapter on Pizarro and the conquest of Peru, too rapid a survey to do full justice to that theme. Some twenty-odd chapters are then utilized to cover the affairs of Central America and the isthmus in about that same number of years. This was a turbulent period. Spanish control of the native population was not yet firmly established, and a recurrent element in the narrative is that of Indian revolt—by the Cakquikels, the Zapotecs under Chief Sinacam, the Guatemalans, the fierce warriors of Chiapas, and others. Among the Spaniards, likewise, there were bitter disputes over jurisdiction and bloody clashes of rival aspirants to power. Pedro de Alvarado is the most famous of these quarreling conquistadores, yet in the contentions he was merely one among many. Upon his death feminism made its first appearance in Spanish colonial government when the control of Guatemala was entrusted to his widow, Doña Beatriz. Her rule was cut short a few months later, as a flood of water poured down from the Volcán de Agua, on the slope of which the capital city was situated. Doña Beatriz was one of the many victims.

In the decades of the 'thirties and 'forties, Central America served as a base from which the Spaniards attempted to extend their conquests to other and richer lands. Best rewarded was the advance to Peru, and Bancroft naturally has much to say about the role of Panama in the conquest and in subsequent contacts with Peru. There is a chapter also on Alvarado's ill-fated expedition from Guatemala to Peru, and another describing his final venture, in which he sought new profit and glory by an expedition northwestward.

The description of life in the area during this epoch is largely in terms of Indian revolts and their suppression, the contentions of the Spaniards, and the constantly renewed hope that another Mexico or Peru would be found beyond the horizon. Along with these elements the church began to play an increasingly important part. There had been churchmen on hand earlier, to be sure, notably the avaricious vicar, Fernando de Luque, whose partnership Pizarro summarily cast off. Yet the church was no more than a feeble power for good until Francisco Marroquín arrived, to be Bishop of Guatemala, and Bartolomé de las Casas came similarly to Chiapas. The latter's instrumentality in procuring the New Laws is well known; his heroic labors in Chiapas were of even greater practical value.

Having reached mid-century, and almost the mid-point of this second volume, Bancroft was prepared to move much more rapidly over the quarter millennium from 1550 to 1800. In the domestic affairs of Central America he saw little to detain him. In economy, in administration, and in relations with the natives, routines had developed which persisted with little change to the end of the colonial period. Therefore, it was necessary only to record the shifting personnel and to notice the colorful episodes that occasionally relieved the monotony. Thus handled, these annals might have been brief indeed, except for two disturbing elements, the *cimarrones* and the pirates. The former were runaway Negroes who had, as this name implies, gone wild. The isthmus, in particular, was beset by them. The pirates were a motley crew in which English, French, and Dutch elements predominated. Central America was but a fraction of the area they ravaged in these two and a half centuries. The high seas, the islands of the Caribbean, and even the Pacific coast of Spanish America were within their field of operations. Yet Central America, with its isthmian transfer of the treasure of Peru and Upper Peru, was the objective surpassing all others. The account of freebooting in this locality thus becomes a fair sample of the depredations on Spanish America in its entirety.

First in the field was Francis Drake, descending on Nombre de Dios, attacking Cartagena, attempting to ambush a treasure-laden pack train, and at length, after much hardship, brave fighting, and perilous adventure, making off with almost thirty tons of gold and silver. Oxenham followed his example. Drake returned, succumbed to sickness, and was consigned to a watery grave off the isthmus he had so sorely ravaged. François l'Olonnois was the next great freebooter. Shipwreck at Campeche did not discourage him. He returned to harry the Honduran coast and to plan a raid on Guatemala, though his men prudently refused to venture so far inland. Wrecked once more, and deserted by most of his men, he set out in a longboat for Costa Rica, where his inhuman cruelties on all who had fallen into his clutches were avenged by the Indians. Capturing this once-dreaded scourge of the Indies, they hacked his body to pieces, which they duly roasted and ate.

Mansvelt, Parker, and divers other buccaneers had lesser exploits to their credit. Topping them all was the sturdy Welshman Henry Morgan. After an apprenticeship with Mansvelt, he became a leader in his own right and launched out on a career of plundering, rapacity, and lust that paled the earlier efforts into insignificance. Whereas Drake had been motivated by patriotism and Protestant piety as well as by a desire for loot, Morgan's motives were exclusively piratical. The sack of Puerto Bello and the capture and burning of Panama were merely the highlights of his work. Bancroft recites the story in all its bloody details, after which he turns to Sharp, Ringnose, Harris, Sawkins, Coxon, Dampier, Grogniet, and other "brethren of the coast."

Implicitly in his text and explicitly in a spacious footnote on pages 567–569, Bancroft admits to an absorbing interest in the expeditions of these wild fellows, "a New World revival of the vikings." "Their daring raids, bloody feuds, and hair-breadth escapes by sea and land" did much to uphold his interest, but he was also aware of their achievements in exploration, their contribution to non-Spanish colonization in the Caribbean area, and their stimulation of international commerce. Piracy is the exciting theme of this half volume on Central America in the latter part of the colonial period. Much of the time the Spanish defenses seem pathetically inadequate, yet Spanish heroism was not lacking, and in the end the Spaniards retained possession of the land, even despite an attempt to plant a colony of Scots at Darién and the onslaughts of regular British forces under Admiral Vernon. All these attacks were a tribute to the prosperity the Spaniards had achieved in their New World empire.

Continuing the survey of Central America, Volume III moves rapidly to the last days of Spanish rule. Though exceptional in achieving its independence through simple declaration, whereas practically all Spanish America won freedom only after the bitterest of fighting, Central America was soon embroiled in bloody internecine strife. For a few months she attached herself to Mexico, then seceded to establish a confederation, which, after a short and stormy life, dissolved into the five republics that now grace the "third America." Through the decades to 1887, when this volume appeared, these states had but indifferent success in living at peace with one another or within themselves. Frequently the issue was between personalities, with one *caudillo* striving to replace another. When principles were involved, they were most apt to relate to boundary claims or to the determination of the clergy and the privileged oligarchy to retain the upper hand.

In the 'fifties an adventurer from the north descended on Central America—William Walker, the "grey-eyed man of destiny." Throwing in his lot with the democrats, or rather appropriating their support to his own ends, this filibuster soon gained the mastery over Nicaragua. But by highhanded action he antagonized the conservatives, and, what was worse, by quarreling with the Accessory Transit Company he called down the wrath of the Vanderbilt interests. When Costa Rica put up an unexpected resistance, Walker was forced to flee from Nicaragua. Upon his return to Honduras, he was worsted in battle, captured, and shot by a firing squad.

Walker's militant interference in Central America is given much more space than the penetration of American capital in the rival transportation lines, the railroad across Panama, and the lake and river steamers performing the Nicaraguan transit. The volume ends with a discussion of projects for developing interoceanic communication, culminating as of 1887 with the work on a ship canal by Ferdinand de Lesseps, a work then languishing because of exhaustion of capital but not yet despaired of by the French.

Not all the reviewers hailed Bancroft's *Central America* as a perfect work. In *Harper's,* for example, the reviewer of Volume I complained:

> His philosophizings run in narrow grooves and are often superficial, sometimes trite, and sometimes, as Sterne would say, "hobby-horsical." Many of his reflections, observations, and judgments are strained and pragmatical, others have an air of mock-profundity, still others are so extravagantly cynical or so unnecessarily objurgatory as to savor of morbidness or affectation, and others again are needlessly or offensively iconoclastic and irreverent. His style, too, is often marred by defects that seriously detract from its general impressiveness and attractiveness, not the least among which are its occasional lapses into turgidity or ambiguity, its labored circumlocutions, abrupt transitions, and capricious digressions, its use of inapt or improper words, and its tendency to paroxysms or rather tumid declamation.[3]

A few of these strictures are undoubtedly appropriate. On the whole, however, the style of the *Central America* volumes will be found more forceful, more lucid, and more engaging than this reviewer's.

As to other elements of historical craftsmanship, the criteria are less subjective. The plan and proportions of the work have already been discussed. The materials utilized included practically every book or pamphlet that had dealt with any phase of Central American history. A certain amount of manuscript material was also available, principally in the

[3] *Harper's,* LXVI (March, 1883), 635.

collection that E. G. Squier had assembled. Yet these were at most an incidental supplement to the printed materials used, and Bancroft's neglect of the official archives of Spain and her former colonies has given modern scholars their chief opportunity to improve on his treatment.

For his narrative of nineteenth-century Central America, Bancroft drew heavily on a third type of material—newspapers. In the tenth chapter, for example, there are 45 citations of newspapers and 75 of other references; in the sixteenth chapter, 33 newspaper citations and 50 others. The newspapers used include several California and a few eastern United States journals, but mostly they were Central American sheets, many of them doubtless available nowhere in the United States except in Bancroft's collection. Nowadays the use of newspapers as historical sources is commonplace; in the 'eighties, however, it was an innovation with regard to which Bancroft must be reckoned a pioneer.

Still another source of information was available for the volumes on Central America. In the first years of his residence in California, Bancroft, it will be recalled, had made ten or a dozen trips by the Panama and Nicaragua routes. This passing through did not make him an authority on the region's history, but it was a help—slightly when it came to dealing with certain phases of the latter history, and more substantially on such matters as the isthmian transit, and the conditions of climate, terrain, and lush vegetation encountered by Balboa, Morgan, the gold seekers, and the canal builders. Furthermore, Bancroft had on his staff several men experienced in Central America, notably Thomas Savage, who assumed a special responsibility on the Spanish American subject matter.

Thus advantaged by his great collection of books, his newspaper files, and his personal contact with Central America, Bancroft was able to produce a history of this area that is still the standard on the subject. Its persistence may be partly accidental; there is a temptation to think that any general history published in the 'eighties could now be improved upon. Nevertheless, the fact that it has not been superseded is something of a proof of merit. The merits, as indicated, lie somewhat in its literary style; more, in the sources of information utilized; and most of all, in the planning, proportioning, and execution of the work.

Next in order stand the six volumes covering Mexico's history through the three and three-quarters centuries from the discovery by Hernández de Córdoba to Bancroft's publication date, 1887, approximately midway in the epoch of Porfirio Díaz.[4] In format these volumes are alike and in general plan they are symmetrical with the ones on Central America. The apportioning of space is also similar. The time span of the six volumes is, respectively, 5, 80, 203, 20, 37, and 27 years—which means, of course, that the Spanish beginnings received particular attention, the rest of the colonial era more cursory inspection, and the erection and the experiences of the Mexican nation careful study. There can be little quarrel with this proportioning. Justification of a sort may be found through comparison with the volume that for the past two decades has been the standard history of Mexico.[5] In this work the conquest of the Aztecs is sketched much more rapidly and the pages thus gained are utilized for the following epoch. Similarly the subject matter of Bancroft's final volume is dealt with in fewer pages, and the earlier experiences of the republic correspondingly expanded. Otherwise, the proportions of this modern volume are substantially the same as Bancroft's.

Like the *Native Races* and *Central America*, the *History of Mexico* is essentially an exhaustive digest of the existing literature on the subject, so far as Bancroft had been able to

---

[4] Hubert Howe Bancroft, *History of Mexico* (6 vols.; San Francisco, 1883–1888).

[5] Herbert I. Priestley, *The Mexican Nation: A History* (New York, 1923).

get hold of it. Again, his collecting was so thorough that little printed matter of significance had escaped him. The vastness of the materials consulted is hinted at by the 92-page list, in the customary fine print, which appears in the preliminary pages of Volume I. From it were omitted most items already listed in *Central America* or to be listed in the *North Mexican States,* as well as many works which were cited only once. Although Bancroft had pieced together a continuous run of leading Mexican newspapers, such sources figure less prominently than they had in the preceding volume. A good number of the printed items, however, are source materials. Included are the more obvious collections of documents and also a host of individual items, both pamphlets and books.

Bancroft's collection had a substantial holding of Mexican manuscripts, derived from the Andrade and Ramírez sales and elsewhere. These were utilized wherever pertinent, yet it cannot be said that any very considerable part of the six volumes was based primarily on manuscript materials. Once more, a major criticism must be that Bancroft did not take full advantage of the rich store of original documents in the official archives of Mexico and Spain. He had some awareness of what was there, as is evidenced in the final volume of his *Works* by a graphic and somewhat detailed description of the principal Mexican archives,[6] yet in the preface to the *History of Mexico* we find him guilty of self-deception when he lists among his manuscript holdings "a copy of the famous *Archivo General de Mexico,* in thirty-two volumes."[7]

To the present generation, a work in six fat volumes, totaling almost five thousand pages, sounds like reference rather than reading matter. For Bancroft's *Mexico* this impression is confirmed by the factual detail in which it abounds. Several features recommend it as a reference work. Its treatment is so exhaustive that the investigator of almost any character

[6] Bancroft, *Literary Industries,* 701–703, 740–751.
[7] Bancroft, *History of Mexico,* I, viii.

or topic in Mexican history to 1887 will find some mention of his subject and citation of references where it may be pursued further. It is the largest history of Mexico in the English language, and it is more exhaustive and more thoroughly documented than any of the histories in Spanish. Consequently, any reference collection on Mexico would do well to start with this set.

Undoubtedly, reference use has predominated—and by a ratio almost astronomical. Nevertheless, the volumes read well. Volume I, on the conquest of the Aztecs, has a theme that is superlatively compelling. Bancroft regarded it as the grandest episode in American history, a military exploit of surpassing brilliance, a conquest basic to Spanish expansion on the continent, and an Indian defeat especially deplorable since it disrupted the most flourishing culture of pre-Cortesian America. The narrative in this volume must inevitably be compared with Prescott's classic. In length and in outline the two are much alike. For style the palm goes to the New Englander's measured periods, but for facts the Bancroft account, utilizing certain materials that had not been available earlier, is somewhat more reliable. Its reader appeal is enhanced by an attitude of strong sympathy for the attacked Aztecs and by a sincere admiration for the heroism and brilliance of the Spaniards and their leader. The concluding sentences give a fair idea of the attitude that pervades:

> If there ever was a hero, a genius of war worthy the adoration of war-worshippers, if ever there were grand conception and achievement, all were vividly displayed in the mind and person of Hernán Cortés. . . .
>
> In some respects, and as compared with his companions, he indeed approached the deity the Mexicans thought him. Behold him out upon this venture, throwing life to the winds that waft him from Cuba, sinking his ships behind him, plunging into the heart of a hostile country, and with a handful of men opposing powerful armies, quelling insurrections, capturing his captors, turning enemies into allies, balancing upon his finger contending powers, and

after the grand cataclysm opened by him on the central plateau has spent itself, he quietly pockets the prize. No Alexander, or Scipio, or Caesar, or Napoleon ever achieved results so vast with means so insignificant. It was indeed a rare piracy![8]

Volume I, to repeat, should reward the reader well. Candor demands the admission, however, that it is not much read; not even, it would appear, by the most recent and one of the most popular biographers of Cortés, Señor Salvador de Madariaga.

The second volume, concerned with the spread of the conquest, the erection of the viceroyalty, and the implanting of Spanish institutions, has important but less fascinating subject matter. The casual reader is apt to find his interest lagging; indeed, he might better be directed to the writings of modern specialists such as Arthur S. Aiton, C. Pérez Bustamente, George P. Hammond, J. Lloyd Mecham, Vito Alessio Robles, Carl O. Sauer, and Lesley B. Simpson, several of whom launched forth on their scholarly careers from researches begun at the Bancroft Library.

The reader will find even less to delight him in Volume III. Here are detailed, in the form of modified annals, the events of the seventeenth and eighteenth centuries. A sample taken at random may prove palatable, but the repetitions encountered in any larger assignment are almost certain to induce tedium. When one encounters chapter titles such as "Five More Viceroys" and "Viceroys Forty-four to Forty-six," one suspects that the writer himself was thus affected. A more serious complaint about this volume is that, in the epoch with which it deals, Mexico, as the Viceroyalty of New Spain, embraced a much larger area than is discussed. Technically, this holds good likewise for Volume IV and much of Volume V; but the objection applies especially to Volume III because in the later colonial period much of the most significant action took place in the more northerly parts of the viceroyalty, which Bancroft segregated as the north Mexican states and

[8] *Ibid.*, I, 694.

Texas, and as Arizona and New Mexico, and California, and which he takes up separately in other volumes thus entitled. A reader of Bancroft's *Works* will have the whole picture, but one who chooses only the set on Mexico probably would not see the vast extent of New Spain toward the close of the colonial era.

The fourth volume benefits from stirring action, heroic deeds, and an achievement of patent significance. In it are depicted the sad state of incompetence into which Spanish rule had sunk, the surging class hatreds that had been engendered, and the fortuitous causes of the revolutionary outbreak. Father Hidalgo as an inspiring but impractical leader, Father and General Morelos as a military genius, General Calleja as a bulwark for the loyalists, and dozens of other participants are not only described, but brought to life. Artistic considerations might call for simplification of the account here offered, but the wealth of detail serves to bring out the dimensions of the struggle and the bitterness of the conflict in which the Mexican republic was created.

Thereafter, the experiences of the nation are an anticlimax, yet possessing frequent appeal. The fifth volume has to do with ambitious but floundering attempts at the operation of a republic. Some of the leaders were well-meaning, Victoria and Guerrero, for example; none, however, was really heroic; and with "his most serene highness," Santa Anna, is reached at last the "apogee of personalism." The neighbor to the north, meanwhile, contributed two dubious favors, the principle of federalism, and a supply of settlers for Texas, which were followed by the annexation of that province and a war of conquest whereby the Mexican nation was shorn of half its territory. Bancroft's treatment of this topic is vigorously critical of the United States.

The final volume opens with Benito Juárez triumphant after the liberal constitution of 1857 had passed its first severe test. His regime was soon threatened by the French intervention. Maximilian and Carlotta were principals in a drama that seems much more distant than Mexico of the 1860's. Their venture came to its tragic but in Bancroft's view its appropriate end, and Juárez and his adherents could again undertake to translate liberalism and reform into law and practice. The difficulties were great. Juárez' death added to the confusion, and Mexico drifted into another period of intermittent rebellion. From this anarchy she had been rescued in the late 'seventies by the strong hand of Porfirio Díaz. Bancroft's history thus terminates on a, for him, happier plane with order benevolently forced upon the country. Treating a subject matter such as this, no book could be completely dull. Bancroft's account, as a circumstantial and veracious narrative, captures the realities of this epoch.

When three volumes of his *Mexico* had been published, Bancroft decided that he should go to Mexico, see the land, interview its leading citizens, and gather additional materials for the volumes on the nineteenth century.[9] It was then that he built up his file of Mexican newspapers; then also, that he acquired a sizable quantity of books and pamphlets. Furthermore, he made the acquaintance of General Díaz, at the moment on "sabbatical leave" from the presidency, yet obviously the foremost man in the republic. Díaz obliged with a series of interviews and then with a fortnight of dictating to a pair of stenographers, which yielded some five hundred pages of manuscript.[10] Having such a start, Bancroft resolved to bring out a biography of Díaz, and forthwith proceeded to do so.[11] It was, in a sense, an authorized biography. Díaz inspected the proof sheets and suggested a few changes, which

[9] The trip is described in Hubert Howe Bancroft, Notes on Mexico in 1883, a manuscript volume of 209 pages, in the Bancroft Library; and in Bancroft, *Literary Industries,* 700–751.

[10] A manuscript of 560 pages, Conversación entre el Sr. Gral. Porfirio Díaz y Mr. H. Bancroft, Bancroft Library.

[11] Hubert Howe Bancroft, *Vida de Porfirio Díaz: Reseña histórica y social del pasado y presente de México* (San Francisco, 1887).

were made.[12] The prevailing tone is laudatory. Herein Bancroft was undoubtedly sincere. It should be borne in mind, however, that this work appeared in 1887, and that even Díaz' sharpest critics deal favorably with this early part of his career, saving their more vigorous denunciation for the later decades of his dictatorship and for his responsibility for the aftermath of revolution. Bancroft's *Díaz,* though apparently little circulated and seldom cited, is a solid and respectable biography. It was a by-product of the larger Mexican venture.

Next in the series are two volumes on the history of the north Mexican states and Texas.[13] Here the published literature was less extensive, and no writer of Prescott's brilliance had preceded. Bancroft's collection, however, included a larger number of firsthand accounts that had found their way into print and a mass of manuscript material, chief of which were the reports and letters of the missionaries who had labored so heroically in the Spanish northward advance. Even more than the *Mexico* proper, these two volumes were a pioneering venture, and the degree to which they were based on manuscript and source materials was correspondingly greater. The nature of the subject matter also called for a larger number of maps and charts, and these are interspersed at frequent intervals.

Volume I is a survey of frontier advance and its attendant problems from the early sixteenth century to the end of the eighteenth. The early chapters relate principally to exploration by land and sea, with Cortés, Nuño de Guzmán, and Francisco de Ibarra as dominant figures. Their ex-

[12] Porfirio Díaz, List of Corrections, n.p., n.d., MS, Bancroft Library. Most of the changes called for substitution of an impersonal expression in place of Díaz' name; for example, "the executive" for "President Díaz," and "present government" for "government of Díaz." Another called for the suppression of several paragraphs which argued that, because the population was so lacking in literacy and responsibility, Mexico required a rule of despotism or tyranny.

[13] Hubert Howe Bancroft, *History of the North Mexican States and Texas* (2 vols.; San Francisco, 1884–1889).

peditions and the more far-flung journeys of Cabeza de Vaca, Coronado, and Cabrillo were soon supplemented by an extension of Spanish control through Indian conquest, the spread of settlements, the advance of agriculture, and above all by the opening up of silver mines in the mountainous area reaching northwestward. At about the close of the century, Jesuit and Franciscan missionaries became the most active agents of frontier advance and continued in this leadership to the end of the colonial period. All through Spanish America this was the golden age of mission activity. The northern frontier of New Spain, and its western portion in particular, supplies one of the best examples; Chihuahua, Sinaloa, Sonora, and the Californias were first occupied through the instrumentality of the mission. The missionaries, furthermore, were the chief chroniclers of this advance.

Proselyting zeal was one of the reasons for the expansion; hope of profits through mining, agriculture, or exploitation of the natives was another; and later, eclipsing these, was the need of improving the defenses of New Spain. In Lower California the Pichilingues threatened. English, Dutch, and French freebooters made themselves at home in its waters to waylay the Manila galleon or to descend on the Mexican and Central American South Sea ports; and Spanish settlement of the peninsula was undertaken so that these foreigners would be forestalled. Across the continent it was the French who threatened, and the Spanish response was to occupy Texas as a buffer province to ward off possible encroachment. In later stages the foreign bogey was English, Russian, or Anglo-American, and Spain answered with colony planting or reinforcement. Yet even without any rivalry from France, England, Russia, or the United States, Spain might have proceeded with defensive colonization of these northern borderlands. The main adversary, after all, was the Indian, and protection of the settled area was most feasible if certain agencies of Indian control were thrown out into the region of the wild tribesmen. Mission, presidio, and pueblo comprised the threesome customarily employed. Uniting religious, military, and civilian pressure, they advanced the frontier; and, more importantly, they formed a bulwark for the older and more valuable parts of New Spain.

Interspersed with such upheavals as the Mixton War, the revolts of the Suaquis and Ocoronis, the Yaqui wars, the Tepehuán revolt, the uprising of the Tarahumares, the Pueblo revolt, the Lower California revolt, the Seri wars, and the Yuma massacre, this period may appear to have been an era of the wildest disorder. In actuality, life and property were fairly safe. The colonial record is chiefly of mission founding and expanding economy, only occasionally splotched with violence and conflict.

Volume II, on the nineteenth century, is the one really filled with blood and thunder. It embraces, of course, certain episodes connected with the struggle to liberate Mexico from Spain, including the capture of Hidalgo, Allende, and Aldama, their execution, the Magee-Gutiérrez imbroglio culminating in the battle of Medina, the quixotic gesture of Mina, and several other holocausts on battlefield or before firing squads. The Texas-Mexico controversy provided another series of massacres and mass executions: at the Alamo, at Goliad, and those growing out of the Santa Fe expedition and the surrender at Mier. On the west coast these were rivaled in the 'fifties as filibusters from California descended on Sonora, Sinaloa, and Lower California.

Indian depredations, meanwhile, were about as bad as they ever had been. Control measures now included such occurrences as the Texan war on the Cherokees, the massacre at San Antonio in 1840 of twelve Comanche chiefs and twenty braves, scalp buying by Chihuahua and Durango, and Indian hunting as a business by James Kirker and other mercenary wretches. Add to all this the fighting in this region during the War with Mexico and during the French intervention; add also the armed revolutions normal to Mexican domestic politics throughout most of the nineteenth century, and you have the recipe for a bloodcurdling volume. Volume II has this quality; it also contains much information about economic development, transportation improvements, governmental changes, and social and cultural advances.

On quite a number of specific topics Bancroft's *North Mexican States and Texas* has been improved upon by subsequent writers: on Francisco de Ibarra by J. Lloyd Mecham, on the early Jesuit missions by Peter M. Dunne, on Kino by Herbert E. Bolton, on the Gálvez visitation by Herbert I. Priestley, on Stephen F. Austin by Eugene C. Barker, on the War with Mexico by Justin H. Smith. Yet in the preface to his *Stephen F. Austin* Barker refers to it as still the best reference on Texas. And no one has attempted to redo the job as a whole. These two volumes remain the only comprehensive account and analysis of north Mexico from the earliest times well into the national period. The work is not always smooth going, the reader is required to do much jumping about, helpful generalizations about the fundamentals of this region's history are sometimes implied rather than made explicit, and on many points something better is now available; but these shortcomings by no means eliminate the usefulness of this two-volume record of 360 years of happenings in what are now eight or ten states and territories.

Turning to Arizona and New Mexico,[14] Bancroft found a subject that proved particularly attractive. Here were the oldest European settlements in the western United States—so old that ten years before the Pilgrims landed at Plymouth Rock a *Historia de la Nueva México* had been published. Here was an Indian civilization surpassing that of any other part of the United States and persisting with the least modification. Here was a land ushered into history with magic words: the

[14] Hubert Howe Bancroft, *History of Arizona and New Mexico* (San Francisco, 1889).

Seven Cities of Cíbola, Gran Quivira, the Strait of Anian. Those who moved into it, Coronado, Oñate, and the rest, did not realize their high hopes of attaining riches and power, but their exploits were nonetheless exciting and at times heroic. In the later colonial period New Mexico tended to be more picturesque than important. In the struggle for existence its *gente de razón* and the Pueblos kept just one jump ahead of the marauding Apaches and Comanches. The Pueblos, though only superficially modified by contact with the Spaniards, were now reduced in numbers. An occasional governor was conspicuous for efficiency and zeal, but the usual official was lazy if not venal, and even the missionaries succumbed to like temptations.

Mexico's fight for independence conferred liberation upon this northern province. Unchanged, however, were the patterns of conduct of the military, the political officials, and the religious. Nor did the sedentary peoples and the seminomads cease their conflict. The main change was economic. The commerce of the province, which had been supplied by the January fairs at Chihuahua, was now serviced by American goods brought over the new Santa Fe trail from Missouri. Accompanying these commodities "southwest on the turquoise trail" came American traders, some of whom became residents, and American fur trappers, who made Taos a base for their operations all over the Mexican Northwest.

In 1846 the United States seized this region. The treaty in 1848 and another in 1854 also involved Arizona, a land the Spaniards had visited repeatedly but which they had developed but slightly. Although American rule conferred some blessings on New Mexico and Arizona, it did not bring immediate surcease from Indian attacks, an immediate era of good government, the immediate blessing of peace, immediate statehood, or immediate prosperity. When Bancroft's volume went to press in 1889, the most he could do was to opine that the danger of serious Indian trouble seemed to be past, and that railroad communications were opening a possibility of economic betterment. Such improvements, however, were mostly for the future.

Notwithstanding its attractions, a comprehensive history of New Mexico and Arizona had not been attempted prior to Bancroft. W. W. H. Davis, it is true, had essayed in 1869 a history of the Spanish conquest, in which he got as far as the year 1700, and L. Bradford Prince, in a volume entitled *Historical Sketches of New Mexico* (1883), had summarized Davis and carried the narrative through the American conquest. In many respects a competent workman, Prince repeated several of Davis' errors, and, because his materials were few, his book was admittedly fragmentary. Bancroft's advantages over these historians were that he attempted a more thoroughgoing study, that he supplemented the broken file of New Mexico's official archives by other manuscripts acquired in Mexico, that he assembled a more complete collection of published works relating to the area (he was the first, for example, to utilize Villagrá's metrical *Historia de la Nueva México*), and that his viewpoint was anything but provincial. Other comprehensive histories have since appeared—by Twitchell and Coan for New Mexico, and by Farish for Arizona. To an appreciable degree based on Bancroft, they have not entirely supplanted his work.

Much of the specialized literature that Bancroft was able to utilize was of superior quality: included are such items as the Benavides memorial, Sigüenza y Góngora's *Mercurio Volante,* Pedro Bautista Pino's *Exposición sucinta,* Zebulon Pike's narrative, Josiah Gregg's *Commerce of the Prairies,* George W. Kendall's *Narrative of the Texan Santa Fe Expedition,* and the several official reports on the Mexican War, the boundary surveys, and the railroad surveys. More recently, New Mexican history has had the particular attention of the state historical society, and its *Review,* and of the Quivira Society and the Coronado Cuarto Centennial Commission. These latter organizations, sponsoring publication of original documents and rare treatises, have greatly enlarged the fund of information available on New Mexico's colonial period. Individual scholars have also been active. The result is that the time appears to be ripe for a new synthesis to incorporate the findings of this research, as well as to cover the development of the half century since Bancroft closed his volume. Until such a work appears, Bancroft's volume will continue to be a first reliance; in the preparation of such a work it would be of great assistance.

In the respective state histories Bancroft allots a few pages to Spanish activities in Colorado, Utah, and Nevada, and in his *History of the Northwest Coast* he gives perhaps two hundred pages to Spanish voyages both real and apocryphal. His other principal contribution as a Hispanic Americanist, however, is represented by the first four volumes of his *California* and the supplementary volume, *California Pastoral*. These will be analyzed in a subsequent chapter; comment here is limited to their function in his presentation of the history of Spanish North America.

His idea is set forth in several of his prefaces and particularly in that to the volumes on the north Mexican states. In brief, it was that, in addition to supplying a general history of Mexico in six volumes, he would take the northern portion of that nation and develop its regional history more adequately in two additional volumes, and then would go into greater detail for New Mexico and Arizona, and finally into still greater detail for Alta California. The region of northern Mexico was to be studied partly for its own sake, but also as a typical region, and as a connecting link between the nation proper and the remoter provinces to the far north. The California annals, similarly, were to be presented partly as a contribution to local history, but also as a type study of a province under Spain and Mexico.

Three observations may be offered. The first is that Bancroft's choice of region and then of locality to be emphasized was influenced by his estimate of their interest and their ultimate importance, and likewise by the quantity of information he had been able to assemble. The second is that his concept of the way in which regional and local history should fit into and illuminate national history was more advanced than that of many so-called regional historians. The third is that he was aware that colonial Spanish America reached far above the Rio Grande and the present Mexican line, and he did not hesitate to select as his type colony a province that has since been incorporated in the United States. Thereby he demonstrated freedom from an astigmatism all too common among present-day historians of Spanish America, who confine their attention to the colonies that were south of the present border.

13

Historian of California

To the Pacific United States is devoted more space comparatively than to southern regions, California being regarded as the center and culminating point of this historical field.

Hubert Howe Bancroft, *History of Central America,* I, vii

In Bancroft's collecting, California had been both the starting point and the area of principal emphasis. In his history writing he likewise regarded it as the center and the rightful climax. Now that California, with a population of eight millions, has taken rank among the states as first in the value of agricultural products, first in motion-picture production, first in airplane manufacture, and first as a tourist mecca, such an emphasis is well justified. In the 'seventies and 'eighties, when he was planning and producing his histories, Bancroft, without presuming to know the exact directions that would be followed, envisioned a bright future for the state. He was also aware that California had become the dominant unit in the American West, the financial and commercial capital, and the cultural leader. Current importance thus called for a more careful analysis of the local past. That past, furthermore, possessed so much of intrinsic appeal that it seemed a historian's grand opportunity. Therein is to be found the chief reason for giving it special attention.

Bancroft noted, for example, that ever since the beginning, when it had been "a mere field of cosmographic conjecture," an unknown land "somewhere on the way from Mexico to India," California had gathered to itself "a liberal share of the world's notice."[1] Visits by early navigators, Cortés and his men in the peninsula, and Cabrillo, Drake, Cermeño, and Vizcaíno farther north, uncovered no immediate treasure and did not result in prompt occupation, but they did contribute to California's fame. Vizcaíno, in particular, with perfervid praise of the Port of Monterey, conferred on the province a mythical resource which promised to be of great utility to the rich Manila galleons and which consequently beckoned the Spaniards northward. Yet, notwithstanding this additional attraction, the land was left to the exclusive enjoyment of its natives, well-nigh the most benighted on the continent, until another century and two-thirds had gone by.

Then belatedly, though with a burst of unmistakable energy, Spain moved to occupy the land. Using institutions tested on other frontiers—the mission, the presidio, and the pueblo,—she erected a society vividly reminiscent of the Middle Ages, though in point of time no more remote than our national origins. Junípero Serra and Gaspar de Portolá were contemporaries of Benjamin Franklin and George Washington, and 1776 dates not only the Declaration of Independence but also the founding of San Francisco. Into the Mexican period the medieval character continued. The ranchos in their vast extent, the retainers who surrounded persons of any importance, the emphasis upon the man on horseback, and the appeal to arms as the method of deciding governmental authority—all these smacked of feudal times. These conditions were in the act of disappearing from northern California at the time of Bancroft's arrival. In southern California they persisted almost to the time of his publishing.

Because of its coastal position, visitors came to California at frequent intervals, contributing both to local enlivenment and to the world's interest in the province. Despite the Spanish restrictive system, some of these foreign visitors began to

[1] Hubert Howe Bancroft, *History of California* (7 vols.; San Francisco, 1884–1890), I, iii.

engage in trade as well as in sea-otter hunting, and throughout the period of the Wars of Independence they were the chief suppliers of the Californians. With the Mexican epoch, whalers began to make California a port of call, beaver trappers entered from across the continent, and hide-and-tallow traders put in their appearance. Anglo-Americans thus engrossed the province's first lucrative export trade. Ingratiating themselves with the provincials, they took on many customs of the country; yet, retaining their Yankee proclivities for business, they soon gained control of the domestic commerce.

Resident traders were followed by settlers intent on farming and ranching. Covered wagons in the early 'forties brought enough of these pioneers to make Mexico's continued hold on the province doubtful. The United States government had occasionally displayed an interest in acquiring California and particularly the bay of San Francisco, and in May, 1846, having found an excuse in Texas, President Polk launched a war for the conquest of California and certain additional Mexican territory. Before tidings of this development could reach the West Coast, some of the Americans in the Sacramento Valley, stimulated by the presence of Captain Frémont and his band of sixty men, raised the Bear Flag and undertook to seize the province. Before this movement reached a conclusion of success or failure, regular forces appeared on the scene to claim California for the United States, a step which the Treaty of Guadalupe Hidalgo confirmed.

American control raised problems of political adjustment. The national authorities were too remote to deal with them efficiently, but the Californians demonstrated a surprising capacity. These matters, and the social problems attending the transition from Hispanic to Anglo-American ways, were soon complicated by the discovery of gold and the descent upon the province of a cosmopolitan horde of Argonauts.

Gold furiously accelerated the indexes of population, of wealth, of prices, of commerce, and of crime; indeed, the excesses of 'forty-nine and the 'fifties gave rise to some head-shakings that California would have been better off without the discovery. Gold, nevertheless, was the factor that first thoroughly publicized California. It brought a new population, won statehood, made San Francisco a city, gave agriculture a new birth, created a market for industries, stimulated the development of transportation, encouraged journalism, rewarded literary endeavor, and gave rise to a distinctive society. By the Gold Rush, California was suddenly elevated to leadership in the American West. Completion of the transcontinental railroad in 1869 confirmed that leadership and laid the foundation for further lusty growth in the decades to follow.

On this wise was California's past as Bancroft could look back upon it in the 'seventies and 'eighties. The state had not yet entered the epoch when the typical citizen would be an orange grower, a seeker after health, or a real-estate agent, nor that later stage when he would be a suburban dweller, dependent on his automobile for transportation, and in all likelihood an employee of some oversize corporation, a bank, utility, oil company, factory, or chain store. Its significance in the West, on the Pacific Coast, and in the nation was, however, unmistakable, and the characteristics of its history were plainly discernible. Stretching back to the Cortesian epoch and within fifty years of 1492, its past was already long. With its primitive Indian culture followed by the mission-centered Spanish era, a pastoral Mexican interlude, sudden Americanization through the Gold Rush, and a solidification of these gains through the railroad, variety abounded. Furthermore, this variety was accentuated by the fact that the most far-reaching changes, those induced by the Gold Rush, had happened only yesterday.

For the writing of this fascinating history Bancroft found an abundance of materials. Indeed, he admitted that he was able to make use of fresher, more complete, and more adequate materials than had any previous historian of any state.[2] Partly this was an assertion of his phenomenal activity as a collector, but more fundamentally it was the consequence of his entering the field early. Elsewhere it has been remarked what a boon it was to him that he was the first and, for years, the only determined collector of Californiana. He was close enough to the most stirring events in that history, the Gold Rush, the American acquisition, the Mexican era, and even the Spanish period, to gather in the ephemera that so often elude collectors. He could gather information directly from participants, and thus he captured much fugitive material that would not have been available a generation later, some of it in print, some of it in manuscript, and some not yet committed to paper. The opportunity offered by this combination of circumstances, he regarded as unique.

As to wealth of materials, it is quickly apparent that Bancroft did not exaggerate. California's past, and certain episodes in particular, had caught the attention of a large number of writers. Publishers, convinced that reader interest would be similarly widespread, had been willing to put much of this writing into print. Consequently, the published literature was far larger than one would have expected in view of the relative unimportance of the province before 1849 and the moderate population and prosperity it had attained by the latter part of the century.

Included were several famous titles: Palóu's *Life of Serra,* a firsthand and documented narrative of the labors of the first father-president of the missions, and virtually a history of the province to 1784; Richard H. Dana's *Two Years before the Mast,* deservedly the most widely read item of all Californiana; John C. Frémont's *Reports,* travel writing that gave a majority of Americans their ideas of the circumstances of overland travel to California; Bayard Taylor's *Eldorado,* the report of the most famous correspondent assigned to cover the

[2] *Ibid.,* I, vii–viii.

Gold Rush; George H. Derby's pseudonymous John Phoenix sketches, which took the nation by storm and set a new style for American humorists; Bret Harte's "Outcasts of Poker Flat" and Mark Twain's "Jumping Frog of Calaveras," short stories that rocketed two other Californians to fame.

Other works, by reason of their historical content, might well have had equal attention: La Pérouse, Vancouver, and Shaler visited Spanish California and wrote vivid descriptions; Petit-Thouars and Duflot de Mofras approximated Dana in informative value on the Mexican period; Alfred Robinson drew on his long experience as resident agent in the hide trade to produce his classic *Life in California,* published in 1846; James Ohio Pattie's *Personal Narrative* and Edwin Bryant's *What I Saw in California* are superior travel books; government officials, in the war and in boundary and railroad surveys, produced reports of significance; on the Gold Rush, Delano is at least as meritorious as Bayard Taylor; Letts and Vischer are memorable as illustrators of early California; local historians, notably Soulé, Gihon, and Nisbet at San Francisco, and Hall at San Jose, assembled data that later writers have drawn upon heavily; and the general histories attempted by Alexander Forbes in 1839 and by Franklin Tuthill in 1866 are highly creditable.

Excellent as these works are, the outstanding feature of this writing is its bulk. Bancroft utilized some two dozen published descriptions by foreign visitors prior to 1848. He found some 475 printed works relative to the Mexican period and more than 1,000 for the first thirty-five years of the American period.[3] Books and pamphlets predominated, but there was much newspaper and periodical material, particularly on American California, and by counting such items individually the figures just given could have been much increased. This was certainly a substantial amount of printing about a land that had emerged so recently from pastoral calm.

[3] *Ibid.*, I, 34–45.

Manuscript materials were even more abundant. Spain's imperial system set great store by full reporting on the part of her various officials. Her soldier-officials and her churchmen in California upheld this tradition by doing their full share of paper work. The practice likewise carried over into the Mexican period, and in consequence there had accumulated a tolerably full manuscript record of California affairs through the first eight decades after the Spanish founding. This record is times over more ample than exists for any Anglo-American frontier province of comparable date.

Preservation of these records, while not letter perfect, had been meticulous. The largest single accumulation of them Bancroft found in what he called the Archivo de California, some three hundred bulky volumes, plus loose papers, which had been turned over to the keeping of the United States surveyor general's office in San Francisco. They were stored in this office because they contained information on land titles, but they were much broader in content. Bancroft characterizes them as "the originals, blotters, or certified copies of the orders, instructions, reports, correspondence, and act-records of the authorities, political, military, judicial, and ecclesiastical; national, provincial, departmental, territorial, and municipal."[4] Similar but smaller collections were discovered at Los Angeles, Monterey, Sacramento, San Diego, San Jose, San Luis Obispo, Santa Barbara, and Santa Cruz. As described in a previous chapter, Bancroft sent copyists and abstracters to assemble the nonduplicating materials of these archives for his collection.[5]

The records preserved at the missions partook likewise of the nature of public-archives material. Usually, such items as the registers of baptisms, marriages, burials, and confirmations were retained at the several missions, and Bancroft consulted them there. Other papers were assembled by the

---

[4] *Ibid.*, I, 46.

[5] Chapter 7, above; see also Bancroft, *Literary Industries*, 468–472.

Franciscans at Santa Barbara. Another collection, known as the Archivo del Arzobispado, had been assembled by Alexander S. Taylor, the pioneer bibliographer, and still another was in the hands of the Bishop of Monterey and Los Angeles. Again utilizing copyists and abstracters, Bancroft availed himself of these manuscript collections. The results he bound in eighteen stout volumes which contained an estimated 10,000 documents.

These he had been able to supplement by an ingathering of some 2,000 original documents and fifteen bound volumes, integral elements in the mission record, but latterly in the hands of private parties. Similarly he had acquired seven blocks of original documents which had once been segments of the Archivo de California. In addition, he had gathered in from private owners a great mass of original manuscripts, about half of which was closely similar to the material in the public and mission archives, the rest consisting of more personal correspondence and papers. Lumped together as Documentos para la Historia de California, these papers filled 110 volumes and amounted to at least 40,000 documents. Notable among them were the Vallejo papers, the Guerra y Noriega papers, and the Larkin papers.

He also had some 550 manuscripts relative to California before 1849—diaries, journals, official reports by military and religious officers, regulations, narratives, *expedientes,* and the like. From residents of Spanish and Mexican California he and his secretaries had also taken down some 160 dictations, half from native Californians and half from pioneers. They ranged from a few pages to five volumes in length. They varied also in reliability, and Bancroft, though prizing them highly for the light they shed on many matters of local history, was aware of the imperfections inherent in reminiscent testimony. Although the discovery of gold had greatly increased the number and distribution of publications relative to California, manuscript material was still important. Of dictations, Bancroft had an additional hundred from forty-niners and twenty-five from members of the San Francisco vigilance committees.[6]

What with books, pamphlets, maps, periodicals, newspapers, scrapbook collections, copies and abstracts from the public and mission archives, original manuscripts, and dictations, Bancroft had an exceedingly rich store of Californiana. He did not exaggerate when he asserted its superiority over the resources at the command of any previous historian not only in California but in any state in the Union. Such were the materials on which his *History of California* was based.

Transitional between his library and the historical narrative stand the bibliographical data with which the set is furbished. The initial item is the customary alphabetical list of authorities quoted. More than a thousand titles utilized incidentally in the preparation are omitted from the list, which still spreads over sixty-four pages.[7] Short titles, the omission of any data on the length, nature, and location of manuscripts, the lack of classification, and the total absence of critical comment subtract much from the utility of this list. A thirty-page chapter on the bibliography of California history[8] partly supplies this defect; at other places in the narrative, discussions of the available literature are worked in; and in a multitude of footnotes throughout the seven volumes individual references are analyzed. The index in Volume VII offers a key to these bibliographical asides. Assembled, organized, and presented as an annotated description of the literature of California's history, this bibliographical lore would surpass anything now in print. Bancroft, however, having no particular ambition to be a bibliographer, subordinated these data to the historical narrative and scattered them through the seven volumes. The information that he had was practically complete, the presentation in the footnotes is full

[6] Bancroft, *History of California,* I, 45–58.
[7] *Ibid.,* I, xxv–lxxxviii.
[8] *Ibid.,* I, 34–63.

enough, but because of the deficiency in organization and emphasis his bibliographical contribution is oftentimes cavalierly dismissed.

The most apparent feature of Bancroft's treatment of California is its bulk. Seven stout volumes are filled with the historical account, one more than had been allotted to the Mexican nation, and, in addition, the writing on the state is allowed to spill over into four supplementary volumes. The total is eleven volumes, some 8,800 pages, and, including the passages in fine print, probably 4,500,000 words.

These dimensions are an indication but not an absolute guaranty of exhaustiveness, a quality at which Bancroft determinedly aimed. To him it meant an obligation to record what had happened from year to year, giving to each episode or development an amount of space in proportion to its importance. A description of selected illustrative events might make better reading, but it would not be a comprehensive or exhaustive history—it would not tell the whole story. To get this entire record into even the generous space made available required the most rigorous condensation, more rigorous than in any other section of the *Works*. Viewed from the outside, these volumes may suggest prolixity, but the reader who looks into them will find that they are presented with an economy of words and that the paragraphs are packed with factual detail. The reference user will be in a still better position to endorse the prediction and promise that Bancroft offered in his preface, that "no intelligent reader desiring information on any particular event of early Californian history—information on the founding or early annals of any mission or town; on the development of any political, social, industrial, or religious institution; on the occurrences of any year or period; on the life and character of any official or friar or prominent citizen or early pioneer; on the visit and narrative of any voyager; on the adventures and composition of any immigrant party; on any book or class of book about California; or on any one or any group of the incidents that make up this work—will accuse me of having written at too great length on that particular topic."[9]

In apportioning space Bancroft was somewhat influenced by the amount of information available, but primarily by his estimate of what was interesting and significant. The first volume, after a hundred pages of introductory matter, is given over to the Spanish founding in 1769, the critical events of the 'seventies, and the less spectacular developments to the end of the century. Volume II spans the first quarter of the nineteenth century, a period when Spain was content merely to hold the colony, when independence was conferred by the heroic efforts of the patriots in Mexico, and when the provincials began a readjustment to the new republican regime. The exhaustiveness of Bancroft's *California* is well illustrated by the fact that he gives approximately as much space to these years in somnolent California as he had in his *Mexico* to the crucial struggle for independence.

Volume III deals with a decade and a half of the Mexican pastoral era. It embraces such matters as the rise of the hide-and-tallow trade, the first visits by whalers, the appearance of American beaver trappers, the secularization of the missions, and the rise of the ranchos. In the next volumes the peak of emphasis is reached. Volume IV is on the early 'forties, when Mexican rule became increasingly chaotic, and when the covered wagon began to deposit pioneer American settlers in the province. Volume V treats of the Bear Flag Revolt, seizure by the United States, the southern California rebellion, reconquest, and military government. Its span is only from 1846 to 1848.

Volume VI has gold as its theme. It describes the "flush times," 1848 to 1856, and carries on to the end of the decade. The final volume moves more rapidly over the decades of the 'sixties, 'seventies, and 'eighties. It has a more miscellaneous

[9] *Ibid.*, I, x.

cast than the others. Seven chapters, XI–XVI, and XXV, supply the chronological framework by sketching political history through these decades, but the other eighteen are topical and oftentimes reach back much further into the past. They discuss such matters as the development of agriculture, 1769–1889; manufactures, 1848–1889; extermination of the Indians, 1849–1887; and population and society, 1849–1889. The compromised plan of this volume illustrates the uncertainty that historians usually feel when they contemplate the recent past. The preponderance of economic topics is indicative of the dominant element in the state's experience from 1860 to 1890.

Doubtless most noteworthy in the arrangement of the *History* is the heavy stress on the thirty-five years from 1825 to 1859; four volumes carry this story, whereas in the *Mexico* one had sufficed. And within this period, the 'forties, to which two and a half volumes are assigned, are the obvious favorite. If the four supplementary volumes are taken into the reckoning, the concentration on the mid-century period becomes all the more striking, because all of them are focused on it; in other words, eight of the eleven volumes are on this comparatively short period.

From the perspective of the 1880's, Bancroft's space allotments can be reasonably justified. T. H. Hittell's four-volume history,[10] published in that decade and in the 'nineties, is similarly proportioned, and the third large history of the state, edited by Z. S. Eldredge in 1915,[11] differs merely in that the latter part of the Spanish period is minimized in favor of the first dozen years. Of modern works, the two volumes by Chapman and Cleland,[12] which became the standard in the early 1920's, give the same fraction of space to the 'forties and 'fifties. They double the ratio for the eighteenth-century

[10] Theodore H. Hittell, *History of California* (4 vols.; San Francisco, 1885–1897).

[11] Zoeth S. Eldredge, *History of California* (5 vols.; New York, 1915).

[12] Charles E. Chapman, *A History of California: The Spanish Period* (New York, 1921), and Robert G. Cleland, *A History of California: The American Period* (New York, 1922).

Spanish colony, which means of course that they give proportionally less space to the period 1800–1840 and, as it happens, still less to the period after 1860. The most recent text,[13] the present writer's, turns out to be the least Bancroftian of any. If Bancroft's seven volumes were redone in its proportions, the first five would shrink to half size, the one on 'forty-eight, 'forty-nine, and the 'fifties would become a double volume, as would likewise the one on the 'sixties, 'seventies, and 'eighties, and other double volumes would be added on the Spanish approaches to California and on the state since 1890. Had it been written in the 'eighties, this book would have borne a closer resemblance to Bancroft's. Even today it is difficult to maintain that anything has been more important to California than Americanization and its golden sequel.

Of the general nature of Bancroft's *History of California* little further need be said. Given the materials in their abundance, the outline proportioned as indicated, and the determination to be exhaustive, the volumes could not be much different from what they are. Chronologically threaded, but with an occasional topical deviation, they follow their methodical course. For the most part they are a recital of what happened in the state and in its parts, year after year. They are not, however, mere annals, for the participants in the history are carefully introduced and characterized, the reasons for their actions are probed, and the course of development is interpreted. The reader of these volumes will be impressed by the minuteness with which California happenings are chronicled. He will be equally impressed by the candor with which gaps are acknowledged in the information available.

The California volumes have features not present in the other histories. There are footnotes, for example, which list and describe the ships that came to California in each of the earlier years. Similar tabulations record the entrance of Americans and other foreigners to become residents in the

[13] John Walton Caughey, *California* (New York, 1940).

province. At the end of Volume I is an alphabetical list of the inhabitants of California, 1769–1800, keyed to show date of arrival, in the earliest period, 1769–1773, in the later 'seventies, in the 'eighties, or in the 'nineties, and specifying category, such as padre, soldier, settler, child, convict, carpenter, weaver, or muleteer. Without claiming perfection for this list, Bancroft properly observes, "It may well be doubted if so complete a list of the earliest inhabitants can be formed for any other state of the United States or Mexico."[14] Volume II has a shorter list of foreign pioneers who came to California before the end of 1830. These are individually dated.

These contributions toward a Who's Who of early California are crowned by the Pioneer Register and Index, a dictionary of California biography, 1542–1848. Set in fine print, conserving space through the utilization of many abbreviations and tucked away inconspicuously in the back pages of the second, third, fourth, and fifth volumes, the Register has had much less than the praise due it. As much as a page is occasionally allotted to one person. More often, a single page has entries for forty or fifty men, not counting wives and progeny. Since the Register fills 370 pages, the aggregate of persons covered may be estimated at eight to ten thousand, truly an impressive roll call for a province so young and undeveloped. With regard to foreign pioneers the aim was to include all. Of Spaniards, Mexicans, and native Californians the selection was a bit more rigorous, yet all missionaries, all traders, all rancheros, and all officials are included, and enough others to make the list thoroughly representative.

In a prefatory note Bancroft served notice that he would not clutter the Register with indiscriminate eulogy. Praise and blame he considered inappropriate to its narrow confines, and he preferred to keep it objectively factual. Concerning those who had figured at all prominently in the state's history, a verdict in the Register would have been redundant since the

[14] Bancroft, *History of California,* I, 732.

History contained analysis and appraisal of almost all of them. A few private individuals, conspicuous for qualities praiseworthy or blameworthy, are suitably characterized. As a rule, however, "no attempt is made to depict the character, to picture them as 'nature's noblemen,' or to point out the fact that they were not members of temperance societies."[15]

The information set down is primarily vital: date of birth, date of arival in California, particulars of marriage and offspring, date of death, and the like. Customarily, occupation is indicated, and often there is brief mention of the highlights of the man's career. The longest sketches have to do with representative citizens whose affairs were of some importance, but whose connection with public affairs had been slight. Public characters of equal or greater importance—Father Serra, for example—are disposed of in fewer lines. Their biographies had become part of the history of the state and thus had been discussed at the appropriate places in Bancroft's narrative of California history. For an individual of this type the Pioneer Register ordinarily would have only a reference to the passage where a biographical essay could be found, and citations of the passages where were described the "historic" events in which he had taken part.

These frequent references had the effect of making practically the whole of the five volumes on California to 1849 tributary to the Register. They justify the additional label "Index." They increase times over the quantity of biographical data systematized in the 370-page Register. They serve, furthermore, to weld the Register to the *History of California*. Offhand, there is a temptation to extract from the *History* the signatures on which the Register is printed and to make of it a separate volume. Yet the convenience thus achieved would be only partial, and the Register apart from the *History* would lose one of its principal values. To bring out the reality, its title might well be expanded to read "Register of Pioneer

[15] *Ibid.*, II, 684.

Inhabitants of California, 1542 to 1848, and Index to Information concerning Them in Bancroft's *History of California, Volumes I–V.*"

Since the Register represents the biographic distillation, not only of the first five volumes of the *History of California,* but also of Bancroft's entire collection of Californiana, the amount of labor necessary to its making was colossal. Fortunately, a good fraction of this work had already been done in the indexing of the collection, preparatory to the writing of the histories. All that was necessary was to separate the biographical portions relevant to California, arrange them in alphabetical order, and add the references to biographical passages in the *History*. Even so, the labor involved was great. Bancroft doubted that immediate appreciation would be commensurate, but he foresaw a time when the marshaling of all these data about the pioneers would have a great usefulness. To the best of his knowledge, nothing of the kind had ever been attempted for any other new country. It is still true that no other state or nation can boast so complete a roster of its early inhabitants.

Appraisal of the supplementary volumes, *California Pastoral,*[16] *California Inter Pocula,*[17] and *Popular Tribunals,*[18] is deferred to a subsequent chapter, where they are discussed with their cousins, *Essays and Miscellany*[19] and *Literary Industries.*[20] Yet no estimate of Bancroft as historian of California would be complete if they were totally neglected. A hint of their merit is found in Phil Townsend Hanna's *Libros Californianos,* a nomination of "Five Feet of California Books." Obviously, Hanna could not include Bancroft's *Works,* because the complete set runs to seven and a half feet. He did elect *California Pastoral,* which he describes as "the best appraisal of Spanish-California life and manners that we have,"

[16] San Francisco, 1888.
[17] San Francisco, 1888.
[18] Two vols.; San Francisco, 1887.
[19] San Francisco, 1890.
[20] San Francisco, 1890.

and *California Inter Pocula,* which he calls "a fine interpretation of gold-days from contemporary records." No other writer is doubly represented in his list.[21]

These volumes are unhurried expositions of elements in California's social and institutional structure in the mid-nineteenth century. Constructed on a generous and rambling pattern, they are freighted with a wealth of anecdote, and this is their excellence, that they describe circumstantially the habits of Californians under Spain and Mexico, the ways of the miners, and the early approaches to the problems of law and law enforcement. They expand upon matters given passing attention in the seven-volume history, but by no means exhaust the possibilities. From the materials utilized for the history, similar volumes could have been prepared on such topics as early voyages, the missions, the American conquest, prerailroad transportation, the impact of the Civil War, and a dozen others. Following the line of his special interest, Bancroft chose rather to elaborate upon mid-century topics.

These extra volumes unquestionably were intended to be read. The Pioneer Register as obviously was designed for reference use. Of the history as a whole, some intermediate remark would seem to be in order. Because of its comprehensiveness and its bulk, one who first approaches it will reckon it a work to be consulted rather than consumed from cover to cover. Times over more students, it seems safe to say, have used the history thus than have read as much as a consecutive one-seventh. Nevertheless, chapters abound that tell their story well. Transition and continuity are handled with care, and the style, though occasionally florid, tends usually to be clear and direct, well suited to the endless flow of carefully attested facts, which itself possesses a certain fascination.

Another criterion by which Bancroft must be judged is in comparison with the work of other historians of California.

---

[21] Phil Townsend Hanna, *Libros Californianos, or Five Feet of California Books* (Los Angeles, 1931), 48–53.

Quantitatively he is well in the lead. It is customary to refer to Theodore H. Hittell's and Zoeth S. Eldredge's as the other large histories. Hittell's four volumes are about of a size with four of Bancroft's; Eldredge's five would not make more than three Bancroft volumes. And, as indicated above, Bancroft's score is seven volumes labeled *History of California;* eleven, with the four supplementary volumes included; and considerably more, if other pertinent sections of the entire set are included. Thus his history of the state is by far the largest; it offers the most lavish assortment of entries, the largest array of facts, and the most generous provision of detail. Furthermore, although the Hittell and Eldredge histories have their merits, the one in stress on legal and political history, and the other in the essays by specialists which comprise the final volume, both are most adequate on the Spanish and Mexican epoch and the early American period, the segments on which Bancroft has made his principal and much larger contribution.

Modern scholarship, rather similarly, has supplemented Bancroft, but without making any pretense of supplanting his history of California. A major addition has been effected by going to the archives of Spain and Mexico and utilizing materials neglected by Bancroft and his generation. Important consequences have resulted, not only in bringing to light further details about the work of Spanish explorers, missionaries, and pioneers, but also in orienting the California province with respect to the policies of the Spanish empire and the exigencies of the Mexican nation.[22] This orientation may be implicit in Bancroft's *Works,* but the division into geographical sections obscured it, and readers of the state's history have not had the fact brought home to them until

[22] Particularly in two volumes by the late Charles E. Chapman, *The Founding of Spanish California* (New York, 1916), and *A History of California: The Spanish Period* (New York, 1921); in Herbert Eugene Bolton, *The Spanish Borderlands* (New Haven, 1921); and in Bolton's numerous more specialized works.

quite recently. Exploitation of the California materials in Spanish and Mexican archives, it should be pointed out, is a process now well under way but by no means completed. These sources have not been exhausted, and their potential illumination of California history has not been fully realized.

Concerning the quarter century subsequent to the Civil War, a period of which Bancroft was somewhat neglectful, and concerning the half century of busy development since the publication of his *Works,* modern scholars have had a great opportunity to make a contribution. A start has been made, but the sum total of energy expended and of illumination effected has been smaller than in the supplementing of Bancroft's account of earlier California. With one possible exception, modern surveys of the state's history taper off rapidly after 1865 or 1890, and monographic studies have tended to cluster in the century from the first mission to the first transcontinental railroad, rather than in the subsequent era of railroad, automobile, and airplane.

The modern supplementation of Bancroft, it might further be observed, has been largely by spot studies which have resulted in monographs on scattered subjects. A few surveys of the entire field of California history have been attempted, but on a Lilliputian scale as compared with Bancroft's. No one has proposed to redo his history for the period it covered, nor has anyone attempted a continuation that would achieve comparable thoroughness for the late nineteenth and twentieth centuries. Our aggregate knowledge of California history, it must also be admitted, derives less from the researches of modern scholars than from Bancroft. Eventually the moderns must excel; theirs is the advantage of scientific training, of access to the treasures in Hispanic archives and recognition of their value, and of eligibility to investigate the stupendous achievements of Californians since 1890. So far, however, the cumulative results of their efforts have not matched, let alone surpassed, Bancroft's contribution as historian of California.

14

Annals of Neighboring States

It is an immense territory, this western half of North America; it was a weighty responsibility, at least I felt it to be such, to lay the foundations of history, for all time, for this one twelfth part of the world. Hubert Howe Bancroft, *Literary Industries,* 581

AS A COMPLEMENT to his history of California, Bancroft envisioned a series of volumes that would present the annals of the neighboring states. Clearly, his fundamental aim was to round out the narrative already begun for Spanish North America and California. He was fully aware that the processes of development there to be recorded were interrelated with those of the Great Basin region, the Rocky Mountain country, and the Pacific Northwest, and that his *Works* would have neither balance nor completeness if the expanse of territory from Nevada, Utah, and Colorado to Alaska were neglected. As it finally worked out, some nine volumes were allocated for the history of these ten states, and they appear in the *Works* as follows:

History of Nevada, Colorado, and Wyoming, 1 volume (1889)
History of Utah, 1 volume (1889)
History of the Northwest Coast, 2 volumes (1884)
History of Oregon, 2 volumes (1886, 1888)
History of Washington, Idaho, and Montana, 1 volume (1890)
History of British Columbia, 1 volume (1887)
History of Alaska, 1 volume (1886)

Considered as a unit, this history of the Great Basin, Rocky Mountain, and Northwestern states is roughly comparable to the history of California. The time of publication happens to be the same, 1884 to 1890; the relative bulk, nine volumes to seven, is not disproportionate; and there is much the same endeavor to produce an all-embracing account. Certain of the California features, such as the Pioneer Register, are not duplicated, yet the searcher for specific information can turn to these volumes with approximately equal confidence.

The sharpest contrast is that the breakdown in this section of the *Works* is by geographical units rather than by chronology. And since some of the states had had a longer and more eventful history than others, the space allotments are far from uniform. Two volumes deal with the Northwest Coast from the earliest times to the end of the Hudson's Bay Company's monopoly and the settlement of the international boundary. Another two volumes chart the history of Oregon through the next four decades, a period in which it was unquestionably the foremost of these states. Utah, British Columbia, and Alaska with propriety draw a single volume each. The other six states and territories share the remaining two volumes, their fractional shares standing in this order: Washington (392 pages), Colorado (336), Nevada (322), Montana (219), Idaho (196), and Wyoming (147). Anyone who undertook to bring the history of these several states up to date would end with a radically different distribution. Washington and Colorado, in particular, have come rapidly to the fore. But counting only up to the 'eighties, Bancroft's apportionment of space seems substantially right.

It is a temptation to say—in fact, critics have said—that Bancroft could have achieved a more evolutionary view of general western development if he had approached these ten states as a regional unit rather than dealing with them separately. Certain factors were common to them all. They were new regions only recently brought to the attention of civilized nations and still more recently brought under occupation. Throughout this vast area the fur trapper and trader had been the forerunner of settlement. Throughout, mining rushes had been the principal accelerators of development. Throughout, California's contribution had been substantial: in example, in prospectors, in commerce, and in stimulation of transportation development. By stressing such common features Bancroft could have produced a significant regional history. Yet it was equally true that the several parts had historical as well as political distinctness: Alaska through its Russian beginnings, British Columbia as a part of the British Empire and the Canadian Dominion, Nevada as a community revolving around silver, and Utah as the Zion of the Latter-day Saints. In a regional treatment these local peculiarities might have been obscured. Furthermore, much of the detail that Bancroft planned to include was undeniably local and would have impeded seriously the flow of a regional narrative.

Bancroft, it must be admitted, had still another reason for choosing a series of state histories in preference to a broad regional account. As a businessman he had an eye to the market for his books, and he was well aware that persons with an acute interest in the region were much rarer than those who could be appealed to on the basis of preference for their particular state. His salesmen found it an advantage to be able to point out that the *Works* would contain, in conveniently accessible form, the history of the prospective purchaser's state. This, however, was but a contributive factor in the decision; the main determinant was that a series of state histories promised to be more logical, useful, and manageable.

The magnitude of Bancroft's history-recording undertaking will come home to anyone who essays the heroic task of reading these nine fat volumes on the neighboring states. Even to subject them to cursory review is a large undertaking. From their arrangement in the series, it appears that they should be approached by moving eastward from California through Nevada, Utah, and Colorado, then swinging northward through Wyoming, Montana, and Idaho, continuing on to the Northwest Coast, and rolling northward through

Oregon, Washington, British Columbia, and Alaska. Such an arrangement, of course, is not grounded in chronology, since these states ran concurrent rather than consecutive courses. Yet it is one of geographical convenience; its trail winds through them with a minimum of doubling back, and it carries one along with gradual transitions from state to state. Nevada, for example, was so closely affiliated with California that its history seems like another installment of the California narrative.

Bancroft opens his *History of Nevada* with a chapter descriptive of the geographical setting. He notes, of course, that Nevada comprises part of the Great Basin, rimmed on the east by Utah's Wasatch Range and on the west by California's Sierra Nevada. He stresses, however, its varied relief, ribbed by a series of north-to-south ranges, and he lays proper emphasis on the significance of the Humboldt Valley as providing a break through these ranges and offering an avenue for east–west travel. He makes clear that aridity is a dominant feature of the Nevada environment, the product of scant and irregular rainfall combined with unusually rapid evaporation. Yet he is at pains to point out that there are spots suited to cultivation and larger tracts where irrigation could be developed. Indeed, on this score his optimism will strike the modern observer as excessive. He does substantial justice to Nevada's mineral wealth, and he pays tribute to its beauties of scenery. He did not, of course, foresee the modern exploitation of divorce mill, dude ranch, and magnesium.

The history proper opens with mention of early approaches and possible entrances by Coronado's men in the 1540's, or by Francisco Garcés, and Domínguez and Escalante, in the 1770's. Some space is also allotted to the conjectural cartography with which mapmakers filled in what might better have been left as a yawning blank. The real discovery is properly dated 1825, when Peter Skeene Ogden led a Hudson's Bay Company brigade into the valley of the Humboldt, which to them was the Mary or the Ogden. American trappers, Bridger, Green, and Jed Smith, entered soon after Ogden, and throughout the 'thirties these fur traders continued to hold the center of the stage, and there was no considerable part of the state that they did not traverse. With the 'forties, California-bound pioneer settlers began crossing Nevada, some of them on the Humboldt Valley route that forked from the Oregon Trail, and others on the Old Spanish Trail, an extension of the better-known Santa Fe Trail and circling north of the Grand Canyon and across the Mojave Desert to Los Angeles. A bit later came John C. Frémont as the first official explorer for the United States government. In 1843–1844 he circled Nevada, cutting across its northwestern and southernmost portions, and in 1845 he crossed westward after passing along the southern side of Great Salt Lake. Frémont contributed to nomenclature, sometimes acceptably, as at Pyramid Lake, then again unaptly, as in conferring the name Humboldt. His writings served to build up interest in the entire West, Nevada included. In the following biennium the United States gained title to Nevada through the War with Mexico, of which none of the action took place within the present state. Of the compensation offered Mexico for the ceded territory only a negligible fraction can be reckoned for Nevada.

Throughout the next nine or ten years Nevada's history was pretty largely a reflection of what was going on in the Mormon community to the east and in gold-mad California to the west. A few settlements sprang up, such as Beattie's and Reese's Mormon station in the Carson Valley. To these were added other settlements, including the nucleus for Carson City, composed of gentiles who had crossed the Sierra Nevada. Prospecting for gold was an active enterprise, occasionally with good reward, while others saw promise of success in farming. Throughout this period, however, the real sustenance for these first residents was through trade with the Argonauts pursuing their weary way toward the California diggings.

Bancroft's pages are replete with detail on these beginnings and on the first steps in governmental organization, land claiming, merchandising, lumbering, journalism, and practically all other activities. The coverage is so cyclopedic that the style is often reduced to pedestrian plodding. Yet not always. Concerning one Clark who built a cabin and called the place Eden, we read: "Like the first Adam, he deserted his paradise after a short residence for a more lucrative existence in the outside world."[1] In a footnote on the same page occurs this remark: "Jacob H. or 'old man' Rose was another atom of humanity which found lodgment about this time at the mouth of King's cañon in Eagle valley."

Other opportunities to enliven the narrative are strangely neglected. Thus the story of what appears to have been Nevada's first divorce is relegated to the fine print of a footnote,[2] and the same is true of highly useful information on the first newspapers,[3] and of the introduction of Eilley Orrum, the character who in folklore, letters, and ballet is the first heroine of Nevada. Technically, this is at the opposite pole from overwriting, and thus doubtless preferable.

With the discovery of the fabulous Comstock Lode, Nevada ceased to be merely a way station for California travelers, a secondary center for gold prospectors, and a farming country of strictly limited possibilities. Silver began its reign with a rush of eager souls from California. Virginia City set a dizzy pace in the bonanza years of the early 'sixties, and went to greater extremes in the early 'seventies when the big bonanza was struck. The Comstock not only accelerated Nevada development; it also became the dominant element in the state's history. In proportion to its dominance it receives major attention throughout most of the remainder of Bancroft's narrative.

Under the influence of the Comstock, Nevada's history be-

[1] Hubert Howe Bancroft, *History of Nevada, Colorado, and Wyoming* (San Francisco, 1889), 72.

[2] *Ibid.*, 73–74. [3] *Ibid.*, 169–170, and 305–308.

came much more complex. For the historian to record were such matters as the establishment of claims, the mushroom growth of Virginia City, the organization of mining companies, the elaboration and improvement of mining techniques (as in the Deidesheimer method of cribbing), the construction and evolution of reduction works, the importation of lumber and timber, the erection of the Washoe aqueduct to supply Virginia City with good water, the building of railroads, the speculation in mining stocks, the manipulation by the Bank of California, and Sutro's fight for his pet scheme, the Sutro Tunnel. Alongside these developments came statehood, with increased opportunity to make politics yield a profit, a burgeoning of journalism in a distinctive style, and a smattering at least of social concessions in schools, the theater, churches, and fraternal organizations.

The reader of Bancroft's *Nevada* will savor much of this silver-rooted fruitage. He will get a clear perception of the state of affairs in Nevada, including insight not only into the mechanical procedures of mining, smelting, banking, and governing, but also into the social and intellectual milieu of the time and place. He will have a fair idea, for example, of the common working conditions, of the prevailing relationship of capital and labor, and of what cultural advantages Nevada's metropolis could boast. Perhaps he will wish for a more forthright denunciation of stock-jobbing by mining directors, of the unblushing corruption of legislatures and courts, and of the deplorable siphoning off of the mineral wealth that was Nevada's greatest natural resource; yet all these criticisms are implicit in the account. Besides the Comstock, he will read about other mining rushes up and down Nevada, and he will encounter some description of the other interests of the state.

Proofreading is below the California standard, and minor errors appear, such as putting wagon tracks into Death Valley in 1848[4] and routing Jed Smith along the Humboldt.[5] Subse-

[4] *Ibid.*, 3. [5] *Ibid.*, 62.

quent writing, such as the general surveys by Davis, Mack, the Writers' Program, and Lillard,[6] and the monographs focused principally on the Comstock, have added to the information available in Bancroft, yet without displacing his work as the first reference on early Nevada.

"In the history of Utah," Bancroft wrote in his preface to that volume, "we come upon a new series of social phenomena.... There is only one example in the annals of America of the organization of a commonwealth upon principles of pure theocracy. There is here one example only where the founding of a state grew out of the founding of a new religion. ... It has been long since the world, the old continent or the new, has witnessed anything like a new religion successfully established and set in prosperous running order upon the fullest and combined principles of theocracy, hierarchy, and patriarchy."[7]

A subject such as this, he continued, imposes embarrassments "which render the task at once delicate and dangerous." Even though a writer manages "to escape the many pitfalls of fallacy and illusion that beset his way," even though he is able "to find and follow the exact line of equity ... between the hotly contesting factions," still "he is pretty sure to offend, and bring upon himself condemnation from all parties."[8]

The materials on Utah history he characterizes as "a mass of mendacity." "The attempts of almost all who have written upon the subject seem to have been to make out a case rather than to state the facts." Among the Mormon writers were many violent partisans, while the opposing treatments, he says, were "full of calumny, each author apparently endeavoring to surpass his predecessor in the libertinism of abuse."[9] The evi-

[6] Sam P. Davis, editor, *History of Nevada* (2 vols.; Los Angeles, 1913); Effie Mona Mack, *Nevada: A History of the State from the Earliest Times through the Civil War* (Glendale, 1936); Writers' Program, *Nevada: A Guide to the Silver State* (Portland, Oregon, 1940); Richard G. Lillard, *Desert Challenge: An Interpretation of Nevada* (New York, 1942).

[7] Hubert Howe Bancroft, *History of Utah* (San Francisco, 1889), v–vi.

[8] *Ibid.*, vi. [9] *Ibid.*, vii.

dence, nevertheless, was abundant. The church authorities had put stress on the entering and recording of historical data, and to their success Bancroft offers this tribute: "Save in matters of spiritual manifestations, which the merely secular historian cannot follow, and in speaking of their enemies, whose treatment we must admit in too many instances has been severe, the church records are truthful and reliable."[10] These he supplemented, as was his custom, by interviewing old residents and searching for privately held papers.

In his history of California, it will be recalled, he had used the method of putting into the body of his work the narrative as provided in the principal or most convincing testimony that had come to his attention, and of putting into the footnotes whatever testimony was divergent. Applied to Utah, this meant that the text would be "from the Mormon standpoint, and based entirely on Mormon authorities," and though the footnotes were filled with "anti-Mormon arguments and counterstatements," the casual reader would probably get the impression that Bancroft endorsed the Mormon interpretation. In his preface he disclaims partisanship,[11] and no doubt with full sincerity, but this scheme of presentation exposed him to the charge of partiality. Only when the criticisms began to pour in did he realize that the writer who paraphrases or quotes another identifies himself, at least in part, with the judgments and sentiments there expressed.

Yet a careful reading of the volume on Utah corroborates the avowal in his preface that he would give this new sect "a full and respectful hearing," though withholding nothing that its most violent opposers had said. Thus the prophet Joseph, whose humble origins and earthly impulses have moved many gentile writers to harsh criticism and ridicule, is so depicted that it becomes understandable how he gathered a following; yet there is no suppression of anecdotes, true or apocryphal, that put him in a bad light. The general impression conveyed

[10] *Ibid.*, vii–viii. [11] *Ibid.*, viii–xi.

is that the persecution of the Mormons in Missouri and Illinois was not only un-American but, for the most part, unprovoked; yet there is no hedging on the fact that the doctrine and practice of polygamy represented a serious tactical blunder and a heavy load for the Saints to bear.[12] Just tribute is paid to Brigham Young's vigorous leadership, to the heroic character of the migration to Utah, and to the epic achievement in conquering a forbidding environment, in transforming the desert into a garden, and in erecting there a metropolis and a commonwealth. In such matters as the contribution of the Mormon Battalion, Bancroft detects more than pure patriotism.[13] He finds no evidence that the Mormons were responsible for the Pah Ute massacre of Lieutenant J. W. Gunnison and his party.[14] As to the Mountain Meadows massacre, on the contrary, he does not gloss over Mormon culpability, though insisting that the church leaders had not planned this atrocity.[15]

His final comment on the Mormon War is that it was "an ill-advised measure on the part of the United States government,"[16] but he properly insists that the basic complaint against the Saints was not on religious or social grounds, but because of the peculiar political institutions of their community. They were organized in a closely knit group, in which respect they were not without parallel in American society. But they regarded far-reaching control of their church authorities as a government of God which should not be subject to man-made governments, and, having made all their arrangements on a basis of coöperative self-sufficiency, they operated as though they were not just a state within a state, but a state apart from the United States. All things considered, this analysis penetrates to the real core of the matter.

At the time of Bancroft's writing, Utah was not yet a state. Population had long been more than sufficient to meet the

[12] *Ibid.*, 36–192.
[13] *Ibid.*, 245–246.
[14] *Ibid.*, 467–471.
[15] *Ibid.*, 543–571.
[16] *Ibid.*, 538.

customary requirement, and the economic and political capacity of the inhabitants of the territory left no room for doubt. The undue influence that the church could exert upon local government was regarded, however, as too great an obstacle, and polygamy, then in process of being exorcised through the Edmunds Act, gave excuse for delay. Bancroft has no kind word for this piece of legislation, but he leaves it almost entirely to the reader to decide whether the Mormons should have had more considerate treatment with regard to statehood. After scanning the record of the Mormons' material and cultural progress in the forty years since their arrival in the Salt Lake region, he concludes that theirs was "one of the greatest achievements of modern times."[17] His principal peroration, however, had been expended a few chapters earlier when he recorded the death in 1877 of Brigham Young.[18] For thirty years and more Young had been the spiritual leader of his people, their bulwark in time of adversity, and the director of their temporal pursuits. Bancroft pays him generous tribute, among other things, for his business sagacity, and he praises him not least for building so well that the Mormon politico-religious entity could go on functioning successfully even after death had taken away the leader who had seemed indispensable. Dramatically and historically Brigham Young certainly was the hero of the story to be unfolded in Bancroft's *Utah*.

In the succeeding decades only Mormon historians have gone into the subject with comparable exhaustiveness, although W. A. Linn in 1902 was almost as generous with detail. Modern research, though not always without prejudice, has applied scholarly measurement to selected subjects within this larger frame, and fictionists have dramatized some of the more pungent phases. Bancroft's *Utah*, however, is still a convenient storehouse of factual data, still a readable narrative of the Mormons' magnificent achievements, and still one of

[17] *Ibid.*, 773. [18] *Ibid.*, 668–676.

the most thoughtful and fair analyses of Mormon theology, philosophy, theory, and practice.

Colorado, neighboring Utah to the eastward, was that much closer to the orbit of American affairs, and therefore might reasonably have been expected to enjoy an earlier development. Another factor of geography decreed otherwise. Colorado is the most elevated and the most mountainous of the forty-eight states. Her ranges offer a particularly stubborn barrier to east–west travel, and in consequence the favored routes lay farther north or farther south.

To be sure, there was contact with the region of present-day Colorado at a fairly early date. Coronado in 1541 may possibly have touched the southeastern corner, though the authorities seriously doubt it. The eighteenth century witnessed several penetrations, notably Villasur's on his way to a disastrous encounter with a French and Indian force near the junction of the North and the South Platte, Juan María Rivera's by the valley of the San Juan, Domínguez and Escalante's in an effort to open a route from New Mexico to California, and Juan Bautista de Anza's on an Indian campaign out of Santa Fe. Early in the nineteenth century Zebulon Montgomery Pike entered as the first official agent of the United States. Somewhat later, Major Stephen H. Long came to do further exploring, and in the meantime fur trappers and Indian traders, the pioneers in opening almost every part of the American West, had begun to push their operations into the Colorado region. In the 'twenties the Santa Fe Trail took shape as an artery of western travel and commerce. Its most favored route passed east and south of Colorado, but the optional route by Bent's Fort and Ratón Pass cut across the state. When the Oregon Trail came into being in the 'thirties and 'forties, it did no more than nick the northeastern corner of Colorado. Consequently, the pioneer settlers bound for Oregon and California, the detachments of troops sent west in connection with the War with Mexico, and the gold seekers en route to

California tended to swirl around rather than to pass through Colorado, and made only slight impress on it.

California's gold, however, roused hopes that all the West might prove auriferous, and early in the 'fifties sporadic prospecting began. Nothing momentous was discovered, and no determined search was undertaken until 1858, when a Cherokee group came out from Indian Territory to investigate an earlier report of gold prospects. They were soon followed by other parties from the Missouri River towns, and by the end of the year gold hunting was rife all up and down the eastern face of the Colorado Rockies. And although no remarkable find had been made, the year 1859 saw the rush reach full intensity. Some 150,000 persons started across the plains for this new Eldorado. A third changed their minds en route and turned back to the States. Another large number, the great majority of those who had come out in 1859, left Colorado before the year was over. Nevertheless, substantial quantities of gold had been discovered, near present-day Boulder in January, 1859, and at Clear Creek on May 6, and the reality of Colorado mining was thus assured. The area of mining was expanded, town planting went forward, and the constitutional convention, which had adjourned to see if anyone was going to remain in the area, reassembled to lay the basis for regular government.

The exciting events of this era of discovery and the subsequent steps of development in diversified mining, stock raising, and irrigated and nonirrigated farming, are matters that mainly receive Bancroft's attention. The span of years is almost exactly that of his Nevada account. The mineral output was considerably smaller, but other elements of development were on a substantially larger scale. That the pages allotted are almost the same in number is a slight discrimination against Colorado, but explainable in terms of Bancroft's Pacific-centered interest and Colorado's peripheral location with respect to the area he had chosen for his histories.

Wyoming was also at the margin of Bancroft's area, but because it possessed South Pass, the most convenient of all gateways through the central and northern Rockies, it was traversed by a host of travelers on their way to Oregon, California, and Utah, or to the mining regions all up and down the West. The French voyageur, the Sieur de La Vérendrye, intent on his search for the Western Sea, as well as on the lookout for new fur country, initiated Wyoming's history in the 1740's. Considerably later, yet near the onset of the nineteenth century, American mountain men began to exploit the resource of beaver pelts, to be had along the headwaters of the Sweetwater, the North Platte, the Green, and the Snake. Lewis and Clark passed around Wyoming, though one of their men, John Colter, turned aside from the return trip and explored the terrain extensively. Astor's overlanders crossed the present state, and after that time it was on the main highway of western travel.

Unfortunately for its own development, that is about all that can be said for Wyoming for the next several decades. Fur trappers, Oregon missionaries, pioneer settlers, government explorers, Mormons, and forty-niners traipsed through without leaving much of a mark. Summoned to protect travelers from hostile Indians, the Army garrisoned Fort Laramie and a few lesser stations, but again without substantially altering the scene. Stage lines and pony express were likewise transitory. The Pacific railroad came to stay, but its presence did not transform the area, which up to this point, indeed, lacked even a name. The essential difficulty was that mineral wealth had not come to light, and without gold or silver Wyoming could not bid against Colorado and Nevada and Montana and her other more resplendent sisters.

What Bancroft found to record was, in consequence, rather sparse and fragmentary. There is mention of parties passing through, of the founding of trading posts and military stations, of stage depots and railroad division points. There was, to be sure, some prospecting, and toward the end of his narrative there were brave beginnings in stock raising and crop production. Politically, the Territory of Wyoming did not undergo the vicissitudes of Utah or display the vagaries of Colorado. Its chief novelty was in setting the nation an example by granting suffrage to its women in 1870. The burden of Bancroft's narrative was the Indian wars, with which Wyoming was well supplied. Modernizing the account, one would still lay heavy stress on through traffic, but with greater attention to agricultural development and the enlarged importance of the wonderland of the Yellowstone.

Several elements of Wyoming's experience were reproduced in the neighboring communities of Montana and Idaho. These also were areas introduced to history by the fur traders; they were regions traversed by sundry individuals on their way to the West Coast; and only belatedly did their settlement occur. Indian troubles likewise loomed large. Wyoming had its Fetterman massacre, Montana was the scene of Custer's last stand, and Idaho provided the principal setting for the Nez Percés' masterly retreat under Chief Joseph. Differentiation was chiefly on two points. Idaho and western Montana had closer association with the developments of the West Coast, Oregon in particular; whereas eastern Montana and Wyoming faced east and were usually supplied by way of the Missouri River and the plains. Still more important, Montana and Idaho turned out to be richly endowed with minerals, and consequently their territorial days were marked by greater prosperity and greater turbulence than was the lot of their neighbor to the southeast.

The Bancroft account of these two states is contained principally in the latter part of the thirty-first volume of the *Works*. Reference, however, should be made to the two volumes on the Northwest Coast, the two on Oregon, and the pages on Washington, where most of the early history of these inland regions is covered. Unless geographic divisions of Northwestern history were to be discarded completely, this arrangement is well justified. In the earlier epoch the present boundary lines did not exist, and Idaho and most of Montana were merely part of the hinterland of the Hudson's Bay Company's Old Oregon empire. The subsidiary relationship continued into the American period, as is illustrated by the shifting political units. Idaho, for example, in 1848 was included in Oregon Territory, in 1853 was a part of Washington Territory, in 1863 was constituted as a territory in its own name with Montana and most of Wyoming included, and in 1864 was carved to its present size through the same act of Congress that created Montana Territory. In a sense, therefore, its earlier history belongs with that of its better-developed neighbors. Bancroft was tempted to say that Idaho's history "properly begins with the discovery of the Boisé mines, in August, 1862."[19] Similarly, in Montana the first gold strikes the first white woman resident, the first vigilante trial and execution, and the first county election were subjects of interest only a short time before the erection of the territory.

Once Idaho and Montana were put on the map, their development proceeded apace. Gold was the cause, and the organization of territorial government was but the symbol of an influx of population to these remote parts of the interior. Western prospectors are traditionally a restless lot. Those who came to Idaho and Montana gave the impression of being more than usually so, perhaps because a fair fraction had, as a secondary or even a primary purpose, evasion of military service in the Civil War. The annals of their mining camps abound in crimes of violence, the most reprehensible being the Magruder massacre in Idaho and the deeds of Henry Plummer, the sheriff-highwayman, and his deputy bandits in Montana. To cope with these cutthroats and road agents, vigilante action was the first recourse, followed more tardily by the blossoming of regular courts, jails, and penitentiaries.

[19] Hubert Howe Bancroft, *History of Washington, Idaho, and Montana* (San Francisco, 1890), 406.

Since the volume covering these two states did not go to press until 1890, Bancroft could record the achievement of statehood. Admission to these full privileges implied, of course, a substantial growth in population, productive economy, and social stability. Mining had been fundamental, but other factors, such as farming, stock raising, town development, political experience, journalism, and educational programs, showed promise. Their rise is sketched in some detail, as are also the equally important matters of Indian pacification and railroad building. If the account were to be extended through the period of statehood, one would look for more particulars on agricultural growth, more attention to Idaho lumbering, and acknowledgment of the influence exerted in Montana by Anaconda Copper; but these are phenomena that postdate the territorial epoch.

For his account of the Northwest Coast, Bancroft's series of volumes on Spanish North America and on California were foundational. They described the process of Spanish advance, between the early sixteenth and the late eighteenth century, from Panama about halfway up the Pacific coast of North America. The last years of the eighteenth century and the first half of the nineteenth were to witness the exploration of the northern half of this coast, the work of Russians, British, and Americans, as well as Spaniards, and the rivalries of these nations for title to this coast line and control of its interior. On the earlier Spanish advance Bancroft had merely to refer to the other sections of his *Works*. On the Indians of the Northwest he could likewise cite his *Native Races*. His first 150 pages, nonetheless, were made introductory. They reviewed the advance of New World exploration from 1492 to its third centenary, noting the intense activity in the first half century and the renewed interest dating from about the 1770's, and they discussed at length the apocryphal voyages and the imaginary geography which had substituted for real investigation and accurate mapping.

Attention to the area began in earnest with the voyages of Pérez, Heceta, and Bodega in 1774 and 1775. The Spaniards, however, did not publish the results of these voyages, and consequently the credit for discovery has been popularly assigned to James Cook, who arrived in 1778, and even to George Vancouver, who put in his appearance in 1792. To the voyages of the British and American sea-otter hunters, and to the Spanish explorations preliminary and consequent to the Nootka controversy, some 200 pages are allotted. The account is detailed, giving particulars about all recorded ventures in trade or exploration, and listing vessels that appeared on the coast. Although recent studies, for example Henry R. Wagner's *Spanish Exploration of the Straits of Juan de Fuca,*[20] have elaborated on phases of the subject, this part of Bancroft is still a useful reference on the maritime approaches to the Northwest Coast.

The remainder of this volume charts the approaches of the overland fur traders. Beginning with the French in Acadia and along the St. Lawrence, the British on the shores of Hudson Bay, and the Anglo-Americans in New England and the Hudson Valley, it traces the expansion of these several trading ventures. The variant techniques of French, British, and Americans are analyzed, and the amalgamation of methods and forces in the North West Company is described. The volume concludes with the heroic feat of the Nor'wester Alexander Mackenzie in completing the transcontinental advance that had been begun almost two centuries earlier.

The second volume carries on the theme of North American fur trade, covering the period from 1800 to 1846. The first three chapters are on the Lewis and Clark expedition, which, though it had other purposes, was integrally related to the extension of American trade. Fur-trade history proper resumes with the work of Fraser, Stuart, and Thompson, with Astor's emissaries by sea and overland, with the regime of the

[20] Santa Ana, California, 1933.

Nor'westers in Oregon, and the merger of their company into that of Hudson's Bay. A hundred-page review of the Oregon question is next inserted, after which fur-trade history again has the central place in the narrative. Dr. John McLoughlin, chief factor for the Hudson's Bay Company and "King of Old Oregon," is the figure around whom this section revolves, but without slighting Jedediah Smith, Nathaniel J. Wyeth, and other Americans who trapped or traded in furs and with space for the visits of botanist David Douglas, propagandist Hall J. Kelley, tycoon Sir George Simpson, explorer Charles Wilkes, and globe-trotter Eugène Duflot de Mofras.

As in other parts of the *Works,* this narrative of the fur-trading period is compendious in detail. It contains mistakes; for example, the curious one on page 128 of the second volume, of accepting David Coyner's tale at face value and tracing two American trappers, Workman and Spencer, to the Colorado River and into Los Angeles in the winter of 1809–1810 with a Mexican caravan from Santa Fe. In the California volumes no such improbable story is recorded, and it is remarkable that Bancroft and his staff gave it credence here.

When one is asked to cite the major references on the fur trade of the North American continent, he usually begins with Hiram M. Chittenden's massive work, *The Early American Fur Trade in the Far West,*[21] and then descends to lesser works on phases of the subject, localized in the Missouri Valley, the Rocky Mountains, the Canadian West, or Old Oregon. Bancroft's *Northwest Coast,* if renamed more realistically as a *History of North American Fur Trade,* might well be put first on the list. Though directed toward Old Oregon, it embraces most of the background elements relating to early French, British, and Anglo-American trade, traces subsequent development in Canada as well as in the United States, brings in the maritime phase of sea-otter hunting, and explains how

[21] Three vols.; New York, 1902.

these several strands were interwoven in the far Northwest. More than any other work, these two volumes attempt an over-all survey of the North American fur trade. On most of the topics where this account is casual—on the Russians in Alaska, the later operations in British Columbia, and on trade and trapping in the Rockies and the American Southwest—the industrious reader could find passages elsewhere in the *Works* that would at least double the space here filled. Even without our throwing out this dragnet, the two volumes entitled *Northwest Coast* deserve consideration as our broadest survey of the fur trade on this continent.

These two volumes on the Northwest Coast are also to be regarded as the initial part of the history of Oregon, which Bancroft continues in two other volumes thus entitled. The first of these, dated 1834–1848, begins with the arrival of the first missionary and ends with the erection of territorial government. The second covers the following twoscore years of Oregon's experience as territory and state. Both, one hardly need say, are compendious treatments incorporating a great mass of factual data. They are based on exhaustive use of the literature on Oregon, supplemented, particularly in the latter volume, by a substantial amount of testimony gathered after the Bancroft method from surviving participants and historic personages.

The first volume has a high degree of subject unity. It opens with the coming of the missionaries, analyzes their methods and the results of their labors, notes their early shift of emphasis from converting the Indians to colonizing Oregon, recounts the coming of other pioneer settlers, and observes the culmination of the work of settlers and missionaries in the acquisition of Oregon for the United States. American acquisition thus is the theme of the volume, and almost every step recorded is seen to have contributed toward that result.

Of the early Americans in Oregon, Ewing Young and Cyrus Shepard are singled out for praise; Young for his initiative in rigging up a whisky still, for his consideration in dismantling it, for his leading role in the Willamette Cattle Company and its cattle drive from California, and for the circumstance that his death spurred the Americans to initiate a government so that his estate might be properly administered; and Shepard for his missionary zeal and his efforts to instruct the natives. The attitude toward the Protestant missionaries as a whole may seem to be one of harsh criticism, yet what we really have is accurate reporting of their work, their misfortunes, their quarrels, their several capacities and dispositions. It is, of course, notorious that so far as regeneration of the Indians was concerned their work was in large part barren. With excellent discernment, the measure of their attainment is expressed rather in terms of the American colonization of Oregon. As a nucleus, as an example, as an advertising agency, and as a rallying point the missions were worth much to the national cause. This is the place in history that Bancroft gives them.

The volume is a storehouse of information on the experiences of the overland parties, on the repeated threats of Indian uprisings, on the generous assistance accorded to countless Americans by McLoughlin, on the conditions of life among the Oregon pioneers, and on the repeated manifestations of the urge for a governmental organization of the American type. The missionary element made Oregon somewhat peculiar among the parts of the American Far West; most of these other phenomena had their counterparts all up and down the West.

After 1848, Oregon's history became more complex and less dominated by any one theme. Bancroft's record follows suit. The final volume begins with a survey of conditions prevailing in 1848 and of the way in which the California gold discovery first blighted and then stimulated agriculture and industry. Thereafter, most of Oregon history had to do with political questions, the Indian problem, and elaboration of the state's economy. Through the first decade, political organization was in the stage of uncertain and experimental development. In 1859, however, Oregon graduated from its minority and became a full-fledged state.

Almost immediately, her citizens had to face the national issue of loyalty or disunion. With the population drawn largely from nonslaveholding states, it may seem that her choice should have been easy. Yet in neighboring California, Confederate sympathizers came near to controlling the state, and in near-by Idaho they did capture control. Oregon resembled California likewise in having been Democratic throughout the 'fifties and in possessing a party boss, Joseph Lane, who was partial to the South. A test of strength occurred in the fall of 1860 over the election of United States senators. By that time Lane had failed of the presidential nomination but was the vice-presidential candidate of the Breckenridge Democrats. His adherents put up a strong fight, but in the end were overcome by a coalition of Douglas Democrats who seated James W. Nesmith and Republicans who backed the famous California orator, E. D. Baker. In the presidential election in November, Oregon surprised itself by going Republican. In the post-Civil War years political choice was less a matter of issues and more a matter of men and party labels.

Under the regime of the Hudson's Bay Company the Indian was regarded as a useful hunter who should be protected and preserved. The American attitude, notwithstanding the humanitarianism of the missionaries, was that his lands could be utilized to better advantage by the whites. American acquisition, therefore, may be interpreted as implying the elimination of the Indians. The process began, even in the early 'forties, with efforts to restrain the Indians from molesting travelers or settlers. As white population grew, the potentialities for conflict increased, and incidents of reciprocal violence became more and more numerous. In the early 'fifties most of the trouble was along the Columbia, in the Willamette Valley, and farther south in the Rogue River country. Later in the decade, campaigns of extermination were waged in eastern Oregon from the military post at Grande Ronde as a base. By the late 'sixties the theater of conflict had been pushed still farther afield, with the major campaigns conducted against the Shoshones and Snakes in eastern Oregon and against Shoshones and Pit River tribesmen on the California border. By the next decade, campaigns passed into the next zone and included the Modoc War in California and the operations against the Nez Percés in Idaho and Montana. Although Oregon's Indians were not exterminated, they were so reduced in numbers and in defiance that white utilization of practically the entire state had become feasible.

In the latter part of the annals of Oregon there is recognition of the increased significance of things economic, the rise of grain farming on the eastern plateau, the expansion of cattle raising, the rise of lumbering, fishing, woolen mills, and the like, the improvements in transportation by water and by rail, the establishment of numerous towns and cities, and the flourishing of Portland as the metropolis of the Northwest. Bancroft's narrative reflects this shift in emphasis, but does less justice to these economic changes and their social consequences than it had to the earlier problems of politics and Indian wars.

Perhaps the essential difficulty is that the volume is not carefully proportioned. It purports to cover forty years, yet almost the entire volume is devoted to the decade and a half to 1862 and less than a hundred pages are reserved for discussion of the economic and cultural progress of the next quarter century. Symbolic of this neglect is the arrangement of the next to the last chapter, which bears the title "Political, Industrial, and Institutional, 1862–1887." The political portion is set in the customary type, but the rest is offered in 69 pages of fine print such as normally was employed in the footnotes. Elsewhere Bancroft had employed the same device to keep his written material from overflowing the 800 pages of his standard volumes. We are justified, however, in making an inference concerning his measure of relative importance on the basis of the material that he selected for reduced type. In general, we may remark that this was the California story repeated, with too hurried and casual a treatment of the more recent past.

Next on Bancroft's list came Washington. Its modern history has been enormously complex, what with railroad building and competition, the boom touched off by the rush to the Klondike, expansion in lumbering and agriculture, shipbuilding and airplane manufacture, an upsurge of transpacific commerce, Seattle's rise to metropolitan rank, and grand-scale development of hydroelectric power and water for irrigation. As of 1889, however, her history was comparatively simple, and Bancroft found it could be compressed into half a volume.

Early voyages, the fur trade, the agitation of the Oregon question, and the missionary labors, so far as they related to what is now Washington, had been discussed in the previous works on the Northwest Coast and on Oregon. He could begin, therefore, with the entrance of the first American settlers, notably a certain Michael T. Simmons, who led the invasion of the Puget Sound district in 1845. Even apart from the objections of the Hudson's Bay Company to American settlement north of the Columbia, these pioneers found the region dreary and difficult. To get along, they had to resort to a combination of farming, fishing, and lumbering, and they soon found that, besides fending off the local Indians, they had to withstand raids by the fiercer northern tribesmen. The early annals thus have much on Indian fighting, including the offering of bounties for the heads of hostile chiefs, and the timely intervention of the warship "Decatur" to prevent the sacking of Seattle. As in Oregon, the western Indians first felt the weight of American military force.

Later in the 'fifties the war was carried to the natives of eastern Washington. The Palouses, Spokanes, and Coeur d'Alenes inflicted a crushing defeat on a force led by Colonel Steptoe, but Colonel Wright invaded their country, seized and executed some of the Indians known to have led the attack upon Steptoe, and likewise disposed of some who were charged with other crimes. Wright also killed most of a herd of 800 horses captured from the Spokanes, thus reducing that tribe to impotence. Continuing his campaign, he forced the Coeur d'Alenes and the Nez Percés to submit, collected hostages from the Palouses and the Walla Wallas, and hanged a few warriors as examples to their fellow tribesmen.

These stern measures of the Army may seem to have exceeded the provocation. When followed by pacificatory steps by the government agents, however, they brought surcease from Indian troubles.

Of the early political figures the most notable was Isaac Ingalls Stevens, who came to Washington as leader of the northernmost of the Pacific Railroad surveys, was the first territorial governor, and for two terms was delegate to Congress. Though a Breckenridge Democrat, he remained loyal to the Union, sought action in the Northern army, and died heroically in the battle of Chantilly. Too many of the other territorial appointees were mere placemen; for example, his successor as governor, whose prime interest in taking the post apparently was to get rid of one wife and marry another.

In the early 'sixties the most exciting happenings in Washington were the gold strikes at Clearwater, Pierce City, Oro Fino, Salmon River, and Boise, all of which are in present-day Idaho. The rush to these diggings quite overshadowed the more remote action of the Civil War. By 1863 it resulted in the severance of Idaho as a separate territory. The even tenor of territorial politics was relieved in 1878 by the drafting of a state constitution, which went unheeded in Congress, and in 1885–1886 by a flurry of rioting against the Chinese. Of greater significance was the completion, at last, of the Northern Pacific Railroad, whereupon population jumped from 75,000 in

1880 to more than twice that figure by the end of the decade. Thereby agitation for statehood gained added support, and in November, 1889, this result was achieved.

Bancroft's account covers the political record adequately. Again we find him resorting to fine type for some ten pages of biographical sketches and for a 65-page chapter on resources and industries, in which is presented a mass of data on economic and social conditions at the end of the territorial era.

British Columbia is separated from the American Northwest by nothing more substantial than a man-made line, arbitrary and artificial. Physiographic elements south of the line have their continuations across it, and the major geographic conditions prevailing on one side are approximately duplicated on the other.

As to history, likewise, the resemblance is close. The annals of all these provinces were bottomed on the fur trade, and, as he had already done with respect to Oregon, Washington, and Idaho, Bancroft found it convenient to report the early happenings of British Columbia as part of the general story of the Northwest Coast. On the eve of the arrangement of the Oregon treaty in 1846, British Columbia began to have experiences that were distinctive. Separate treatment begins at about this point, yet much that is recorded for the following forty-odd years is strikingly like that put in print for the states below the 49th parallel. Agriculturists began to take an interest in the region. There were experiments in lumbering, in coal mining, in commercial fishing, and some attention was given to the problems of government. Later in the decade of the 'fifties a gold rush brought thousands of prospectors and created sudden prosperity. Years later, the construction of the Canadian Pacific Railway supplied an even more powerful impetus to economic development. In all these matters, and likewise in the presence of an Indian problem and in the attainment of a provincial status corresponding to statehood, British Columbia closely resembled her American neighbors.

In broad outline, therefore, Bancroft's *History of British Columbia* runs parallel to his histories just described. Nevertheless, it has individuality, and this seems to be ascribable chiefly to two distinctive qualities on the part of Canada's Pacific province. One of these was the initial presence of the Hudson's Bay Company as an entrenched monopoly, with rights antedating those of individual settlers, and with a disposition to discourage, or even to prevent, the occupation and development of the land. The dog-in-the-manger attitude of this great house, though logical enough in terms of fur-trade profits, led to bitter conflict with the pioneer settlers.

The second and more important distinction was that the province throughout all its history was British. Its people were prevailingly British, their ways more akin to England's than to those of the United States; and the tone of Victoria society, abetted by the officers of the naval vessels customarily in port, likewise savored chiefly of Old England. On these associations was overlaid, in 1871, membership in the Canadian dominion, but, when Bancroft wrote, this connection had not overshadowed the province's sense of relationship to the empire.

These two factors—the peculiar influence of the Hudson's Bay Company and the British-Canadian orientation—stand out prominently in Bancroft's account. They provide a sort of obbligato embellishing the main theme of the book, which is the rise of British Columbia as a Pacific state. They add thus to the artistry of the volume and help to make it one of the most readable of the thirty-nine. They doubtless supplied the chief reason for allotting an entire volume to British Columbia, whereas Washington, with equivalent material progress and more protracted Indian troubles, received only half as much space. Finally, they seem to have contributed toward a better-balanced volume. The early years, after the custom of historians, are treated in more generous detail, but almost half the pages are reserved for the developments of the 'sixties, 'seventies, and 'eighties.

Since 1887 much has been written on British Columbia. Besides particularized literature, one would want to consult *From Fur Trade to Airplane,* by Angus, Howay, and Sage;[22] *The Pacific Province,* Volume XXI of *Canada and Its Provinces;*[23] and the four-volume history by E. O. S. Scholefield and F. W. Howay.[24] These works extend Bancroft's account and have corrected it on occasional details. They have not supplanted it, nor have they surpassed it as the first reference on the early decades of British Columbia's history.

Alaska, the northernmost of Bancroft's provinces, would now be recognized as large enough and important enough for a separate volume. The Klondike rush, Alaska's twentieth-century tourist appeal, and its place in the strategy of World War II produced an awareness and an appreciation that previously had been lacking. In 1885, when Bancroft's volume went to press, none of these things had happened. Seward's wisdom in arranging the purchase was still not thoroughly vindicated; furs ranked as the first resource of the area; its vast expanse was most sparsely populated; and American ignorance on the subject of Alaska was still abysmal. In his preface Bancroft insisted that this great sprawling land had a history, and that one valid reason for studying this history was that the land also had promise. The prospects he saw were less in gold, tourists, and strategy, and more in farmlands, fisheries, and standing timber, yet the soundness of his general conclusion would today be admitted.

In the preparation of his history of Alaska, Bancroft employed his usual methods. He sent an agent, Ivan Petroff, thrice to Sitka to interview informants and to gather historical data. Another agent extracted materials from the official archives in St. Petersburg, while copyists assembled additional documentation at Sitka and Washington. These materials, together with the printed matter already in his collection, were marshaled, through the index, into usable form.

---

[22] New York, 1942.

[23] Twenty-three vols.; Toronto, 1914.

[24] Toronto, 1914.

The narrative that resulted was primarily the epic of Russia's eastward expansion. The rapid advance across Siberia, "a century-long sable hunt half round the world," that brought the Russians to the shores of the Pacific, is pungently summarized. Three chapters then treat of Bering's heroic voyages, probing the strait between Asia and North America and achieving the first Caucasian contact with Alaska. The next half-dozen chapters deal with the swarming of the *promyshleniki,* the rough and unruly traders who were the pioneers throughout the Aleutian Islands. When imperial control of this distant frontier proved ineffective, the czar borrowed a leaf from British practice and instituted the device of trading-company control. At first there were two companies, the Shelikof and the Lebedef, which fought each other almost as did the North West Company and the Hudson's Bay Company. In 1796 the Shelikof faction came off victorious as a consolidation was ordered and the Russian American Fur Company received a monopolistic charter.

These events and those of the next quarter century brought Russian America to a climax. To this epoch Bancroft allots twelve important chapters, and he makes its dominant figure, Alexander Baranof, Shelikof's agent and resident manager for the Russian American Fur Company, the real hero of the Alaskan drama. Baranof's weaknesses are admitted and there is no glossing over of his indifference to the program of missionary work undertaken among the Alaskan natives. He is honored, however, for active prosecution of fur gathering, for fair and resolute dealings with the natives, for persistence despite most uncertain support from Siberia, for his achievements in shipbuilding in Alaska, and for putting Russian Alaska on a secure footing.

Single chapters describe company operations under the second charter, 1821–1842, and in the final twenty-five years of Russian control. Another chapter recounts the circumstances of the transfer to the United States, and the final hundred pages survey fur trade, fisheries, other economic pursuits, social conditions, and political arrangements. Treatment of the American period is necessarily inconclusive. American neglect is amply demonstrated, and lack of interest in Alaska is clear from the record. What the future would hold in the way of political concessions and provisions, settlement, and economic development, Bancroft had no way of knowing. To other pens he had to leave the chronicling of American Alaska; his volume is essentially the story of Russian endeavor there. In that category it remains today a well-constructed survey and a principal reference.

Such, in brief, is the nature of the nine volumes in which Bancroft presented the history of the ten states that are California's neighbors to the east and north. There was unevenness in treatment, and unfortunate neglect of the later phases of several of these state histories. It may be objected also that the arrangement adopted stressed individual peculiarities at the expense of regional perspective. Yet the work was done with such thoroughness and such candor that for most of these states Bancroft's history is still the basic reference for the period covered. The persevering reader, furthermore, who works through these 7,000 pages will have a general comprehension of the processes whereby the northwestern quarter of the continent was discovered, explored, and made to yield a profit in furs; of the steps determining its ultimate ownership; and of the foundations laid by prospectors, settlers, Indian fighters, railroad builders, politicians, and divers others for the commonwealths that now adorn this region. The account is less unified than for California, and in exhaustiveness of detail it is not quite up to Bancroft's California standard. No modern writer, however, has undertaken to redo this history for the entire Rocky Mountain and Pacific Northwest, and no one has essayed, on a like scale, to bridge the gap between the late 1880's and the present. Here, then, is another vast field of regional history in which Bancroft stands alone.

15

Essayist

In the supplementary works I indulged in a wider latitude as to the choice of subjects, the expression of opinion, and giving my faculties freer play in the execution.... They were more myself than almost any of my other works.

Hubert Howe Bancroft, *Literary Industries,* 655

BEYOND THE FIVE VOLUMES on the aborigines and the twenty-eight comprising the history of the Pacific states, Bancroft projected an additional six, which he entitled *California Pastoral, California Inter Pocula, Popular Tribunals* (in two volumes), *Essays and Miscellany,* and *Literary Industries.* These books were designed to complement rather than supplement those that had preceded. Since the obligation of comprehensiveness had already been discharged, they could be more leisurely and less rigid in design. And because they were less formal, they could be more revelatory of their author's outlook on life and his concept of history. In the anthropological and historical surveys Bancroft, of course, had disclosed many of his ideas and interpretations, as well in the selection of materials and the organization employed as in the outright voicing of judgments and conclusions. The added volumes, however, offer a more open expression of his philosophy and his opinions. Although these volumes are first to be considered as contributions to the history of the West, it will be appropriate, therefore, to reëxamine them as a mirror in which their author is reflected.

California Pastoral, the first work in this group, depicts the province in its Arcadian period, the fourscore years from 1769 and the founding of the first Spanish establishments to 1848 and the discovery of gold. Historical events in the conventional sense—wars, conquests, political upheavals, and governmental actions—are attended to but slightly; stress is laid rather on the life of the people, the elements of the local economy and, more especially, the prevailing social practices and customs. In the forepart of this era the provincials, few in number, were barely able to eke out a living, and their ways were necessarily simple. Influenced also by the greater adequacy of his information on the later years, Bancroft dealt rapidly with the folk habits of Spanish California and concerned himself primarily with the customs and mores of the Mexican period. It was, indeed, to this epoch, of the 'twenties, 'thirties, and 'forties, that the phrase "California Pastoral" was most appropriate.

By way of introduction his first three chapters analyze the Spanish and Mexican thought patterns that were the matrix from which California's provincial society was fashioned. Spanish national characteristics are presented with some attention to their origin in feudalism and chivalry, in the bitter contest against the Moors, and in the poverty of the land. That Spanish methods would yield an advantage over the natives of America is freely admitted. The point stressed, however, is that neither side had a monopoly of culture and enlightenment, or of barbarity and superstition. Each represented a compound of "civilization and savagisms." The application of Spanish colonial policy is discussed against a background of appraisal of colonization in general. Then, in lieu of an essay on Mexico as the immediate motherland of pastoral California, appears a chapter-long summary of Alexander von Humboldt's inspection and description in the opening years of the nineteenth century. Bancroft contrives to pay handsome tribute to this great German scientist, and at the same time to reveal the conditions prevailing in the land from which California was an offshoot.

The next chapter, though lyric in its tone and entitled "Lotus-Land," is an accurate and particularized description of the California environment, its mountain ranges and valleys, its harbors and rivers, the factors governing its varied climates, and its potentialities for agriculture and industry.

The life of the Spanish pioneers at the missions, presidios, and pueblos is treated in succeeding chapters. Generalizations are supported, or even avoided, by illustrative anecdotes drawn from the extensive literature that had been worked over in compiling the history of this era. The same technique prevails in the remaining five or six hundred pages, which concern the Mexican period; in fact, in some of them a succession of anecdotes tells the entire story. These latter chapters explore almost every phase of economic and social history. They include discussions of "Pastures and Fields," "Occupations and Industries," and "Inland Trade and Coast Traffic," and of "Woman and Her Sphere," "Food, Dress, Dwellings, and Domestic Routine," and "Amusements." Others attack the problems of law, government, religion, courts, and crime. Under the caption "A Futile Fight with Ignorance" appears a survey of the faltering progress of schools and schooling. Comments on the speech of the pastoral period are assembled as "Californianisms," while a glossary lists Spanish words and phrases that had persistent use in the California vernacular.

Of somewhat doubtful eligibility is the chapter on "Banditti." True enough, several of the most spectacular highwaymen, including Joaquín Murrieta and Tiburcio Vázquez, were Spanish Californians, and the field of their operations was chiefly in southern California, which continued rural and pastoral. Yet they flourished after 1848 and in some degree because of the Gold Rush. Inserting them into the description of the preceding epoch is somewhat misleading.

The penultimate chapter, curiously omitted from the table of contents, is a fitting conclusion to this description of the provincial beginnings. "Founding a Great Metropolis" is its title, and it describes the very gradual development on the shores of San Francisco Bay from 1776 to 1846, the slightly more rapid pulsations in the next two years, including the change of name from Yerba Buena to San Francisco in January, 1847, and the status attained about a twelve-month hence on the eve of the startling transformation that the Gold Rush was about to bring on. Finally, as the twenty-third chapter, there is a forty-page essay on the "Bibliography of Pastoral California," in which manuscripts as well as printed works are catalogued and described.

The outline of this book is almost exactly what one would have it. No phase of life in the halcyon days comes to mind which might better have been discussed than these elements that are included. The several chapters, furthermore, are proportionate. The style may seem to be burdened with an excess of allusions to classical mythology and the masterpieces of world literature, yet often these comparisons characterize California customs with perfect aptness. Even the rambling and unhurried style befits the tempo of the period, and the diffuseness of Bancroft's writing is balanced by a number of well-turned phrases and by an occasional eloquent passage. The device of piling up the evidence is a sound approach to the problem of social history, and the vast amount of detail that is encompassed gives the reader a feeling of intimate acquaintance with the days of the dons. Furthermore, this sense of authoritativeness is conveyed without resort to footnotes, and in view of their prodigal employment in his histories this is a departure of no mean significance. These are some of the qualities of excellence possessed by *California Pastoral*. In 1929 it acquired a competitor in Nellie Van de Grift Sánchez' *Spanish Arcadia,* but it is still the classic on the life of early California.

California Inter Pocula pursues this description of folkways into the days of gold. The geographic setting is first blocked in, especially for the valley of California, whence, by the eastern tributaries of the Sacramento and San Joaquin, the reader is conducted to the diggings. After various irresponsible references to California gold in the first three centuries of its history are reported and scouted, the circumstances of the actual discovery are set forth. Then follows a description of the experiences of the overland forty-niners and of those who came by Panama. The latter account, spread over a hundred pages, is notable because it recounts Bancroft's own experiences as a California-bound traveler in 1852. A chapter on the Cape Horn route would seem to have been called for, but is not included.

The introductory matter thus disposed of, the greater part of the volume is given over to description of the California folk pattern. Under such headings as "El Dorado," San Francisco," "Society," "Business," "Classical Abnormalities," and "Further Abnormalities" are marshaled reports of the conduct of Californians of the flush times. Again the approach is anecdotal, and in places there is a veritable cascade of illustrative incident. Information of the most diverse sorts is included—on the diet and costume of the miners, on the mining laws and regulations, on the operation of stages, on the eager reception of mail from the States, and on the style in profanity. Squatterism, prisons, courts, Indian episodes, Chinese episodes, drinking, gambling, and dueling have each a chapter. The only phases slighted are those, such as politics and the record of economic development, that were accorded full treatment in the history of the province. This, of course, was intentional so that duplication would be avoided and so that this volume might stress the character of California society.

Since it has the profile of an accumulation of data rather than a carefully worked-out argument, the plan of the volume is not of the utmost importance. Slight revision might have improved the organization. For example, two chapters descriptive of conditions of life and labor at the mines might better have been consecutive instead of separated by one on

San Francisco. The other principal flaw is in the chapter on Indian episodes. The heartless attitude of the forty-niners toward the Indians was, of course, one of the most striking sociological phenomena of the times, and recognition of it was an essential element for the description Bancroft was attempting. A chapter on the subject thus was amply justified. Bancroft's introduction to it is admirable. He quotes De Quincey:

> Believe me, it is not necessary to a man's respectability that he should commit a murder. Many a man has passed through life most respectably, without attempting any species of homicide. A man came to me as the candidate for the place of my servant, just then vacant. He had the reputation of having dabbled a little in our art, some said, not without merit. What startled me, however, was, that he supposed this art to be part of the regular duties in my service. Now that was a thing I would not allow. So I said at once, 'if once a man indulges himself in murder, very soon he comes to think little of robbing'; and from robbing he comes next to drinking and Sabbath-breaking, and from that to incivility and procrastination. Once begin upon this downward path you never know where you are to stop. Many a man has dated his ruin from some murder or other that perhaps he thought little of at the time.[1]

He proceeds then to tell how the coming of the miners affected the Indians, how they took to digging gold, how they gradually acquired some knowledge of its value, how they were misunderstood and mistreated by the miners. He tells of occasions when Indians were casually killed, and of others when whole villages were massacred for wrongs committed by one or two of their number, or by other Indians entirely. For other atrocities, robbery of the Indians was the motive. Without straying far from the diggings or from 'forty-nine, Bancroft could have adduced a score or more of such incidents. Instead, after some ten pages of such matter, he elected to take up the Modoc War of 1871 and to allot some 115 pages

[1] "On Murder as One of the Fine Arts," second paper, *Blackwood's*, November, 1839; as quoted by Bancroft, *California Inter Pocula*, 436.

to narrating its course. This war, to be sure, was the largest that California was to witness, and, although it had more in common with the Indian wars of the Pacific Northwest, it can be traced partly to the mishandling of the Indians by the California prospectors. He describes this famous contest thoroughly, accurately, and fairly. The discussion, however, adds little to the picture of California in its flush times.

As a proportioned whole, *California Inter Pocula* is not quite on a par with *California Pastoral.* It shares many of the merits of that volume—a generous offering of detail, a dependence on factual array rather than elaboration in the telling. It possesses a further advantage in that much of the description of California, as well as of the Panama route, came out of Bancroft's own experience, as well as out of his historical researches. The title, furthermore, is priceless; "California in her cups" is a most apt characterization for the province in its period of intoxication with gold.

From these descriptive tasks Bancroft turned to a problem that called for analysis and measured judgment. In the headlong advance of the American frontier in the Far West, the law had lagged behind. This West was so remote that the United States had trouble in setting up the machinery of government and in staffing it adequately. The people who poured into this farthest frontier were exceedingly diverse. They came from all the states and from most of the nations. They came as individuals and brought no functioning government with them. Many came with no intention of remaining permanently, and consequently they had little interest in stabilizing western courts or law. And when to all this was added the heady wine of gold, the natural result was an impatience with the delays and the formalities of conventional court actions. When crime became a problem—and this happened almost at once—the regular procedures of the law were neglected in favor of an impromptu justice which Bancroft calls popular tribunals.

These irregular people's courts were one of the most distinctive features of this frontier. They have a prominent place in the literature of the period, both in the firsthand reports and in the later, more contemplative surveys. The subject, furthermore, is of such a character that seldom does one find a dispassionate evaluation. Almost all easterners, as residents of better established and less hurried communities, were shocked at the recourse to extralegal punishments, and most westerners who had a background of legal training were equally critical of the disrespect of the law. Better, they said, that a host of criminals go unpunished than that one man be hanged or whipped or otherwise disciplined without having had his day in court. A number of writers put on record this criticism of the West's peculiar institution, and in terms almost as denunciatory as those directed against another section's peculiarity, Negro slavery.

Against these critics was arrayed a school of writers who found much to praise in western vigilance. It was not, they insisted, mere lynch law or mob violence. The provocation, they said, was usually great, the law impotent or hopelessly corrupted, the necessity for action so pressing that something must be done. Often, these advocates continued, the accused person had a fairer trial than would have been his lot in a regular court. Again, we find it argued that the law was not sacred, that it was too much encrusted with British abuses to be appropriate for America, that its red tape was an abomination. The law, said the spokesmen of vigilance, had force and justification only because of the will of the people, and if the majority chose to redirect the law through revolution, rather than through the slower processes of election and legislation, well and good.

Bancroft's view, as expounded in the two volumes entitled *Popular Tribunals,* was emphatically that of the justifiers of vigilance. He saw defects. He admitted that a few innocent men had been victimized. He realized that certain self-styled vigilante groups were in fact mobs. He was aware also that the preference for direct action persisted in many western localities long after the regular agencies had been made adequate. Yet he greatly admired the resourcefulness with which the westerners had improvised courts when they found themselves outside the pale of regular jurisprudence, and he had a profound respect for the methods and achievements of the San Francisco committees. The two volumes are consistent throughout in making his stand clear. The second pricks it out even more sharply through a dedicatory note that reads "To William T. Coleman, Chief of the Greatest Popular Tribunal the World has ever Witnessed, I dedicate this volume." Incidentally, this is the only volume among the thirty-nine that carries a dedication.

The story that unfolds in *Popular Tribunals* is in some measure that of western vigilance in general, but primarily that of the San Francisco committees of 1851 and 1856. After a short discussion of the theoretical basis for resort to extra-legal justice, Bancroft describes the conditions that engendered the first San Francisco committee: the Hounds' association; its metamorphosis into the Society of Regulators; the orgy of theft, robbery, murder, and arson loosed upon the city; the utter inadequacy of the courts in dealing with this crime wave; and the example of direct action which had become standard procedure in the mines.

Then follows a 200-page report of the work of this committee. Public sentiment seems to have been ready for heroic measures, and once the idea was broached to a leader of sufficient determination, the not always admirable Sam Brannan, organization and action quickly followed. This committee faced several knotty problems. One was to establish the identity of a man in custody, supposedly James Stuart. Forbearance in this case was amply justified when at length the real Stuart was apprehended and the innocent Thomas Berdue could be released. The organized criminal element was perhaps no more than a challenge to the committee, but the city's officeholders, a majority of the legal profession, and a part of the press made up an important opposition.

On several occasions the committee was almost frustrated. Hanging John Jenkins under cover of night seemed a confession of weakness, if not of cowardice. The verdict of the coroner's jury in the inquest that followed, placing responsibility upon nine of the vigilante leaders, was a telling blow, which the committee effectively parried by publishing its entire roster of 180 names. It blundered badly in publishing a resolution claiming the right to search any premises for suspicious characters or stolen property. On the whole, however, it acted with commendable circumspection. The four men it hanged were clearly guilty of high crimes. Its sentences of banishment were well directed, and though, on the part of a regular court, exiling would be a shirking of responsibility, on the part of a vigilante body it is a more acceptable device. The committee's donation of $15,000 for the completion of the county jail was irreproachable. And at the end of its crusade, with the regular courts quickened and bolstered in the performance of their duties, the committee could break off its work without so much as a formal adjournment or disbanding.

Quoting freely from the press of Philadelphia, New York, Boston, and points east, Bancroft surveys contemporary world opinion of San Francisco's first popular tribunal. The London *Times* characterized it as a precedent "of which no man can calculate the evil." The Vermont *Union Whig* saw in the committee a demonstration of the moral inadequacy of the Californians to maintain a constitutional government. "In the absence of fire to keep up a pleasant popular ferment," said the Philadelphia *Ledger*, "the citizens [of San Francisco] resort to a different species of amusement," and the *Ledger* went on to view the sequel with alarm. The New York *Herald* branded the sway of Judge Lynch as "a terrible state of affairs," and the New York *Journal of Commerce* opined that the committee had perpetrated abuses more dangerous than those it had sought to remedy. So ran the comments of the majority, but a few eastern journalists expressed views which Bancroft found more agreeable. The Albany *Knickerbocker* asserted, "If the action of the people is to be regretted, it is only because they did not move earlier." And the Buffalo *Express* observed, "From the vigorous, sensible, active state of California comes to the older states a hint and a suggestion that they would do well to heed." The suggestion, of course, was for elimination of the delays and technicalities encrusted upon the regular processes of the law.[2]

Since these judgments were arrived at in the distant longitude of the Atlantic seaboard, their finality is open to question. Bancroft adduces them to illustrate the general temptation to criticize California's resort to direct action, and he uses them as strawmen to demolish in vindication of the committee. In the remaining 320 pages of this volume, however, he puts on record the evidence that justifies one of the major forebodings of the critics of San Francisco's first committee. These critics had been alarmed that the vigilante principle would spread and that San Francisco's example would be followed generally. Such, indeed, was the result. Popular tribunals rose again in the diggings, spread to rural California, and became standard devices in the southern cow counties. Beyond the state the same pattern extended into all parts of the West. The incidents Bancroft relates of "necktie sociables" and "strangulation jigs" in Montana, and Idaho, and New Mexico, are expressions of the same philosophy that pervaded the metropolitan group. Yet with this difference: frequently the rural practitioners of extralegal justice were less orderly, less moderate, and less scrupulous to see that guilt was thoroughly established.

The narrative of San Francisco vigilance is then resumed

[2] Quoted in Hubert Howe Bancroft, *Popular Tribunals* (2 vols.; San Francisco, 1887), I, 407–426.

with a book-length treatment of the committee of 1856, which to Bancroft was the Grand Tribunal. Its origin may be ascribed to conditions reminiscent of 1851, or, indeed, to the failure of the first committee to achieve a lasting reform. That earlier terror had checked crime for the time being. It had also stiffened the courts, and if we may take capital punishment as a measure, an improvement can be discerned. Prior to 1851, San Francisco had witnessed no regular execution. On December 10, 1852, with much fanfare and with half the town on hand to witness it, the first legal hanging took place, the victim a certain José Forin, "a stranger, without money, friendless, and unable to speak the English language,"[3] and guilty of killing another Mexican. On July 28, 1854, before ten thousand spectators, William B. Shepherd paid with his life for having killed a reluctant father-in-law; and early in 1856 Nicholas Graham was hanged for the murder of a steamboat fireman. These three executions, however, must be set against an appalling crime record, for San Francisco's six-year tally of murders is put confidently at 1,400. With respect to the West in general, Bancroft calls this the Augustan age of murder.

Unrestrained crime, nevertheless, was not the whole story in 1856. A companion evil had grown up, a complicating factor, which was the utter corruption of the municipal government. The San Franciscans, to be sure, had only themselves to blame—themselves or, more accurately, the townspeople of a year or two earlier, who had permitted ballot stuffing and intimidation to sweep the wrong candidates into office. The citizens of 1856, far more urbane than those of 'fifty-one, deplored the sad condition of their city. They were distressed over gambler Charles Cora's cold-blooded murder of United States Marshal Richardson, but they responded only with headshakings. Nor did the scathing editorials of James King of William prod them to action. Yet when Super-

[3] *Ibid.*, I, 746–747.

visor James P. Casey, incensed at King's flaunting of his term in Sing Sing, shot down his determined critic, public indignation suddenly boiled over. For the immediate purpose the regular courts clearly would not do. A popular tribunal was erected instead, more decorous, more formalized than the previous one, but fully as inexorable.

Bancroft's narrative keeps pace with the rapid sequence of events that followed Casey's fatal shot. One senses the surge of public indignation, the streets seething with aroused men, and the wrath of the citizens that lacked only a gesture of leadership to produce an immediate lynching. William T. Coleman, Clancy J. Dempster, and other vigilante leaders are credited with blocking any such action, but the populace itself was reluctant to descend to this level of mob violence. Bancroft's narrative keeps pace, yet he permits himself a number of philosophical digressions on such matters as the injustice of King's strictures against gambling and gamblers, and the servility which a newspaper must show to its master, public opinion.

This latter axiom was illustrated by the fate of the San Francisco *Herald*. Under the direction of John Nugent, whom Bancroft characterizes as "the deepest, clearest, most logical and eloquent journalist ever upon this coast,"[4] the *Herald* had been the ablest journal in the state. It had supported the first committee, but in 1856 it refused to admit the necessity of vigilante action because of what it called the "affray" between Messrs. Casey and King. No sooner was the second committee organized than it caused a boycott of the *Herald* through cancellation of subscriptions and withdrawal of the advertisements of jobbers and auctioneers. On Thursday, May 15, the *Herald* was the largest paper in town; on Friday, May 16, it was the smallest; nor did it ever recover. Whereupon Bancroft comments: "A newspaper, though professedly a leader of public opinion, is, it is almost needless to say, the most

[4] *Ibid.*, II, 81.

servile of slaves. It leads by watching narrowly the direction public opinion tends; then circling to the front, it shouts, 'Come on!' "[5]

Bancroft's narrative of the subsequent work of the committee is particularly successful in recapturing the atmosphere of dramatic tension that prevailed. This is partly the result of his thorough knowledge of the vigilantes. Knowing them so well, and assisted by their statements, records, and reports, he is able to present what is essentially the inside story of what the committee did. Furthermore, he never minimizes the opposition. Though professing no respect for the friends of Casey and Cora, the local officeholders, the professional politicians, and the vacillating governor, and no agreement with those who on principle inclined toward the law and order party, he makes no denial of their strength. The reader is constantly reminded that forces of some strength might at any moment thwart the efforts of vigilance. The committeemen themselves were aware of the danger. Their initial concern about the perfection of their organization was to strengthen their hands, and not merely to satisfy a sense of propriety. In the parleys with the governor; in the march on the jail; in the trials and execution of Casey and Cora; in the arrest and trial of Judge David S. Terry—in fact, in all the actions of the committee, the menace of popular, municipal, state, or federal interference was always proximate. Suspense, therefore, is a quality of this narrative throughout. Can Governor J. Neely Johnson be held off? Can the committee get hold of Casey and Cora? Will it resolutely proceed to their execution? Will federal authorities keep hands off? Will Hopkins recover? What shall be done with Terry? Thus crisis follows upon crisis, and even with the formal adjournment of the committee the uncertainties are prolonged. Will the courts of California, or of New York, hold the vigilantes to answer for the deeds of the committee? One by one, these

[5] *Ibid.*, II, 79.

questions are resolved, but the impression conveyed is that it was never a foregone conclusion that the committee would prevail.

In this narrative Bancroft occasionally makes use of verbal pyrotechnics. Such, for example, are his apostrophe of the martyred King and his soliloquy on the hanging in effigy of the Rev. William A. Scott. At times he waxes eloquent over the villainy of the opposition or the heroism or genius of the vigilantes. For the most part, however, he tells the story simply, with graphic detail and with a realism that stems from the directness of his sources, but without extravagant rhetoric. Having completed the narrative, he allows himself two chapters to measure the fruits of vigilance and to reflect on the moral and philosophical issues that had been involved. He concludes that the beneficial effects were easily preponderant and that a right more fundamental than any codified law justified San Francisco's evocation of a popular tribunal.

There, if artistic considerations alone were to prevail, the book would end. But in 1877–1878, in response to the labor agitation led by Dennis Kearney, vigilance was briefly recrudescent in the pickhandle brigade directed by the lion of the vigilantes, William T. Coleman. For the plight of the workingmen Bancroft reveals a genuine sympathy. For their subservience to demagogues he has only regret, and he characterizes the whole affair as an unfortunate illustration of what Macaulay had foreseen in 1857, when he warned of grave danger that the United States would be plundered and laid waste by barbarians, Huns and Vandals engendered within the country and by its own institutions.

Popular Tribunals emerges from analysis as a monograph of unusual merit. The materials that went into its making were extraordinarily good. Bancroft had full newspaper reports and the testimony of many contemporary observers. He was also fortunate enough to uncover the official records of the first vigilance committee and to persuade a number of leading participants in the second to testify in detail about its operations. Furthermore, he was personally acquainted with many of the men involved, and he was thoroughly conversant with the conditions that had prevailed in San Francisco in the 'fifties. He had first come to the city less than a year after the flourishing of the first committee, and had returned only months after the adjournment of the second. In his preface he refers to his work as well-timed. If it had been attempted earlier, few of the participants would have been willing to divulge information; a decade later, few informants might have been left. All that has since been written on the vigilantes stems from his work, and the tenor of judgment in specialized studies, such as those of Mary F. Williams, James A. B. Scherer, and Stanton A. Coblentz,[6] or in the more general works on California, is substantially that expressed in *Popular Tribunals.*

Essays and Miscellany, standing next on the shelf, displays its author in a variety of moods. Chapter I is a diatribe against Lewis H. Morgan and his disciples, who denied the reliability of the early American chroniclers, Bernal Díaz, Cortés, Sahagún, and the rest, and refused to admit that Maya and Aztec civilization had outstripped that of the Iroquois. Today, this is almost whipping a dead horse. Modern anthropology has accustomed us to think of these Middle Americans as the culture leaders of the entire continent and in some respects the peers of the Old World leaders. At the time, however, it was an act of courage to differ with the acknowledged dean of American anthropologists.

Chapter II, in less bellicose vein, notes the westward tend-

[6] Mary F. Williams, *History of the San Francisco Committee of Vigilance of 1851* (Berkeley, 1921); James A. B. Scherer, *The Lion of the Vigilantes: William T. Coleman and the Life of Old San Francisco* (Indianapolis, 1939); Stanton A. Coblentz, *Villains and Vigilantes: The Story of James King of William and Pioneer Justice in California* (New York, 1936).

Perhaps it should be mentioned here, for the benefit of readers not yet acquainted with King's story, that "of William" (i.e., son of William) was his way of distinguishing himself from numerous other James Kings.

ency of civilization, gently chides the East for its conservatism, and points to the Pacific seaboard as the probable "terminal of the great Aryan march," whereon already the "New Civilization" had begun to take shape. Further comment on the nature of development in the Far West is to be found in subsequent essays on "Social Analysis" and "Nation Making." Western applications are frequently adduced in essays on general topics such as "Work," "The Jury System," and "Money and Monopoly." In the last-named, for example, railroad building and operation are the chief illustrations offered. Still other essays focus on problems distinctively western.

Thus Chapter III is a meditation on gold. It opens with the musings of a "philosophic savage" as he surveys the gold diggers hard at work on the middle prong of the American River in July, 1848. His thoughts on the irrationality of prizing gold are answered, in part, by allusions to the power of gold in the world called civilized, and are corroborated, in part, by further comments on the illogic of worshiping this relatively useless metal. The fable is brought to a close with a surprise ending that would have done credit to O. Henry.

Chapter IV, appropriately, is a commentary on the policies of Indian treatment put into practice by the Spaniards, the English colonials, and more latterly by the United States. Later in the volume Bancroft returns to the problems of race and has something to say about the Africans in slavery and out of it, about the difficulty of assimilating immigrants from eastern Europe, and particularly about the tangled logic of opposition to the Chinese. His position, in brief, was that the United States would have been better off if it could have remained as homogeneous in population as were the seventeenth-century English colonies. After importing Negroes and accepting immigrants drained, as he inelegantly phrased it, "from the cess-pools of Europe," the United States, he insisted, was straining at a gnat when it objected to the Chinese.

These are essays with a western flavor, many of them concerned with topics that would have been of merely incidental concern to a New Englander, and all are handled in a fashion reflecting the influence of Pacific slope environment.

Another group of essays reflects Bancroft's interest in scholarship, writing, and publication—the note, it will be remembered, on which the volume had opened. In discussion of the factors producing success he has much to say about the motivation of writers, and in separate essays on history and criticism he analyzes these two branches of learning and literature. "The writer of history," he observes, "need not be a genius—indeed, genius is ordinarily too erratic for faithful plodding—but he must be a fair man, a man of sound sense, good judgment, and catholicity of opinion; of broad experience and a wide range of knowledge. While guarding against a too free indulgence in . . . love of personalities . . . he will never hold himself above anything which affects human nature, however humble, nor below those abstract generalities which are a later product, the result of study and experience."[7]

Criticism is characterized as a necessary evil, an art susceptible to grave abuses, and a temptation to small men to inflict indiscriminate and malicious damage. Among a host of observations, some of which are much more epigrammatic, we find these suggestions: "The lack of honesty and sincerity in praising a poor book is as culpable as in condemning a good one. And even worse than this is so magnifying the non-essential faults of a really good book, and omitting to mention its merits, as to leave the impression that it is wholly bad."[8]

In a vein reportorial but still somewhat philosophical he then surveys the literature of Central America, of colonial Mexico, of nineteenth-century Mexico, and of early California. In 25 pages on Central America he has something to say about the pre-Columbian literature, the Popul Vuh and the

---

[7] Hubert Howe Bancroft, *Essays and Miscellany* (San Francisco, 1890), 103.

[8] *Ibid.*, 116.

like, makes an itemized analysis of the narratives of the conquistadores, and goes on to the chronicles of Dominicans and Franciscans and the writings of later scholars. Assessing the revival of learning that began in the late eighteenth century, he comments on the increase of secular writing and printing. Finally, he takes stock of what was doubtless the most popular form of literary expression in Central America, verse.

Mexico had much more of literature, and the survey of achievement in its several branches required 110 of Bancroft's pages. Again the spread is from before Columbus to the late nineteenth century, and the discussion covers all sorts of writings: by the indigenes, by conquistadores, churchmen, revolutionists, scientists, and political leaders, by historians, novelists, dramatists, and poets.

California's literature, to which 60-odd pages are allotted, flourished but slightly under Spain and Mexico. Indeed, for this entire epoch Bancroft's verdict is that "not a single literary effort appears worthy of note."[9] As a possible exception he offers Palóu's *Vida de Junípero Serra* (1787) and Robinson's *Life in California* (1846), originally intended as introduction to a translation of Father Boscana's *Chinigchinich*. He notes earlier activities in printing and follows in detail the introduction of journalism as the American element became predominant in the 'forties. This awakening was followed immediately by a golden avalanche of writing and publishing, here reviewed under such varied headings as short stories, poetry, biography, history, narratives, reminiscences, descriptive handbooks, compilations of information, and works of philosophy and economic theory. With so great a quantity of writing to describe, Bancroft could not tarry long with any single item. Frequently, however, he compresses into a sentence a most apt judgment. Concerning the reminiscences of an old-time resident we read, "Bandini conveys his less valuable memoirs under a pretentious title, and regards them

[9] *Ibid.*, 593.

evidently as admirable; yet he disclaims any attempt at writing history, or any striving for elegance and method, and this declaration he certainly adheres to."[10] Of *The Annals of San Francisco,* after commenting on the many personal notes injected and the fulsome flattery therein contained, he remarks, "It may be classified as a book intended to sell."[11]

From his roll call of California literary achievement Bancroft modestly omitted any reference to his own contribution in *Native Races* and the *History of the Pacific States.* Many of the more substantial items in the nonfiction list had been produced by his publishing house, and several had been done at his instigation. Among these were the first real history of California, by Franklin Tuthill; the two most voluminous descriptions of western resources, those by Cronise and Hittell; and the two fat tomes edited by Professor Alonzo Phelps, *Contemporary Biography of California's Representative Men,* which is rightly called "the most pretentious specimen of book manufacture on the coast."[12] In writing of the expansion of California letters, Bancroft was thus treating of a development in which he had taken an important part.

Autobiographical material, however, was for the most part reserved for the thirty-ninth volume, *Literary Industries.* Concerning this volume nothing is more striking than the fact of its inclusion in the *Works.* No other author or editor of a multivolume history—neither Gibbon, nor Macaulay, nor Parkman, nor Winsor, nor McMaster, nor Channing, nor any other that I can think of—has incorporated his own biography as part of his history. Yet Bancroft considered it an appropriate thing to do. Perhaps more accurately we should say that he used the story of his life as the thread on which to present an account of his purposes as collector and historian, of the objectives of his great series, and of the methods employed in its production. His methods, all will agree, were novel enough to require some such explanation.

[10] *Ibid.,* 603. [11] *Ibid.,* 615. [12] *Ibid.,* 614.

His autobiography begins, therefore, with a synoptic view of the field of Pacific states history to which he had devoted thirty of the prime years of his life. There was, he insists, "no part of the globe equal in historic interest and importance . . . which at the time had not its historical material in better shape, and its history well written by one or more competent persons."[13] Another sheaf of pages examines the atmosphere of California, then and now so suspiciously regarded as too pleasant and diverting to prompt intellectual activity. Bancroft's testimony is that he was never aware of any climatic or environmental handicap. On page 47 he begins to explore his family tree, and nine pages later he records his own birth. Thence the narrative proceeds unpretentiously and straightforwardly, though not without digressions.

Toward the middle, autobiographical detail is outbulked by narrative of the growth of the historical collection, organization of the staff for research and writing, and operation of the literary workshop. Four chapters, for example, concern Enrique Cerruti and his campaign for Vallejo's documents and support. Toward the end, biographical data is further subordinated to the story of the final phases of publishing the *Works,* a process rendered dramatic, as well as heroic, by the fire that laid waste the bookstore and publishing plant in April, 1886. *Literary Industries* thus ends with assurance of the rounding out of the set of thirty-nine volumes. Bancroft's life was by no means over; the *Works,* however, stood complete. It was inevitable that the book should be a more satisfactory biography of the history project than of the historian.

From these six supplementary volumes, nevertheless, one derives clear impressions of the man. Summarizing such impressions, I would remark, first, his great capacity for work; second, the clarity of his views; and third, the remarkable fluency of his pen. On the first point it will suffice to quote Bancroft's description of the daily routine he set himself.

[13] Hubert Howe Bancroft, *Literary Industries* (San Francisco, 1890), 8.

"For years it was my custom to rise at seven, breakfast at half past seven, and write from eight to one, when I lunched or dined. The afternoon was devoted to recreation and exercise. Usually I would get in an hour's writing before a six o'clock tea or dinner, as the case might be, and four hours afterwards, making ten hours in all for the day."[14] As to the second point, these volumes carry their own testimony. He was not blind to contrary evidence, and except on a few matters his opinions were expressed with urbanity; yet, by and large, he was a man of pronounced views.

The easy discursiveness of these volumes is proof of the readiness of his pen. On this head he reports that, when he first began to write, composing was a labored operation. Later he learned to concentrate on what to write, rather than how to express it. When full of his subject, he sometimes turned out twenty or thirty pages in a day. His average over a period of time he puts at "not more than eight badly scratched manuscript pages a day," a phenomenal rate and sufficient to account for approximately three volumes a year. He adds that in the latter part of his literary career his mind became "more tractable," and he "never waited for either ideas or words."[15]

[14] *Ibid.*, 682.
[15] *Ibid.*, 682–683.

16

Process of Authorship

I have tried many occupations, and there is no kind of work, I venture to say, so wearing as literary labor.

Hubert Howe Bancroft, *Literary Industries,* 236

EVEN MORE than by their bulk, Bancroft's *Works* are rendered distinctive by the coöperative method of their authorship. They were produced in a literary workshop, by a division of labor which had many of the attributes of the factory method, the assembly line, and mass production. Coöperative research lay behind them, and they were, at least to a degree, staff-written. Bancroft took great pride in having devised a system whereby many hands and many minds could be brought to bear upon the tremendous task that he had outlined. Yet, because the method was novel, it was not generally understood; and because it was not understood, it was not universally approved. Criticism has tended to center on this process of authorship, rather than on the intrinsic qualities of the *Works,* and it has been the primary factor in determining the estimate of them by the press, the historical profession, and the people generally.

From the moment of his decision to do the history of the Pacific states Bancroft realized that he would need to employ assistants. He was not immediately aware of the magnitude of the task—initially he was thinking in terms of much less than thirty-nine volumes,—nor did he envision at the outset the extent to which he could make use of fellow workers. The technique evolved with the project, and in the end both were far more elaborate than originally expected. The coöperative method thus rose out of necessity. It was not invented at one stroke, but developed gradually through experimentation and by trial and error. Though never completely satisfied with it, Bancroft reckoned the system one of his principal contributions to scholarship and insisted that only by some such method could real unity be achieved in a coöperative work.

Bancroft's histories began, as all books should, with an idea. His idea—hit upon, as previously related, after much toying with the project for a Pacific states cyclopedia—was to write the history of these far western states, from the sources and comprehensively. It was not, as yet, a detailed plan; neither how many volumes would be required, nor what should be the distribution of space to the various topics, was clearly in view. On both these points, and also on particularized tables of contents for the separate volumes, Bancroft was content to wait until work on the materials could yield familiarity with the many ramifications of his vast subject and thus point out the space distribution that would be most appropriate.

In the beginning he was thinking in terms of just a few volumes. As late as 1878, after the Indian detour had led him to publish five unexpected volumes on *Native Races,* he was still counting on no more than fourteen volumes of history.[1] Four years later, on the eve of the release of the first installments of the histories, the plan had expanded, but thirty-nine was not to be recognized as the magic number until a year or two later. By 1884 the plan began to acquire rigidity. Issuing the volumes in chronological sequence, for example, meant that it was necessary to know how many volumes would be given to Central America, Mexico, the north Mexican states, and California, so that the first Oregon volume would bear the proper number in the set. The later installments of several parts of the *Works,* therefore, had to be moulded to fit the

[1] Hubert Howe Bancroft to Mrs. Frances Fuller Victor, August 1, 1878. Cited in W. A. Morris, "The Origin and Authorship of the Bancroft Pacific States Publications," *Oregon Historical Quarterly,* IV (1903), 335.

intervals of shelf space that had been reserved for them. Usually this meant compressing the narrative, though sometimes the problem was met by printing sections in smaller type.[2]

Meanwhile, Bancroft and his staff had been trying their hands at historical research and writing. The first efforts on record were Oak's cutting up of duplicate copies and severalizing the parts, Bancroft's fling at the conquest of Mexico, the enthusiastic reading program on the part of his medievalist, and the copying *in extenso* of divers voyage narratives. From these fruitless experiments they moved on to an attempt at indexing. Again the method first employed was not satisfactory, but after some tinkering and simplifying the results improved. Bancroft continued the indexing to the extent of some $35,000 worth of time. This investment was essentially one of tooling for production.

The index was susceptible of two uses. Often it was employed to lay before a researcher or writer the complete literature on a given subject; as Bancroft put it, "each volume opened at the page." At other times it was used to guide the note takers, who were another principal element in the literary workshop. Their work, like that of the indexers, was pedestrian. It required a certain knack, which not everyone had, but it reduced itself to a fairly simple task of reading and abstracting. Those who participated in the writing did some of the note taking, but much of it was done by subordinate members of the staff, under the direction of Oak or Nemos. Quantities of these notes are still preserved in the library, where they have had a much greater continuing utility than the index. Indicative of the amount of note taking carried on is Bancroft's estimate of $80,000 as its expense. This also may be classified as tooling for production.

In format, however, the notes are something of a shock. They are uniform in being clearly labeled with respect to source and subject, but they are on slips of paper of assorted

---

[2] See chapters 13 and 14, above.

sizes, having been made on sheets of foolscap which were then cut up to separate the individual notes. The filing system was still more fantastic. Instead of the tabbed manila folders that modern office practice would recommend, Bancroft used clothesline, clothespins, and paper bags such as one is accustomed to associate with the grocery. In these bags the slips of the note takers were filed by subject until wanted in the writing.

Nothing else so primitive figured in the procedure, but there were other reminders that this was the pre-typewriter, pre-fountain pen age. Index, notes, first drafts, rewritings, and copy for the printer were all handwritten, usually in ink, but occasionally in pencil. The work was done at tables or desks as the worker chose. The proprietor's own preference was to work at a standing desk, with his materials spread out on a revolving table at his elbow. An unusual library practice was that smoking was permitted. The workday was also that of a bygone generation—from 7:15 A.M. to 6:00 P.M., with half an hour off for lunch.[3]

Many of the details of indexing and note taking were designed to fit the special requirements of his project, but in using assistants for these purposes Bancroft was merely doing what many historians had done before and many since. It was more revolutionary for him to propose to put assistants to actual writing, but this he did, and on a considerable scale.

In making these assignments Bancroft's first expectation was that his assistants would be able to give him rough drafts that would expedite his writing. As early as the Indian volumes, he discovered that some of his men could do much more, and he encouraged them to turn out printable copy.

---

[3] So described on the card entitled *General Rules of the Bancroft Company,* Bancroft Library. Elsewhere it appears that the hours were eight to twelve and one to six; Bancroft, *Literary Industries,* 562–563. From the Bancroft Library Time Book, March 1883—May 1887, a manuscript volume in the Bancroft Library, it appears that, although some men worked ten or twelve hours, a nine-hour day was standard.

HUBERT HOWE BANCROFT IN 1879

HUBERT HOWE BANCROFT IN 1882

Indeed, his concept of the ideal assistant came to be one who could supply copy that would need a minimum of revision. Although the theory still was that he would go over everything and would be responsible for the final manuscript, he accepted without modification much that they wrote. Wherefore his assistants might better be called collaborators; indeed, they have often been hailed as joint authors of the *Works*.

The fact that they participated in the writing was never a secret. Bancroft did not deny it, did not try to conceal it, and never apologized for it. On the contrary, he gloried in it. In his prefaces, in his releases to the press, and in his advertising brochures he stressed the coöperative authorship as an evidence of the great quantity of compacted erudition which his set of volumes represented. Over and over he proclaimed that no individual working alone could possibly have produced them. His frankness, however, did not extend to a specification of the parts written by particular members of the staff. Except in the preface to *Native Races,* where he made a fairly precise statement of the contributions of Harcourt, Fisher, Goldschmidt, and Oak, he studiously avoided tabbing any chapter or volume as written by a specific staff member.

To justify this action he adduced two reasons, one practical, the other purposeful. On the practical side, he insisted that to clutter the set with names of contributors would handicap the sales campaign. Here he probably was correct. In authorship his name at the outset was as obscure as that of any of his assistants, but it was established in the realm of publishing and bookselling, and a single name, furthermore, could more readily win acceptance with the public. Over and above this practical consideration was his determination to stress the essential unity of the set in its interrelated coverage of the histories of the Pacific states. He published the books, therefore, without by-lines, and as "The Works of Hubert Howe Bancroft."

Besides calling forth severe criticism, the merits of which will presently be discussed, this action drew a veil over the actual authorship of any particular passage and gave rise to a protracted debate concerning where the credits should go. Through internal criticism of the published *Works,* through scrutiny of such notes, manuscripts, proofsheets, and corrected copy as have been preserved, and through analysis of statements of persons who were in position to know—through these three methods it is possible to approach the question of authorship.

Any reader or sampler of the *Works* will discover that they are not absolutely uniform throughout. Some parts are more florid than others; some are written with greater terseness; others, with a plodding style, with a larger number of digressions, with more classical allusions, with more frequent shafts of humor, with more dispassionateness, or with greater fervor. These variations, together with certain shifts in vocabulary and rhetoric, seem to betoken diverse authorship. Before accepting this evidence as conclusive, however, it should be recalled that the writing was spread out over a score of years, a period long enough for any writer to develop different skills and new habits. The subject matter, furthermore, was so diverse that it called for different styles to fit its varying moods. Narratives of the Spaniards in search of Monterey, of the recreations of the southern California *paisanos,* of the Donner Party snowbound in the Sierra, of the increased acreage planted to wheat, and of a vigilance committee in session might come from the same pen and yet exhibit great variety in style. Stylistic multiformity thus indicates, but falls somewhat short of proving, multiple authorship.

The notes, manuscripts, revised manuscripts, proofsheets, and so on, that have been preserved are fragmentary.[4] Intrastaff memoranda, interlined changes in contrasting handwrit-

[4] They fill several fair-sized bins in the Bancroft Library, but do not contain the complete preliminary paper work for a single one of the thirty-nine volumes.

ing, and marginal notations prove what we already know, that a number of persons were at work. Some of the manuscript is in the form of clean copy, evidently transcribed for the printer, and corresponds to the final typescript such as might be struck off by a present-day stenographer. These naturally offer few clues to individual contributions. The less clean copy is more revealing.

That for Chapter XXIII of *Literary Industries*,[5] for example, clearly illustrates Bancroft's use of a draft supplied by one of his assistants. The chapter begins in Nemos' hand, with corrections, word changes, deletion of sentences, insertions of sentences and paragraphs in Bancroft's hand, and ends with a dozen pages written out by Bancroft. In the first paragraph Bancroft deleted one unnecessary word, and added a quotation from Maudsley and a closing sentence. The second and third paragraphs are his. The fourth is Nemos', with two words struck out. The fifth saw two changes in wording, the addition of two sentences, and the elimination of one of Nemos'. In the sixth paragraph Bancroft changed one word. Then follow fourteen successive paragraphs in Bancroft's hand.[6]

Nemos' next paragraph was accepted with three alterations: The clause "Not that I am disposed by any means to prolixity" is made to read "Not that I am inclined to prolixity." The phrase "absolutely impossible" is shortened to "impossible." And the expression "I trust I never for a moment forgot" is changed to "I could not but remember." Each revision is an improvement. The same might be said of the changes in a paragraph a half dozen pages farther on, telling about the departure of two of his assistants who had been offered the editorship of the *Overland Monthly*. This is Nemos' wording as modified by Bancroft. "The young men behaved very honorably [Bancroft substituted: *very well*] about it. They immediately informed me of the offer, asked me to

[5] Bancroft, *Literary Industries*, 562–591.

[6] *Ibid.*, 564–568.

advise them what they should do, and assured me they would not accept unless with my full approbation [*with my approbation*]. Although they were deep in my work, although I must lose in a great measure the results of their last year's labor [*their last year's training*], and although I should have to teach new men and delay publication, yet I did not hesitate. I told them if I were they I should go [*I told them to go*]: the pay was better, the position was more conspicuous [*more prominent*] and their work would be lighter."[7]

The middle third of this chapter[8] is in the main as Nemos wrote it. Changes average two or three to a page, and include, besides mere revisions in wording, injection of comments and addition of detail. For example, to what Nemos had written about the fire hazard in the Market Street building Bancroft added a paragraph describing the steps taken toward greater safety after the narrow escape in November, 1873. Twenty copyists were put to work transcribing all that had been written, but that could not at once be printed; letterpress copies were made and kept at Oakville and at Bancroft's home, the original being retained on the fifth floor.[9] Several of the revisions in this chapter partake of this same character; they are not merely stylistic, but enrich the account.

Who, then, should be acclaimed author of this chapter? It is obvious that Nemos produced the first draft, after which Bancroft went over it with care, and through changes, insertions, and additions was the actual writer of more than half the chapter. Clearly, he made the whole chapter his in the sense of seeing to it that each sentence and paragraph carried the content that he wanted it to have. Yet in terms of origin it was not entirely his. In terms of responsibility, however, Nemos cannot be held accountable. He merely started the writing; Bancroft took it over and determined the final content and reading. Though not the complete author, he was completely responsible.

---

[7] *Ibid.*, 576. [8] *Ibid.*, 570–579. [9] *Ibid.*, 573.

Other manuscript fragments preserved in the Bancroft Library supply similar evidence. In certain of them it appears that the draft supplied by an assistant, though doubtless read and considered, was replaced by an entirely new write-up. In others, whole paragraphs were incorporated; and in still others, the changes were merely verbal and nominal. The manuscript copy preserved represents hardly more than a tenth of the 39-volume set. It happens, furthermore, to be most abundant on *British Columbia, California Inter Pocula, Literary Industries,* and the early chapters of *Central America* and *Nevada,* of which Bancroft admittedly was the primary author. And, of course, the notes, drafts, and manuscripts have no endorsements testifying to the extent of their use by Bancroft or other members of the staff. They provide, therefore, an insecure basis for generalization, except as they make clear that at times the process of authorship was exactly as Bancroft described it:[10] indexing and note gathering by assistants, preparation of a draft by a number of the staff, and revision and rewriting by Bancroft in person.

Although this description implies that the method described was always followed, Bancroft elsewhere records that he expected his assistants to write for publication. Savage, Nemos, Oak, and Mrs. Victor corroborate and allege that large parts of the set had only perfunctory attention from the chief and were really the work of other members of the staff. Their allotments of credit, though not complete and not in perfect coincidence, are the best basis we have for specifying the parts on which the several staff members worked. A summary analysis of their reports is presented here in tabular form.[11]

---

[10] *Ibid.,* 564–568.

[11] It is based on Henry L. Oak's Estimate of Authorship of Bancroft's *Works,* MS, Bancroft Library; on William Nemos' estimate, incorporated in the foregoing; on Henry L. Oak, *"Literary Industries" in a New Light* (San Francisco, 1893); on Thomas Savage, Autobiography, MS, Bancroft Library; and Frances Fuller Victor, as reported in W. A. Morris, "The Origin and Authorship of the Bancroft Pacific States Histories."

Work		Bancroft	Harcourt	Fisher	Gold-schmidt	Oak	Nem
Native Races	I	1/3	1/6	1/6		1/6	1/6
	II		All				
	III			11/16	5/16		
	IV					All	
	V					All	
Central America	I	1/2				1/6	1/3
	II	1/18					1/2
	III						
Mexico	I	1/5–1/4					3/4–4
	II						2/3
	III						1/3–1
	IV	1/12					1/4
	V						1/4
	VI						2/3
North Mexican States and Texas	I					All[d]	
	II						1/4
Arizona and New Mexico						All	
California	I					All	
	II					All	
	III					All	
	IV					All	
	V					All	
	VI	1/14				1/15	5/8
	VII						3/8
Nevada, Colorado, and Wyoming		1/17					
Utah		1/3					
Northwest Coast	I	1/2				1/2	
	II	7/8				1/8	
Oregon	I						
	II						
Washington, Idaho, and Montana							
British Columbia		1/2					1/4
Alaska		1/2					
California Pastoral		All					
California Inter Pocula		9/10[g]					
Popular Tribunals	I	All					
	II	All[g]					
Essays and Miscellany		All					
Literary Industries		9/10					1/1
Total volumes		9 5/6	1 1/6	41/48	5/16	10	5 1/

APPORTIONMENT OF AUTHORSHIP CREDITS FOR BANCROFT'S "WORKS"

Peatfield	Bates	Kuhn	Savage	Griffin	Victor	Bowman	Petroff	Remarks
								[a]Rewritten by Kuhn [b]With Peatfield [c]Rewritten by Nemos
1/12	1/4	1/3 1/5 [c]	All					
1/12 1/12 1/4 1/12 1/12			1/4 1/3 1/3 2/3 1/4	1/12				
3/4								[d]Using an earlier MS by Harcourt
					1/3 5/8			
					16/17			
	2/3							
					1/8 [e]			[e]Rewritten by Oak
					All All			
	1/4 1/3				All	1/4	1/4	[f]With Bowman
					1/10			[g]Some assistance by wife and daughter
1 5/12	1 1/2	1/2	2 5/6	1/12	4 9/10	1/4	1/4	

APPORTIONMENT OF AUTHORSHIP CREDITS FOR BANCROFT'S "WORKS"

The table reveals several facts about the operations of Bancroft's literary workshop. The scattering and haphazard distribution of assignments, particularly for the earlier volumes on Central America and Mexico, suggests that the governing factor was the availability rather than the expertness of individual members of the staff. Of Bancroft and Nemos, versatility was expected in the later stages of the work also. For others we can discern at least a measure of specialization: Savage on Spanish America; Peatfield on Texas and related phases of Mexican history; Oak on the Spanish borderlands, including northern Mexico, New Mexico, and early California; and Mrs. Victor on the American Northwest. Mrs. Victor's specialization is the more pronounced if it is borne in mind that her contributions to the *Northwest Coast* and to *California Inter Pocula* were originally intended for the Oregon volumes and were shifted because that manuscript had become too long.[12]

For all its complexity, the chart is in places misleadingly simple. In *Mexico* I, for example, Bancroft's and Nemos' shares are intermixed as well as indeterminate. In *Central America* II and *Mexico* III, to take other examples, the fractions are approximate and their location uncertain. In *California* VI and *Alaska* there is obvious inaccuracy, because the sum of the parts is an improper fraction. Thus any attempt to attach names to the several parts runs afoul. For certain parts no name can be mentioned with assurance; for others the workers obviously were several, and their exact contributions are a matter of uncertainty.

A number of overlaps in credit are also to be considered. We notice Nemos writing with Peatfield, Nemos writing with Bowman, a Nemos draft rewritten by Kuhn, a Kuhn draft rewritten by Nemos, Harcourt's manuscript on Lower Cali-

[12] As set forth in Henry L. Oak, *"Literary Industries" in a New Light,* 38, 43; W. A. Morris, "The Origin and Authorship of the Bancroft Pacific States Histories," *Oregon Historical Quarterly,* IV (1903), 353.

fornia utilized by Oak and Nemos, a Bancroft draft redone by Mrs. Victor, one of hers rewritten by Oak, and Bancroft assisted by members of his family. Consultation within the staff must have been a common occurrence; Savage, for example, is referred to as the acknowledged expert on the Spanish language, to whom difficult problems of translation were carried as a matter of course. More significant, the general plan of procedure was the same for all the histories, not merely in the budgeting of space and in the setting up of a rough outline, but also in such matters as the chronological approach, the use of the best source as the chief basis for a given part of the narrative, the quotation in footnotes of variant testimony as assembled by the note takers, the citation of authorities as marshaled through the index, and the generous use of biographical footnotes. The set's high degree of uniformity in philosophy, interpretation, and general tenor also points to staff writing rather than individual attack upon the job of authorship. Oak and Nemos unquestionably passed upon much that was handed in by other members of the staff; and Bancroft, though he did not achieve his ideal of a 100 per cent check, went over much of the manuscript before sending it to the printer.

A hint of Bancroft's proclivity for advising and directing his assistants is afforded by the series of letters he sent to Mrs. Victor in the latter part of 1884, when she was taking up the history of Nevada, Colorado, and Wyoming. He wrote that Franklin D. Richards would send extracts of Mormon material on Nevada in accordance with a prepared memorandum. Then he advised Mrs. Victor to draw up a general plan for the volume "as the men do on Mexico," so that each section could be given its due proportion. He recommended the Utah volume as a model for treatment of the earliest explorations, reminded her that Oak's work on New Mexico would tie in, suggested several books to be consulted, forwarded dictations with instructions on their use, and counseled against the adoption of Helen Hunt Jackson's views on the Colorado Indian wars. He suggested additional references and reported that he was getting a dictation from the editor of the *Rocky Mountain News* that was "almost pure history" and would serve as the basis of the narrative on that state. He indicated how many pages he would allot to each of the three states, and he instructed that special attention be accorded to the cattle industry, which he characterized as "one of the most marvelous and important of modern times."[13]

This detailed advice and much more was directed to the one person on his staff who had previous experience as an author. It would seem reasonable to suppose that his direction of other staff members was even more detailed and specific. The exact extent of this supervision, however, cannot be established by documentary evidence, by testimony, or by internal criticism of the *Works*.

Mrs. Victor, soon after retiring from the staff, became insistent that she deserved recognition as an author. In Oregon and Utah newspapers she set forth her claims at length, and at the San Francisco winter fair in 1893 she exhibited four of the Bancroft volumes with a special preface inserted and her name displayed as the author.[14] Oak, likewise, put in a belated bid for fame. He issued a pamphlet to correct Bancroft's picture of procedures in the literary workshop, and presented to his alma mater, Dartmouth College, a set of ten Bancroft volumes with his name inserted as author. The press, before and after, raised a hue and cry about the manner in which Bancroft had been "a purloiner of other people's brains." And Morris, in 1903, damned him roudly for unprofessional conduct, for confusing the purchase of publishing rights with the

---

[13] Hubert Howe Bancroft to Mrs. Frances Fuller Victor, September 11, 21; October 7, 11, 13, 25; November 2, 8, 9, 1884; October 9, 20; November 1, 9, 17, 1885; cited by Morris, "The Origin and Authorship of the Bancroft Pacific States Histories," 324–330.

[14] Morris, "The Origin and Authorship of the Bancroft Pacific States Histories," 344–345.

right to claim authorship, and with stigmatizing the *Works* with anonymity.[15]

To the earlier of these complaints and charges Bancroft made emphatic response; thereafter he ceased arguing. In his rebuttal he made much of the fact that, at the time of their first employment, all his assistants had been given to understand that whatever they produced would be his to use as he saw fit—to publish as it was, to revise or rewrite, or to discard. Proceeding then to a less legalistic argument, he insisted that the staff members had not been working on their own. All had been on his payroll, operating under his direction and on projects of his selection. All had been the beneficiaries, furthermore, of the extraordinary aids to research and writing that he had made available: the great collection of books, newspapers, and original documents, the index, and the voluminous notes.[16] Bancroft was somewhat less than frank in maintaining that he was personally responsible for the final write-up of every portion of the *Works,* but he certainly might have added that he took complete charge of all the details of publishing, including the proofreading, indexing, and other drudgeries that often fall upon authors, and that he supplied the will to get the job done.

The conclusion perhaps should be that neither side was right. The staff members owed so much to their chief and the facilities he had provided that they could not with propriety claim authorship of individual volumes. Bancroft, on the other hand, was confusing the right to publish with the rights of authorship. And, having leaned so heavily on some of these helpers, he should have made more open and precise acknowledgment of what they had done.

Just how these acknowledgments should have been made is not easy to say. Even for the most independent member of the staff a by-line on a title page would have been inexact and

[15] *Ibid.,* 290.

[16] Well summarized in Henry L. Oak, *"Literary Industries" in a New Light,* 52–53.

misleading. Elsewhere in the set, where the merging of effort was much greater, such a device would have been impossibly cumbersome and meaningless. In the prefaces, however, statements could have been made giving recognition to those to whom it was due. Such acknowledgments would have done no damage to the sales campaign, would have gratified the staff members, and would have protected Bancroft from much of the criticism subsequently leveled at him.

The arguments recited above relative to the employment of his assistants, the plan of revising their drafts, and the desire to stress the unity of the entire set, had much to do, I am convinced, with determining Bancroft's line of procedure. Reasonable conjecture offers two additional elements in explanation. First, his background as a businessman, bookseller, and independent publisher had not given him an adequate realization of the pride of authorship that almost every writer has, or of the store that scholars would set by an explicit statement of authorship. Second, having begun to issue the set as his *Works,* he found that the line of least resistance was to continue, in spite of having shifted the process of authorship in the direction of finished writing by staff members. This combination of circumstances accounts for the inadequate credits to the members of the staff.

Omission of these credits was a serious mistake, probably the most serious of Bancroft's entire career. Opening the door to criticism, it invited a number of savage diatribes,[17] which

[17] For example, the following: "Apropos of our great Pacific Coast 'historian' whom the New York *Sun* so admires, I am told that in the 'literary exhibit' at the Mechanics' Pavillon are publicly displayed several volumes of 'Bancroft's Works' labelled on the back with the name of Frances Fuller Victor, who wrote them. That is her way of claiming her own, and it is to be hoped that the same thing will be done at Chicago by not only her but every living writer whose work Mr. Bancroft claims as 'his' because he paid for it. Most of the names are now adorning little headboards out in the cemeteries—a result of Mr. Bancroft's scale of wages. It was he who, estimating the number of his hack-writers who were dead of overwork and undereating, wept to think that Nature allowed him nothing for their skulls as 'returned empties'." Ambrose Bierce, "Prattle," San Francisco *Examiner,* January 29, 1893.

led many persons to believe that the set was altogether the work of hired hands and that Bancroft's contribution was merely financial. Even to the more discerning, this effort to stress the integral character of the *Works* obscured the coöperative method of historical research and writing which Bancroft regarded as one of his major contributions.

The truth of the whole matter is not best represented by the caption "The Works of Hubert Howe Bancroft," nor by the schedules made by Oak, Nemos, Savage, and Mrs. Victor, where the work of the several writers is rather sharply segregated. In charting the authorship it would be more realistic to take a sheet of paper; stipple its entire surface to indicate the detailed planning of the thirty-nine volumes; shade its entire surface to represent the gathering of the collection, its regimentation by means of the index, and the assembling of pertinent data by the army of note takers; crosshatch the entire surface to represent the subsidizing of the workers through the wages paid them; enter then with appropriate symbols the particular assignments and contributions of the individual writers—Bancroft, Oak, Nemos, and the rest; and finally, retouch the entire chart to indicate the revisions and rewriting, some of it done by Oak and Nemos, but much by Bancroft in person. A chart fashioned on this wise would be the most valid representation of the process of authorship whereby the *Works* were built. Parts of the structure were erected by separate artisans, but upon a common foundation, out of materials supplied by the enterpriser, in accordance with a detailed master plan, and with alterations ranging from minor to major made under the supervision of the chief builder.

Coöperative writing of American history, though occasionally proposed, had not been applied to a large project prior to Bancroft's day. In the 'eighties and 'nineties it was invoked for three other monumental sets, Winsor's *Narrative and Critical History of America,* the American Commonwealths series, and the American Statesmen biographies. Since that time, coöperative ventures have become more common, the most conspicuous examples being the American Nation volumes, the Chronicles of America, the History of American Life, and the Dictionary of American Biography. A measurement of the Bancroft method is possible through comparison with these other efforts.

Bancroft, it will be recalled, built his staff out of nonprofessional recruits. Winsor enlisted a coterie of Harvard historians to contribute to his set, but relied more heavily upon amateurs of standing. Approximately the same observation may be made concerning the American Commonwealths and Statesmen volumes. Professional historians participated, but some of the most notable contributions came from outside the fold, for example, Josiah Royce's *California,* Carl Schurz's *Henry Clay,* and Theodore Roosevelt's *Gouverneur Morris.* As a protest against certain shortcomings in the Winsor volumes, and in determination to represent the best that scientific history had to offer, the American Nation series was made strictly professional. A few historians by avocation wrote for the Chronicles, the American Life authors were historians all, while the editors of the D.A.B. enlisted 2,243 assorted contributors. The trend certainly has been in the direction of greater dependence upon trained, professional personnel, though not to the complete exclusion of others. That Bancroft did otherwise was a function of his time, place, and topic, and not an indication of a distrust of institutionalized scholars.

Several of these sets are dwarfed by Bancroft's *Works,* and even the most ambitious does not match his bulk. With the possible exception of the monographs in the American Life series, furthermore, they have been to a large degree synthetic. Most of the sketches in the Dictionary, for example, summarize the information available in print and are contributions to the convenience of scholars rather than products of original research. Certain volumes in the American Nation series, notably Frederick Jackson Turner's *The Rise of the New West,* were hewed out of the sources, and a few of the Chronicles "contain the concentrated essence of much special research."[18] The avowed purpose of the latter series, however, was to dramatize and popularize; while, in launching the American Nation, Albert Bushnell Hart, the editor, had stressed the need for an intelligent summarization of the present knowledge of American history. In the Winsor history the primary aim was to make accessible to students a summary of scattered material and to give them a guide to the sources. This purpose was implemented by extensive editorial notes and by critical essays on bibliography attached to each chapter, and it is these bibliographical appendages that make the *Narrative and Critical History* useful still.

Bancroft certainly purported to do something different. Parts of his *Works* were tabulations of data, most of which had existed in print, though so scattered as to be not conveniently available. *Native Races,* for example, contained large sections of this kind. Other portions—instance, *California Pastoral*—were expositions calculated to attract the general reader. The core of the *Works,* however, though written in the light of a thorough combing of the existing literature, was bottomed on source materials, including oral, manuscript, newspaper, and pamphlet. To a far larger degree than in any of these other coöperative works, he was breaking new ground and cultivating soils that had not previously yielded a crop.

In methodology also a distinction should be drawn. Each of these enterprises began with central planning—which determined the general nature of the series and the space allowable to individual items. Having drawn his assignment, however, together with the specifications governing length, form, and tenor, the contributor to any of these sets worked independ-

[18] Michael Kraus, *The Writing of American History* (New York, 1937), 587.

ently, in his own town, in his own cell, with such materials as his own initiative could turn up, shaping, formulating, and interpreting solely in the light of his own knowledge and judgment. Referring to the Winsor volumes, for which only the preliminary planning and the final general editing were centralized, Bancroft scouted the setup as a mere pretense at coöperative writing.[19] In his establishment, by contrast, the whole process of authorship was brought under one roof. Marshaled there were the necessary materials, systematized by the index, and prepared by the note takers. There Bancroft and his collaborators made a joint attack. Leeway was left for individual effort and for personal achievement, but under circumstances offering every facility for conference, interchange of ideas, and correlation of work.

Logic would argue that the procedure in the literary workshop must have been thus. The chart of credits points to the same conclusion and is corroborated by the testimony of Josiah Royce, who was a guest researcher in the library throughout the summer of 1884. "From both Mr. Bancroft and his able collaborators," says Royce, "I received, during all this time, frequent and most friendly oral advice." Further, "I am much indebted, for the formation of many of my opinions and arguments, to the suggestions gained through conversation and correspondence with Mr. Bancroft and his collaborators."[20] In Bancroft's library, one would gather, coöperation was a reality.

Although coöperative writing in the Bancroft manner has not characterized the larger joint enterprises in American history, there have been modern applications of methods strikingly similar. The editors of *Time* and *Fortune,* Walt Disney in his earlier productions, and the Writers' Program of the Works Progress Administration afford what seem to be close parallels, not to mention a number of eminent historians who,

---

[19] Bancroft, *Literary Industries,* 763–768.

[20] Josiah Royce, *California* (Boston, 1886), viii, ix.

TIME BOOK for the Month of March 1883

NAMES.	1–13	14–31
Murray	/ / / S / / / / / / S / –	/ / / / S ½ – / / S / / ½ ½ /
Kuhn	½ ½ ½ Gone to	Los Angeles to see
Peatfield	½ / / S / ½ ½ ½ ½ ½ / S Sick	rainedkee S ½ / / / – / S – ½ ½ ½ ½ /
Allsopp	/ / / S / / / / / / S / /	/ / / / S / / / / / / / S / / / / / /
Mrs Victor	/ / / S / / / / / / S Trip	to S Oregon S ——
Savage	/ / / S / / / / / / S / /	/ / / / S / / / / / / S / / / / / /
Gilmour	/ / / S / / / / / / S / /	/ / / / S / / / / / / S / / / / / /
Benson	/ / / S / / / / / / S / /	/ / / / S / / / / / / S / / / / / /
Rasmuss	½ ½ / S ½ ½ ½ ½ ½ / S / ½	/ ½ ½ / S / ½ ½ ½ ½ / S ½ ½ ½ ½ / /
Matthies	—— S died in S 6th	Hospital S 28.2.03 S
De Lery	/ / / S ½ / ½ / ½ / S / /	½ ½ / ½ S Left – S
Newkirk	/ / / S ½ / ½ / ½ / S / /	/ / / / S ½ / ½ ½ / / S ½ / / / / /
Pearson	/ – / S / ½ / / ½ / S ½ /	– / ½ / S ½ / / ½ / / S / ½ / ½ / /
Black	/ / / S / / / / / / S / /	/ / / / S / / / / / ½ S / / / / / /
Bates	/ ½ / ½ / ½ / / / – S ——	½ ½ / / S ½ / / ½ / / S – / / / / /

*Overdrawn $170

BANCROFT LIBRARY TIME BOOK, MARCH, 1883

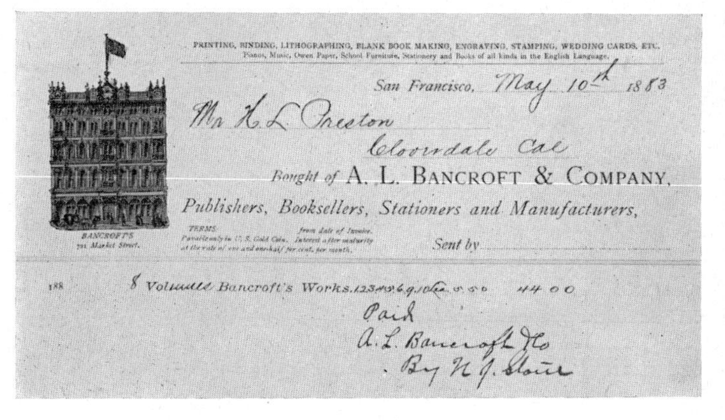

PRINTING, BINDING, LITHOGRAPHING, BLANK BOOK MAKING, ENGRAVING, STAMPING, WEDDING CARDS, ETC.
Pianos, Music, Owen Paper, School Furniture, Stationery and Books of all kinds in the English Language.

San Francisco, May 10th 1883

Mr H. L. Preston
Cloverdale Cal

Bought of A. L. BANCROFT & COMPANY,
Publishers, Booksellers, Stationers and Manufacturers,

BANCROFT'S
721 Market Street.

TERMS from date of Invoice. Payable only in U. S. Gold Coin. Interest after maturity at the rate of one and one-half per cent. per month.

Sent by

188 8 Volumes Bancroft's Works. 1 2 3 4 5 6 9 10 Ea 5.50 44 00

Paid
A. L. Bancroft Co
By N. J. Stone

RECEIPT FOR PAYMENT BY A SUBSCRIBER

PAYABLE JANUARY 31, 1889

(3)

No. 1054.

The History Company

PUBLISHERS OF THE

Works of Hubert Howe Bancroft

History Building

San Francisco, January 21st, 1889

H. L. Preston, Esq

Cloverdale, Cal.

Dear Sir: In accordance with the terms of the special agreement we have with you, to wit: to pay for TWO VOLUMES JANUARY 31st AND TWO VOLUMES JULY 31st EACH YEAR, by draft, we have this day drawn upon you for collection of the amount due, $ 11.00, through Cloverdale Banking & Com'l Co. ~~Bank.~~

Volume 35 shipped 7.12.88 $ 5.50

" 23 " 10.12.88 $ 5.50

$ 11.00

Yours truly,

THE HISTORY COMPANY

By A. S. Latham

DRAFT ON A SUBSCRIBER

if the general belief is correct, have learned how to make full use of research assistants.

Notwithstanding this contemporary revival, the prevailing attitude is to frown upon Bancroft's method. His critics have been legion, have been harsh, and, if my estimate is correct, have been picayunish. Comprehension of his process of authorship, nevertheless, would not be complete without some notice of the charges preferred.

One such complaint is that he was a hard taskmaster. In the operation of his literary workshop he naturally followed the standards of his day and of his world, which was that of business. His printed card setting forth the general rules of the Bancroft Company specified the hours as "7:15 Sharp to 6 P.M., Half an Hour for Lunch." Salaries, the card continued, would be paid on the last day of the month. Employees might purchase goods at wholesale rates for cash; no books would be lent; and holidays were listed as "22d February, 4th of July, Thanksgiving, Christmas and New Year's Afternoons."[21] Not satisfied with a ten-and-a-quarter-hour day, some of Bancroft's men wanted to add to their earnings by returning for night work. For a while he permitted it, but, finding that the total output was not increased, he called a halt to this practice. Subsequently the standard day was reduced to nine hours. There are time sheets that certify to a sixty-hour week.[22]

Accustomed as we are to such phrases as the "eight-hour day" and the "forty-hour week," this program seems archaic. For literary work in particular the hours seem unconscionably long, yet not impossibly so. As late as the 1920's the present writer throve in a clerical job for which the ten-hour day prevailed, and among his acquaintances today he numbers several researchers and writers who maintain that pace. Bancroft unquestionably was equal to it. Elsewhere he speaks of his

---

[21] Card, *General Rules of the Bancroft Company,* Bancroft Library.

[22] Bancroft, *Literary Industries,* 562–563; Bancroft Library Time Book, March, 1883–May, 1887, and various payroll sheets, for example, that of August 6, 1887, MSS, Bancroft Library.

customary hours when working at home: rising at seven, breakfast at seven-thirty, at his desk from eight to one, lunch, followed by a few hours of out-of-door activity, another hour at the desk before dinner, and an after-dinner session until eleven.[23] This also is a recipe for a ten-hour day. Nevertheless, if Bancroft were reconstructing his literary workshop today, the hours certainly would be shorter.

Apart from the matter of hours, Bancroft had some other attributes of the taskmaster. Pay was never figured on a piece-work basis, but there was a natural tendency to expect to see results and to measure them quantitatively. The medievalist, for example, who read with such enthusiasm but procrastinated so long about putting anything on paper, was not regarded as a satisfactory employee. Others on the staff were encouraged to produce. Mrs. Victor was praised for making rapid progress with the first Oregon volume and was chided for lowered output on her later assignments. Bancroft's attitude was determined not merely by his desire to get his money's worth, and not merely by his wish to see the job finished. Influenced also by his own capacity to turn out copy for the printer, he had difficulty in understanding why his associates had so much trouble attaining half his speed.

Subtly and otherwise he applied pressure. The most effective device doubtless was through advancing parts of the set to publication even before the manuscript for a given volume had been completed. Certain portions were written with the compositor nagging the heels of the writing staff. Such acceleration jeopardized and perhaps damaged the quality of what was written. Yet, despite these tactics that smacked of the sweatshop, Bancroft kept the respect and the good will of his men. He was able to assert, "I believe I never have had a serious misunderstanding with any one of my regular assistants. We worked together as friends, side by side, as in one common interest."[24]

[23] Bancroft, *Literary Industries,* 682. [24] *Ibid.,* 585.

Again, it is asserted that he employed an erudite gentleman to supply literary quotations and classical allusions with which to spice the prosaic narratives. Harcourt certainly applied for such a post, representing that it would be consistent with Bancroft's general program of coöperation and specialization. Bancroft's own insistence is that he rejected the proposal, on the grounds that he might as well turn to one of the published anthologies of quotations as to use another's selections. He read omnivorously, that much is certain; and it is easy to believe his assertion that he kept on the lookout for quotable morsels of wisdom or phrasing. His technique apparently was not to rely on spontaneous inspiration, but to go back over a completed chapter or two and insert the adornments. And though some of the quotations in Latin, German, Italian, and French can hardly have been Bancroft's personal discoveries, it is likely that many of the others were gleaned from his reading.

A more serious charge is that the *Works* are shot through with bias, commonly identified as anti-Catholic, derogatory of the Indians in their natural state but sympathetic toward them in their contacts with the whites, pro-British, anti-pioneer, pro-Mormon, pro-Vigilance, and antimonopoly. This criticism takes the line that Bancroft inculcated these opinions in his assistants or revised their work with such thoroughness as to make his interpretation pervade the entire set. It is valid at least to this extent: the *Works,* volume by volume, do express the ideas that Bancroft wanted expressed, and, no placid fence-sitter, he took a firm stand on many controversial matters. As a recent writer has observed, however, "His prejudices are open, well known, and easily adjustable."[25]

Still more grave is the accusation that, because of skimped revision and rewriting, his volumes lack integration, do not present a unified, consistent, and complete interpretation, and do not express a defined and elaborated philosophy of

[25] Bernard De Voto, *The Year of Decision, 1846* (Boston, 1943), 525.

history. Superficially this recrimination would seem a logical contradiction of the one immediately preceding to the effect that throughout the *Works* a consistent prejudice runs. Certainly Bancroft did not row up his thirty-nine volumes to argue a thesis as directly as, say, the Beards in their four volumes on the rise of American civilization, or Von Holst in his constitutional history of the United States. But to deny that he had a philosophy of history is to overlook the repeated statements of his purpose and of his concept of his function as historian of western North America. His duty, as he envisioned it, was to assemble and present the facts about the course of development in this vast and little-studied area, to measure their meaning as far as possible, but without obscuring or beclouding the basic record. The prescription was not for all historians and for all history, but for himself and his subject. Recalling the nature and the status of the latter, few would gainsay the wisdom of his choice. Nor is it infallible that the interpretative essay, though a subsequent step, is a higher form of historical endeavor.

These criticisms and others that have been voiced against Bancroft are the counsel of perfection. One critic regrets, for example, that Bancroft did not attain "such style as that of Parkman, such dignity as that of Oncken or Winsor, such mastery of his splendid subject as is shown by Gibbon."[26] Tarrying not to inquire who Oncken was, we may second the wish that Bancroft could have been such a paragon. He had his shortcomings, and his critics—too often out of spleen, out of jealousy, out of shortsightedness, or out of unawareness of certain of his merits—have magnified them. In a sense their excess of rebuke matters only to his biographer. In another respect it has broader significance; for out of this criticism, most of it relating to the process of authorship, grew a tend-

[26] Rockwell D. Hunt, "Hubert Howe Bancroft: His Work and His Method," Historical Society of Southern California *Publications,* VIII (1911), 173; see also Rockwell D. Hunt, "My Interview with Hubert Howe Bancroft," *Ghost Town News,* III (December, 1943), 5.

ency to disparage the *Works* or, worse, to assume that they could not have much value.

Time, in its inexorable healing of wounds, has worked a cure. In a little more than five decades of use Bancroft's volumes have proved themselves and have earned a much more general appreciation of their magnitude, their solidity, and their quality. By extension, this increased respect has conferred honor on Bancroft himself and, at least in part, has vindicated his process of authorship.

17

Marketing the Works

Money enough to establish a university has been expended on this work. . . . For fifty cents a week you can secure what is equivalent to the entire results of Mr. Bancroft's expenditure of half a million dollars, and a quarter century of time.

Pamphlet, *A Few Words concerning the Historical Publications of Hubert Howe Bancroft,* 8, 9–10

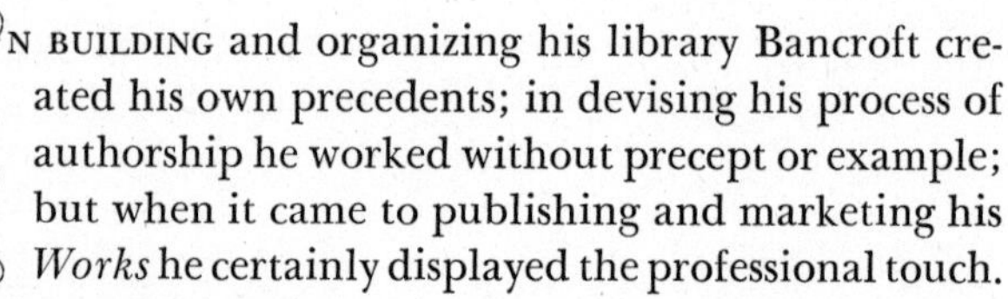

IN BUILDING and organizing his library Bancroft created his own precedents; in devising his process of authorship he worked without precept or example; but when it came to publishing and marketing his *Works* he certainly displayed the professional touch. Therein he was in sharp contrast to the majority of historical scholars. A few write with such grace or on such compelling topics that publication is never a problem. Another few find angels who exorcise all worries about paying the printer. Once in a long while there is a José Toribio Medina who can be his own compositor and printer's devil, or a Reuben Gold Thwaites who can set in motion series after series of edited documents. For the most part, however, the scholarly historian is innocent of real knowledge about printing and publishing, is a timid suppliant before the lordly publishers, and would be handicapped by restraint and uncertainty if called on to conduct a sales campaign.

In this field, of course, Bancroft was a professional. By the time the histories began to roll out he had behind him a quarter century of bookselling and publishing in San Francisco, he had made his concern by far the largest of its kind west of Chicago, and he had become a past master at promotion and salesmanship. He was ideally fitted, it would thus appear, to take personal charge of the sales program. He did plan its general outline, and from time to time he suggested steps that would lift sales, but its detailed direction he delegated to a subordinate.

This willingness to delegate responsibility was, of course, quite in accord with his long-established practice. In 1856, when he opened his bookstore, he had put Kenny in the position of prominence as salesman. As the business expanded, he assigned increasing authority to the various department heads, thereby making possible his excursions to the East and to Europe and his retreat to the fifth floor. When it came to collecting, he demonstrated his capacity to use the services of Whitaker, Stevens, and others, by empowering them to act at discretion. His setup for history writing, as we have seen, involved use of assistance on a grand scale. Similarly, in the handling of the marketing program, he appointed a sales manager and entrusted to him the design and direction of the sales campaign. Preserved memoranda record occasional suggestions from the proprietor, but always with the reminder that the final decision would be by the department chief. Throughout, therefore, he was consistent in this high trait of executive ability, this willingness to permit staff members to make decisions and to exercise authority.

Still another reason seems to have prompted Bancroft to relinquish active direction of the sales campaign. It was partly a matter of delicacy—a realization that it would not look exactly right for him to head the drive for subscribers, and that another person might be more effective. More, it was a conviction that his talents were more pressingly needed in the writing department. This does not necessarily mean that he considered himself a better historian than businessman; repeatedly he asserts that money-making was no problem to him, and the record of his success fully bears out this claim. It does mean, however, that selling was not his forte, and that he preferred to concentrate on writing, leaving the commercial end to someone else. This fact in Bancroft's career as businessman-historian is perhaps the one most often lost sight of.

He had, nevertheless, a most practical view of the problem of giving currency to his *Works*. He distinguished sharply between printing and publishing. To get his books printed and bound and then merely to have them stacked in some cellar or warehouse would not have satisfied him at all. To have circulated them by free distribution would have pleased him little better. He was convinced that the only way to be sure that books would be read and appreciated was to see to it that they were purchased.[1] Like every other author, he hoped for a wide circle of readers, he was convinced of the importance of the ideas and information he had to present, and he coveted attention thereto. Successful marketing, therefore, he regarded as a prime object of the arduous program through which he had struggled. Furthermore, he thought it not unreasonable that he should strive to recover on his investment of hundreds of thousands of dollars in collecting, indexing, note taking, writing, setting up in type, proofreading, printing, and binding. To that extent his motives were mercenary, but underneath was the determination to make the *Works* a successful expression.

In 1874 and 1875, when the *Native Races* were launched, Bancroft thought it better that they appear under the aegis of an established eastern publisher. Manufacture, to the point of stereotyping the plates, was done in his Market Street plant. Presswork and binding were done under contract at Houghton's Riverside Press. The services of D. Appleton and Company, the nominal publisher, were thus enlisted in the enterprise only at the stage of final distribution. *Native Races* sold acceptably well; indeed, considering their solidity and

[1] For an emphatic pronouncement on this matter consult Bancroft, *Literary Industries*, 792.

bulk, they sold remarkably well. Only a modicum of the credit, however, was due to Appleton. Bancroft's energetic onslaught on the reviewers and his own advertising put these Indian volumes over. Beyond noting that Appleton had not pushed the set, he made no complaint, but when it came to publishing the histories, he decided to rely on his own house.[2]

In taking note of this decision, the leading trade journal of the booksellers commented on "the magnitude and permanent importance of the series of Pacific States Histories on which Mr. H. H. Bancroft has so long been engaged." "The work," it continued, "is of especial interest to the trade. . . . It is to be regretted that it was thought necessary, in order to properly push the work, to place it in the hands of canvassers rather than to issue it through the regular trade channels, as it is a work which it should be the pride of every bookseller to have on his shelves."[3]

With regard to the mere production of the books this decision is worthy of comment. Even today there are few, if any, western houses equipped to set type, print, and bind on so grand a scale, yet Bancroft's Market Street plant had facilities both in machines and in skilled workmen that were more than adequate.

Much more remarkable was his essaying to market the printed volumes, for, both on the surface and under scrutiny, it appears the largest and most difficult task that has arisen in the publication of American history. The histories of George Bancroft, Parkman, McMaster, and Channing were ponderous, yet appreciably smaller than Bancroft's thirty-nine volumes. Each was brought out piecemeal, usually with an interval between volumes, and the problem thus was reduced to the marketing of a single book. The American Nation and the Chronicles of America usually sold as sets. They are not comparable to Bancroft, however, in size or cost

---

[2] *Ibid.*, 346–347, 588.
[3] *Publishers' Weekly*, September 16, 1882.

of production, their appeal was nation-wide, and the backbone of their support came from library and classroom sales. Thwaites's great set of *Jesuit Relations* and his *Early Western Travels,* though likewise simpler and less expensive in preparation and manufacture, provide what is probably a better hint of what an eastern publisher would have done with Bancroft's *Works.* These sets were brought out in limited editions, priced high, and disposed of primarily to libraries. Applied to Bancroft's seven-and-a-half-foot shelf of books, this method would have offered almost no likelihood of succeeding. The Pacific states, where the *Works* should have their greatest appeal, were sparsely populated, only sparingly equipped with libraries, and by no means addicted to the reading of their own history.

From the beginning, Bancroft was aware that the standard procedures of bookselling could not be counted on to float his set. He was convinced, however, that an interest in the history of their region could be awakened in the people of the West. His sales program was posited on that assumption, and he listed as prospects not merely libraries, collectors, and specialists in western history, but bankers, lawyers, businessmen, farmers—in short, every westerner who could muster the purchase price.

As a preliminary to the sales drive proper he made bids for publicity in western periodicals and newspapers. At his suggestion members of his staff prepared copy on his exploits as a collector, on the remarkable character of his library, on his method of authorship, on the magnitude and importance of the work he had under way, on the dimensions of his flourishing business firm, and on the more picturesque milestones in his career. The press was generally disposed to regard these items as newsworthy, printed some of them intact, and used others as a basis for write-ups. This sort of promotion began just before the publication of *Native Races,* but was also used to pave the way for the histories. By way of encouraging the press Bancroft occasionally ordered five hundred or a thousand extra copies of the more satisfactory notices for use as dodgers.

The testimonials and reviews that *Native Races* had elicited afforded another opportunity. A sheaf of excerpts from these comments was put into pamphlet form as early as 1875, under the caption "What the World Says about It." Supplemented by extracts from later notices and relabeled "What is Being Said of Mr. Hubert H. Bancroft and His Literary Work," this material came to be a standard element in the advertising. It was appended to a number of brochures.[4] Translated into Spanish and accompanied by signatures in facsimile, several were used to furbish a brochure designed to promote sales in Mexico.[5] They occur also in the prospectus placed in the hands of the salesmen, and, in modified form, they were incorporated in the fourteenth chapter of *Literary Industries.*

Still other pamphlets were issued, notably *A Few Words concerning the Historical Publications of Hubert Howe Bancroft,*[6] *A Brief Account of the Literary Undertakings of Hubert Howe Bancroft,*[7] and *Reviews of Hubert H. Bancroft's History of the Pacific States from the British Quarterly Review and the London Times.*[8]

Devices such as these are customarily the means of stimulating orders from libraries and collectors and of promoting over-the-counter sales. Having little hope that these normal outlets could be made even reasonably large, Bancroft aimed his publicity toward another goal. Its chief function, as he saw it, would be to ease the way for the salesmen who were

[4] Such as Hubert Howe Bancroft, *The Early American Chroniclers* (San Francisco, 1883, 45 + [5] + 13 + [2] pp.), and *The Historical Works of Hubert Howe Bancroft in Their Relation to the Progress and Destiny of the Pacific States* ([San Francisco], n.d., 14 + 12 pp.).

[5] *Obras Históricas de Huberto Howe Bancroft,* n.p., n.d., 24 pp.

[6] Eleven pages and map (San Francisco, 1882).

[7] Twelve pages and map (San Francisco, 1882).

[8] Nineteen pages [San Francisco, 1886].

to canvass the West, customer to customer if not door to door, and, by selling direct, were to build up the necessary volume of sales.

Actual direction of this campaign was put in the hands of Nathan Jonas Stone. A native of New Hampshire, a farmer and schoolteacher, Stone came to California in 1863 at the age of twenty. According to Bancroft, he arrived with a working capital of ten cents, which he promptly invested in Bartlett pears and ate. Though times were dull, he immediately found a job with a dairy. Three months later he became superintendent of an industrial school farm. In 1867 he entered Bancroft's employ as manager of the subscription department, from which, after a time, he was transferred to the wholesale department. In 1872 he resigned to open an importing and exporting house in Yokohama, which grossed a million dollars a year. Ill health brought him back to California. In 1882, fully recuperated, he was persuaded to take charge of marketing the *Works*. Abundant energy, marked executive capacity, expertness in the psychology of salesmanship, and high appreciation of the Pacific states histories made him an ideal sales manager. "No one," Bancroft asserts, "could have been better fitted for this arduous task than he."[9]

Stone was responsible for the detailed execution of the campaign; he formulated the instructions to the agents; he was fertile in ideas for the advancement of sales; and he doubtless contrived several of the arguments that were repeatedly employed. It is clear, nevertheless, that the program had Bancroft's approval in principle and in detail, that it was conducted along lines of his choosing, and that, with all due recognition to the sales manager, it had a Bancroftian design.

Its cardinal point was that the books should be sold on their merits, that every prospective customer should be made aware of the magnitude of the subject attempted, of the comprehensive gathering of materials, especially the sources in

[9] Bancroft, *Literary Industries*, 795.

Bancroft's collection, of the degree to which the histories were a pioneer effort, and of the tremendous number of man-hours that the completed set would represent. Bancroft was willing—indeed, he recommended—that the salesmen present the *Works* as a service to the community and worthy of support by public-spirited citizens, but he would countenance no begging and was not willing that any appeal should be made that would hint at charity.[10]

Equally fundamental was the principle that the *Works* should be presented as a unit, and that orders should be sought, not for just a single volume, and not for just the California or Oregon section, but for the entire set. From a pecuniary standpoint this procedure was obviously advantageous; Bancroft argued, for example, that only by working on this basis could he compensate salesmen of the caliber that the *Works* justified. It could also be argued that the *Works* were constructed as a unit, that there were frequent cross references from one section to another which had saved much repetition, that no volume or section was complete without the rest, and that an understanding of the history of one part of the coast presupposed some knowledge of the history of the neighboring states. Furthermore, the point was made that the investigation of the history of the entire region had been carried on as a common task, that the costs were considerable and interrelated, and that a person whose interest was limited to a particular state should support the entire project, because only thus had the publication of the state history been made possible. There was reciprocal advantage, Bancroft argued, if the citizen of Oregon placed on his shelves the *History of Colorado,* and vice versa. Besides, only by orders for the entire set could the publisher get a fair return. Fractional orders were occasionally accepted, but the endeavor was to get commitments for the entire set.[11]

---

[10] *Ibid.,* 791–793.
[11] *Ibid.*

What this program called for in terms of salesmanship will be better appreciated if the cost is figured out. The books were priced at $4.50 a volume, "bound in extra English cloth, neat and attractive"; at $5.50, "bound in fine leather, library style"; at $8.00, "bound in half calf, half Russia, or half morocco"; and at $10.00, "bound in Russian leather, or tree calf." Depending on the binding, then, the thirty-nine volumes would come to $175.50, $214.50, $312.00, or $390.00. This was the obligation that subscribers to the set were asked to assume.

Bancroft's advertising, however, did not stress these totals; in fact, I nowhere find them multiplied out. Though doubtless partly a device to shield subscribers from awareness of the full cost, this stress on the price per volume rather than per set had a justification. For no one was expected to pay the entire amount in one lump sum. Instead, what was essentially an installment plan prevailed, payments were to be made only as the books appeared, and this was not expected to exceed the rate of three or four a year. The actual outlay, therefore, as Bancroft pointed out in the best installment-selling manner, would be less than fifty cents a week, in exchange for which one would get a product that had cost half a million dollars to produce.[12]

Tradition hands down to us a vivid, though perhaps not accurate, account of the work of the solicitors. A pamphlet entitled *Information for Agents to Assist in Selling the Works of Hubert H. Bancroft* affords a reliable insight into the intended methods of the canvass. Though unsigned and undated, it is doubtless the work of Nathan Stone and presumably was written at the start of the campaign. It calls, first of all, for agents "of the highest integrity and ability" who would pledge to work on this job full time for several years. Each should familiarize himself with the background and

[12] *A Few Words concerning the Historical Publications of Hubert Howe Bancroft* (San Francisco, 1882), 9–10

aims of Bancroft's publications, preferably by spending several days at the library, and should be convinced of the excellence of the set. "Any one who does not thoroughly believe in this work of Mr. Bancroft's, that it is as important as any other, as the building of a railway, or the cutting of an isthmus canal, and that it is being well done, is not a suitable person to place it before the people."[13]

Before approaching a prospect, agents were advised to learn something of his character and interests, to arm themselves with a letter of introduction, and, if possible, to get an appointment. After a few preliminary remarks the agent was advised to launch into a description of Bancroft's new departure in authorship, his collecting, his use of assistants, and, with a world map to enforce the point, his endeavor to do the history of one-twelfth of the earth's surface. The better part of a page of eight-point type supplied a discourse on these points such as an agent might use.

Then, with the prospectus in hand, he should make description of the set and its component parts, interjecting comments on the excellence of the presswork and binding, giving assurance that the work would be carried to completion, and playing up the importance of ordering the entire set. The temptation to put off ordering until publication should be complete was, however, to be resisted. "It may not be so convenient to take and pay for them all at once as to pay for single volumes as they appear. And then even if he does this he will be all this time years behind his neighbors in matters of general information. Most of the knowledge contained in these books has never appeared in print before. People will be talking about it, and he will not understand them if he has never read the books. Besides, say he waits and buys them all at once, how is he then going to sit down and read and digest them all at once? It is something like a man's saying

[13] [Nathan J. Stone], *Information for Agents to Assist in Selling the Works of Hubert H. Bancroft* (n.p., n.d.), 2.

he would not bother about buying meat at the butcher's every day, but would buy a drove of cattle for his dinner at the end of the year."[14]

The prospectus was made up in several variations so that agents in California could feature sample backstrips of California volumes, those in Oregon the *History of Oregon,* and so on. This detail was not without its importance; it would tend to persuade the customer that his state had a prominent place in the work.

The grand scheme having been set forth, the customer's response was to be noted. Again the injunction was to try to get him to take the whole work. "What better use can be made with money than the purchase of all this knowledge? What more magnificent legacy can a man leave his children?"[15] Perhaps he would enter his subscription then and there.

If he was not yet convinced, argument concerning the value and importance of the work would not be amiss. "There is not a nation, people, or country on earth whose earliest annals have been presented as thoroughly and truthfully"—the agent here to flash "What Is Being Said" as corroboration. He might explain that the value of the work did not mean that Bancroft was "the greatest writer that ever lived." "He does not think so either.... All great men are modest.... There may be fifty as good writers in the United States as Mr. Bancroft, but not one of them could write this history to-day, or any day."[16] The explanation, of course, was in terms of the collection amassed, the great amount of work invested in its study, and in the timeliness of the undertaking. Fifty years earlier would have been too soon; fifty years later, and "three fourths of all he gives would have been forever lost." "It was not all the man; it was partly the time when it was done that makes it so valuable."[17]

Then the agent might launch upon a detailed description of the contents. The introduction to the first volume of *Cen-*

[14] *Ibid.,* 4–5. [15] *Ibid.,* 7. [16] *Ibid.,* 8. [17] *Ibid.*

tral America was worth comment, especially the way in which Bancroft had reduced it to less than seventy pages. A sample might be read. Oak's "Summary of Geographical Knowledge" should be commented on, with some display of the maps, and, farther on, of the sketches of sixteenth-century ships. A full page of fine print, a part of one of Bancroft's notes, was also to be pointed out as an evidence of his thoroughness. More rapidly, then, the contents of the next several volumes should be indicated with reference to the increasing attention to detail as northern Mexico and New Mexico were reached. "But it is all interesting and instructive, all exceedingly valuable. Why should Mr. Bancroft print uninteresting or valueless matter when he had as much as he could possibly use of the very best quality? Please write your name there"; and in italics the solicitor was instructed to present *"a blank which you have been filling up with a complete set of Bancroft's Works, possibly while in the midst of your last appeal."*[18]

A suggested commentary on *Native Races* was then supplied,[19] after which the agent was advised to stress that his primary purpose was to convince the listener that Bancroft had turned out "a good work, good for the country, for the world, and for every man in it, and that it has been well done." Once more "What Is Being Said" was to be called into play. "Then," the agent was exhorted, "bring out your blank order, at the same time handing your pen or pencil to the listener, as though he would subscribe as a matter of course."[20]

The instructions went on to chart a graceful retreat should the prospect refuse to subscribe. Without appearing in the least disconcerted, the agent was then to say that he would see to it that reports on the progress of the Bancroft histories were sent to the listener, together with samples of authoritative comment. Thus he would be informed of developments and have a basis for arriving at a decision. "I want your favorable consideration of Mr. Bancroft's work," the agent was

[18] *Ibid.*, 9. [19] *Ibid.*, 9–14. [20] *Ibid.*, 15.

instructed to say, ". . . think well of it, and speak well of it; give it your moral support, if nothing more, and this, I can tell you, is no small matter to a man like Mr. Bancroft, who is engaged in a life-long and arduous work."[21]

Bidding his prospect a cordial goodbye, the agent then was to depart, immediately after which he was to make a written report to the company, listing name, address, occupation, standing in the community, and estimating the prospect's credit rating, A, B, C, or D.[22]

Some of these reports re-create the scene. Agent H. C. Osmurt, for example, wrote as follows:

Mr. Stone!

I called on this man Ed Randall with every confidence in the world of success, but his wheat crop is an entire failure and he is down in the dumps. The price of land he says has fallen 25 per cent in the past 2 years, and his 2 boys wanted the work the worst way. But I could not induce him to be a subscriber, though I spent all of 2 hours with him.[23]

Or, consider F. A. Gilly's report after interviewing G. D. Mecum of Orland.

Well to do. Out of debt. Has 4 children the oldest 18 the youngest 6 years old. See statistics. This family needs the work more than any I have yet interviewed but the cry is poor crops and could not shake their decision. The boys all go to the Normal school here and they have the idea that the work would do them no good till through with school.[24]

Gilly's report on George Mudd of Germantown mentions another variety of sales resistance:

A man of large means. Likes history. Out of debt. See statistics. Will take the work as soon as he can possibly get books on hand read so that he can see way clear to read them. He is a gentleman who has

[21] *Ibid.*

[22] *Ibid.*, 16.

[23] Report of H. C. Osmurt on interview with Ed Randall, n.p., n.d., MS, Bancroft Library.

[24] Report of F. A. Gilly on interview with G. D. Mecum, Orland, August 23, 1886, *ibid.*

literary taste. Has 3 little children oldest 9 years. Think we can secure the nassary [*sic*] order upon my return.[25]

By the canons of business psychology this blueprint for salesmanship was almost letter-perfect. It appealed to the prospect's pride in intellect, to his desire to be well informed, to his wish to keep pace with his neighbors, to his intention of doing the right thing by his children. His patriotic motives were played upon through the representation of the *Works* as a contribution to local history which he certainly would want to support. Cajolery was present, subtly but lavishly, in the plea that Bancroft wanted understanding, approval, and support from him as a substantial and influential citizen. Finally, his business sense was flattered through the demonstration that the books were a bargain, that they were the result of a large expenditure, that they had permanent merit, and would prove a sound investment. These certainly were high-pressure methods, yet what was said of the collection, the sources, the method of writing, the thoroughness, and the importance of the publication was no more than the truth, though it was the truth presented in the most favorable light.

As the campaign progressed, other artifices were brought into play, some of which were irreproachable, some open to criticism. When sales resistance was on the score that the set might never be completed and the subscribers left with an unfinished narrative, Bancroft countered with two arguments. He reminded that, although the history of the world is one complete story, it is seldom written or read as such. Most often it is written in parts, and the most brilliant histories, such as Macaulay's *England* or Motley's *Dutch Republic,* are usually confined to short episodes, yet for what they set out to do are regarded as complete. Individual volumes of Bancroft's *Works* would have this sort of completeness whether the set was rounded out or not. But he hastened to add that

[25] Report of F. A. Gilly on interview with George Mudd, Germantown August 14, 1886, *ibid.*

all thirty-nine volumes would be published.[26] To prove it he broadcast an affidavit by Governor Geo. C. Perkins and Mayor M. C. Blake, who, at his request, visited the library in January, 1882, inspected the work there in progress, and thereupon affirmed, "Judging from what is already in print, the mass of manuscript ready for the printer, and the number and efficiency of the assistants engaged, we entertain no doubt of the completion of the series within the time promised to subscribers."[27]

The follow-up letter, mentioned as a parting shot by the unsuccessful solicitor, was high in Bancroft's favor. Writing from Mexico to his sales manager, he endorsed it enthusiastically, not only for customers who had not yet ordered, but also for those who had entered their subscriptions. "What they want," he remarked, "is occasionally a nice letter speaking a good word, not long—but something that will make them feel that we remember them in some other way than simply the price of a volume. . . . I believe it to be important that our subscribers everywhere should be kept in a good humor. I believe a good letter writer will save to the Dept. hundreds of orders that otherwise would be dropped."[28]

A custom also developed of having the agents gather information on "California [or Oregon, or Washington] as It Is," the while they sought to make sales. Forms were prepared on which data of almost all conceivable variety might be entered: acres of vines, boxes of raisins, gallons of wine; number of orange, lemon, and olive trees; acres of orchards, wheat, barley, oats, corn, alfalfa, potatoes; number of head of cattle, horses, sheep, goats, hogs; amount of honey, butter, and cheese; artesian wells, nurseries, timber, tillable lands, quality

[26] A *Few Words concerning the Historical Publications of Hubert Howe Bancroft,* 10–11.

[27] Reproduced in a dodger headed "The Literary Works of Hubert H. Bancroft." The circumstances are reported in Bancroft, *Literary Industries,* 587.

[28] Hubert Howe Bancroft to Nathan J. Stone, Saltillo, September 13, 1883, MS, Bancroft Library.

of soil, depth to water, average temperature and rainfall; manufacturing, itemized under flour, lumber, lumberyards, machine shops, woolen mills, carriage factories, brick factories, stone quarries, planing mills, and minerals; and papers published. The instructions read: "In collecting statistics of the country, the agent will get as reliable a report as is possible to obtain, omitting *nothing* that might be of interest to the world at large."[29]

Probably a hope was entertained that this information would be useful in the preparation of the final chapters of the histories or for some later project, yet the major purpose apparently was to enable the agents to maneuver prospective purchasers toward signing on the dotted line. The device seems occasionally to have been abused. Some persons appear to have subscribed because they were under the impression that the information they supplied about themselves would be written up with prominence in the appropriate part of the histories.

In Montana, in particular, a furor arose over unscrupulous canvassing. To forestall disappointing the four hundred who had subscribed, Bancroft sent a trusted lieutenant, R. D. Faulkner, to find out what promises had been made and whether the agents had gathered the necessary information. He went on to expostulate: "We certainly do not want to allow ourselves to be placed in a false position by our agents and then have a great howl raised in 2 or 3 years. It is unnecessary. They can't take any more orders that way. We certainly cannot make anything at it. It all comes from the agent's being too lazy to write out what he has promised, and not caring for us or for the work or the people or the subscribers or country further than to get their money out of it. We are not [in] on it, and Stone is going to stop every man if he can't make this canvass without fooling people."[30]

[29] Quoted from one of several specimens in the Bancroft Library.

[30] Hubert Howe Bancroft to R. D. Faulkner, Denver, November 26, 1884, MS, Bancroft Library.

Faulkner carried a certificate that Bancroft would "make the best use possible of all the information given to him." He was also "fully authorized to adjust any differences with subscribers to the series."[31] His pacificatory efforts were not completely successful. Ten months later, under the heading "Still They Come," the Helena *Daily Independent* complained: "The Bancroft book swindlers are still sending in carloads of books to the farmers and ranchmen throughout Montana. The Prickly Pear valley is being flooded with them, some men receiving as high as fifteen huge volumes, which they never ordered and never wanted and cannot afford to pay for. Some of the victims declare their intention of testing the matter in the courts."[32]

Another five months later, the Montana subscribers still not being quieted, A. L. Bancroft & Co. sent what amounted to a formal apology. "We lay no claim to perfection," this communication read, in part, "nor do we pretend to judge *always* soundly of the morals of our agents. In spite of *every precaution possible,* the volume of our business being so great and extending over so large an area, we have to expect to be misrepresented and injured at some time or other, by some one or more of our numerous employees. Others may be hurt and aggrieved by such conduct; but, as you must know, we suffer therefrom much more than any other individuals or any community." The letter went on to deplore the work of the "rogues who have bilked us out of thousands of dollars directly, in addition to the serious damage they have done us indirectly," and to promise continued efforts to see these scoundrels lodged in the penitentiary.[33]

In May, 1886, Bozeman, Montana, was the scene of a mass

[31] Hubert Howe Bancroft to "All Interested in the History of Montana," San Francisco, November 22, 1884 [actually penned in Denver], MS, Bancroft Library; A. L. Bancroft & Co., Letter of introduction, San Francisco, November 25, 1884, MS, Bancroft Library.

[32] Helena, Montana, *Daily Independent,* October 14, 1885.

[33] A. L. Bancroft & Co. to John S. M. Neill, San Francisco, February 9, 1886, Helena, Montana, *Daily Independent,* February 25, 1886.

meeting at which were adopted resolutions "condemnatory of the deceptive course resorted to by the canvassing agents in procuring subscriptions." These dissatisfied subscribers were warned, however, by the editor of the Bozeman paper "to consider carefully whether they are not legally bound to the contracts they voluntarily signed . . . and whether a set of resolutions will release them from such obligations if A. L. Bancroft & Co. determine otherwise."[34]

The fact of misrepresentation is clearly established, though the measure of it is harder to determine.[35] It is the sort of thing that frequently—in fact, almost inevitably—accompanies subscription salesmanship, and by his selection of that method Bancroft was to a degree responsible. Thereafter, it would be difficult to charge him with complicity. His deploring of unscrupulous dealings by the agents has the ring of sincerity, and I am convinced that he really meant it when he condemned such actions as dishonest and unnecessary.

He did, it is true, make some effort to correlate personal mention in the histories with the help proffered. The sales agents, so far as the evidence goes, were not authorized to make any such promises, though in soliciting family papers for his collection Bancroft had let it be known that he would have to write the history from such materials as he was able to get, and that if papers were supplied, mention of writers and recipients was probable, whereas if they were withheld a measure of neglect was inevitable. There is direct evidence, also, that he wanted "coöperative" persons played up in the histories; in fact, the biographical notes that are so abundant in the latter pages of the histories of a number of the states can be justified on no other score. Incidentally, Frances Fuller Victor claims the credit for suggesting this device.[36]

---

[34] Bozeman, Montana, *Weekly Avant Courier,* May 13, 1886.

[35] One of the overzealous agents was Bancroft's nephew, Ashley Bancroft. See Hubert Howe Bancroft to H. G. Struve, San Francisco, January 18, 1887, MS, Bancroft Library.

[36] W. A. Morris, "The Origin and Authorship of the Bancroft Pacific States Histories," *Oregon Historical Quarterly,* IV (1903), 331.

There are other instances of modification of content, apparently for the sake of insuring better sales. Thus, at the very outset of the presentation of the histories, proof sheets of the introductory matter in the first Central American volume were submitted to a committee of churchmen. They found so much to take exception to, in thrusts and insinuations against the Roman Catholic Church in Spain and its colonies, that a majority of the pages had to be reset. Pride of authorship is generally so acute that changes such as these would be sanctioned only with great reluctance. Bancroft, however, gave in with no indication of hesitation or regret. Oak records a similar occurrence sometime later in connection with objection by a group of clerics to certain statements in the California volumes. "Rather than make any changes," he says, "I would have consigned them to the highest temperatures known to their respective faiths," but his chief with great complacency ordered the proposed alterations made.[37]

Changes strictly promotional were made in the Texas portion of the narrative. As an initial step the words "and Texas" were added to the title *History of the North Mexican States.* Then Peatfield was put to work on a revision of the 1884 edition of the first volume of this series. By condensing parts of the Mexican material he made room for an added chapter on Texas, which appeared in the edition of 1886.[38] Herein no external pressure was involved; the aim was simply to appeal to prospective subscribers in Texas.

There are instances also of textual variations for the sake of gaining a single customer. For example, the first printing of the *History of Oregon* carried a skeptical and unflattering account of Judge O. C. Pratt's conduct of the trial of the Indians charged with responsibility for the Whitman massacre.[39] In a later printing this account was revised and made much less uncomplimentary to the judge. The impulse be-

[37] Henry L. Oak, *"Literary Industries" in a New Light,* 36–37.
[38] Entitled "Annals of Texas," pp. 630–669.
[39] Bancroft, *History of Oregon,* II, 97–98.

hind this change appears to have been neither pressure from the Pratts nor change of heart on the part of the historian, but that the judge was giving favorable consideration to commissioning Bancroft to do his biography in the *Chronicles of the Builders.*

Bancroft's dealings with Leland Stanford offer a comparable illustration, though in this instance the direction was reversed. The railroad magnate was likewise a prospect for a place in the *Chronicles;* in fact, his name was down for $10,000, material on his life had been gathered, and a laudatory biography of some 300 pages was ready for the printer. Things standing thus, it is not surprising that Bancroft should have prepared to say in his *History of California,* in reporting Stanford's nomination for governor in 1858: "The choice was a strong one, the strongest beyond doubt that could possibly have been made. . . . By his strength of will, his continuity of purpose, his originality of thought, his large and liberal views, and above all by his rare administrative faculty, he was admirably fitted for the executive office." A footnote on the same page promised that the *Chronicles* would contain a complete history of his life.

These statements now occur only in the set of the *Works* that was Stanford's personal copy.[40] Presumably they were intended for general circulation, though it is possible that they were meant for his eyes alone. It is clear, at any rate, that they were deleted from the regular edition after Stanford had taken umbrage at what he called misrepresentation by Bancroft's sales agent. As a patriotic gesture Stanford had subscribed to forty sets of the *Works,* expecting that they would run to no more than five or six volumes. Late in 1889 or early in 1890, having accumulated a roomful of the not yet completed publication, Stanford came to the end of his

[40] As reported in George T. Clark, "Leland Stanford and H. H. Bancroft's 'History,' a Bibliographical Curiosity," *Papers* of the Bibliographical Society of America, XXVII (1933), 12–23. The quotations are from page 753 of the sixth volume.

patience. He read the riot act to a Bancroft representative, refused to accept any more of the volumes, and canceled his order for a write-up in the *Chronicles*. In pique, or in relief from any further need of truckling to Stanford, Bancroft thereupon expunged from the regular edition the complimentary passages quoted above.[41]

As a sidelight on Bancroft's sales procedure, this incident carries several implications. Chief among them is the complaint often voiced, that the salesmen got many of their orders under false pretenses by neglecting to specify that the *Works* would run to thirty-nine volumes, or even by representing that there would be but five or six. Oak records that a Mexican visitor to the library, who was asked if he would not like to enter his name for the history of his state, signed what proved to be an order for the entire set.[42] This particular inequity was promptly rectified, but many other subscribers felt that they had been taken in by the sales agents.

In the nature of things, documentary proof on this point is not to be had. Many assert that they were victimized, and resentment against the sales methods attained considerable dimensions. Yet even when his own mood toward Bancroft was tinctured with aversion, Oak firmly denied that his employer had ever instructed the agents to deceive or misrepresent. He was lax in curbing overzealous and unscrupulous salesmen, but the size of the *Works* was thoroughly publicized, the wording of the contracts was plain, and the majority of those who complained were alert, intelligent, successful men of the world, presumably well aware of the force of contracts and thus not in the habit of signing blindly.

The rapidity with which the set grew and its apparently interminable progress did call forth editorial expostulation. In 1885, for example, the editor of a Nevada journal remarked: "The APPEAL owes Herbert [*sic*] Howe Bancroft an

[41] *Ibid.*

[42] Henry L. Oak, *"Literary Industries" in a New Light,* 16.

apology for receiving Volume V of his History of Mexico, and allowing it to lie a couple of months on the editorial table without finding time to read and review it. But Mr. Bancroft has himself to blame for a good deal of this. Every three months he throws a volume of history at the editorial head, and expects a review. . . . These histories contain enough matter to keep a man a year reading and thinking, and under the circumstances it is not strange that we fall behind. If Mr. Bancroft would run the press a trifle slower, and print books not quite so thick, we will endeavor to review them, but just now he cuts off chunks of history meat a good deal bigger than we can chew."[43]

Enthusiasm among the purchasers certainly tended to wane as the *Works* strung out. Many doubtless persuaded themselves that they had been misused. In this antagonism toward the historian-publisher they were encouraged by Ambrose Bierce, the acerbic columnist on Hearst's San Francisco *Examiner*. Bierce overlooked no opportunity to get in a dig. For example, a few days after a serious accident in the Market Street shop, he inserted this quip: "One of the men frightfully injured in the elevator accident in the Bancroft building was intending to subscribe for *The History of the Pacific States*. He had a narrow escape."[44]

Notwithstanding such mockery the canvass went on. It was pursued most actively in California and the neighboring states, but to some extent in the East and in foreign lands. When Bancroft went to Mexico in the latter part of 1884 to gather material for the later history of that region, he busied himself occasionally as a salesman. Originally he had not supposed that Mexico would provide much of a market, but he was agreeably surprised. Orders poured in. He could write back to Stone that Mexico was a field inviting to the canvasser, and that if it were worked assiduously and intelli-

[43] Carson, Nevada, *Appeal*, 1885; clipping in the Bancroft Library.

[44] Ambrose Bierce, "Prattle," San Francisco *Examiner*, September 23, 1888.

gently it would yield a fair number of subscribers.[45] Shortly thereafter, in a pamphlet entitled *Obras Históricas de Huberto Howe Bancroft,* there were listed some 162 subscribers in Mexico. On the basis of the response to his sales campaign, Bancroft was ready to conclude that the whole world was a potential market for the thirty-nine volumes. "Some parts of it," he admitted, "are better than others, but the firm of A. L. B. & Co. will make the greatest mistake of their lives if they don't continue this work all over the world as time and opportunity offer to do it profitably."[46]

In actuality the sales fell a bit short of this goal. They quickly mounted, however, to more than 6,000 sets, at least 234,000 volumes, and a gross return of more than $1,000,000. Although the costs of writing and publication were not sharply segregated from those of the commercial house, and although some allowance for uncharged rent, shop services, and interest ought to be made, it still appears that Bancroft managed to recoup on his great investment and did not sustain a loss. Considering the length, weight, and solidity of the set, this outcome is nothing short of remarkable.

What is more important, this large sale gave the *Works* excellent availability. Ever since publication the set has been easily accessible to readers, students, and researchers. No library need be without it, and in the book markets today it may be had at prices ranging sometimes below a dollar a volume. This current availability is, in a direct way, a tribute to the success of the sales program initiated by Bancroft, elaborated by Stone, and carried out by their enthusiastic cohorts.

[45] Hubert Howe Bancroft to Nathan J. Stone, Monterrey, Mexico, September 11, 1883, MS, Bancroft Library.

[46] *Ibid.* On another occasion he wrote that Canada, Australia, or the Cannibal Islands could be made a market if properly worked; Hubert Howe Bancroft to R. D. Faulkner, Denver, October 22, 1884, MS, Bancroft Library.

18

Near Disaster

Here was my own corpse, my own smouldering remains, my dead hopes and aspirations, all the fine plans and purposes of my life lying here a heap of ashes, and I could not bear to look upon them. Hubert Howe Bancroft, *Literary Industries,* 776

IN 1882, BANCROFT had launched upon the ambitious program of producing and marketing the ponderous volumes that he called his *Works.* By 1890, as the preceding chapters have narrated, he had carried these two heroic tasks to a remarkably successful conclusion. En route he had had much good sailing, but he had also encountered sundry storms, one of which threatened his enterprise with disaster.

It happened on the last day of April, 1886. Bancroft was with his family in San Diego, where he had acquired extensive property holdings both in town and at Helix Farm in Spring Valley. Oak, Nemos, and the other members of the literary staff were hard at work in the library on Valencia Street. From the Market Street building A. L. Bancroft had gone out at three o'clock to attend a meeting of the Horticultural Society, but the building hummed with the activities of the three hundred or more employees.

At approximately ten minutes to four, two of the clerks in the law department noticed smoke arising from the basement. They promptly called the fire department. At almost the same time, some women who were passing along Market Street likewise noticed the smoke, ran into the furniture store of L. and E. Emmanuel, and reported it. A call was also put in from the box across Market Street at Geary and Kearny. Meanwhile, Joseph Page ran upstairs and sounded the alarm in the printing department and the bindery.[1]

"The scene which ensued," according to the *Chronicle* reporter, "was one of intense excitement and confusion, and that many of the employees were not burned to death was owing to the fact that some among them remained cool and were able to assist and direct their panic-stricken fellows. A number of the girls employed in the bindery fainted away, others became hysterical and not a few of them were prevented from leaping from the windows to the sidewalk."[2]

The flames, which had started in the furniture storeroom and factory in the west half of the basement, spread rapidly. Reaching the two elevator wells, they shot upward and soon enveloped the entire top floor. Fortunately, the stairways were not immediately affected, and the three hundred employees, despite their impulse toward panic, were able to make their escape.

Before any flames broke through the roof, the first firemen arrived on the scene. They carried a hose line in the front door and up the stairs and endeavored to confine the fire to the fifth floor. The bindery stock was so highly inflammable, however, that it was problematical whether they would succeed. Whatever hopes they had were dashed when smoke began to billow up from the basement, which they had not known was on fire, and they had to retreat.[3]

By this time, of course, a large crowd had gathered. Its attention was chiefly upon the firemen who were manning hoses in front of the building. Then all eyes were turned to one of the upper windows where a boy appeared, too much unnerved to make for the stairs. Through the billowing smoke

[1] The fire was reported in detail in the San Francisco *Chronicle,* the San Francisco *Examiner,* and the San Francisco *Alta California,* of May 1, 1886; see also Bancroft, *Literary Industries,* 772–790.

[2] San Francisco *Chronicle,* May 1, 1886.

[3] *Ibid.*

came a policeman, clasped the boy in his arms, and hurried him away from the window. The suspense of waiting for their appearance below was hard to bear, and a shout of joy greeted their emergence on the sidewalk.[4]

Rumors, meanwhile, circulated of others trapped in the basement; in particular, two of Emmanuel's mattress makers, Patrick Beatty and James Brannan. They were said to be "calling for help and begging some one for God's sake to cut through the sidewalk, as they were suffocating."[5] At some risk, the firemen got to Beatty, lifted his almost lifeless form to an express wagon substituted for an ambulance, and sent it at a gallop toward the receiving hospital. Beatty died before the journey was half completed, and the driver made delivery instead at the morgue and hurried back for a possible second load.[6]

Meanwhile the crowd grew and the police had trouble holding it out of danger and out of the way of the firemen. More fire companies arrived—in fact, all that San Francisco possessed—and got to work, Chief Scannell directing his forces from a vantage point on the far side of Market Street. His appeal for help was promptly answered by firemen from Oakland, who galloped their horses to the pier, caught the five o'clock ferry, and were soon at the scene. They were held in reserve to answer any supplementary alarms.

Despite all exertions the fire increased. With a crash the top floor caved in. The flames roared through the roof—an awe-inspiring spectacle. Other crashes followed, and several small explosions. The collapse of the west wall showered bricks on the frame building adjacent on that side, and it was soon a mass of flames. The rear wall soon followed, falling across Stevenson Street and carrying the fire to a row of small stores and rooming houses, which were soon consumed. As further spread of the flames threatened, some of the neighboring businessmen began frantic efforts to remove their

[4] *Ibid.* [5] *Ibid.* [6] San Francisco *Examiner,* May 1, 1886.

goods, and the firemen turned much of their attention to trying to save the adjoining properties. The roof of the Grand Opera House caught fire, but with the assistance of a bucket brigade the firemen were able to save this landmark. They also stopped the flames short of the Nuclear Building and the Palace Hotel.[7]

With the Bancroft Building the firemen did their best, carrying in hose lines in the early stages of the fire, chopping a hole from the sidewalk to the basement to get at Beatty, maintaining the fight in Stevenson Street until just before the rear wall tumbled down to fill the street with rubble, and retiring from the front of the building to the center of Market only after several of their hoses had broken, several of their ladders had caught fire, and there was imminent danger that the heavy cornices would fall on them. Within a few hours the building was almost completely consumed. The wreckage smouldered through the night, but in the morning only the front wall was still standing, and it was regarded by Chief Scannell as a menace to Market Street traffic.[8]

An estimated quarter of a million persons watched the conflagration.[9] It began when Market Street was crowded with afternoon promenaders, and it continued through that thoroughfare's busiest hours. At ten o'clock the crowd seemed to be still as large. A good many commuters remained perforce, because cable-car service was halted on the Market, Turk, Mission, Howard, and Folsom lines. On the Market Street line cars did not run until the next morning, when an architect certified that the front wall of the Bancroft Building would not fall into the street.[10]

They had seen a brilliant spectacle, though one reporter

---

[7] San Francisco *Chronicle,* May 1, 1886.

[8] *Ibid.* Five days later, A. L. Bancroft and Chief Scannell were still arguing whether to guy this wall or tear it down; San Francisco *Examiner,* May 5, 1886.

[9] San Francisco *Alta California,* May 1, 1886.

[10] *Ibid.*

remarked that if it had happened by night instead of day the display would have been still more dramatic.[11] He mentioned two effects, however, that would not have been produced without the bright rays of the setting sun. The grotesquely carved caryatids above the fifth-floor windows, when caught in the light of the sun and the flames, seemed to him "to take life, and appeared as if holding high carnival over the scene of destruction."

"A pretty sight was afforded those in the foreground," this reporter continued. "The myriad of streams playing upon the building, crossing and recrossing and breaking into sparkling jets, was caught by the sunlight, and for a few minutes there hung over the whole front of the doomed building a large and beautiful rainbow. The sight seemed to impress the crowd, which stared and stared at the spectacle in apparent amazement."[12]

On the fringes of the fire the reporters found material for many human-interest stories. At Third and Stevenson a hose burst, and the onlookers were drenched. Near by an old graybeard shouted, "It is the will of the Lord. This is a judgment sent upon this wicked city. Flee from the wrath to come, ye wicked sinners!" A policeman collared him and flung him into a pool of water.[13] A certain Michael Barry was arrested for trying to pick a pocket, Al Stewart, "the noted pugilist and Rock-roller," for snatching a watch, and a certain Alfred Hampton for driving over a hose.[14]

"One of the saddest incidents attending the fire," according to the *Alta,* "was the utter destruction of the magnificent wardrobe of J. J. Maloney, the celtic orator, who occupied luxurious apartments at 233 Stevenson street. He mourns the loss of a handsome cream-colored overcoat and the historical gripsack that has so often been seen on dress parade upon our

[11] San Francisco *Chronicle,* May 1, 1886.
[12] *Ibid.*
[13] San Francisco *Examiner,* May 1, 1886.
[14] San Francisco *Chronicle,* May 1, 1886.

main thoroughfares, besides many articles of *bijouterie* and *vertu*, which cannot be replaced on this side of the continent."[15] The *Chronicle*, in similar vein, commiserated "Mark Antony" Maloney on the loss of his wardrobe and two volumes of Shakespeare, but rejoiced with him that he had saved "a pair of Foster kids, a pair of embroidered suspenders, and several cravats."[16]

Maloney, of the Stevenson tenements, was but one of the ancillary victims of the fire. Emmanuel's loss was heavy, and Spear the painter, Schussler Brothers, the Pacific Trunk Company and various others suffered from $2,000 to $15,000 damage, but the brunt of the loss, amounting to almost $1,000,000, fell upon the Bancroft Company. Less than half of the loss was covered by insurance. It was San Francisco's worst fire in a decade.[17]

Three men lost their lives: Beatty and Brannan, Emanuel's mattress makers, and John Fleming, an extra fireman, who fell from a ladder and suffered internal injuries which proved fatal.[18] A flying brick broke the arm of one fireman, T. F. Barrett; and another, Patrick Curran, caught his foot in a bight in the hose and suffered a broken leg; a third, Thomas Bender, was thrown from Engine No. 2 on the run to the fire; and a fourth, John Soap, fell off a ladder, and his right eye was destroyed. The full list of injuries would be much longer.[19] In addition, Cashier T. A. C. Dorland and Robert Fleisher, a bookbinder, were reported missing, though both showed up the next day.[20]

Supervisors Williamson and Valleau took advantage of the fire and "expressed themselves in emphatic terms regarding

[15] San Francisco *Alta California*, May 1, 1886.

[16] San Francisco *Chronicle*, May 1, 1886.

[17] Rivaled only by the California Mills fire in 1881, the O'Connor-Moffat fire, and the H. S. Crocker fire in October, 1885.

[18] San Francisco *Examiner*, May 2, 1886.

[19] *Ibid.*; San Francisco *Chronicle*, May 1, 1886; San Francisco *Alta California*, May 1, 1886.

[20] San Francisco *Examiner*, May 1 and 2, 1886.

the inadequate number of hydrants."[21] The *Chronicle* likewise editorialized on the lessons of the fire. San Francisco, it said, clearly needed a building code that would ban frame construction for elevator shafts, would insist on fire-resistant cross walls in structures as large as the Bancroft Building, and would prohibit "such dangerous excrescences" as the "enormous cornices" that had proved a constant menace to the fire fighters. In the long run, the *Chronicle* also insisted, citing Chicago's experience as proof, it would be good economy to increase the tax rate so that the city could have an enlarged fire district, a greater number of firemen, and additional equipment.[22]

The editors, however, did not neglect to notice the victims of this "great calamity" and "the train of misery" it left in its wake. To the tenement dwellers of Stevenson Street, to the various shopkeepers, to the hundreds of persons thrown out of work, and particularly to the Bancroft Company, various editors expressed sympathy. The *Chronicle* reminded its readers that Bancroft's was the leading publisher on the coast, the principal stationer, almost the sole reliance of the legal profession for its supply of books and forms, and "the only place to which the book-buyer could resort with some assurance that he could find what he wanted." "Such a convenience will be sadly missed," the *Chronicle* went on, "and until the facilities are restored, San Franciscans will suffer the drawbacks experienced by smaller cities and towns."[23]

The *Alta* was even more generous. "The destruction of Bancroft's Publishing and Stationery house by fire," it proclaimed, "is something more than a personal loss. It is a calamity shared by many people, and a misfortune to this great city in which it was a mark of enterprise most honorable to San Francisco. . . . Our people will promptly encourage the rehabilitation of this San Francisco institution, for the Bancrofts

[21] *Ibid.*
[22] San Francisco *Chronicle,* May 1, 1886.
[23] *Ibid.*

are as much a part of California as the mountains which keep solemn guard upon our boundaries."[24]

Bancroft's first word of the fire was in a telegram from Nathan J. Stone, "Store burning. Little hope of saving it." He finished the day's routine and stowed himself away on the northbound train, his mind reeling with thoughts of the ramifications of the disaster: the loss of the building and its stock, the destruction of his business establishment, the disemployment of faithful workers, the halting of his plans to buy and build in San Diego, and most of all the probably fatal blow to his project of history publishing, which with the twentieth volume had just passed the midpoint.[25]

Arrived at San Francisco, he was at first too much distraught to tackle his problems. He could hardly bear to look at the charred ruins, and he had no relish for the wry humor of a neighboring shopkeeper who put up a sign that read, "Owing to climatic changes which our weak constitution could not stand, we decided to 'go west.' Swan, the painter, is now convalescent at 851 Market street, opposite the Baldwin."[26]

Bancroft found his "boys" installed at 110½ Geary Street, with a stock of a "few ink bottles, three small busts of Cleveland, and a complete set of books belonging to the History Department."[27] This was bad enough, but not so bad as it sounds. The firm had a print shop in another building. It had some stock stored elsewhere, and other goods in transit. Within a few days it moved to larger quarters at Sacramento and Davis streets. Furthermore, the books that were saved were the account books of the history department and, though doubtless not worth the million dollars that the press reported, they had a substantial value.

At first Bancroft though he would have to sell the lot on which the building had stood. But no one offered anything

[24] San Francisco *Alta California*, May 1, 1886.
[25] Bancroft, *Literary Industries*, 772–773.
[26] Quoted in the Woodland *Daily Democrat*, May 7, 1886.
[27] San Francisco *Chronicle*, May 1, 1886.

like a fair price, insurance companies paid off promptly, and the savings banks encouraged him to borrow. And so, in the end, he decided to rebuild.[28] Major considerations were to take care of his employees and to fulfill his promise of completing the histories rather than leaving the subscribers with broken sets on their hands, though of course it was also a great personal satisfaction to be able to carry on. Significantly, the branch of the business that he chose to revive first was the history department.

On May 3 he got out a circular to all subscribers announcing that publication of the *Works* would *"positively proceed to completion,"* with only a slight interruption due to the fire.[29] On May 7 he sent out a longer letter assuring that, although the publishing house, its entire stock of goods, some thousands of bound volumes, and the plates of several volumes had been destroyed, all manuscript was saved; that materials to resume manufacturing had been ordered by telegram; and that his "monumental undertaking" would unfailingly be carried out. Actually, the manuscript of the first Oregon volume was lost, but by good fortune two copies of the newly printed book had been taken to the library, and from them it was possible to reset the type. Otherwise the book would have had to be rewritten.[30]

On May 5 a communication of like tenor was broadcast to the press. It reminded of "what Mr. Bancroft is doing for American literature and for the Pacific States. His work is accepted everywhere on the judgments of the most eminent and capable critics as authority on his subject, and is recognized universally as a standard history; while, also, it presents this part of the United States in its true light to the East and to Europe, from which we desire first-class immigration and capital." It disclaimed any plea for sympathy, but each editor

[28] Bancroft, *Literary Industries,* 774–782.

[29] Examples of this and the subsequent circulars are preserved in the Bancroft Library.

[30] San Francisco *Chronicle,* June 6, 1886.

was asked, in his own "appropriate and forcible way," to call upon generous subscribers, who were in arrears, to forward the amounts due, and thereby to contribute "in the most helpful way and at the most opportune moment towards carrying on to a happy consummation, the most important and most thoroughly approved literary publication of this age."

Editors all across the land complied with this request, some in virtually the words of the circular,[31] and at least one subscriber responded to the appeal. This was J. D. Farwell of Niles, who on May 10 wrote that he was not only paying up his arrearages, but would show his sincerity by remitting the whole amount of his subscription. Bancroft reproduced his letter as still another circular.

With the fifth California volume substituted for the first Oregon, which had been next on the schedule, the set got under way again. It continued without further hitch to 1890 and the publication of the thirty-ninth volume. The fire, tending somewhat to popularize the Bancroft house, may have made the work of canvassers and collectors a bit easier, but, with 12,000 volumes burned and the plates of a dozen volumes to be replaced, it entailed a large addition to the cost of production.

On the total number of copies now in existence and on the content of the volumes the fire had no effect. Upon the library, also, safely housed some three miles away, there was no direct damage. The business house and Bancroft's personal fortune were the things that suffered.

At San Diego, where he had been buying speculatively in expectation of a rise in prices, he sold some of his outlying property and erected a business building, which brought a good rental. At San Francisco, instead of selling the site on

[31] For example, Santa Barbara *Independent,* May 12, 1886; Salt Lake City *Tribune,* May 16, 1886; Waco *Texas Baptist Herald,* May 20, 1886; Las Vegas, New Mexico, *Chronicle,* May 20, 1886; New York *Tribune,* May 22, 1886; Philadelphia *American,* May 29, 1886; and Boston *Evening Journal,* June 1, 1886.

Market Street, he bought an additional twenty-five feet of frontage on Stevenson and began construction of a better building than the original.[32]

The main problem, however, was to develop a source of income. Through the thirty years since 1856 the business house had performed that function and had supported the collecting, the literary workshop, and the publishing ventures. At the library the most that could be done was to economize. By this time the collection was regarded as satisfactorily complete, and no great outlays were being made for new materials. The staff, with Oak taking the lead, voluntarily reduced their salaries, which lessened somewhat the financial burden that Bancroft had to meet. Nathan Stone's department, reorganized now as the History Company, was able to remedy part of the difficulty. Although the histories at the time of the fire were $200,000 in the red, revenue from the subscribers was beginning to come in at a satisfactory rate, and in the period following the fire this department supplied a principal part of Bancroft's income. It was, almost, the ugly duckling reaching maturity.

Meanwhile, Bancroft labored to revive his business house, which had been shattered as well as disrupted by the fire. His nephew, Will B. Bancroft, had opened his own print shop at 49 First Street. Three other nephews, Charles, George, and Harlow, had organized a schoolbook and supply house which they called Bancroft Brothers. Albert had taken the law department and merged it with Sumner Whitney's in a new firm of which he became president, the Bancroft-Whitney Company. Under the old firm name he also operated a music shop at 114 Dupont Street and a bookstore at 607 Market. The residue in Hubert Howe Bancroft's hands was little more than the Market Street site and the History Company.[33]

Upon completion of the new structure, which he chose to

[32] Bancroft, *Literary Industries*, 789–790.

[33] *Ibid.*, 788–789; *Langley's San Francisco Directory for the Year Commencing May, 1887* (San Francisco, 1887), p. 198.

call the History Building, Bancroft persuaded Will to rejoin him, and under the firm name of the Bancroft Company he reopened most of the former departments. In some respects the new establishment was better than its predecessor. Much of the rebuilding of business, however, was done by competing firms, including A. L. Bancroft and Company, Bancroft Brothers, and the Bancroft-Whitney Company, which continued their separate existence; and though 721 Market resumed its place as the ranking book mart of San Francisco, its margin of leadership was considerably reduced.[34] This relative decline and the reduced earning potential actually exceeded the $500,000, in excess of the insurance, which Bancroft had had to write off as a direct loss from the fire.

[34] The Bancroft-Whitney Company still operates. By 1892 A. L. Bancroft and Company had become only a music store and by 1897 it ceased to function. Bancroft Brothers continued till 1898, at which time the Bancroft Company likewise went out of existence and the History Building became rental property. See *Langley's San Francisco Directories* for 1888–1895, and the *Crocker-Langley Directories* for 1896–1899.

19

Subscription Publisher

I confess to a profound admiration for men of superior efforts and accomplishments, for men of strength and ability, of applied genius,—great men if you will; for no man ever yet performed a great work who was not entitled himself to be called great. Hubert Howe Bancroft, *Chronicles of the Builders*, I, xii

NO SOONER had the presses finished their marathon run on the thirty-nine volumes of the *Works* than Bancroft was ready to set them going again. He had copy in hand for a sequel in seven volumes of the customary fatness. Originally he contemplated naming this set Kings of the Commonwealth, but when actually issued, in 1891–1892, it was entitled *Chronicles of the Builders of the Commonwealth: Historical Character Study.*

This enterprise, besides representing the momentum gathered in Bancroft's literary workshop, had a twofold inspiration. It arose partly out of the circumstance that the histories had necessarily subordinated the biographical element. Their basic framework had been geographical and chronological; their thread, topical narrative. The men who made the history had been mentioned and credited and described, occasionally their careers and characters had been sketched, and in the Pioneer Register and elsewhere thousands of lives had been epitomized. Yet Bancroft could say that something less than justice had been done to the participants in the fabulous development of westernmost America.

Furthermore, the gratifying success of the campaign to market the *Works* suggested a continuation. If those solid, ponderous volumes of history could be made to pay for themselves, it seemed altogether probable that a biographical venture would yield a profit. And this result, it appeared, could be made doubly certain by resort to a device long hallowed in biographical publishing—the collection of a fee for each biography included.

By no means the inventor of subscription publishing, Bancroft had behind him at least one experience with it. In 1881 his house had brought out, presumably on a subscription basis, a sumptuous two-volume work, *Contemporary Biography of California's Representative Men,* edited by Alonzo Phelps, and with an introductory essay by Bancroft himself.[1] From the pattern standardized and especially popular in the field of local history the *Chronicles* deviated only in requiring fees considerably above the average in amount, and in intermingling the biographical sketches with the supporting text whereas the usual method in "mug books" was to present a historical section followed by an appendix of biographies.

This latter variation Bancroft chose to regard as a tenfold improvement. The recipe as he states it runs as follows: "Take one by one the more important of these men of strength and influence, and after a thorough character study, place their portraits in the midst of the work which they have done, and in company with kindred industries accomplished by others, and round the whole throw the framework of history." In a vein somewhat less felicitous he goes on to describe the result. "Here, then, are embalmed in the annals of their own time and country the men and their deeds, there to remain, the benefits and blessings conferred during life thus being made perpetual."[2]

[1] Hubert Howe Bancroft, "California's Biography," in Alonzo Phelps, ed., *Contemporary Biography of California's Representative Men* (2 vols.; San Francisco, 1881), I, 7–26.

[2] Hubert Howe Bancroft, *Chronicles of the Builders of the Commonwealth: Historical Character Study* (7 vols. and index, San Francisco, 1891–1892), I, x.

Anyone who leafs through the *Chronicles* will concede the validity both of the recipe and of the statement of results.

The steel engravings, first of all, present a formidable array of bearded oldsters. Their air is resolute, sturdy, self-confident, domineering; the majority appear both weighted and hardened by success; almost every visage comports with the reality of rugged individualism.

Going beyond the portraits to the biographical sketches, one encounters further similarity. These builders started as poor boys. They worked hard. They saved. Some eschewed borrowing as the blackest plague; others used their credit repeatedly and with daring. By collecting an unearned increment as the West grew, and by their own heroic efforts in making the West flourish, they emerged wealthy, prominent, influential, and powerful. Speculation and luck had enhanced their fortunes, but almost without exception they were self-made men. They were the aggrandizers, the enlargers, the builders, and, in that sense, the benefactors of the American West.

They were, in sooth, men pretty much like Bancroft, and in writing up their lives he was, to a degree, merely writing variations on his own biography. This fact, as well as the subscription character of the set, doubtless inclined him toward favorable comment and unstinted praise. These were men he could understand and whose worth he could appreciate. Such, at any rate, is the tenor of the sketches. The builders are presented as paragons of industry, honor, virtue, and public-spiritedness. Occasionally a between-the-lines reading carries a hint of intolerance, hardness, or even meanness, but the more general assertion is that they were the salt of the earth, the West's nobility, if not actually to be called its kings. And the cumulative effect upon the reader, it must be admitted, is apt to be overpowering.

An inevitable defect in the subscription method of biography publishing is that selection of subjects is put upon a completely arbitrary basis. In the usual work of this type the characters described are too often obscure and unimportant, the real reason for their inclusion being that they were affluent and gullible. With relatively few exceptions Bancroft's list was drawn up on this basis. The end result, however, was a fairly representative line-up of significant figures. Bristling with millionaires, his hundred names included half a dozen governors, half a dozen United States senators, a chief justice of the United States Supreme Court, San Francisco's most distinguished vigilante, several railroad tycoons, a number of leading bankers, captains of industry in mining, lumbering, shipbuilding, flour milling, and real-estate development, pioneers in the new techniques of western agriculture, and the founders of the University of Southern California and the Medical College of the University of California. Thus, although amendments would have improved it, the roster was respectable and distinguished.

The wisdom of several of Bancroft's choices has been corroborated by subsequent biographers who have published full-length treatments of Fray Junípero Serra and President Benito Juárez, who were included in the *Chronicles* without fee; of John Jacob Astor, Justice Stephen J. Field, and Cornelius Vanderbilt, for whom the actual fees are not on record; and of William T. Coleman, Henry Miller, E. J. "Lucky" Baldwin, and H. A. W. Tabor, who subscribed and paid. What Bancroft said of these men still retains considerable interest.

More usefulness attaches to his treatment of others comparable in significance but to the present not honored with a longer biography. Such, for example, were Frederick Billings, attorney and chief promoter of the Northern Pacific Railroad; Charles Crocker and Collis P. Huntington, kingpins for the Central Pacific and Southern Pacific; and George H. Sisson, enterpriser in Mexican railroads, mines, and colonization projects. In the realm of industry, many of the careers were worth recording, as for example that of Irving M. Scott of the Union Iron Works of San Francisco, designer and manufacturer of much heavy mining machinery and builder of ships, among them the battleship "Oregon." The achievements of Asa Mead Simpson in lumber, of Isaac Elder Blake as a pioneer in the transporting of oil by tank car, of Austin Sperry in the milling of flour, of Benjamin K. Porter as a tanner, of John Barton in salt, and John S. Morgan in canning oysters, were less spectacular, but in the aggregate they go far toward describing the production of wealth in the West in the generation then approaching its close. When supplemented with accounts of the high-pressure sales methods of the real-estate dealer Wendell Easton, of town founding as managed at Inglewood by Daniel Freeman, of irrigation construction as handled in the Fresno area by Moses J. Church, of fruit cultivation and marketing by refrigerator car as pioneered by Augustus T. Hatch, and of the undertaking business as made to flourish at San Francisco under the skillful hands of Nathaniel Gray, the panorama of building the West is lighted up throughout practically its entire extent. The majority of the hundred men here immortalized made a contribution large enough to assure that a record of their lives is worth having. En bloc these sketches provide an excellent biographical illustration of the history of the West in its emergence from frontier conditions.

In the *Chronicles,* furthermore, the biographical sketches are compounded with a series of historical essays and discussions which amount to some 1,897 pages, approximately 41.5 per cent of the set, or virtually the equivalent of three of the seven volumes. These essays are not footnoted or supported by bibliographies. They were written, however, out of the vast fund of information gathered and organized in the production of the histories, and consequently have a higher factual content and a greater reliability than is usual in offhand writing, such as they appear to be. For a survey of political development in the Pacific states the 292 pages on the subject in Volume II are an excellent reference. In the next volume appears a similar view of agricultural history. Volume IV deals with mines and manufactures. To the history of western railways the equivalent of an entire volume is devoted, and commerce, education, and religion are each treated at length.

Almost universally these essays have been regarded as adulterants thinning out the biographical content of the *Chronicles.* Furthermore, the derivative nature of the scholarship involved, the small circulation and the comparative rarity of the set, and the shadow of the subsidies upon it have minimized their actual use. Abstracted from the *Chronicles* and collected as a series of popular monographs, they would deserve attention and praise as competent summaries of the economic and social history of western America, in the light, of course, of the information available in 1890. The Bancroft Library has one such specimen, a 160-page gathering of the signatures from Volume VII that pertain to society, education, and religion.[3] The discussions of agriculture, commerce, mining, manufacturing, and transportation development would make an even better impression.

Memoranda and correspondence preserved in the Bancroft Library supply graphic detail on the way in which the *Chronicles* were promoted and produced. Early in 1888, for example, Bancroft was writing to his representative in Mexico that preliminary matter would soon be available on the projected volumes of biographies of notable men, "set in a fine framework of history, and conditions and resources of the country." After remarking that "it will best anything of the kind that has ever been done," Bancroft went on to say: "I have no particular desire of our straining ourselves in the matter of Mexico and Spanish America, but if there are any men there who want to put up from $1,500 to $10,000 Mexican money,

[3] Hubert Howe Bancroft, *Society—Past and Present; Education in the Western United States, Central America, and Mexico; Science, Art, and Literature in Mexico; The Church in the Western United States, Central America, and Mexico* [San Francisco, 1892].

in advance, for a woodcut or steel portrait and biography, the latter to be in extent and power according to the coin, (which the Mexican office can have 25% of), they are now offered the opportunity. . . . Here is a good chance for the coming president, González, and others."[4]

In July, 1890, to take another example, solicitor Washington Davis wrote from Chicago concerning a prospect, George M. Pullman:

> Got well started on dictation by 11 a.m., when Mr. Pullman had to stop to meet important business engagement on account of dividend. He begged to be excused for the day and thinks we can finish tomorrow after eleven o'clock. Has had his private secretary gathering material for me for two days. I may be able to forward same and photograph tomorrow night. Nothing said about money. Huntington's portrait had fine effect. A good subject.[5]

A few days later Davis reported again:

> Have been with him all day from 10:30 a.m. He took me down to his town in his private car, and it was 5 p.m. before we returned. He is now thoroughly interested, has given fifteen pages dictation, and an abundance of other material, from which can be made one of the finest biog's in the "Chronicles." But the dictation cannot be finished until after Aug. 14. He wants to get some information from his mother at 1,000 Islands, and will also furnish photo then when he will be looking better and feeling better.
>
> "The bars are not put up."
>
> Everything in good shape with him. His name goes a long distance with the others. "Old Hutch" goes the other way.[6]

There, unfortunately, the record of this episode ends. The life of Pullman, which would have been "one of the finest biog's in the 'Chronicles,' " was not put into print, and one is left to infer that, when something finally was said about money, the sleeping-car magnate declined to coöperate.

[4] Hubert Howe Bancroft to R. D. Faulkner, San Francisco, January 5, 1888, MS, Bancroft Library.

[5] Report of Washington Davis, Chicago, July 1, 1890, MS, Bancroft Library.

[6] Report of Washington Davis, Chicago, July 9, 1890, MS, Bancroft Library.

Although part of the writing was done by the solicitors, a larger amount was done in the library on Valencia Street. Here Bancroft was assisted by several men held over from the original staff, among them Thomas Savage, William Nemos, and Alfred Bates. The experience they had gained must have facilitated greatly the task of preparing the copy for this second series of volumes. There is little testimony on the exact manner in which the work was carried on, but a letter from the proprietor to one of the workmen supplies at least a hint.

> In regard to your work on Biographies, it stands simply in this way. I am pledged to give the biographies to the History Company promptly as soon as they can be done after they are handed in. This is imperative. If you don't do it, I shall have to get someone else. This I should dislike to do as I know you and your work, and am in the main satisfied with it.
>
> And so far as you are concerned, I am sure you will never find so good, pleasant, and permanent work again if you lose this.
>
> This work will probably last for years, but it won't do at all whenever I leave town for you to stop work, for I shall be away a great deal of the time, and the work will *have* to go on.[7]

A sidelight on the soliciting in southern California is provided in the next to the last chapter of Horace Bell's *On the Old West Coast.* So far as Bell was concerned, the biography business was a monstrous and ludicrous graft; he had only contempt for those who were a party to it, and what he had to say about it was in the nature of a diatribe and lampooning. After describing how a woman commissioned by the *Golden Era* wrote fantastically embellished lives of "forty fools" whom he had pointed out among his acquaintances in southern California, and how Col. R. S. Baker paid her *not* to write up his life, Bell turned to the work of Dr. Edwin W. Fowler, who canvassed for Bancroft in that part of the state. Bell was particularly scornful that John G. Downey, a former governor, allowed Fowler to invent for him a distinguished ancestry in Ireland, a castle and the like. According to Bell, when

[7] Hubert Howe Bancroft to Alfred Bates, n.p., n.d., MS, Bancroft Library.

Downey's check for $5,000 was presented for payment, banker E. F. Spence refused to honor it. "I am Downey's business agent," he quotes Spence as saying, "and if this is the sort of thing he is spending his money for then he is incompetent to manage his own affairs."[8] Apparently there was a hitch in collecting from Downey. The proof sheets of his biography have a notation in Bancroft's hand: "Hold till 5M is paid."[9] Bell admits that Downey was perfectly willing to pay. He asserts categorically that the *Chronicles* were never published.[10] But of course they did appear, with Downey's biography very much in evidence,[11] which would seem to prove that the reluctant banker finally cashed the check.

A memorandum certified by H. B. Hambly sets forth the amounts subscribed and paid by the various candidates for inclusion in the *Chronicles*.[12] The accuracy of this list may not be absolute, but it agrees with the relevant evidence at hand. It records no subscriptions for the biographies of the Astors, Benito Juárez, Junípero Serra, Stephen J. Field, Lorenzo Sawyer, Matthew P. Deady, Richard Gird, the Vanderbilts, and Daniel Ream. Unpaid subscriptions are listed for Irving M. Scott, Watson C. Squire, George W. Hunt, and Robert Whitney Waterman, and partly paid subscriptions for William T. Coleman, Annis Merrill, Jeremiah F. Sullivan, Dean J. Locke, and Elias J. Baldwin.

On the average, there was one page of biography for each hundred dollars of subsidy, and quite a few of the thousand-dollar contributors were rewarded with their steel-engraved likeness and the normal ten pages. Others drew more space: Austin Sperry at the rate of 2.0 pages per hundred dollars,

[8] Horace Bell, *On the Old West Coast: Being Further Reminiscences of a Ranger* (New York, 1930), 288.

[9] Meaning, of course, $5,000. Notation on page proof in the John G. Downey folder, Bancroft Library.

[10] Bell, *On the Old West Coast,* 289.

[11] Bancroft, *Chronicles of the Builders,* II, 120–137.

[12] Harry B. Hambly, "List of Subscribers to 'Chronicles of the Builders of the Commonwealth,' Stating Amount Subscribed and Paid," October, 1936, MS, Bancroft Library.

Elias J. Baldwin 2.7, Alban Nelson Towne 3.3, Governor Francis Emory Warren 3.5, Moses Hopkins 4.2, Alonzo Erastus Horton 4.3, the Ames brothers 5.0, and William T. Coleman 18.1. Others got less than a page per hundred dollars; for example, William Gilpin 0.61, George H. Sisson 0.45, Joseph Failing 0.40, John G. Downey 0.32, and Daniel C. Freeman 0.30. The interpretation perhaps should be that lives that were not of much interest or importance were written up briefly, no matter what was subscribed. Or it could be that the solicitation was on a catch-as-catch-can basis, and each man was struck for what it was thought he might pay. Whatever the explanation, the ratio between amount subscribed and length of biography was not constant; or, in other words, the sketches were not done on a straight space-rate basis.

Financially the *Chronicles* were a brilliant success. Omitting from the reckoning the Astors and Vanderbilts, Scott, Gird, Deady, Ream, and certain others who may or may not have paid, the total subvention amounted to $219,225,[13] which must have been several times the cost of preparation and manufacture.

Manifestly, it would have been impossible to keep the subscription nature of the *Chronicles* a secret. Bancroft did not openly proclaim it, but, on the other hand, he made no real effort to conceal this element in the arrangements. As an open secret it became general knowledge. Thereupon certain critics, reasoning by analogy, were ready to charge that Bancroft's histories must have been done on the same pattern, with space and favorable treatment open to purchase on substantially the same basis.[14] This conclusion had very little direct evidence to stand on. Concern for the financial success of the *Chronicles* did, however, at times exert an influence upon the content of the histories.

[13] *Ibid.*

[14] William A. Morris, "The Origin and Authorship of the Bancroft Pacific States Publications: A History of a History," *Oregon Historical Quarterly*, IV (1903), 334.

Leland Stanford's biography, in consideration of a promise of $10,000, was written and set in type. On the eve of its release, however, he took umbrage at the interminable nature of the *Works,* complained that he had been duped into agreeing to take forty sets, and refused to pay any further tribute. The long article on his life was therefore killed; Volume VI of the *Chronicles* had to be padded out with additional nonbiographical matter; and the laudatory comment that appears on page 753 of the sixth volume of the *History of California* in Stanford's personal set was suppressed so far as general circulation of the *Works* was concerned.[15]

Judge Orville C. Pratt's retaining fee of $2,600 not only insured a eulogistic biographical sketch in the *Chronicles,* but also prompted revision of a passage in the *History of Oregon* reporting the trial in 1850 of five Indians charged with responsibility for the Whitman massacre. As first set in type this report was somewhat cynical. The editor of the *Oregon Spectator* had praised the judge for being "firm and fearless." Adverting to the determination of the Oregonians, especially the old settlers, that these Indians should be punished, Bancroft had written: "There was not the slightest danger that Pratt would go against the people in this matter. But he ruled as he did, not so much from any just or noble sentiment, as, first, because there was present no inducement to do otherwise, the fifty horses not going to the judge [an allusion to the mode of compensating the counsel that the court had appointed for the defense]; and secondly, he well knew the country would be too hot to hold him should he do otherwise."[16] For a later printing this passage was deleted in favor of an encomium on Judge Pratt, praising his knowledge of the law, the courage and dignity with which he conducted

[15] George T. Clark, "Leland Stanford and H. H. Bancroft's 'History,' a Bibliographical Curiosity," *Papers* of the Bibliographical Society of America, XXVII (1933), 12–23; see also chapter 17, above.

[16] Hubert Howe Bancroft, *History of Oregon,* II, 97–98. The Bancroft Library has a copy with this wording.

this trial, his awareness that violent measures might be precipitated if the defendants should be allowed to escape through a technicality, and the general confidence and respect that he won throughout Oregon. The *Spectator's* adjectives "firm and fearless" are used without a blush and without quotes. They reappear in a virtually identical paragraph in the *Chronicles*.[17]

Conceivably, the original statement reflects Frances Fuller Victor's slant, and the revised version Bancroft's. It seems more likely, however, that the cynical and facetious tone first employed was not intended to express harsh criticism or ill will, and that the subsequent mellowing of judgment was accomplished by the commission to cover Pratt in the *Chronicles*.

Another issue on which Bancroft's opinion shifted was that of the degree of obligation resting upon the Central Pacific Railroad Company to repay interest and principal on the bonds advanced by the United States Government. In the *History of California* Bancroft set forth the arguments pro and con and left the reader to take his choice.[18] In the *Chronicles,* in the essay on Collis P. Huntington, he voiced only the railroad's contention that it was not originally contemplated that there should be repayment in cash, that repayment in services by transporting troops and military supplies had fallen far below expectations because the mere existence of the railroad had curbed the Indians, that the government's mismanagement of the sinking fund under the terms of the Thurman Act cost the company $2,000,000, and that authorization and subsidizing of competing railroads made it impossible for the Central Pacific to repay.[19]

Twenty years later, when Bancroft again took pen in hand, he saw this problem in another light, berated the railroad

[17] Bancroft, *Chronicles of the Builders,* II, 245.
[18] Bancroft, *History of California,* VII, 621–624.
[19] Bancroft, *Chronicles of the Builders,* V, 83–85.

company for attempting to defraud the nation through the Funding Bill, and excoriated Huntington as the highest criminal among those who had held California in thralldom through the four decades of what he called its dark age of graft.[20] Unquestionably this was Bancroft's real opinion as of 1912. By that date crusaders of the Lincoln-Roosevelt League had spread this conviction among the majority of Californians. A paragraph in *Essays and Miscellany,*[21] protesting the "wholesale robbery" that had characterized railroad building, suggests that Bancroft's earlier attitude was less favorable toward the Big Four than is indicated by the Huntington biography in the *Chronicles.* This would appear, then, to be another occasion when the retaining fee colored the interpretation.

Partly because of this coloring of judgment, but largely because of the fee system that was employed, the *Chronicles* have come in for heavy abuse. Horace Bell used the phrases "bogus book" and "the top of the biographical graft,"[22] while Henry L. Oak scornfully remarked, "Great men, who happen to be rich, may have their greatness put on record by the historian of the Pacific Coast."[23] Today's verdict would be a trifle less severe; yet, even so, the stigma has not worn off. The stain tended likewise to spread, blackening Bancroft's name and sullying the reputation of his histories. In the competent topical surveys and in the wealth of biographical data illustrating and enlivening the latter portion of the histories, the *Chronicles* possess real merit. Yet, notwithstanding these good points, it is clear that Bancroft's standing among his contemporaries and in the estimate of the historical profession would have been better if the idea of doing these biographies had never occurred to him.

Encouraged by the profits accruing from the *Chronicles,*

---

[20] Bancroft, *Retrospection,* 232–239.
[21] Bancroft, *Essays and Miscellany,* 441.
[22] Bell, *On the Old West Coast,* 287–288.
[23] Henry L. Oak, *"Literary Industries" in a New Light,* 55.

Bancroft indulged in two other elaborate publishing ventures, *The Book of the Fair,*[24] occasioned by the Columbian Exposition at Chicago, and *The Book of Wealth,*[25] occasioned by the upwelling prosperity of the United States and the rise of large fortunes. Neither of these works was a "vanity publication" in which biographical data might be inserted for a consideration, but both were sumptuous and expensive works, beyond the reach of the masses, designed in format to grace the tables of the ultrawealthy, and in content to appeal to this same clientele.

Beginning in 1876 with the centennial of the Declaration of Independence, the American people were deluged with a succession of historic events to celebrate. Grand fairs or expositions came to be the favorite commemorative device, and the climax, though by no means the last example, was the Chicago fair, marking the four-hundredth anniversary of the discovery of America. By its pretensions alone this exposition was worth the attention of historians. It was, furthermore, a moulding force upon the nation, exerting influences on architecture and loosing other impulses that were to be felt for a generation.

While the Chicago fair was still in the blueprint stage, Bancroft displayed a lively interest in it, especially in arranging as a complement to it a historical exhibition in the Far West. He prepared a long memorandum on the subject,[26] in which

[24] Hubert Howe Bancroft, *The Book of the Fair: An Historical and Descriptive Presentation of the World's Science, Art, and Industry, as Viewed through the Columbian Exposition at Chicago in 1893* . . . (5 vols.; Chicago and San Francisco, 1893).

[25] Hubert Howe Bancroft, *Achievements of Civilization: The Book of Wealth: Wealth in Relation to Material and Intellectual Progress and Achievement; Being an Inquiry into the Nature and Distribution of the World's Resources and Riches, and a History of the Origin and Influence of Property, Its Possession, Accumulation, and Disposition in All Ages and among All Nations, as a Factor in Human Accomplishment, an Agency of Human Refinement, and in the Evolution of Civilization from the Earliest to the Present Era* (10 vols.; New York, 1896–1908).

[26] Hubert Howe Bancroft, Memorandum concerning the Holding of a Pacific Coast Historical Exhibition at Sacramento in 1892, MS, Bancroft Library.

he argued that, in the East, "the great event cannot come home to them as it should come home to us." "Spanish discovery and occupation in America," he added, "is in the direct line of our history." "There is no place in the world more appropriate and fitting for a historical celebration of the discovery by Columbus than this western seaboard . . . where civilization itself must pause and make a retrospection."

Among other things, he proposed quarter-acre relief maps of the New World as it was in 1492 and as it had become in 1892, exhibits of Indian artifacts and ways of life, exhibits to show the real life of mines and mining camps and the evolution of the mining industry, displays of Mexican and Central American products, and presentations to illustrate the material progress of the West in agriculture, industry, and transportation.

With respect to most of the older communities he was of the opinion that their early history was "too traditional and too remote from the busy present to be intelligently given in a line of material exhibits in natural and comprehensive sequence." As for the West, however, he was confident that an exhibition of a historical character would "do much to quicken the study of our past," would "broaden intelligence concerning the Pacific Coast," would attract the attention of people at a distance, and would "address the fancy and excite the curiosity of every class." To insure that this intellectual stimulation should result, he proposed exhibits of books and manuscripts, conferences, lectures, and discussions, through which an awareness of the historical evolution of the Pacific states "from Alaska to Patagonia" would be inculcated in all. Every visitor to such a fair would come away "wiser, intellect brighter, blood and brain aglow with new food and fire."

This elaborate concourse at Sacramento did not become a reality. Some of its material features were incorporated in the Mid-Winter Exposition at San Francisco in 1894, which, however, was essentially a reëxhibit of Russian furs, French art,

German manufactures, and the like, that had been on display at Chicago. But it was not the Pacific Coast Historical Exposition from which Bancroft had such great expectations for "progressional inspiration." The Chicago fair came nearer realizing these expectations, and to it he had turned his attention.

As a manifestation of his interest he published in 1893 a sumptuous work in five lush volumes, *The Book of the Fair: An Historical and Descriptive Presentation of the World's Science, Art, and Industry as Viewed through the Columbian Exposition at Chicago in 1893*... Done in de luxe format, on heavy paper twenty-two inches by seventeen, with a profusion of illustrations, and in a limited edition of 400 sets, this work was at once a tribute to the fair and an exaction of tribute from purchasers such as had shown by their support of the *Chronicles of the Builders* that they could be counted on to order a work of this sort.

On at least two occasions columnist Ambrose Bierce supplied his readers with advance notices of this set. Late in 1892 he announced: "That eminent *littérateur,* Hubert Howe Bancroft . . . is engaged in another peculiarly Bancrovian project . . . *The Book of the Fair*—not, as might be inferred from the title, a history of the female sex, but a volume on the Chicagonese exposition. A volume indeed!—is Hubert a paragrapher that he should do this thing? There are to be *twenty* volumes and no two alike."[27] Again, a circular inquiring about exhibits at the fair happened to fall into Bierce's hands. "My exhibit," he wrote, "(how did you know that I was to have one?) is to consist of a brazen plate inscribed with the names of the foremost eight of California's literary and commercial impostors . . . as follows: (1) Hubert Howe Bancroft; (2) Hubert H. Bancroft; (3) H. Howe Bancroft; (4) H. H. Bancroft; (5) Bancroft, Hubert Howe; (6) Bancroft, Hubert H.; (7) Ban-

[27] Ambrose Bierce, "Prattle," San Francisco *Examiner,* November 27, 1892.

croft, H. Howe; (8) Bancroft, H. H."[28] Bancroft, needless to say, was undaunted by this gratuitous invective and went on with his plan.

As "companion and consort to the Book of the Fair," he then proceeded to issue another folio set, comparable in format, but of ten volumes and in an edition of 950 sets. Again the title was descriptive. *Achievements of Civilization: The Book of Wealth: Wealth in Relation to Material and Intellectual Progress and Achievement; Being an Inquiry into the Nature and Distribution of the World's Resources and Riches, and a History of the Origin and Influence of Property, Its Possession, Accumulation, and Disposition in All Ages and among All Nations, as a Factor in Human Accomplishment, an Agency of Human Refinement, and in the Evolution of Civilization from the Earliest to the Present Era.* This grand design was accomplished in some twenty-nine chapters, beginning in Chaldea and Egypt, progressing through the Far East, Central Asia, Greece, Italy, western Europe, Africa, Australia and Hawaii, South America, Central America, Mexico, and Canada, to the United States. In the final seven chapters the role of wealth was pursued from the Pacific states to the Rocky Mountain, Midcontinent, the Southern, the Central Lake, the New England, and finally to the Middle Atlantic states.

The ideas set forth in this thousand-page survey of wealth through the ages are not profound. As an example of luxurious book making and as a commercial venture it is of somewhat greater interest. With it Bancroft closed the career as a subscription publisher which had been foreshadowed in his *Works* and brought to its most important expression in the *Chronicles of the Builders.*

---

[28] *Ibid.*, February 26, 1893.

20

Bitter Harvest

There were hundreds in California who damned me every day.
Hubert Howe Bancroft, *Literary Industries,* 310

As he entered upon his sixties, Bancroft could look back upon an eventful and productive career. In the forty years since his first arrival in California he had built a business and a fortune, had assembled the most remarkable collection of western Americana in existence, had brought out half a hundred massive volumes of history and biography, and had marketed these commercially forbidding tomes with such genius that they were made to yield a profit. By 1892 he had accomplished most of the things on which his fame must ultimately rest.

He was, at sixty, a trifle stooped from bending over the writing desk. Asthma tortured him periodically, but otherwise he was hale and hearty, and would yet live on for a full quarter century. This outcome is a happy irony after the apprehension he had felt that his allotted years might run out before the *Works* could be completed, and after the way he had driven himself and his staff to get that job done.

It ought to be the lot of a historian who has a monumental achievement to his credit to spend his declining years basking in the honors he has earned. Had Bancroft lived still another quarter century, such plaudits would have come to him. As it was, he received scant honor. In fact, his "retirement" in 1892 from active duty as a historian was to the accompaniment of a chorus of abuse in which the catcalls of Ambrose Bierce were no more than the leitmotif.

There may be individuals so detached and self-sufficient that they are indifferent to what is said about them, but certainly Bancroft was not such a person. He was sensitive in the extreme and felt every thrust, although oftentimes he wisely chose to ignore attacks. To criticism, of course, he was accustomed, though not inured. In the early 'eighties the men of Morgan had belabored him unmercifully for his disagreement with their chief. Others had derided the folly of a merchant purporting to be a scholar. The high-pressure methods of some of his collectors and salesmen supplied still others with grievances. The bulk of the *Works* was an irritant to some, and the subscription character of the *Chronicles* gave others an excuse to recoil. Throughout the 'eighties and at intervals thereafter Bancroft was the target of snipers and potshooters, but the heaviest salvo of recriminations came in the early 'nineties.

There was, for example, the complaint voiced by Henry L. Oak, for eighteen years the chief assistant in the literary workshop.[1] In the early stages of his work for Bancroft, Oak was a warm admirer of his employer and an enthusiast for the grand project at which they were working. As time went on, his admiration somewhat cooled, and he felt and expressed regret that the quality of the *Works* was suffering because publication was too much rushed, but his heart was still in the work and his loyalty was evidenced, as late as 1886, after the great fire, when he voluntarily reduced his salary by 25 per cent in order to help Bancroft carry on. The next year, upon the completion of the volume on Arizona and New Mexico, ill health made necessary his retirement from the library.

During the next few years, while Oak was, as he called himself, "a hermit invalid,"[2] the waves of criticism of Bancroft and

---

[1] Henry L. Oak, *"Literary Industries" in a New Light: A Statement on the Authorship of Bancroft's Native Races and History of the Pacific States, with Comments on These Works and the System by Which They Were Written* . . . (San Francisco, 1893).

[2] *Ibid.*, 8.

his *Works* stirred mixed emotions in his breast. As the designer of several of the methods employed in the library and as the dean of the workmen there, he had a personal interest in the acceptance and the reputation of the *Works*. He had contributed much to them and could not help feeling that denunciation of them was a reflection on his work. On the other hand, aware of certain shortcomings in Bancroft, and contrasting his early protestations and promises with subsequent neglect, he was inclined to second certain of the criticisms. Particularly when *Literary Industries* was issued, with its description of the methods employed for the production of the *Works,* Oak felt impelled to plunge into the argument.

In December, 1891, he busied himself with the preparation of a statement, subsequently printed as an eighty-page pamphlet, in which he undertook to correct the Bancroft version of what had been done in the literary workshop. His chief purpose—and on this point he was emphatic—was to insist that Bancroft's assistants, himself in particular, had in fact been collaborators and were entitled to recognition as authors. Supplementary to this argument he gave an account, at variance with Bancroft's, of the processes used in the library, and he supplied much incidental information about happenings during his connection with the enterprise. For example, it is here set down that the send-off review of *Native Races,* substituted for President Gilman's cautious effort, and published in the *Overland Monthly* over the signature of J. Ross Browne, was actually written by Oak. "In my haste," he added, "I cribbed one or two elegant phrases from President Gilman's previous effusion."[3]

Although the central core of Oak's argument was that Bancroft had misrepresented, he gave a good deal of space to combating unjust charges that had been festooned upon those that he considered legitimate and justifiable. He objected, for instance, to the abusive articles and cartoons in

[3] *Ibid.*, 57.

which "the *soi-disant* author [Bancroft] was represented as incapable of writing grammatical English, using his great wealth to hire at starvation rates needy men and women of some literary experience or ability to write his volumes, and purchasing with money favorable notices in the press."[4] He denied that historical materials were collected under false pretenses, or borrowed and not returned, and he insisted that, within his knowledge, "no part of the Bancroft collection was improperly acquired."[5] He dismissed as incredible the charge that any considerable number of intelligent men subscribed for thirty-nine volumes on the supposition that there were to be only a few.[6] Concerning another calumny, that Bancroft accepted pay for space or favorable treatment in the *Works*, Oak, reminding his readers that he had been in a position to know what was going on, testified that Bancroft certainly never attempted to "deliver the goods."[7] Part of the criticism he ascribed to disgruntled employees, and part to jealousy among university historians. He thought it ridiculous that Theodore H. Hittell should refuse to consult Bancroft's *Works* in the preparation of his history of California.[8]

He was ready to stand up for the necessity and the significance of local annals and to defend the *Works* as an excellent example thereof. Of them he observed, "Thus while the defects are superficial, the merits go deeper, and are such as in my opinion are chiefly to be desired in a work of reference on such a scale, and on such a subject."[9] Except that "the manuscript archives of Spain and Mexico were practically not searched," he accepted every claim that Bancroft had made concerning the thoroughness of the collecting.[10] He hailed his chief as the worst compiler but the best writer of the entire staff. "Give him a topic which he understood and in which he was interested, and he would present it in a manner to hold the reader's attention in a far higher degree than any

[4] *Ibid.*, 12.
[5] *Ibid.*, 14–16.
[6] *Ibid.*, 16.
[7] *Ibid.*, 17.
[8] *Ibid.*, 20–21.
[9] *Ibid.*, 23.
[10] *Ibid.*, 26.

of his associates."[11] Perhaps because the parts of the *Works* for which he had been responsible were annalistic, Oak deplored that Bancroft had insisted on proffering his *Works* as history rather than annals.[12]

Concerning the annals of the Spanish Northwest on which he had worked, Oak pointed out that they were based on an abundance of source materials, that the space allotted had been adequate, the time permitted sufficient, and the general subject matter of intrinsic significance. Although the entire series was at the moment "under a cloud of disapproval and distrust," it was for reasons largely independent of its real qualities, and Oak was confident that in the long run the *Works,* and especially the California volumes, would be acclaimed of great value and high importance.[13]

His statement, thus, contained generous praise of the *Works,* as well as a measure of compliment for Bancroft as a writer, a fair and liberal employer, and a man "who, by his force of character, would have achieved success in almost any direction."[14] Yet it contained a strong denunciation of the policy of withholding credits for authorship and of other defects in Bancroft's methods, and Oak felt constrained to give notice that he intended to release the statement.

Accordingly, on April 3, 1892, he addressed a long letter to his former patron.[15] "Dear Sir," he began, "I write to inform you of my intention to publish a statement respecting the authorship of the *Bancroft Works* and my connection with the same, with some comments on the methods of writing the works, and some criticism of statements in the *Literary Industries*." He expressed, then, a degree of diffidence about joining the ranks of Bancroft's detractors, with whose enmity he had in most phases no sympathy. He hesitated also because of "old-time assurances" that he "had nothing to fear finan-

[11] *Ibid.,* 35.
[12] *Ibid.,* 72.
[13] *Ibid.,* 72–76.
[14] *Ibid.,* 36.
[15] Henry L. Oak to H. H. Bancroft, Seigler Springs, April 3, 1892, printed in Oak, *"Literary Industries" in a New Light,* 66–67.

cially" so long as Bancroft had any money. He assumed that these promises had "ceased long ago to be valid," but not wanting to leave it in Bancroft's power to say, "I always intended to do something for Oak, and if he had given me notice all might have been arranged," he included in his letter this curious proposal: "If in addition to courteous treatment and a fair salary for work done for you, I had ever accepted from you any financial favors of any amount, I should of course feel bound to silence on certain matters. And even now if you are willing to give me for past services, say $20,000—an immense sum for me and a very small one for you,—I should still feel myself so bound, destroying my statement and all memoranda, and whenever I could not conscientiously speak in your favor, keeping strict silence."

Under ordinary circumstances, one would read here a demand and a threat. Oak protested that he did not so intend, and when we read his entire statement and bear in mind his characterization of himself as "a hermit invalid, brooding, perhaps too much, over the only piece of literary work he has ever done, or is ever likely to do,"[16] it is clear that this was something short of blackmail.

"I have received your very remarkable letter," runs the reply which Bancroft dashed off, "and as I know that you are neither fool, knave, nor blackmailer, I conclude it's your liver, and also that you have more friends than you know what to do with, as you are so ready to sacrifice the oldest and best you ever had."[17] Asserting that Oak had always had from him kindness and liberality, pleasant and congenial employment, good pay, and more credit than he had a right to expect, Bancroft observed, "Indeed, I doubt if authors are in the habit of giving their employees any credit at all, and oftentimes not very much pay."

"In regard to the threat you make," he added, "that if I

[16] *Ibid.*, 8.

[17] Hubert Howe Bancroft to Henry L. Oak, Helix, April 14, 1892, printed in Oak, *"Literary Industries" in a New Light,* 67–68.

don't give you $20,000 you will publish something against me, I say, Proceed. . . . The work is done, and you may say what you please, and people may think what they please." The truth, he was confident, could not hurt him. "If you are sick I am sorry, but making an ass of yourself will not make you feel any better." And with this unconciliatory remark, Bancroft took leave of his former librarian and chief assistant.

A reader of this exchange of letters is almost sure to get the impression that Oak, for all his admirable traits, was inept and ineffectual. As a pathetic figure, he wins sympathy. Bancroft, on the contrary, appears brusque and hard, if not heartless. He was, of course, a man of great determination, which sometimes expressed itself as obstinacy, and there was not the remotest likelihood that he would pay out the $20,000. Nor, under the circumstances, is it desirable that he should have done so. For, as Oak admitted, it was not financially that he had been ill used. The recompense he really wanted was to have his authorship put clearly on record, and the suppression of his statement would have been the longest possible step in the opposite direction. It is better that at this stage Bancroft said to him, "Proceed."

Yet instead of mitigating the wrongness of Bancroft's earlier decision about withholding credit from his collaborators, this pathetic incident points up the fundamental error of his procedure, which was indeed his tragic flaw. His original decision to use only his name was a commercial one and reflected his unfamiliarity with the ways of scholars. In time, the idea that he expressed to Oak, "I doubt if authors are in the habit of giving their employees any credit at all," became his real conviction. His critics have pounced on this notion as a complete falsehood. It was at least a half truth, but unfortunately Bancroft persuaded himself that it was entirely correct. Repeatedly in the course of publishing the *Works* he passed up opportunities to set matters right by an open avowal of the nature of the assistance he had used. In *Liter-*

ary Industries, in particular, he might have told the whole story. A $20,000 check to Oak, nevertheless, would have been no proper remedy.

In February, 1893, Oak made arrangements with the Bacon Printing Company in San Francisco to bring out his statement. Containing much that was pro as well as some that was contra, it was a temperate criticism. To judge by the infrequent references to it and by the small number of copies that seem to have survived,[18] Oak gave it little circulation, and it attracted much less attention than Frances Fuller Victor's claim to authorship. Superimposing her name on the covers and inserting a special preface, she exhibited four volumes of the *Works* at the Mechanics' Fair at San Francisco in January, 1893, and in a display of writings by New York women, later in the year, at Utica.[19] In various newspaper articles she also asserted her claim to authorship.[20]

Later in 1893, Bancroft was sued for libel by his nephew, Will B. Bancroft, for years the manager of the printing department in the Bancroft house. Alleging that his uncle had charged him with making improper use of moneys held in trust, Will asked $200,000 damages. Bancroft telegraphed from Chicago that to avoid the nuisance and notoriety of the suit he would compromise with his nephew for $2,500 or $3,000. On his return, however, he decided to fight the charges, and in September, 1893, the case came to trial before a jury in Judge Slack's court.[21]

[18] There are copies in the Bancroft and the Huntington libraries, but the work is not mentioned in Cowan's *Bibliography of the History of California.*

[19] William A. Morris, "The Origin and Authorship of the Bancroft Pacific States Publications: A History of a History," *Oregon Historical Quarterly,* IV (1903), 344–345. See also *San Francisco Women's Literary Exhibit, Columbian Exposition, 1893: List of Books by California Writers* (San Francisco, 1893).

[20] Salt Lake City *Tribune,* April 14, 1893; New York *Mail and Express,* November 23, 1893; Salem *Oregon Statesman,* February 24, 1895; cited in Morris, *op. cit.,* 332, 353, 357.

[21] Reported in various San Francisco papers; for example, the *Examiner,* September 19 through October 8, 1893.

The essential facts brought before the court were as follows: After having to call on his uncle to pay off certain gambling debts in San Diego, Will had come to San Francisco and had gone to work at $40 a month as an advertising solicitor for A. L. Bancroft and Company. Transferred to the printing department, he became its manager and advanced in salary to $300 a month. After the fire of 1886 he established his own printing business on Stevenson Street, where, according to his assertion, he made $6,000 in ten months.

Bancroft subsequently induced him to come back into the firm as manager of the printing department at a salary of $350 a month and with a quarter interest, some 1,350 shares, in the History Company. Will contributed his printing business, which was of little or no book value,[22] and gave his note for $50,000. He soon found that he could not meet the interest payments on the note. A new one without interest was drawn and then cancelled, but the 1,350 shares were left in his possession, though on condition that they were not to be hypothecated. Nevertheless, he did put them up as security for a loan of $3,500 at the People's Bank. As soon as Bancroft learned of this, he got the shares "out of pawn" by paying the "$3,500 or so" that had been borrowed and by covering Will's overdraft of $12,000. He preferred no charges against his nephew, but promptly discharged him.[23]

Subsequently, Bancroft so far relented as to put his nephew back on the payroll at $25 a week "for certain services, because he said he had no money and he thought he could get some orders for the printing office. He agreed to reform and do better." The arrangement cannot have been satisfactory to either party. In two brief notes addressed to his nephew Bancroft bluntly said he had no expectation that Will would pay him back, either the $25 a week he was receiving, or the

[22] He testified that its assets were $24,000 and its liabilities $23,000; Bancroft's attorney put the liabilities at $26,000. San Francisco *Examiner*, September 19, 1893.

[23] As reported in the San Francisco *Examiner*, September 27, 1893.

$5,000 that had been put up a decade earlier to pay off the gambling debts. As plainly, Will was distraught. Evidently he hinted at suicide, for in one of the notes from his uncle there appears this postscript, "I would like back the pistol you borrowed of me, not that I am afraid you will kill yourself, but I want it."[24]

At this stage of the game, in 1891, Will resorted to the law in an attempt to force a dividend payment by the History Company. It was in this connection that Bancroft assertedly called him an embezzler. At the trial, in 1893, Bancroft's attorneys sought to prove that his statement to reporter Joseph T. Cooney had been merely that his nephew "never owned the stock, that he merely held it in trust and pledged it for his own use." Will's attorney got Cooney and several others to give what the reporter for the *Examiner* called "testimony to show that some people thought the irate uncle was charging his nephew with embezzlement."[25]

In the courtroom there were fireworks aplenty. Bancroft's attorneys, with Thomas A. C. Dorland, secretary-treasurer of the History Company, as a principal witness, maintained that their client had not committed a libel, that the language attributed to him had not been proved, that there was no proof of malice on his part, and that on the contrary he had greatly aided his nephew. The attorneys for the plaintiff were more sensational. Former Judge Van Fleet asked the jury to award heavy damages as the only way to punish a defendant worth at least $1,500,000. And Eugene Deuprey in his closing argument declaimed that "Dorland, instead of being a Man Friday to Crusoe Bancroft, was more like a Sancho Panzo to the Don Quixote Bancroft."[26] With this sage observation to ponder, the jurymen retired. After deliberating for a while, they asked the judge what amount of damages would com-

[24] Hubert Howe Bancroft to Will B. Bancroft, San Francisco, n.d., printed, *ibid.*, September 19, 1893.

[25] *Ibid.*, September 20 and 21, 1893.

[26] *Ibid.*, October 6, 1893.

pensate the plaintiff for court costs, and, being told "anything over $300," they brought in an award of $350. Attorney Deuprey moved that the verdict be set aside as "outrageously against the evidence."[27] The court took the matter under advisement, but in the end it was the defendant's demurrer that was sustained by the superior court.[28]

Throughout, the San Francisco newspapers regarded the trial as good copy. The *Examiner* sent a staff artist as well as a reporter, and its write-up on September 20 was embellished with sketches of Bancroft and Will, their attorneys, and the judge. Two days after the verdict, Ambrose Bierce added a postscript in his column in the *Examiner*.

> During the trial of the Bancroft case on Thursday last an attorney who desired to insult a witness with impunity got himself inside the rail surrounding the Judge's desk in order to have protection. The Judge promptly hunted him out of his hole and made him take a more exposed position, with obvious advantage to his civility. The name of the attorney is Van Fleet; he used to be a Judge, but appears never to have been a Colonel. The Humane Society should bestow upon his tongue a great gold medal for saving life.[29]

Thus the curtain was rung down on the incident of the alleged libel. From the evidence and the arguments one may learn something about Bancroft's personality and his problems. With greater certitude it may be seen as an unpleasant experience for him to endure. Aside from the possibility that heavy damages might be assessed, there was the certainty of unflattering, if not unfavorable, publicity.

Meanwhile, a still heavier siege gun was being wheeled into position to blast at Bancroft's reputation. There had been, it should be noted, rumblings of dissatisfaction with the treatment accorded in the California volumes to the Bear Flag episode and John C. Frémont. The tendency among Californians had been to regard the Bear Flaggers as great heroes

---

[27] *Ibid.*
[28] San Francisco *Call*, October 28, 1893.
[29] Ambrose Bierce, "Prattle," San Francisco *Examiner*, October 8, 1893.

and Frémont as the man primarily responsible for the American conquest. Since the evidence brought to light seemed clearly to controvert this legend, Bancroft took pleasure in debunking it and in excoriating Frémont as a filibuster and adventurer. Before the California Historical Society, Professor William Carey Jones found some fault with this treatment,[30] but, as Oak observed, "so mildly and vaguely as to create the impression that he was voicing not so much his convictions or the critical talent of a professor of history, as his duty to Mrs. Frémont, his aunt."[31] In the *Overland Monthly* W. B. Farwell published a much more violent attack, roundly condemning the Bancroft interpretation, repeating fragments of pro-Frémont evidence, and ignoring completely the new evidence and arguments.[32] To these critics Bancroft made no rejoinder.

In August, 1893, one month before Will's libel suit came to trial, Farwell returned to the attack. For a sounding board he chose the Society of California Pioneers, of which he was a member and past president, and in which Bancroft had been elected to honorary membership because of his distinguished services as a collector and historian. The Society, as set forth in its constitution, was designed to be "a Moral, Benevolent, Literary, and Scientific Association." It was exclusive, admitting to senior membership only those persons who had arrived in California before the end of 1849. It was affluent, with assets totaling almost half a million dollars. To judge from its annual reports, its major function was to insure a proper attendance at the funerals of its deceased members, but there was also the maintenance of Pioneer Hall with its billiard, reading, and smoking rooms, the observance of Admission Day, Christmas, and January 24 with banquets,

[30] William Carey Jones, "The First Phase of the Conquest of California," *Papers* of the California Historical Society, I (1887), 61–94.

[31] Oak, *"Literary Industries" in a New Light*, 80.

[32] Willard B. Farwell, "Frémont's Place in California History," *Overland*, second series, XVI (1890), 519–530, 575–593.

balls, and speechmaking, and occasional gatherings for lectures and concerts. Their advanced years impelled these Pioneers to give much thought to California's early days. The nature of their organization, furthermore, tended to give them a high sense of the importance of what they had done toward winning the West. Consequently, it was not with idle words that Article I of their constitution avowed that their purpose was to "perpetuate the memory of those whose sagacity, energy and enterprise induced them to settle in the wilderness and become the founders of a new State."[33]

To this august body Farwell presented a set of resolutions. His first two whereases reminded the Society of its zeal for the correct remembrance of the early history of the state and its responsibility to guard that heritage. The third whereas charged that "Hubert Howe Bancroft, in his so-called 'History of California,' has . . . distorted the facts and truth of such history and maligned the memory of many of the men conspicuous as participants in these early events."[34] To substantiate this charge, several paragraphs recited details of the critical treatment accorded by the *History of California* to John C. Frémont, Robert C. Stockton, the Bear Flaggers, and Johann A. Sutter. Because of "this monstrous series of libels upon the memories of departed illustrious Pioneers and monstrous perversion of the facts of history," Farwell asked the Society to resolve that these passages were "plainly the vaporings of a mind distorted by prejudice, or envenomed by malice," and further, "that upon the principle of 'false in one thing, false in all,' Bancroft's 'History of California,' so-called, is, in the opinion of this Society, unworthy of credence as authority, or as a source of correct information for present

[33] *Constitution, By-Laws, and Annual Report of the Officers of the Society of California Pioneers, July 1, 1894,* p. 9.

[34] Society of California Pioneers, *Misrepresentations of Early California History Corrected: Proceedings of the Society of California Pioneers in regard to Certain Misrepresentations of Men and Events in Early California History Made in the Works of Hubert Howe Bancroft and Commonly Known as Bancroft's Histories* (San Francisco, 1894), 6.

or future generations, and merits the just condemnation of every fair-minded man."[35]

Farwell went on to list additional examples of what he called "malicious misrepresentations of the characters of early pioneers, respected members of this Society, and of various other Americans who were early settlers." He accused Bancroft of establishing his propositions "by arrogant and unscrupulous dictum, instead of by presentation of historical facts." He stigmatized a criticism of U. S. Grant as a "monstrous wrong," a "cruel slander," and a "mean, cowardly and unpatriotic attack."[36] Then, loading his cannon with grape and chain, he laid down this barrage:

"Throughout this never-ending series of books known as 'Bancroft's Histories,' there runs such a monstrous perversion of facts, such glaring contradictions, such a spirit of prejudice and seemingly malignant dislikes and hatreds of the men of whom he has written, and such a willful distortion of events concerning which they claim to be a faithful record, that it would be a public wrong, if not a public crime, for this Society to give countenance to them, by permitting further association with Mr. Bancroft in the relation of 'Honorary Membership.' "[37]

The bill of particulars went on to point out variations in later editions of Bancroft's *Works,* in passages relating to Pratt, Marsh, Haraszthy, and Terry, and to protest his imputation of lack of veracity to Drake's Chaplain Fletcher, Hastings, Stockton, Colton, Phelps, Revere, Tuthill, Lancey, Vallejo, and Larkin. Bancroft, Farwell charged, gave the lie, directly or by inference, to these writers, "and this, too, usually without the support of evidence to sustain his arrogant and ill-bred dictum, taking it for granted that such dictum will be held by the general public as an imperial edict, not to

[35] *Ibid.,* 10. [36] *Ibid.,* 10, 14, 19.

[37] *Ibid.,* 19. Bancroft had been elected to honorary membership in the society in 1876 at the urging of John S. Hittell; see *Literary Industries,* 577–578.

be gainsaid or disputed as coming from so high an authority as himself, as the historian of historians of the age we live in."[38]

At their regular monthly meeting on August 7, 1893, the associated Pioneers listened to the reading of Farwell's resolutions, which were adopted a month later by unanimous vote of the members present. At the October meeting Dr. Washington Ayer introduced a resolution worded as follows:

WHEREAS, Statements have been made by an honorary member of this Society in a quasi-history published by one Hubert Howe Bancroft, which are at variance with historical records, and reflect upon the honor, dignity and integrity of the California Pioneers, and

WHEREAS, All such statements have no foundation of truth, and are unworthy the labors of an upright historian, and only becoming to one, who in our judgment strayed far from the domain of an honest writer, with the purpose in view to mislead the reader and wrong the founders of a new State upon the western boundary of our country, and by such statements did wantonly and maliciously wrong the old Argonauts; therefore,

Resolved, That the name of Hubert Howe Bancroft be stricken from the list of Honorary Members of this Society, and that the Secretary be requested to send him a copy of this preamble and resolution.[39]

After some debate this resolution was adopted. In the best parliamentary fashion, Dr. William S. Simpson then served notice that at the next meeting he would move for a reconsideration. On November 6 he did so, whereupon the Society voted to refer the resolution to a committee with instructions to communicate the action to Bancroft and give him opportunity to appear and show cause why his name should not be struck from the roll of honorary members.[40]

Through the marshal of the Society, by regular mail and then by registered mail, the committee caused a copy of this indictment and the accompanying bill of particulars, in all some twenty-four typewritten pages, to be served upon their honorary member. The committee set 7:30 P.M., December

[38] Society of California Pioneers, *Misrepresentations of Early California History Corrected,* 23.

[39] *Ibid.,* 4–5. [40] *Ibid.,* 5.

12, as the time for him to present himself, with counsel if he wished, at the committee room in Pioneer Hall. When he neither answered nor appeared, the hearing was postponed to December 26, then to January 9, and then to January 16. Finally, Bancroft still not deigning to make any response, the committee took up the indictment, found all its counts fully sustained, and on February 5, 1894, reported to the Society that the name of Hubert Howe Bancroft should no longer be permitted to remain upon the roll of honorary members. By unanimous vote of the eighty members present the Society thereupon adopted the report of this special committee, adopted Ayer's resolution to strike Bancroft's name from the roll, and adopted a supplementary resolution extolling the Bear Flaggers. Furthermore, the proceedings in the case were ordered printed as a means of referring the whole subject "to the deliberative judgment of a discriminating public." This was done in confidence that "the common verdict of that public as well as that of posterity" would be that Bancroft's "so-called" history would "forever be held to be unworthy of credence," and would "deserve and find no place in the public or private libraries of the world."[41]

From the perspective of the present the wrath of the Pioneers is amusing if not ridiculous. Consider, for example, that Oak, just a few months earlier, had elaborately and explicitly laid claim to almost every passage to which the Pioneers now took such violent exception. One might argue that it was his sins that were now being visited upon his chief. Yet since Oak's name had not appeared on the volumes it is appropriate that he should have escaped all this criticism.

Bancroft's attitude was that he had not asked for honorary membership in the Society, was indifferent whether he retained that connection or not, and would not lift a finger to keep his name on the roll. Infuriating though this attitude was to the Pioneers, there can be no doubt that it was the

[41] *Ibid.*, 3.

course of wisdom. The charges touched subjects on which the Pioneers were extremely sensitive; their prosecution of the case, despite the careful regard for parliamentary usage, showed them to be seething with righteous indignation; and no conceivable evidence or argument could have budged them from the verdict already pronounced. Bancroft really had no choice but to let them proceed. Outwardly he maintained a show of indifference; inwardly he felt discomfiture. And in the popular mind, where his refusal to debate seemed a tacit admission of the validity of the charges, the episode seriously depreciated his reputation as a historian.

Now, after a fifty-year cooling-off period, and with a change of venue, the case of the Pioneers vs. the historian can have a fairer trial. To a majority of the moderns, though such experts as Nevins and Scherer would dissent, the Bancroft interpretation of Frémont seems essentially correct. As to the Bears, likewise, his version is the one now accepted. The mistaken fears that existed are seen as sufficient explanation for the uprising, but the outbreak is regarded as unnecessary and unfortunate, and by no stretch of the imagination can the Bears be seen as the conquerors of California. With regard to Commodore Stockton, the Pioneers would also have great difficulty in convincing a panel of modern experts. The latter see him, much as Bancroft did, as a welcome change after the hesitant Sloat, but they are critical of his provoking the southern California rebellion, and they consider him in the wrong in the quarrel with Kearny. In Sutter the latest biographers find a bit more to praise, but they admit that he came to California as an adventurer, that he had a shady past, and that he was prone to exaggerate his achievements. On these four points, the principal items in the bill of particulars, today's authorities would not agree that Bancroft's writings were "the vaporings of a mind distorted by prejudice or envenomed by malice."[42]

[42] *Ibid.*, 10.

Certain others of the charges would be as speedily dismissed. It is not the practice, for example, to apply to histories the principle "false in one thing, false in all." The copious citations of sources and authorities and the abundant detail in Bancroft's *California* render completely specious the accusation that its propositions were established "by arrogant and unscrupulous dictum, instead of by presentation of historical facts."[43] With regard to the charge that Bancroft had a propensity for calling other writers liars, several of the passages upon reading prove to be ever so much milder than the Pioneers assumed, and others apply to men whose reliability rating is poor.

Remaining then would be the charges relating to variants in later printings in the comments on Marsh, Haraszthy, Pratt, and Terry, all in the direction of moderating criticisms that first were harsh. With regard to Marsh and Haraszthy the changes may reflect merely an honest conviction that the earlier denunciation was too extreme. As for Pratt, it was a shift from cynical to more straightforward reporting, and would be dismissed as trivial except for the suspicion that it was influenced by the prospect of a commission for a biography in the *Chronicles*. The Terry changes, in *Popular Tribunals,* were induced by threats. They were numerous and represented a slight toning down, but the account remained such a round condemnation of Terry that the concession to censorship seems to have been only a formality.

We prefer, of course, that historians formulate their interpretations with such care that they will not have to be changed. We also prefer that they be impervious to monetary suasion and adamant against dictation. Bancroft's revisions are not entirely to be excused. Yet professional historians, as part of the "discriminating public" and the posterity to which the Pioneers submitted their case, do not endorse the Society's judgment that Bancroft's *Works* "will forever be held to be

[43] *Ibid.*, 14.

unworthy of credence, and will deserve and find no place in the public or private libraries of the world."[44] On the contrary, the *Works* have won recognition as honest and reasonably accurate. They are regarded as the basic item and incomparably the most valuable for any collection on the American West.

Thus whereas Oak's charges had a considerable measure of validity and reveal Bancroft's chief flaw, and whereas Will's charges were at worst the result of a misunderstanding, the accusations of the irate Pioneers may be regarded as almost pure fabrication, ridiculous in their pomposity, and disgraceful in their disparagement of the man who had done more than any other to insure the ultimate fame of California's early settlers. Such was the harvest that Bancroft reaped at the culmination of his prodigious work as collector and historian.

[44] *Ibid.*, 3.

21

Time His Ally

There is no American collection with which this can fairly be compared.... There is no other state or country whose historic data have been so thoroughly collected at so early a period of its existence, especially none whose existence has been so varied and eventful, and its record so complicated and perishable.

Hubert Howe Bancroft, *Literary Industries,* 213–224

SPRINTERS, lyric poets, and fighter pilots, as everyone knows, reach their zenith in early manhood. There are other pursuits in which youthful vitality is requisite if a mark is to be made. In the history profession, on the other hand, the most that the young can do is to show promise, and lasting greatness can be won only by sustained effort over a period of years. If a historian is to be great he must be long-lived; he will need other advantages too, but he must have Time as his ally.

In the 'eighties, when he was struggling for the fulfillment of the ambitious design for a comprehensive history of the western half of North America, Bancroft was keenly aware of this necessity. As it turned out, he not only lived to see the *Works* completed and their sequel the *Chronicles,* but he overshot that mark by a full quarter century. He had opportunity, therefore, to weather additional buffetings from the critics, to add another cubit to the long shelf of his books, to take quiet enjoyment in his children and grandchildren, and, as an alert and interested observer of the world about him, to round out the abundance of his experience. He also had time to perform one other task that was essential to the secure establishment of his reputation. Although anticlimactic after the grandiose achievements of his middle decades, this period affords a revealing insight into his attitudes, his mature convictions, and the essential features of his personality.

The chief task confronting Bancroft in this final quarter century was to make arrangements for the disposition of his library. In order that the collection should achieve its full cultural usefulness it was imperative that it be kept in the West, kept intact, assured of safekeeping, and made available to qualified researchers. It was desirable, furthermore, that its new owner should have the means and the wisdom to preserve the vitality of the library by continuing its growth. A multimillionaire might have solved this problem, as a few have done with regard to projects they had set on foot, by establishing a sufficient endowment to cover all contingencies. Only moderately wealthy, Bancroft did not have it in his power to perpetuate his library as a private institution. His alternatives were to try to recover his investment by breaking up the collection and selling it piecemeal through the regular auction channels, or to persuade the state of California or the state university to purchase it intact.

As early as the 'seventies, prior to the publication of *Native Races,* Bancroft was invited and urged to put his library under the protective wing of the University of California. President Gilman came to him with an offer to have a fire-resistant building constructed on the campus in Berkeley in which to house the collection "with full liberty at any time to remove it." Bancroft was appreciative of the offer and gratified at President Gilman's assertion that destruction of his collection would be a "national calamity." He declined, however, because of the implied obligation and because, for the carrying out of the writing project in which he was engaged, it was more convenient to have the collection in San Francisco.[1] With the construction of the library building on Valencia Street in 1881 and the achievement of comparative

[1] Bancroft, *Literary Industries,* 320–321.

safety from the hazard of fire, the prospect of early transfer to state or university control was considerably reduced.

Fire was the agency, nevertheless, that shortly revived the question of the ultimate disposition of the collection. On April 30, 1886, when the Bancroft Building on Market Street was gutted by flames,[2] the library, thanks to the earlier removal to a separate building, suffered no physical damage. But with a loss, over and above the insurance, of at least half a million dollars, and with the derangement and temporary prostration of his great business, Bancroft had to reconsider all his plans. He felt morally obligated to reëstablish his business house. He was equally determined to carry out the publication of the histories as he had announced and promised. For the time being, the library was a necessary tool for the production of those histories, but its further retention looked like a luxury he could ill afford, and Bancroft began to think and talk about the necessity of selling.[3]

These hints roused a number of San Franciscans, among them the editor of the *Evening Post*. In his columns of May 19 he sounded a warning that San Francisco was in danger of losing "a treasure that has won her a unique distinction among American cities," the library whose "wealth of material" had given "such a solid basis" to Bancroft's histories. "Enough public spirit must be found to retain this institution," he continued, "or we must see it mutilated, its parts dispersed throughout the world, its value in great measure destroyed, and this city humiliated in the eyes of lovers of knowledge." "San Francisco," he reminded his readers, "boasts of being the richest city of her size in the country, and now she has a chance to show that she knows how to use her wealth." Going on to positive proposals, he added, "There are half a dozen courses that might be adopted. The Library might be bought to remain just where it is. It might be given

[2] See above, chapter 18.
[3] Bancroft, *Literary Industries*, 772–782.

to the new Historical Society. It would make an admirable nucleus for the collections of the Palo Alto University. It would double the value of the University library at Berkeley. The important thing is that it shall remain an undivided whole, and that it shall not be removed from the vicinity of this city. We cannot believe that our millionaires will let this opportunity slip."[4]

Across the bay, President Edward S. Holden of the University of California likewise took note of Bancroft's predicament. In his biennial report to the Governor on behalf of the Regents of the University he mentioned the probable disposal and dispersal of the 40,000 printed volumes and the thousands of manuscripts that had been assembled at a cost of $250,000. Voicing the opinion that this irreplaceable collection should not be allowed to leave the state, he expressed the hope that it could be secured for the University.[5]

Since neither the Nob Hill millionaires nor the Regents nor the state government responded to these appeals, Bancroft's attempt to sell in 1886 was unsuccessful. By dint of his own heroic efforts, however, he was able to weather the crisis. Reestablishing the business house, he kept the literary workshop in uninterrupted operation and held the library intact.

Nevertheless, the underlying necessity, or at least the compelling wisdom, of disposing of the library was still present, and in 1892, as soon as the *Works* and the *Chronicles* were out of the way, he took up once more the problem of finding a purchaser. This time he directed his attention toward the state and caused to be introduced before the legislature a bill authorizing purchase of the collection for $250,000.

The auspices seemed to be favorable. Since the panic of 1873 and the hard times of the later 'seventies, California had enjoyed steady prosperity. Business was flourishing in 1892,

[4] San Francisco *Evening Post,* May 19, 1886.

[5] Edward S. Holden, *Biennial Report of the President of the University [of California] to the Governor, 1886,* pp. 30–31. See also Benjamin P. Kurtz, *Joseph Cummings Rowell* (Berkeley, 1940), 45–46.

and the state government was not faced with the necessity for stringent and conspicuous economies. Equally favorable was the circumstance that the cuarto centennial of Columbus' voyage of discovery had made the average American more history-conscious than usual. In that respect also the proposal of state purchase was especially timely.

By the program of publicity that he had carried out during the preceding decade and a half, Bancroft had done much to increase the marketability of the collection. His publicity program had been directed toward other ends, such as the procurement of a favorable reception for the *Native Races* and the enticement of subscriptions for the *Works*, but, throughout, a principal talking point had been the superlative excellence of the collection. Press releases had stressed its unparalleled richness in the field of Californiana and its strength for other areas, the high market value of some of its rarities, and the uniqueness of the manuscript holdings. In a dozen or more advertising brochures these claims had been repeated and amplified as vouching for the worth of the Bancroft histories. The salesmen who drummed up subscriptions for the *Works* were likewise instructed to play up the excellence of the collection as one of the main points in their sales arguments.[6] In the *Works* themselves the high praise of the collection had been reiterated, notably in the bibliographical survey included in *Essays and Miscellany* and in the discussion of the library contained in *Literary Industries*. This praise of the library had been for the purpose of justifying and endorsing the *Works;* now it might pay an extra dividend by enhancing the likelihood of state purchase.

Bancroft, however, was too astute and energetic a businessman to rest the case merely on the evidence previously presented and on the arguments already advanced. For the enlightenment of the legislators he prepared another pam-

[6] See *Information for Agents to Assist in Selling the Works of Hubert Howe Bancroft* [San Francisco, 1881], and the discussion of the sales campaign in chapter 17, above.

phlet setting forth the special and outstanding merits of the collection,[7] while to influence them toward the proper decision petitions were circulated endorsing the purchase by the state.[8]

The petitioners asserted that the Bancroft Library was the largest and most complete collection of California historical data in existence, the largest and most complete collection of historical and judicial data on the western half of North America, and the largest and most complete collection of original historical data extant concerning any state or nation in the world. They pointed out that the collection could never be duplicated or replaced; they gave as their opinion that it was offered at a fair price; and they argued with some vigor that to allow this collection "to go abroad, become scattered, and pass beyond the reach of California forever, would be a public calamity, a loss felt through all time, and regretted in ever increasing degree as time rolls by."

An impressive group of notables attached their signatures to this petition, among them Horatio Stebbins, Starr King's successor in the Geary Street Unitarian pulpit; Wm. Ingraham Kip, Episcopal Bishop of California; and P. W. Riordan, Roman Catholic Archbishop of San Francisco. From the University came an entire page of signatures including those of Bernard Moses, Professor of History; the LeConte brothers; E. W. Hilgard, Professor of Agriculture; J. C. Rowell, Librarian; Geo. H. Howison, whose title was Mills Professor of Intellectual and Moral Philosophy and Civil Polity; and G. E. Colby, Second Assistant in the Viticultural Laboratory. Prominent among the professorial signers was Wm. Carey Jones, Professor of Roman and Constitutional Law, whose dissent from the Bancroft-Oak-Royce judgment on Frémont did not blind him to the importance of the collection.

[7] *Analysis and Valuation of the Bancroft Library* [San Francisco, 1891].
[8] Several of these petitions are preserved in the Bancroft Library.

Valuable, too, were the additional signatures gathered in San Francisco from such men as Lorenzo Sawyer, J. Frank Smith, Ogden Hoffman, Hall McAllister, John H. Boalt, A. A. Sargent, John S. Doyle, and John Swett. Because Doyle and a few others wrote in qualifying phrases to the effect that the purchase should be at a fair valuation, a supplementary statement was drawn up certifying that the library would be "a fair and proper purchase" at $250,000, and to this document George Davidson, Wm. Ashburner, Horatio Stebbins, Lorenzo Sawyer, Ogden Hoffman, Jno. B. Barber, and Ralph C. Harrison affixed their signatures.[9]

Unfortunately, however, all was not plain sailing; for Bancroft's name, though widely known throughout the state, was not universally held in high esteem. In the marketing of the *Works,* in the commercializing of the *Chronicles,* in what he had written about the pioneers, and in the mere fact that he, a businessman, had vaunted himself as a scholar, he had antagonized sundry persons. The press, or at least certain portions of it, delighted to criticize him. On the basis of such hostility, rather more than on the merits of the case, the purchase proposal of 1892 fell through.[10]

In 1898 the project was revived, only to strike a snag in an unexpected quarter. In hopes of silencing the criticisms of the price asked, the University Librarian, J. C. Rowell, was invited to make an appraisal of the collection. He went over it with some care and arrived at a figure of $130,000 which because of duplicates he further reduced in terms of "value to the University" to $116,000. To say the least, this was discouraging, for Rowell's opinion carried much weight. In the University Library he was doing an excellent job, albeit primarily in economical administration and efficient management. He was interested in Californiana and one of his prides

[9] Also on file in the Bancroft Library.

[10] For a pithy summarization of the denunciation then current one may turn to Ambrose Bierce's column in the San Francisco *Examiner* of January 22, 1893.

was a collection of local novels, together with autographs, pictures, and appraisals of California writers, but he was not a specialist on rare books and manuscripts and not particularly qualified to appraise the Bancroft collection. He seems, indeed, to have had a few qualms about his performance, for he concluded his report thus:

"I submit this unofficial report to you as the result of an unprejudiced attempt to arrive at the value of the Bancroft Library, in a commercial sense; and yet, if by an untoward fate the collection should be taken away from California and dissipated to the four ends of the earth, I am not sure that a century or so later some person will not be damning that fool of a librarian who valued the manuscripts at $81,000 instead of $150,000. *Quien sabe!*"[11]

Since the ending turned out happily, Rowell need not be damned, but the error of his appraisal was demonstrated just seven years later when a qualified expert put the value at more than $300,000. At that time Rowell turned again to his report of 1898 and in red ink gave it this signed and italicized endorsement, apologetic and engagingly frank:

"*Never issued nor circulated,* (signed) *J. C. Rowell.*

"This estimate of value, reduced to *lowest possible limit,* was made by me for the purpose [of] securing that limit from Mr. Bancroft.

(Signed) "*J. C. Rowell.*"[12]

For the moment, however, Rowell's report blocked any prospect of transfer. Popular opposition still ran strong, its spirit well expressed in the following squib that appeared in the San Francisco press:

"If Hubert Howe Bancroft is as anxious as ever to get rid of his Library, and the appearance of a Senate bill to authorize its purchase would seem to indicate that he is, why not

[11] J. C. Rowell to Charles O. Richards, Berkeley, September 19, 1898; printed as a three-page pamphlet. See also Kurtz, *Joseph Cummings Rowell,* 46.

[12] President's Office files, University of California, Berkeley.

collect a few carloads of his histories and trade them to him for his reference works and literary bric-a-brac? Subscribers to his works would doubtless contribute to the same most liberally. Then if the Library had to be dumped into the bay there would be an acquisition of room in book cases which would be of value."[13]

All things considered, the prospects for advantageous sale of the library seemed very poor. There were a few men, however, who would not let the idea die. One was Charles Mills Gayley, Professor of English at the University and one of the most distinguished of its faculty. On December 1, 1898, he wrote to Rowell:

"I have no hesitation in saying that the acquisition of the Bancroft Library would be one of the greatest benefits historical and literary that could accrue to the University. I sincerely trust that the opportunity may come our way, for we have, and shall have for years to come, no greater need than that of materials and sources with which to develop investigation and first-hand scholarship."[14]

Another enthusiast was Frederick J. Teggart, at the time a lecturer in the University Extension Division and Librarian of the Mechanics' Institute in San Francisco. To them in 1899 was added another recruit, Benjamin Ide Wheeler, the dynamic new President of the University. Almost from the day of his arrival in Berkeley, Wheeler stressed the importance of a university library as the core and heart of a university. In November, 1900, in his first report to the Governor, he put in a strong plea for expanding the holdings of the University Library and for providing it more adequate housing. In view of California's remoteness from the established collections in the East, he spoke of the absolute necessity of building and maintaining a great library "as a citadel and refuge

[13] San Francisco *Weekly Register,* August 5, 1898.

[14] Charles Mills Gayley to J. C. Rowell, Berkeley, December 1, 1898, MS., Bancroft Library.

for the creative scholarship of the Pacific Coast."[15] Thus far he was speaking of the University Library in general terms, but with an enthusiasm that might readily be channeled toward acquisition of Bancroft's collection.

That Wheeler's interest took this turn was primarily due to Henry Morse Stephens. English-born and English-trained, and an associate of Wheeler's at Cornell, Stephens came to the University in 1901 as Professor of European History and Director of the Extension Division. He at once became immensely popular with the students, and through his public lectures developed an enthusiastic following up and down the state. He was, furthermore, Wheeler's closest friend and most constant adviser. As a specialist in European history, and the French Revolution in particular, Stephens might have been excused for lack of interest in the Bancroft collection, but his tastes were catholic, his vision was broad, and he could see what a boon it would be to his department and to the University to have the Bancroft Library at Berkeley. In time he became the most effective advocate of the purchase.

Bancroft, meanwhile, returned to the attack by publishing another illustrated brochure on what had come to be his favorite theme. As in *Literary Industries,* he recited the story of forty-two years of collecting which had brought together some 60,000 volumes. In particular he mentioned the "creating of material" through putting on paper the testimony of participants such as Vallejo and Alvarado. After further description, he listed nine claims that might be made respecting the Bancroft collection. With repetition a few of these claims had grown a bit too large; for example, that his was "the largest collection of American historical data in the world," and that it contained "more of original American historical data than all the libraries in America put together." Others, though sounding equally extreme, could be fully substantiated; for example, "that no state or nation . . . had had its early annals

[15] Benjamin Ide Wheeler, *Biennial Report of the President of the University [of California] to the Governor, 1900.*

so [thoroughly] gathered and preserved" as he had done for western America, and that, "the peculiar conditions under which this collection was made having passed away, it can never be duplicated."[16]

The situation, to say the least, was anomalous. Bancroft was anxious to sell, and the University authorities, on their part, very much wanted to buy. They were deterred by the hue and cry against Bancroft with which the state had resounded, and by the price. Finally, in 1905, Stephens brought matters to a head. Besides talking to Wheeler, he roused the interest of several of the Regents, notably Rudolph J. Taussig, and he made a series of calls on the Bancrofts to discuss with them the advantages of having the collection at the University. These conversations led at length to an offer on Bancroft's part to contribute $100,000 toward the purchase if the University would buy at $250,000, which had been his asking price almost twenty years earlier. This offer was incorporated in a sixty-day option, clothed in suitable legal terminology, witnessed by Stephens and Taussig, and made binding by a consideration of five dollars paid him in hand by the Regents of the University. In ten numbered paragraphs it provided that the library should always be known as the Bancroft Library; that it should be kept intact and suitably housed; that the University should have six months in which to remove the library from the Valencia Street building; that the library was understood to contain all the items catalogued about fifteen years earlier, but that if any were missing the uncatalogued materials should be accepted as full equivalents. It was further provided that the Regents should establish, "when they shall have sufficient funds available for that purpose," a chair to be known as the "Bancroft Professorship of Pacific Coast History."[17] Stephens,

---

[16] [Hubert Howe Bancroft], *Evolution of a Library,* The Bancroft Company of New York [1901].

[17] Option to purchase the Bancroft Library, September 15, 1905; signed copy in the President's Office files, University of California, Berkeley.

in the courtly manner that was second nature to him, sealed this agreement by kissing Mrs. Bancroft's hand.[18]

Next, he went before the Regents and spoke strongly in favor of the purchase—an appeal in which he was enthusiastically supported by Regent Taussig.[19] The Regents, however, were confronted by three difficult questions: Was the collection worth a quarter million, or a quarter million less 40 per cent? If so, where might the hundred and fifty thousand dollars be found? With that money in hand, how could the University protect itself against public opinion and the press, both of which were perennially inflamed against Bancroft? With Rowell exuding dubiety and Stephens and Taussig incontinent with praise of the collection, debate was not apt to settle the first of these questions. It was decided, therefore, to call in an expert to make an appraisal. A favorable report by such an expert would also safeguard the University in its public relations and reduce the problem to one that would be merely financial. With infinite wisdom the University chose the man above all others competent to make such an evaluation, Reuben Gold Thwaites. Not only was he famous as the editor of several great sets of historical sources, including the *Jesuit Relations,* the *Original Narratives of the Lewis and Clark Expedition,* and *Early Western Travels,* but as superintendent of the Wisconsin Historical Library he was experienced in the care and use of a historical collection in many respects comparable to Bancroft's.

On September 18 the finance committee of the Regents authorized an invitation to Thwaites and an honorarium of $500. To Wheeler's first telegram, Thwaites wired back that he was "tremendously busy" and could not come at once. Wheeler responded that the week after next would do and promised to try to provide transportation.[20] Thwaites, there-

[18] As recalled by Philip Bancroft.

[19] Berkeley *Gazette,* September 19, 1905.

[20] Copies of the telegrams, dated September 19–22, 1905, are in the President's Office files, University of California, Berkeley.

upon, agreed to make the trip early in October. "After full consideration," he wrote, "I came to the conclusion that in the interests of Western history, my duty lay in trying to help you out relative to the Bancroft library."[21] The Santa Fe and the Southern Pacific rose to the occasion with passes for the distinguished visitor; the steward at the Faculty Club readied the California Guest Room for his accommodation; and President Wheeler inquired of Rowell, Teggart, and Professor Bernard Moses for someone, expert in the Spanish language, to assist Thwaites in the inspection, work for which the University was ready to pay at the rate of twenty-five cents an hour. Don Smith, lecturer in the Extension Division, was ultimately selected as the interpreter.[22]

With Teggart and Smith at his elbow Thwaites repaired to the Valencia Street building and methodically surveyed its contents. He confessed that he approached the task with some fear that the library's importance had been overestimated in the natural enthusiasm of its owner. In the end, however, he recorded his conviction that Bancroft's several statements had "in no sense been exaggerations of the fact." His report,[23] indeed, was a thoroughgoing substantiation of the claims that had been made for the library, which he found to be "astonishingly large and complete, easily first in its own field, and taking high rank among the famous general collections of Americana."[24] In it he found more books, more rare books, more newspapers, and a considerably greater number of manuscripts than Bancroft had claimed. The strength on California, on the Pacific slope from Alaska to Panama, and on the

[21] R. G. Thwaites to Benjamin I. Wheeler, Madison, September 23, 1905, *ibid.*

[22] Further correspondence relative to Thwaites's coming, *ibid.*

[23] *A Report Submitted to the President and Regents of the University of California upon the Bancroft Library* (Berkeley, 1905); reprinted as "Report on the Bancroft Library," *University* [*of California*] *Chronicle*, VIII (1905–1906), 126–143. For convenience, citations are to the more accessible reprint.

[24] *Ibid.*, 127.

Rocky Mountain states was all that he had been led to expect, and in addition he found significant holdings on other areas such as the West Indies and Spanish Louisiana. Without putting any price tag on the dictated narratives, the indexes, catalogues, and notes, though for the last-named in particular he had high praise, he arrived at a figure of $315,000 as the probable market value of the collection. The real value to California, he hastened to add, was obviously far greater—"any sum available to that end."[25] Particularly in view of Bancroft's offer to contribute $100,000, he pronounced the library a bargain of which the University, in the interest of Pacific Coast scholarship, should take advantage.

Thwaites's report was filed on October 14 and at once was prepared for circulation to the Regents. Wheeler followed the astute policy of thanking Thwaites for this report before he had had a chance to read it. "It will be of great value," he said. "Its character will undoubtedly be of great importance in determining whether we get the library or not, though I confess with fear and trembling that it is in the dollar that the difficulty rests." Elaborating his pessimism, he added, "There is very slight likelihood after all that we shall acquire the library; the great trouble will be the money. I am in favor of it and regard it as more or less a life and death matter, but I find it is very difficult to get money for a library that bears another man's name or a name other than that of the giver, and Mr. Bancroft is furiously unpopular in this state, and the furiosity is raised to the tenth power when the library and the history are brought into the field of vision."[26]

The only alternative seemed to be to look within the finances of the University. In terms of the present-day budgets of our major universities the sum involved would be incidental. In 1905, however, it represented the equivalent of

[25] *Ibid.*, 130. This remark, though applicable to the entire collection, was made with particular reference to the manuscripts.

[26] Benjamin Ide Wheeler to R. G. Thwaites, Berkeley, October 16, 1905, copy in the President's Office files, University of California, Berkeley.

30 per cent of the annual budget for instruction at Berkeley. Happily for all concerned, the Regents, a few years earlier, had set a precedent by dipping into the University's Permanent Improvement Fund to enlarge the campus by purchasing what was known as the Hillegass tract. In six years that tract had appreciated rapidly in value and was now reckoned worth twice its cost. The Regents were heartened, therefore, to employ the same device in purchasing the Bancroft Library. Bancroft met them halfway by agreeing to accept three annual installments of $50,000 each, instead of one lump sum, and further placated the opposition by waiving the clause concerning the Bancroft professorship.[27] The Regents, thereupon, agreed to make the purchase. They would buy with University funds, distributing the expense over five or six years as a charge against the Permanent Improvement Fund. This last detail, of course, was merely a bookkeeping technicality, yet there is appropriateness in the fact that the Bancroft Library came to the University as a Permanent Improvement.[28]

The formalities of the transfer were fittingly simple. On November 25, 1905, President Wheeler, his secretary Victor Henderson, and Teggart appeared at Bancroft's offices on Market Street, where they found Bancroft and his wife. Henderson handed Bancroft the University's note for $250,000 payable in three annual installments. Bancroft then presented to Wheeler a certified check for $100,000 and the key to the Valencia Street building. Wheeler immediately passed the key to Teggart, remarking as he did so, "From now on you are in charge."[29]

---

[27] Hubert Howe Bancroft, Extension of the option to purchase the Bancroft Library, San Francisco, November 9, 1905, signed copy in the President's Office files, University of California, Berkeley.

[28] Albert H. Allen, "University Record," *University* [*of California*] *Chronicle,* VIII (1905–1906), 186–189.

[29] *Ibid.;* Benjamin I. Wheeler to H. Morse Stephens, Berkeley, November 27, 1905, copy in the President's Office files, University of California, Berkeley; Kurtz, *Joseph Cummings Rowell,* 47.

For the University the occasion had an inescapable significance. Although its full import was not to be realized until years later, President Wheeler glimpsed it. "The purchase of the Bancroft Library," he asserted, "marks a great day in the history of the University.... It means the inevitable establishment at Berkeley of the center for future research in the history of Western America; it means the creation of a school of historical study at the University of California; it means the emergence of the real University of study and research out of the midst of the Colleges of elementary teaching and training."[30]

A few journalists expressed violent dissent. "Hubert Howe Bancroft has finally succeeded in dumping his library on to the State of California," buzzed the Sacramento *Bee,* adding that it was "a job-lot of old books and manuscripts," "a pile of rubbish," and "only fit for the garbage crematory."[31] The San Francisco *Wasp* stung deeper. Hard cash had been thrown away for "a heap of old literary lumber," the donation of $100,000 was "imaginary," the greater part of the library should have gone to a paper mill, and the Regents had shown "scant literary taste and still less business acumen." "Students," declared the *Wasp,* "have not any time to burrow in a mountain of musty manuscripts of Spanish priests and California gold-seekers and ranchmen. Young men do not attend a university to search for one or two grains of wheat in a wagon-load of chaff. Neither do we know any professor at Berkeley who will spend a lifetime in 'original research' amongst Mr. Bancroft's literary debris."[32] Other journals, however, expressed complete agreement with Wheeler's sentiments and hailed the library as "a splendid acquisition," "a mine of wealth for future historians," and "the finest reference library

[30] Press release by President Wheeler, Berkeley, November 27, 1905, copy in the President's Office files, University of California, Berkeley; see also the quotation in the *University* [*of California*] *Chronicle,* VIII (1905–1906), 187–189.

[31] Sacramento *Bee,* December 4, 1905.

[32] San Francisco *Wasp,* December 2, 1905, p. 811.

of its own State's history that is owned by any educational institution in the United States."[33]

To Bancroft the occasion was doubtless even more gratifying than to the University, for it represented the consummation of a long and, at times, hopeless effort. He had the mild pleasure of appearing as a benefactor, and the much greater satisfaction of having been vindicated in the valuation he had put on his holdings. Furthermore, he could now rest assured that his collection was in good hands. It would remain in its proper place in the West, it would be preserved as "an undivided whole," and the prospect was that the University would treat it, not as "literary bric-a-brac," but as the "living organism" that it actually was. At least he had done everything in his power to insure it this treatment, even to holding out for an appraisal and a purchase at something like the actual monetary value. Herein he was consistent with the theory he had put into practice in the circulation of his *Works,* that men are more apt to appreciate and value what they buy than what is given them. What the University would ultimately do with the library was beyond his effective control, yet he could take leave of his collection on that November day in 1905 with a feeling that he had provided for its future wisely and well.

[33] San Francisco *Chronicle,* November 26, 1905; San Francisco *Examiner,* November 27, 1905; San Francisco *Call,* November 27, 1905; Oakland *Herald,* November 27, 1905; Sacramento *Union,* November 28, 1905; Los Angeles *Times,* November 28, 1905; Los Angeles *Express,* November 30, 1905; New York *Evening Post,* December 9, 1905; and various others.

22

Successful Retirement

He is the exception rather than the rule, the old man who can look about him and see only the best of children and grandchildren, who on looking back upon an active life can see amidst the errors and mistakes common to human inperfections much that is good, much that will prove useful and beneficial to those who come after him, with no serious lapses into devious ways; give this man a mind at rest and money sufficient for his needs and that is all the world can do for him. That happiness is mine.

Hubert Howe Bancroft, *In These Latter Days,* 132–133

ONE OF OUR most persistent folk beliefs is that the hard-driving businessman, in proportion to the success that he has attained, runs the risk of unhappiness, physical breakdown, and sudden death if he retires from active duty. Bancroft, though he had been as hard a worker as anyone could ask, refused to conform to this pattern. To be sure, he had cushioned the shock by taking partial and temporary leave from business proper soon after attaining the ripe age of thirty-seven. Pursuit of his hobbies as collector, historian, and biographer then assumed the ascendancy, but at sixty he retired from them also, foregoing any systematic efforts to add to his library, and closing down the literary workshop whence had issued the *Works* and the *Chronicles.* Then, according to the formula, ennui, anguish, and disintegration should have befallen him. On the contrary, he survived for another twenty-five years, found that the world still afforded generous opportunity for enjoyment, and responded vigorously to the stimulus it offered to an alert mind.

Three features of these latter years have already been discussed: the prolongation of his career as a subscription publisher, the buffetings from hostile critics, and the campaign to lodge his collection in capable and appropriate hands. Concurrently with these experiences he was shaping the pattern of a successful retirement. His recipe was to take an active interest in what was going on in the world about him.

His background being what it was, the most natural and logical expression of that interest was through writing and publishing. How busy his pen was may be seen from a listing of his later writings. In 1892 appeared his *Resources and Development of Mexico;* in 1899, *The New Pacific;* in 1907 two pamphlets, *Some Cities and San Francisco* and *Resurgam;* in 1912, *Retrospection,* to which in 1915 was added a supplementary chapter in pamphlet form, *Modern Fallacies;* in 1914 appeared his *History of Mexico,* a reissue with elaborations of his *Popular History of the Mexican People,* originally published in 1887; in 1916 another pamphlet querying *Why a World Centre of Industry at San Francisco Bay?;* and in 1917 still another volume, entitled *In These Latter Days.* Furthermore, several of these works were revised for second printings, including the last-mentioned, which was supplemented in 1918 on the very eve of Bancroft's death.

The volume on Mexican resources had close kinship to his earlier books. It grew out of the broad interest in things Mexican which Bancroft had evidenced by journeying thither to gather material to enrich the fifth and sixth volumes of his history of that country. It was related also to the biography of Porfirio Díaz, which was an almost complete casualty in the great fire of 1886. Besides supplying information about himself, Díaz had facilitated the collection of data on his nation and had encouraged the publication of this handbook. As a further link with the *Works* and the *Chronicles,* collaborators Savage and Nemos had a hand in its preparation. For descriptive data on Mexico as it was in the midst of the reign of Porfirio this volume is an excellent reference, and the

1914 edition of the *History* is one of the earliest endeavors to cover the Madero revolution that brought about his downfall.

In several respects the most noteworthy of Bancroft's prolific later writings is the volume on the Pacific. It was written when the War with Spain was rekindling the spirit of Manifest Destiny, thenceforth to be called Imperialism, and when the American people were stirring to contemplate what the future held in store for them on this latest frontier. The New Pacific that Bancroft hailed had not yet been brought into full being, but he envisioned that it would be achieved, in the centuries to come, by applying to that vast area of water, islands, rim, and hinterlands "the world's foremost civilization." America would be the bearer of that civilization, chiefly by extending her trade, and in so doing she would give a new meaning to Berkeley's prophetic quatrain,

> Westward the course of empire takes its way;
> The first four acts already past,
> A fifth shall close the drama with the day:
> Time's noblest offering is the last.[1]

The New Pacific was one of the spate of war books that issued from the presses in 1898 and 1899. It shared some of the shortcomings of other books written in haste and prior to a real shakedown of the historical facts. In eulogizing the year 1898, for example, Bancroft went to extremes. He spoke of it as marking the creation of a new power among the nations, which had demonstrated "the sublimity of war" and introduced "a new age of human emancipation." He cast undeserved aspersions upon Aguinaldo, calling him "an ingrate, a trickster, and a traitor," and gave immoderate praise to McKinley, predicting that with Washington and Lincoln he would "always be remembered by a grateful country as one of its few great presidents."

In this 700-page monograph, however, he marshaled a

[1] Reproduced, with the two preceding quatrains, on Bancroft's title page.

H H [illegible] SONS
SAN FRA[illegible]FORNIA

Wilbur Springs
April 16/13

My dear Young Leddy

Certain eminent physicians, in their diagnosis of the universe, or I might say pessimistic cranks, hold to the opinion, or pretend to carry it about with them, that there are no curative properties per se in 'ot sulphurous waters, emerging 'ot from the bosom of mother nature, — no curative properties, I say, and I hope I make myself clear, other than the horful smell, which is bad enough to clear the premises of all diseases except bribery and graft.

As the poet sings: —

Oh the malodorous waters
The stinky inky waters
The Pukey ukey waters
Savoring of rotten eggs
Savoring of the rotten sea
and [illegible] water & odor de Cologne
and, and, everything.

Hiawatha.

FROM A LETTER OF BANCROFT'S, 1913

(See pages 377–378)

Which means that you
are a very nice little girl
pleasant to live with, good for
the blues, good for a little brother
who would like to rule the roost,
promoter of peace and harmony,
who never loses her temper except
when some one wickedly pulls
her leg — though I don't know
exactly what that means — and
then I would'nt give a cent
for her if she did'nt fight back.

Now if you will come and
live with me and be my little
girl I would like to have you.
This is a genuine offer, and you
can record it as such.

Then come, oh come,
and be my little girl, and
I will throw the present cook
into the bay and get a new
one, and I will turn my present
palace into an opium
den (even though Mr Wilson does
double the duties on the divine
drug) and I will buy you a nice
little bungalow by the lake of Como,
with alabaster trees and all that,
you shall have slaves to whip, and ostriches
to ride, and high spit gowns to wear, {or goats}
and, and a teddy bear.
Good bye. From your dear grandfather —
the last of them.

FROM A LETTER OF BANCROFT'S, 1913

(See pages 377–378)

great fund of information about the resources of the Pacific area, about the approaches of the various peoples of the earth toward this immense ocean, and about their several achievements in utilizing what it had to offer. Dipping into history, he found material for chapters on notable voyages, piracy, Crusoe Island, and projects for an interoceanic canal. A main feature was his discussion of the upwelling of American interest, culminating in the events of 1898 and heralding the New Pacific. He was frankly an expansionist, or, in the phrase of the day, a Large American, and it was with enthusiasm and approval that he greeted America's acceptance of its destiny and the removal of the center of the United States from Kansas to California.

Reviewers, while pointing out a number of blemishes, hailed it as the best of the war books, an able argument for American Imperialism, and the most informative volume on the backgrounds of the Pacific problems that the United States was facing.[2] Its excellence the Boston *Journal* was inclined to attribute to the author's long experience in the study and writing of Pacific Coast history, coupled with his "aggressive western temperament and true historical imagination." It was, the *Journal* continued, "the greatest of his literary achievements."[3]

Public and professional esteem of *The New Pacific* is somewhat reflected in its publication record: printings in November, 1899, March, 1900, and May, 1900; revision and reprintings in September, 1912, October, 1912, and again in 1913. Works that are timely have a special hazard of falling into disuse. Without its really being superseded, this is approximately what has happened to Bancroft's volume.

[2] For example, see the New York *Herald,* November 12, 1899; the Philadelphia *Inquirer,* November 19, 1899; the Boston *Journal,* November 20, 1899; the Washington *Post,* December 3, 1899; the New York *Times,* December 9, 1899; the *Outlook,* December 9, 1899; and the Springfield *Republican,* December 10, 1899. Clippings on file in a scrapbook in the Bancroft Library.

[3] Boston *Journal,* November 20, 1899.

The western meeting of the American Historical Association in 1915 produced a volume ambitiously entitled *The Pacific Ocean in History,*[4] and the Institute of Pacific Relations has sponsored a whole series of monographic studies of localized contemporary problems in the area. Foster Rhea Dulles and George Taylor have each assessed the work of the United States in the Pacific,[5] and in 1940 Felix Riesenberg and Hendrik Willem van Loon used the Pacific as title for popular works stressing the achievements of the early navigators.[6] Renewal of war in the Pacific of course brought forth another flood of combat narratives and inspired many a writer to point to the Pacific as the ocean of the future and the age to come as the Pacific Era. No one, however, has undertaken to cover backgrounds, resources, and potentialities for the area as a whole and thus to chart the further course of the New Pacific.

Of the other items in the Bancroft list, three may be classified as occasional pieces and outlines for city planning. *Some Cities and San Francisco* and *Resurgam* were soliloquies written after the great earthquake and fire of 1906. The burden of his argument was that cities the world over had been ravaged by disasters of all conceivable sorts and had been rebuilt. He reminded San Franciscans that theirs was a city "which a merciful providence has five times burned . . . , the last time thoroughly, giving the inhabitants the opportunity to build something better."[7] He mentioned the disappointed hopes for quick settlement by the insurance companies, for remission of duties on building materials, and for federal aid, and he advocated a federal subsidy to provide "a little fresh gilding for our Golden Gate."[8] Having referred to the Tuilleries, the

---

[4] Edited by H. Morse Stephens and Herbert E. Bolton (New York, 1917).

[5] Foster Rhea Dulles, *America in the Pacific* (Boston, 1932); George Taylor, *America in the Pacific* (New York, 1942).

[6] Felix Riesenberg, *The Pacific Ocean* (New York, 1940); Hendrik Willem van Loon, *The Story of the Pacific* (New York, 1940).

[7] Hubert Howe Bancroft, *Some Cities and San Francisco* (New York, 1907), 23.

[8] *Ibid.*, 64.

Louvre, and Versailles, created for Paris by dissolute monarchs, he asked, "Have we not dissolute millionaires enough to give us at least one fine city?"[9] His main appeal, however, was to the entire citizenry of San Francisco to erect at "the portal of the Pacific" a city of beauty and utility worthy to be the mistress of that ocean, and therefore the mistress of the world.

In *Retrospection,* a few years later, he again adverted to San Francisco's prospects and the steps whereby they might be realized. Noteworthy here was his caution that the Panama Canal, from which so much was expected, would not of necessity prove a great boon to San Francisco. He well remembered how, when the Pacific Railroad approached, "the legitimate profits of half a dozen decades were discounted," and he was disturbed at the prevalence of the same attitude of expecting automatic dividends from the canal. Of the major cities of the world, San Francisco, he said, stood to profit least by the canal.[10]

From the pessimism of this warning he turned in his pamphlet of 1916, *Why a World Centre of Industry at San Francisco Bay?,* to measure the superlative advantages that Nature had conferred upon the city by the Golden Gate, in climate, in contour, in position, in resources, and in tributary area, and to outline the means whereby this greatness might be attained.

Retrospection and *In These Latter Days,* it should be remembered, are the works of an octogenarian. As its title implies, the former is partly reminiscence, and as such it is less detailed and somewhat less accurate than his earlier autobiography, *Literary Industries.* He was looking back, however, not merely at his own career but also at California's and the West's, and one finds in this volume his summary observations on the course of this historical development. The early

[9] *Ibid.,* 12.
[10] Bancroft, *Retrospection,* 475–484.

chapters on some general phases of the subject are effectively done, but greater interest attaches to his discussion of subsequent episodes, particularly in such chapters as "The Dark Age of Graft," dealing with the forty-year epoch of domination by the railroad; "An Unholy Alliance," reviewing the record of San Francisco's graft prosecution; and "Progressive Government," tracing the crusade of the Lincoln-Roosevelt League. On all these issues his convictions, like those of almost all other students of California history, were strong. In refreshing contrast to some other practitioners he wrote without equivocation and straight from the shoulder.

Besides its discussion of the Lincoln-Roosevelt League, which in 1912 was practically a current event, *Retrospection* contained much other comment on problems of the day. Here Bancroft was equally outspoken. We find him putting in a good word for the Chinese and insisting that California's prosperity could best be served by a supply of Chinese labor. Other elements in our immigration program he roundly condemned. He was pessimistic about the effects on American stock through earlier admission of the Irish and "the impossible African," and through the current welcome extended to "the scum and the dregs of eastern Europe." Journalism as it then flourished, the decadent rich, the ruination of prospective mechanics or housewives by subjecting them to higher education, and the shackling of San Francisco's industry and commerce by the arbitrary actions of labor unions—these likewise were on the list of current evils which he viewed with alarm. His "added chapter," *Modern Fallacies,* which appeared in 1915, contained more of the same, with the further adjurations: "Better the United States should join the Allies than that Germany should win. . . . Beware of Nippon [though Japan was soon to become our ally]; beware of breeding Japanese in America for American citizenship; safeguard China; hold the Pacific."[11]

[11] Summarized thus in Bancroft, *In These Latter Days,* vii.

From the vantage point of the Second World War these pronouncements have a prophetic ring and seem to be evidence of great astuteness on Bancroft's part. What he was engaged in, of course, was tract writing—vigorous, persuasive declamation to which his pen was particularly suited. For the moment he was not writing history, though he bolstered his contentions by citing historical parallels and trends.

The same vein continues through his final volume. It opens with the question, "What is the matter with the United States?" and is devoted to "the none too pleasant task of pointing out some of the more glaring faults that retard the progress of our commonwealth."[12] The issues discussed are essentially those that had been on his agenda for some years past: the menace of Germany and Japan; the enemies within the United States in such matters as neglect of honest government, the selfishness of special interests, and the tendency of too many persons to expect the government to pamper them; and the shortsightedness that was preventing San Francisco from attaining its real destiny. The prevailing tone is critical, yet the writer does not impress one as sour or embittered. Inspecting his fellow men and their handiwork, he found much that was amusing and much that was praiseworthy. The amusement more often found expression in a chuckle rather than a broader laugh, in a penetrating phrase or an unexpected observation rather than an elaborate anecdote. The praise was most lavish in connection with the San Francisco graft prosecution and the Lincoln-Roosevelt League, but he gave out other compliments, including a handsome one to the University of California, which he predicted would develop a cultural sphere of influence throughout the entire Pacific area.[13]

The honest essayist divulges, not only his reasoned judgments, but also his various attitudes and emotional responses. Through the medium of his final volumes Bancroft's person-

[12] *Ibid.*, I, vii. [13] *Ibid.*, 302–310.

ality is clearly discerned, both through the opinions expressed and through the manner of their statement. The surface impression afforded is that he was stern, assertive, didactic, and almost crotchety. He was, it appears, a man easily provoked to disdain; and when he took thought of the selfish folly of the California Republican politicos that had led to Woodrow Wilson's reëlection, of organized religion as it functioned in America, or of the philanthropies of an Andrew Carnegie, a James Lick, or a Leland Stanford, his comment was apt to be pungent. He was impatient at the timidity that kept Americans or Californians or San Franciscans from attaining the goals that were within their reach.

Nevertheless, most of his criticism was voiced with cheerful candor. When he referred to the California Pioneers as the "Society of Incurables" it was in gentle irony. He was amused at the smugness of New Englanders, and he remarked the futility of trying to legislate mortal perfection by prohibiting drinking, smoking, cardplaying, Sunday papers, and the like. He was intolerant of lack of courage and lack of efficiency, but he was unreservedly approving of the social and political ideals that had developed in America and thoroughly optimistic about the opportunities that lay ahead, particularly in the West. He had mellowed, though not to the impairment of his critical faculties.

Observe, for example, his commentary on old age,[14] which he frankly admitted was not the best part of life. He objected to the decline in physical strength and in mental alertness, and beyond this, that "the victim of old age has death continuously staring him in the face," death "a nuisance and altogether unlovely." "Those," he remarked, "who expatiate on the felicities of old age as a rule have never tried it." Yet he was quick to add that he had no quarrel with his own fate, that he had found happiness and contentment. "I have all this world can give," he continued. "There are many diseases I

[14] *Ibid.*, 130–135.

have never had; there are some sins I have never committed; many blessings have come to me, more than I deserve; for I cannot claim with Mr. Ford, the peace-maker, that I never indulged in a wrong act in my life. I have done many wicked and foolish things, and like our worthy president have been able to get away with them." In this blending of whimsy and sincerity he is revealed at eighty-five as an unrepentant realist.

In a more sentimental vein, yet still without taking himself too seriously, he sat down in 1905 to prepare a keepsake for his youngest son.[15] He made it partly a scrapbook of pictures, clippings, and other mementos concerning the Granville of his youth, supplemented, however, by reminiscent comment. The tone is accurately indicated by the introductory sentence, "This, to Philip from his father, a passably good man, with bad breathing and not the best of tempers." Further on: "I was what was called a good boy in my infantile days, so my mother used to say—that is, I used to manage to escape more than two lickings for one offense [Nota bene, Licking county was not so called because of the lickings the boys got, but because of a deer lick where the deer came to lick salt. Historical note, When deer come to lick at a deer lick in Licking county it is usually because of the sand which is there, the salt I should say, that the deer come to the deer lick to lick]." Then is recounted the anecdote of the stolen rake teeth, and the "two several prayers and switchings," after which, he writes, "I was put to bed lying on my stomach." This entry is attested "Hubert Howe Bancroft his X mark."

The Rev. Jacob Little is introduced, and his wife "with the expression she used to wear at the annual gift meetings." A picture of the brick schoolhouse called forth memories of the Howe grammar, of playing truant, of coasting on the hill behind the school, and of the thumping of his heart "when he came swiftly flying to the jumping-off place which the dis-

[15] Hubert Howe Bancroft, Ohio Yankees: Philip Bancroft, His Book, MS volume in the possession of Philip Bancroft.

criminating reader will observe at the left." Concerning the meetinghouse where he was taken as a five-year-old, he comments that he understood "all that was said as well or better than he could now."

Clippings on "The Old Granville and the New" and on the history of Welsh Hills carry on the account. In a postscript added to the latter he tells how as a very small lad he was taken by one of his father's hired men to the Welsh church and there for the first time heard the lines,

> For hell is crammed with infants damned
> Beyond the hope of grace.

Whereto he comments, "It doesn't sound so horribly in Welsh when one is asleep." Still other clippings follow, most of them items published in 1905 in connection with the Granville Centennial Celebration. One concerns the organization of the Granville Historical Society, in which Bancroft was elected the first honorary member. Another is a reminiscent description of Granville in 1832 and bears the annotation, "The year in which H. H. B. was born."

With these clippings the small volume ends. As an autobiography it is fragmentary. The personal jottings, in fact, were put in merely to illuminate and perhaps to correct the description of the Granville of the 'thirties and 'forties. Bemused and jocular in tone, they betray a more kindly and good-humored person than his published writings imply.

Certain anecdotes point in this same direction. On one occasion, when he was about eighty, a passer-by inquired "How old might you be?" Choosing to put a literal meaning upon the words, Bancroft without a change of expression replied, "A hundred and ten." Five years later this same questioner met a member of the family, asked if old man Bancroft was still alive, was assured that he was, and marveled that anyone could live to be a hundred and fifteen.[16]

[16] As reported by his daughter-in-law, Mrs. Philip Bancroft.

Another incident concerns his granddaughter Lucy, who gave promise of musical talent. In his youth Bancroft had scraped and saved for years to buy a violin and then had been astounded to find that the purchase of the instrument did not immediately make him able to play it. He worked away without lessons until he could play simple tunes, but that was as far as he got, and among his children only Paul showed special aptitude. Consequently, it was a special joy to him that, when Lucy was about five, equipped with a half-size violin, she went about learning to play for grandfather. At length the day came when she was ready to perform a favorite melody of his, "Flow Gently, Sweet Afton." Grandfather listened attentively and then bestowed a compliment of compliments. "Lucy," he said, "that was beautiful, that was perfect. You play so well that I don't see why you need to practice any more or take any more lessons."[17]

Further indication of his understanding of child nature and, more broadly, of human nature is afforded by a letter that he wrote to Lucy a short time after her performance on the violin. It is, in some respects, a letter that would mean more to her twenty or thirty years later. Yet after a rather pompous beginning, its whimsy, its abandon, and much of its talk seem to be correctly pitched for the enjoyment of a youngster. It reads as follows, verbatim:

Wilbur Springs
[Colusa County, California]
April 16, 1913

My dear Young Leddy

Certain eminent physicians, in their diagnosis of the universe, or I might say pessimistic cranks, hold to the opinion, or pretend to carry it about with them, that there are no curative properties per se in 'ot sulphurous waters, emerging 'ot from the bosom of mother nature,—no curative properties, I say, and I hope I make myself clear, other than the horful smell, which is bad enough to clear the premises of all diseases except bribery and graft.

[17] As reported by Mrs. Philip Bancroft.

As the poet sings:

Oh the malodorous waters
The stinky inky waters
The puky uky waters
Savoring of rotten eggs
Savoring of the rotten sea,
And bilge water, & odors de Cologne,
And, and, everything.
Hiawatha.

Which means that you are a very nice little girl, pleasant to live with, good for the blues, good for a little brother who would like to rule the roost, promoter of peace and harmony, who never loses her temper except when some one wickedly pulls her leg—though I don't know exactly what that means—and then I wouldn't give a cent for her if she didn't fight back.

Now if you will come and live with me and be my little girl I would like to have you. This is a genuine offer, and you can record it as such.

Then come, oh come, and be my little girl, and I will throw the present cook into the bay and get a new one, and I will turn my present palace into an opium den (even though Mr. Wilson does double the duties on the divine drug) and I will buy you a nice little bungalow by the lake of Como, with alabaster trees and all that, and you shall have slaves to whip, and ostrages or goats to ride, and high split gowns to wear, and, and a Teddy bear.

Good bye.

From your dear grandfather—the last of them.

On a second sheet, labeled No. 2, he supplied a postscript.

Young Leddy

Better ask your mother to run her eye over this letter to see if there is anything improper in it for a little maid to hear, just as your father's mother used to do before she read her children a chapter in the bible.[18]

Into his latter years Bancroft was able to carry a number of the habits of a lifetime. He continued, for example, to enjoy robust health, and even, toward the end, outgrew his susceptibility to asthma. He continued also to be an inveterate reader. His custom was to bring home a whole circulat-

[18] Hubert Howe Bancroft to Lucy Bancroft, Wilbur Springs [Colusa County], April 16, 1913, MS in the possession of Philip Bancroft.

ing library, and not uncommonly he read several volumes in a night. Until well into old age he had no need of glasses.

Another penchant in which he persisted was that for travel. His later writing and publishing ventures took him to Chicago and New York. He divided his time between the fruit ranch at Walnut Creek and his residence in San Francisco. Occasionally he visited San Diego, and more frequently he repaired to thermal spring resorts in Napa Valley and Lake County.

Among strangers he seemed to be restrained by timidity and reserve, but to his intimates he displayed a livelier self, voluble and exuberant. He could be, and often was, an absorbing conversationalist, never lacking for the right word, and full of wit and ideas and humor. Indeed, one recollection of him is that he had many of the qualities of Mark Twain. He was happiest in the bosom of his family, and it was with his children and grandchildren and for them that he revealed himself at his best. Whatever impression others might gather, those in the inner circle were always aware of kindliness, warmth, and generosity. In the many things he did for his dear ones he had a horror of ostentation. One Christmas, for example, his gifts to his son and daughter-in-law, Philip and Nina, were ordinary editions of Epictetus and Cressy's *Battles* and a check for $5,000. In presenting the books he made a long and elaborate speech, but of the check he said nothing.[19]

It was fortunate for him that his chief joys were in his books and in his family, for the rest of the world continued to pay him scant honor. Many years earlier, when he was but a beginner in scholarly publishing, Yale had conferred upon him a Master's degree. Now, though his stature was immeasurably greater, no institution grasped the opportunity to honor itself by awarding him a higher degree. That Stanford University should not have lauded a persistent detractor of its founder is understandable, but from the University of Cali-

[19] Information supplied by Philip Bancroft and Mrs. Philip Bancroft.

fornia more adequate recognition should have come. The one honor actually bestowed was by the Pacific Coast Branch of the American Historical Association. At its annual meeting in 1911, this society, upon nomination by E. D. Adams, Maude F. Stevens, and R. F. Scholz, chose Bancroft as its president. Normally he should have presided over the sessions in 1912 and delivered a presidential address. Actually, however, he was not able to attend and the duties and honors devolved upon the vice-president, Rockwell D. Hunt, of the University of Southern California.[20]

Meanwhile, Bancroft's detractors, though perhaps no less numerous than they had been, became somewhat less vocal. Almost every harsh thing that could be said about his methods as collector, employer, and marketer had already been uttered. There was little that was fresh that could claim space in the public prints, and the Pioneers had no more honorary memberships to retract. In the mind of the people, however, the idea was well fixed that Bancroft had been an unprincipled collector, a picker of other persons' brains, and a tricky salesman, and that his *Works* abounded in error. These familiar charges were echoed, furthermore, in two papers that were more professional than any that had previously appeared.

The first of these was by William A. Morris, a specialist on the medieval English sheriff, an astute scholar of England's constitutional history, and an Oregonian who was a good friend of Frances Fuller Victor, from whom he had *ex parte* testimony concerning the Bancroftian methods. In the article[21] that he published in 1903, Professor Morris sought to win a better acceptance of the *Works* by removing from them the stigma of anonymity. The general effect of his paper, however, was to underline the criticisms that were already current of

[20] American Historical Association, *Annual Report, 1911,* p. 68; *Annual Report, 1912,* pp. 71–73.

[21] William Alfred Morris, "The Origin and Authorship of the Bancroft Pacific States Publications: A History of a History," *Oregon Historical Quarterly,* IV (1903), 287–364.

Bancroft's alleged methods, particularly of authorship. Its long-term and cumulative effect has been to disparage Bancroft as a historian and his *Works* as a trustworthy reference.

The second paper was an address to the Historical Society of Southern California by Rockwell D. Hunt soon after Bancroft's election as president of the Pacific Coast Branch.[22] Largely a résumé of Bancroft's authorial technique as set forth in *Literary Industries* and further expounded by Morris, Hunt's article added a few bits of hearsay criticism: for example, that writers on the staff "faked wantonly."[23] Although admitting that Bancroft had completed "a stupendous labor," Hunt ended by regretting that "he was not able to leave us some such style as that of Parkman, such dignity as that of Oncken or Winsor, such mastery of his splendid subject as is shown by Gibbon."[24]

Presumably these two papers came to Bancroft's attention. It would have been quite out of character for him to have made any public rejoinder, and there is no record that he ever uttered a comment. Clearly, neither paper can have afforded him gratification, yet in substance they were accepted as the verdict of the profession. All of which makes it the more fortunate that Bancroft could find satisfaction in writing, and in reading, and above all in quiet association with his family.

[22] Rockwell D. Hunt, "Hubert Howe Bancroft: His Work and His Method," Historical Society of Southern California *Publications*, VIII (1911), 158–173.
[23] *Ibid.*, 170.
[24] *Ibid.*, 172–173.

23

Recognition

The writer of history need not be a genius—indeed, genius is ordinarily too erratic for faithful plodding—but he must be a fair man, a man of sound sense, good judgment, and catholicity of opinion; of broad experience and a wide range of knowledge.
Hubert Howe Bancroft, *Essays and Miscellany,* 103

FINALLY, IN MARCH, 1918, Bancroft's long life came to a close. Some days earlier he had been jostled by a streetcar. He seemed to recover, but on March 1 he suffered a relapse, and the next day he was gone. How much notice would his death receive? The times were crowded and eventful. The United States was then girding itself for the heroic task of delivering enough fighting men in France to make up for the collapse of the eastern front. Chief interest was naturally in the bulletins from the St.-Mihiel sector, where American doughboys were battling German troops. There was concern also about developments in Russia. On March 1, William Randolph Hearst regaled the readers of the San Francisco *Examiner* with a signed editorial calling for immediate recognition of Bolshevik Russia, which, he said, was "the truest democracy in Europe, the truest democracy in the world to-day." Emblazoned across the next day's front page was the banner, "Supreme Court Rules Mooney Must Hang." Yet on Sunday, March 3, both the *Examiner* and the *Chronicle* found space on page one to report Bancroft's death.

"Hubert Howe Bancroft," said the *Examiner,* "noted Pacific Coast historian, the one man who preserved the history and materials of all of old California, died suddenly of acute peritonitis at 5:30 o'clock yesterday afternoon at his home at 2898 Jackson Street. The end came quietly after an illness of only 26 hours."

Bancroft was survived, the *Examiner* continued, by three sons and two daughters. Paul, a former San Francisco supervisor, and Griffing, of San Diego, were at the bedside. The other son, Lieutenant Philip Bancroft, was with a motor-truck company at Camp Johnston, Jacksonville, Florida. The two daughters, Mrs. Charles O. Richards (Kate Bancroft) and Miss Lucy Bancroft, resided in New York.[1]

The *Chronicle,* as if to illustrate the difficulty of attaining historical accuracy, informed its readers: "Hubert Howe Bancroft, one of the most prolific writers of history America has produced, died shortly before five o'clock last evening at his country home in Walnut Creek. Bancroft was 86 years old...."[2]

Although time, place, and attained age were wrongly given, the *Chronicle* story was correct in the basic truth. It was not a report such as the one Mark Twain had characterized as "grossly exaggerated," and it improved in exactitude as it progressed. Charting Bancroft's achievements in business, in collecting, and in publishing, it mentioned his principal publications and bestowed generous though measured praise.

A simple funeral service was conducted the following morning. The Rev. W. K. Guthrie officiated, and the honorary pallbearers were Henry Morse Stephens, Charles S. Wheeler, Rudolph Taussig, Dr. T. W. Huntington, Edward H. Hamilton, and Edward Mitchell. Interment was at Cypress Lawn.[3]

What was said in the way of a eulogy is not on record. In the *Examiner*'s notice of Bancroft's death, however, there had appeared an appraisal by Professor Henry Morse Stephens which was more of a tribute than had come to Bancroft at

---

[1] San Francisco *Examiner,* March 3, 1918.
[2] San Francisco *Chronicle,* March 3, 1918.
[3] San Francisco *Call and Post,* March 4, 1918.

any time since his tour of New England with the proof sheets of *Native Races:*

> Bancroft was the greatest of a half dozen great American historians, and the only one who had an adequate understanding of the historical West.
>
> His greatest value was as a collector of writings concerning the Pacific Coast, for the Bancroft collection is the chief historical glory of the University, which owns it.
>
> His histories constitute a museum of information on Mexico, California, Nevada, Oregon, and all the West, based on his study and knowledge of the country.
>
> No one seeking to know anything about the West can do anything without consulting the Bancroft histories and the Bancroft collection.[4]

Because Stephens was one of the most widely known professors on the staff at Berkeley, his words would command attention. Yet the medium of their expression was not likely to yield more than evanescent result, and it was not to be expected, furthermore, that mere pronouncement, even by Henry Morse Stephens, would eradicate the pattern of thought that had become customary with regard to Bancroft and win him recognition as a great historian.

Among professional historians more caution was evident. In memorial resolutions and in obituary notices in their journals they acknowledged Bancroft's achievements, but in those very tributes, which customarily contain unalloyed praise, they voiced certain of the standard criticisms. The members of the Pacific Coast Branch, assembled at San Francisco in November, 1919, made only an indirect allusion to such criticism, and the major part of their resolution constituted high praise:

> In the death of Hubert Howe Bancroft the Pacific Coast of America has lost one of its most useful and uniquely picturesque pioneers. With enterprise unbounded and with audacious courage, he created the conditions which made possible the first scientific treatment of

[4] San Francisco *Examiner,* March 3, 1918.

HUBERT HOWE BANCROFT IN 1912

My conception of the province of history is a clear and concise statement of facts bearing upon the welfare of the human race in regard to men and events, leaving the reader to make his own deductions and form his own opinions

Hubert Howe Bancroft

My conception of the province of history is a clear and concise statement of facts bearing upon the welfare of the human race in regard to men and events, leaving the reader to make his own deductions and form his own opinions.

HUBERT HOWE BANCROFT

A DEFINITION OF THE PROVINCE OF HISTORY

the history of one-half of our continent. His labors also endow the States and peoples of this coast with a priceless heritage of historical treasures. . . . As his heirs and beneficiaries, in a special sense, of the work which illustrates his enthusiastic devotion to a life ideal, it is fitting that this association should recognize the great debt which all workers in any portion of his field owe to Mr. Bancroft as writer, as publisher, and as collector of the far-famed Bancroft Library.[5]

In the *Oregon Historical Quarterly,* to cite a somewhat different example, the editor wrote: "Mr. Bancroft, the most voluminous of Pacific West historians, may have left a fame more enduring in the long lapse of time than that of any other person who has lived and wrought in this area. His thirty-nine volumes show immense labor and perseverance, and represent large sacrifice of personal fortune. . . . [They] are a reference library that will last for all time." These compliments, however, were interspersed with references to the criticism of Bancroft's "compilation" rather than "digestive" methods, and with reminders that Frances Fuller Victor wrote six of the Bancroft volumes. "The *Quarterly*," the editor concluded, "in recording the great and indispensable services of Mr. Bancroft, has thought it fitting to remember also that of Frances Fuller Victor."[6]

Thus the 1918 attitude of Bancroft's fellow craftsmen is a curious mixture. On the one hand, they were willing to credit him with a magnificent contribution to Pacific slope historiography in the library that he had built, and with a substantial and enduring contribution in his published volumes. On the other, they were ready to inject into memorial notices bits of the hostile criticism that had become endemic.

The reputation of a historian seldom improves after his death. A few classical historians like Herodotus and Thucydides have a current repute comparing favorably with that which they enjoyed in their lifetimes. Another few, more re-

---

[5] *Annual Report of the American Historical Association for the Year 1919* (2 vols.; Washington, D.C., 1923), I, 114.

[6] *Oregon Historical Quarterly,* XIX (1918), 74–75.

cent, including such brilliant literary craftsmen as Gibbon, Prescott, and Parkman, have retained most of their original luster. More commonly, as new sources are uncovered, new techniques developed, new methods of evaluation devised, and new bases of interpretation discovered, the historians of a bygone era tend to depreciate. The saying is that for each generation history must be rewritten, and, to a degree, this is what the reading public and the profession have demanded. It is therefore a matter for remark that Bancroft is much more praised a quarter century after his death than he was by his contemporaries. This fact would seem to be indisputable.

Charles Edward Chapman, for example, in the bibliographical essay appended to his *History of California,* asserts that "Bancroft's works constitute the greatest single achievement in the history of American historiography," that he rendered a greater service than any other American historian, and that "as concerns California history there can be no doubt that he has decided the form it has taken."[7]

Phil Townsend Hanna, in turn, when drawing up a list of the twenty-five most essential, authentic, and entertaining works on California, reluctantly omitted Bancroft's history as too ponderous, but did him double honor by including *California Pastoral* and *California Inter Pocula,* which he characterized as "the two foremost works of their type by any California author."[8]

Although Texas was on the periphery of Bancroft's chosen area and was covered far less thoroughly than the Pacific Coast states, the dean of Texas historians asserts that the *History of the North Mexican States and Texas* "is written with critical objectivity and a wealth of bibliographical equipment, and is the most satisfactory comprehensive history of Texas available." The six volumes on Mexico he characterizes as "perhaps the best work in its field in either English or Spanish. Like

---

[7] Charles Edward Chapman, *A History of California: The Spanish Period* (New York, 1921), 499.

[8] Phil Townsend Hanna, *Libros Californianos* (Los Angeles, 1931), 48.

all Bancroft's writings, it is based on exhaustive acquaintance with bibliography and is profusely documented."[9]

Similarly, Bernard De Voto, having essayed an interpretation of the American West in 1846, says: "I cannot imagine anyone's [*sic*] writing about the history of the West without constantly referring to Bancroft. His prejudices are open, well known, and easily adjustable. A generation ago it was easy for historians to reject much of what he wrote; in the light of all the research since done, it is not so easy now. . . . I have found that you had better not decide that Bancroft was wrong until you have rigorously tested what you think you know."[10]

A more extended appraisal appears in Franklin Walker's recent commentary on early California letters. Although critical of the obscuration of authorship, Walker says that Bancroft "adhered remarkably well to an objective attitude," that his collecting was an extraordinary achievement, and his sifting and organizing of this material "a marvelous accomplishment." His collection is described as "an indispensable library of source-materials," and his *Works* as "thirty-nine volumes of intelligently arranged facts," which "have to date maintained their preëminence as the basic authority on the half continent with which they deal. One would not go far wrong," this writer continues, "in asserting that Hubert Howe Bancroft, the frontier bookseller who turned historian, accomplished the greatest feat of historiography since Thucydides."[11]

The explanation of this changed attitude is relatively simple. Time, though not the solvent for all undeserved aspersions, does tend to rectify. In the past quarter century, researchers in ever-increasing numbers have undertaken investigations of various parts of the Bancroft field. By experience this scholarly army has learned that for its purposes the

---

[9] Eugene C. Barker, *The Life of Stephen F. Austin* (Nashville, 1925), 534, 532.

[10] Bernard De Voto, *The Year of Decision, 1846* (Boston, 1943), 525.

[11] Franklin Walker, *San Francisco's Literary Frontier* (New York, 1939), 302–315.

Bancroft Library is the prime collection of materials, and that the Bancroft volumes are not merely the bulkiest but by all odds the most valuable reference. Thus by pragmatic test the collection and the set, by proving themselves, have vindicated their creator and won him a belated appreciation. Consequently, one who praises Bancroft today is on safer, or at least on more accepted, ground than those who had the wisdom and the courage to do so in the 1890's or in 1918.

Obviously the measure of Bancroft's achievement must be three-dimensional, embracing his work as businessman, as collector, and as historian. In each of these categories it is apparent that the fates smiled upon him, but also that he fully earned his successes. He was fortunate to arrive in San Francisco when it was starting out to become the metropolis of the Pacific slope. He was fortunate in the Civil War years to be able to buy for greenbacks and sell for gold, and he was advantaged even more by the able assistance of such men as George L. Kenny, A. L. Bancroft, and T. A. C. Dorland. Yet his genius for money-making is not to be gainsaid. The Bancroft house is sufficient proof, and the profitable marketing of the *Works* is a still more striking demonstration.

In collecting, as in business, he exhibited wisdom and energy approaching the inspiration of genius. He spurned selectivity and swept in everything that appeared to have any bearing upon his field. He was catholic enough to accept newspapers, and when he could not buy or otherwise acquire materials of obvious importance, he was willing to resort to copying and abstracting, notwithstanding expense, inconvenience, and some recognition of the lesser value of such copies. Furthermore, though initially a collector of Californiana, he soon recognized the artificiality of the state lines and expanded his want list to embrace an entire half continent. Good judgment and skill thus made the most of the opportunity that circumstances presented. And with means that were exceedingly modest as compared with those of

Huntington and other multimillionaire collectors, he assembled a store of data that is not only the best for its province but hardly surpassed by the archives of any region.

Turning historian, where his lack of training and experience made the chances of success appear most remote, he had equal good fortune in discovering a hitherto neglected subject, rich in human interest, which seemed to be the last great chapter in the transit of civilization from Greece and Rome to western Europe, across the Atlantic, and to continent's end on the shores of the Pacific. Here also he displayed great good sense. He chose to deal with his grand subject in its entirety rather than to be satisfied with the annals of some minor locality. Because the task patently outreached his individual capacity, he chose to surround himself with a staff, the members of which, he freely admitted, did much of the work. Disparities in style remind readers that he was not the sole author, yet his was the idea, his the compelling force that kept the project alive, and his the directing hand throughout. Increasingly, with the passing of the years, his is the credit.

Wisely he chose to subordinate generalization and moralizing and to concentrate on presentation of ascertained and unadorned facts. It is of such stuff that the thirty thousand pages of the *Works* largely consist. Essentially they are a recital in endless detail of the particulars of Pacific slope history, for California unbelievably complete, for other areas only less so. Subsequent research has wrought scattered and incidental improvements, yet without by any means supplanting these volumes. They are the core around which every library of western history is built, and, though long since out of print, they are the most cited, the most used, and the most followed of all references in the field. In actual practice, therefore, Bancroft is honored above all other historians of western North America.

In the pattern of his career Bancroft may be thought of as the symbol of his generation. Other westerners were creating businesses and amassing fortunes, some much larger than his. Others, though not so many, were using their wealth to bring cultural improvement to what had been a rough frontier: Adolph Sutro by collecting English pamphlets, Mexican imprints and manuscripts, and early Californiana; James Lick by endowing an observatory; and Leland Stanford by establishing a university. Still others were turning from the literature of entertainment that had characterized the Gold Rush era to attempt more serious, scientific writing. Henry George's *Progress and Poverty* is the most famous example, but in the field of history the *Works* would qualify as an equally meritorious contribution. Bancroft's business success thus conformed to the West's economic pattern, his collecting expressed its cultural aspirations, and his publications illustrated its intellectual maturity.

In the fullness of time he may prove to have been the greatest of them all. Already he has eclipsed many of his better-publicized contemporaries, including Thomas Starr King and E. D. Baker, the Union orators; William C. Ralston, "the man who built San Francisco"; the Big Four; the Kings of the Comstock; and Francis Bret Harte, Joaquin Miller, and Ambrose Bierce, once luminaries of considerably greater luster. The prominence of these men was based, it now appears, on a political cause, a bank, a mere accumulation of wealth, a style in poetry, or some other transitory factor, which, though impressive at the time, in the longer run has diminished or disappeared. Bancroft, on the contrary, in his library and his histories set up durable and viable assurances of lasting and growing recognition. A prodigious historian he certainly was; generations hence he may loom up as the most significant figure that the West has produced.

24

Epilogue: The Bancroft Library

A library is not merely a depository of learning but a society for the promotion of knowledge. . . . If it be a library of history, then sooner or later its influence is felt in the direction of historical investigation and elucidation. . . . Who shall say what might . . . be [its] effects upon the graduating members of a great institution of learning?

Hubert Howe Bancroft, *Literary Industries*, 201

AN INSTITUTION, proverbially, is the lengthened shadow of a man. The Bancroft Library, as administered since 1905 by the University of California, bears some such relationship to its founder. It is not, of course, the only concrete reminder that the present generation has of Bancroft. Nor is everything that has happened within its bounds entirely attributable to him. Yet no appraisal of his achievements would be complete without notice of what the University has been able to make of the materials he collected and what it has been able to build on the foundation he laid.

At the time of the purchase there had been high optimism that possession of this great collection would operate to transform what President Wheeler called a group of "Colleges of elementary teaching and training" into a "real University of study and research."[1] Congratulatory letters from various eminent scholars strengthened this hope, notably one from

[1] Statement of President Benjamin Ide Wheeler, quoted in the *University [of California] Chronicle*, VIII (1905–1906), 187.

Professor Albert Bushnell Hart of Harvard, who expressed amazement that the University had been able to acquire "this incomparable collection" for the sum stated, and predicted that it would be "a place of pilgrimage for all students of Western America."[2]

A necessary preliminary to utilization of the collection was the preparation of some place on the campus in which to house it. That the problem was not easy may be gathered from President Wheeler's statement on the ensuing Charter Day, March 23, 1906, "Most of our buildings are outgrown, overcrowded, ill-equipped, flimsy, and altogether unworthy the name of the State they herald."[3] The University had in prospect a substantial library building through the generous bequest of Charles Franklin Doe,[4] in which the Bancroft collection might eventually be put, and in 1905 it had one new building, California Hall, described as of the most perfect construction then known, and designed to accommodate all the regular administrative officers, the University Press, and the Extension Division, and to furnish several faculty offices and seminar rooms, several large lecture halls, a room for meetings of the faculty, a palaeontology storeroom, and space for a botany museum.[5] To its alumni and friends the University announced in March, 1906, that steel shelves were being installed in the third floor of this building preparatory to receiving the Bancroft Library. "The south end of this floor," ran the announcement, "will be occupied by books and manuscripts, while in the north end will be stored the great accumulations of periodicals and newspapers."[6]

Before these plans could be carried out, the 18th of April arrived, visiting upon San Francisco earthquake and fire.

[2] Quoted in Albert H. Allen, "University Record," *ibid.*, 285.

[3] Benjamin Ide Wheeler, "The Condition and Needs of the University," *ibid.*, 239.

[4] Benjamin P. Kurtz, *Joseph Cummings Rowell, 1853–1938*, 45.

[5] "California Hall," *University* [*of California*] *Chronicle*, VIII (1905–1906), 44–48.

[6] Albert H. Allen, "University Record," *ibid.*, 292.

From across the bay at Berkeley it looked as if the holocaust would be complete. The University heads went through an anxious period, sadly contemplating the writing off of the library purchase as a loss, and, with greater poignancy, the deferment of their hopes to make the University a real institution of learning. Tradition has it that Professor Henry Morse Stephens rallied a group of students, rushed them across to San Francisco, organized them as a bucket brigade, and saved Bancroft's collection. The more prosaic fact is that the library was outside the fire area and that what was seen from Berkeley was some 28,000 other buildings in flames. The Bancroft, as it happened, was the only major library in the city that escaped severe damage or complete destruction.[7]

As soon as possible, then, the transfer to Berkeley was begun, and before the end of May the collection was safe on the top floor of California Hall,[8] where, under Teggart's direction, the work of arranging and classifying got under way.

In the ensuing months there was active publicizing. Several noteworthy additions of material were made. In June it was announced that the library would be the depository for the great mass of documentary material being collected for the official history of San Francisco's great disaster, which Professor Stephens would write.[9] A few months later the University acknowledged receipt from Señor Ezequiel A. Chávez, on behalf of the government of Mexico, of a rich collection of works on that country, several sets of lantern slides, and sixty-seven sections of the official map of the nation.[10]

Treasures exciting particular remark were turned up in the library itself. On the afternoon of July 2, 1906, Professor Stephens lectured in the art gallery of the University Library. He spoke on works of western history in the Ban-

---

[7] F. J. Teggart, "Note on Fire and Earthquake Damage in San Francisco," *Public Libraries,* XI (1906), 273–274.

[8] *News Notes of California Libraries,* I (1906), 14, 56.

[9] Albert H. Allen, "University Record," *University* [*of California*] *Chronicle,* VIII (1905–1906), 401.

[10] *Ibid.,* IX (1907), 71–73.

croft and is reported to have said that the manuscripts in the collection "would make it necessary to rewrite the history of Mexico and French Louisiana."[11] It would have been more accurate to have said Mexico and Spanish Louisiana. Again there was great excitement over the discovery of "the lost 'Corondelet' papers, which for more than a century eluded the search of historians of the world." These were papers of Baron de Carondelet, governor of Spanish Louisiana in the 1790's. Now it was Teggart's turn to be quoted as saying that the discovery of these papers would "make necessary the re-writing of the history of the Southwest," meaning, of course, the Old Southwest.[12]

No sooner was the purchase announced than inquiries be-gan to come in. "I am getting a great many letters from people who are interested in our acquisition of the Bancroft Library," Wheeler reported to Stephens, early in December, 1905. "At least two persons have written asking for any kind of position in the University which would enable them to use the Library for the advancement of their studies."[13] These applications multiplied, and to them were added questions about the avail-ability of research materials. James R. Robertson wanted to know if the library would be open in the summer of 1906; Professor P. E. Goddard sought access to manuscripts with an ethnological bearing; Professor Herbert E. Bolton of the University of Texas requested a transcript of a Texas manu-script cited by Bancroft; and George Wharton James asked for a loan.[14]

The University, meanwhile, was groping toward a policy. Back in October, when the purchase was under consideration,

[11] San Francisco *Chronicle,* July 4, 1906.

[12] San Francisco *Examiner,* September 19, 1907; Albert H. Allen, "University Record," *University of California Chronicle,* IX (1907), 372–373.

[13] Benjamin Ide Wheeler to Henry Morse Stephens, Berkeley, December 8, 1905, copy in the President's Office files, University of California, Berkeley.

[14] Wheeler to Stephens, February 23, 1906; Secretary of the President to Stephens, January 9, 1907, and May 2, 1907; Stephens to Wheeler, April 12, 1909; *ibid.*

Wheeler had expressed great surprise over Thwaites's suggestion that Stephens, the Europeanist, would be the ideal man to have charge of the Bancroft Library.[15] Yet by December he was sounding him out on a relaxing of his activities in Extension and an assumption of supervision of the Bancroft.[16] Shortly thereafter it was so arranged.

From the Baltimore meeting of the American Historical Association that same winter Stephens came back with an idea that was rich with consequence for the library. It had to do with the method of instruction in the large lecture courses in history. At Harvard an experiment had been conducted in supplementing such work by having graduate students take sections of twenty to twenty-five students for the purpose of making the instruction more real through explanations, discussions, conferences, and quizzing. Wheeler was persuaded to authorize introduction of this Harvard method, and in the summer of 1906 it was instituted with the appointment of three teaching fellows, Professor James R. Robertson of Pacific University, Forest Grove, Oregon; Vice-President Rayner W. Kelsey of Whittier College, Whittier, California; and Don E. Smith, formerly fellow and assistant at Cornell. Such fellowships, as Stephens and the University conceived of them, should operate for the encouragement of advanced work. Accordingly, each fellow thus appointed was to be required to spend two hours a day in the Bancroft Library "where an opportunity will be afforded them of calendaring manuscript material and thus getting practical experience in historical work."[17] A little more than a year later the press could report: "Remarkable progress has been made within the past few months by Prof. Henry Morse Stephens and his corps of student assistants in editing and classifying the manu-

[15] Reuben G. Thwaites to Benjamin I. Wheeler, Berkeley, October 14, 1905; Wheeler to Thwaites, Berkeley, October 16, 1905; *ibid.*

[16] Wheeler to Stephens, Berkeley, December 8, 1905, *ibid.*

[17] Stephens, Circular to the faculty [June, 1906], and letters from Stephens to J. R. Robertson, R. W. Kelsey, and Don Smith, June 8, 1906, *ibid.*

scripts of the Bancroft Library. Professor Stephens has placed the work in charge of John Fletcher, graduate with the class of '07."[18]

Another noteworthy development in the summer of 1906 was the Regents' appointment of a commission consisting of President Wheeler, Regent Taussig, Librarian Rowell, and Professor Stephens to draft a program for the organization, regulation, and maintenance of the Bancroft Library.[19] In January, 1907, the report of this commission was made public.[20] Duly appreciative of the Bancroft's potentialities as "the indispensable nucleus of a great research library, like that of the British Museum," the commission recognized three essential needs. An adequate appropriation was required for the work of cataloguing, binding, classifying, and arranging. Substantial purchases were equally necessary to complete the collection with works published since 1887 and to keep it up-to-date. And, if the library was to attain "its rightful position among the great collections of the world," it was imperative that a trained curator be put in charge. These requirements, the commission estimated, would call for an annual expenditure of at least $10,000.

Since this sum was larger than the University Regents could provide, and since, furthermore, the scope of Bancroft's collecting had been so much larger than California, the commission advocated recourse to outside support for this ambitious program. Recommended was the establishment of an Academy of Pacific Coast History as a supporting and advisory body, with membership in its Council contingent on subscription of $500 a year.

The commission proposed transfer from the University Library of all historical material pertaining to the Pacific

[18] Oakland *Tribune,* October 14, 1907.

[19] Memorandum, August 15, 1906, in the President's Office files, University of California, Berkeley.

[20] "Report of the Commission on the Future Organization, Maintenance, and Regulation of the Bancroft Library," *University of California Chronicle,* IX (1907), 48–53.

Coast, and also that all California newspapers currently received should be deposited in the Bancroft collection. Eventually, the commission pointed out, the relationship of the Bancroft to the University Library would have to be carefully defined, though so long as the collection remained in the attic of California Hall such a decision was not imperative.

Complimenting Mr. F. J. Teggart, Librarian of the Mechanics' Institute in San Francisco, for the invaluable services that he had rendered without charge "in caring for the Library in San Francisco, in arranging its transfer to Berkeley, and in getting things into some sort of order in California Hall," the commission recommended his continuance as Honorary Custodian. It further approved the Regents' allotment of $75 a month for the operation of the library, and it endorsed the budgeting of $60 of this sum as the salary of Assistant Custodian W. H. Garnett, and $15 for janitor service and cleaning.

Regulations approved specified the hours for the library, and for the Assistant Custodian, as 9 A.M. to 12 M. and from 1 P.M. to 5 P.M. every weekday. Reading privileges were to be accorded only to graduate students actively at work upon graduate theses and to qualified researchers. Visitors, however, the commission directed, "shall be courteously received and shown around the Library by the Assistant Custodian, but shall not be permitted to use books or other historical material."

Measuring solely in terms of this initial material support—the quarters in the attic of California Hall, the Honorary Custodian in San Francisco, the Assistant Custodian at $60 a month, the janitor service at $15, and the three teaching fellows briefly each day,—it appears that the Bancroft Library at Berkeley started on a shoestring. Yet expressions of interest were strong and repeated and sincere. In September, 1907, for example, when Stephens requested $700 to equip the library with three desks, a swivel chair, several manuscript filing cabinets, "a catalogue card cabinet of considerable size," and seventy-five yards of cork carpet to protect the staff and visitors "from the chill of the concrete floor," the Regents responded by appropriating $1,000.[21] In the Academy of Pacific Coast History, furthermore, there was at least a portent of solid backing.

On May 29, 1907, the Council of the Academy met in San Francisco. On June 11 the Regents approved the Academy's constitution.[22] And the next month, the press could state with candor, "Prof. H. Morse Stephens will soon carry out his plan to make the Bancroft Library the center of an Academy of Pacific Coast History."[23] In 1910, 1911, 1918, and 1919 the Academy vindicated its existence with published volumes consisting largely of edited documents drawn from the Bancroft collection. Included were translations of diaries of 1769–1770 by Portolá, Vila, Costansó, and Fages, by Font in 1775–1776, Fages in 1781–1782, and Durán in 1817. A Donner Party diary and a narrative of 1849 also appear. The final volume presents the papers of the San Francisco Vigilance Committee of 1851.

At least one item in the publications of the Academy came to Bancroft's attention and drew a comment from him. It was Priestley's translation of Fages' diary, concerning which Bancroft wrote: "Thanks for your kind remembrance. The Fages translation is very neat—perfectly done in every respect. The facsimile page is a thing of beauty."[24] On the whole, the Academy publications, though not brilliant, were workmanlike performances, but with the death of Stephens in 1919 the Academy disintegrated.

Stephens rendered the library two other services that were

---

[21] Stephens to Wheeler, Berkeley [September 15, 1907]; Wheeler to Stephens, Berkeley, September 20, 1907; Stephens to Wheeler, Berkeley, October 9, 1907; in the President's Office files, University of California, Berkeley.

[22] Printed in the *University of California Chronicle,* IX (1907), 258–261.

[23] Oakland *Enquirer,* July 18, 1907.

[24] Hubert Howe Bancroft to H. I. Priestley, San Francisco, July 10, 1913, MS, Bancroft Library.

even more worth while. In 1909 and 1910, in collaboration with President Wheeler, he persuaded the Native Sons of the Golden West to establish two annual traveling fellowships of $1,500 each to promote the study of California history at its sources in Spain and elsewhere. And systematically he rounded out his department with specialists in the Bancroft field. In 1911 he induced Herbert Eugene Bolton to transfer from Stanford, to be Professor of History and Curator of the Bancroft Library. Bolton had already gained a national reputation for his work in western American and Spanish American history and was "ideally equipped by training and temperament to take charge of graduate work in history."[25] Shortly thereafter the recruitment of Herbert I. Priestley and Charles E. Chapman made this branch of the department the most distinguished in the United States.

In the years that followed, the Berkeley history department and the Bancroft Library achieved a particular brilliance.[26] Professor Bolton contributed a dynamic leadership that consisted, in approximately equal parts, of an ability to see hundreds of research tasks that were at once feasible and worth doing, and of a genius for encouraging researchers. Through previous experience in the archives of Mexico he had a first-hand awareness of the fresh materials for American history that had been accumulated by imperial Spain, and he and his colleagues and his students became the chief exploiters of this vast documentation in Mexico and more especially in the Spanish archives. Bolton also became the chief exponent of the hemispheric viewpoint in the study of American history, and championed the idea that this perspective be applied to the study of local history. The idea had strong appeal because of its logic; it opened up a new vista; and it revealed a great array of subjects inviting to the student.

---

[25] Charles E. Chapman, *A History of California: The Spanish Period* (New York, 1921), 508.

[26] Discussed at greater length in John Walton Caughey, *California* (New York, 1940), 600–603.

Because of its rapid growth as an undergraduate institution and because of the popularity of Bolton's lecture course on the Americas, the University could offer each year several teaching fellowships in history. These were crowned by the Native Sons fellowships, which by an indeterminate but palpable quantity swelled the graduate enrollment at Berkeley. Still other factors were favorable. Successful graduate instruction calls for a well-rounded department and for strength in affiliated disciplines; the budding Americanists at Berkeley through the next third of a century owed much to the distinguished personnel that the University built up in European history and in anthropology, geography, economics, English, Spanish, and political science. Over these years also, the University made rapid strides in building up its general library. From some 133,779 titles at the time of the acquisition of the Bancroft, the number of volumes has mounted to more than a million.

Nevertheless, an essential element, and in some respects the basic element, in the flowering of this graduate work in American history was the presence of the Bancroft collection. Its acquisition imparted the initial impulse, and the materials in it nourished a large fraction of the researches carried on. Alongside the growing "California school" of historians, amateur and professional students of western American history grew in number and increasingly beat a path to the Bancroft Library. As early as 1921 it was observed that "all earnest investigators" of California history "are sure to appear there at some stage in their researches."[27] Their coming added to the prestige of the Bancroft, which became one of the University's most famous possessions.

Despite the library's becoming the focal point and fountainhead of historical research on California, western America, and much of Spanish America, the University has given the impression that it was neglectful and unappreciative.

[27] Charles E. Chapman, *A History of California: The Spanish Period*, 507.

In 1911 it transferred the collection to the first floor of the new University Library and some years later moved it away from undergraduate traffic to the fourth floor. These quarters soon proved inadequate and had to be supplemented by storage space in the basement of that building and under the grandstand at Edwards Field. These quarters, furthermore, are poorly designed for the care and administration of manuscripts, rare books, pamphlets, maps, and newspapers. Slight provision has been made for scientific cleaning and preservation of materials, and comparatively little use has been made of the modern techniques of microfilming and photocopying. With the exception of an affiliation with the revived Cortés Society, the library has done no publishing since the expiration of the Academy series. Its staff is small and the allotments for book purchases have been exceedingly small. Despite the early proposal of a coördinated program for the University's libraries, the main library and more recently the library on the Los Angeles campus have competed in the Bancroft field. The Regents, for example, to purchase the Cowan collection of Californiana, which was wantonly scattered through the general library at Los Angeles, expended as much as has gone into book purchases for the Bancroft in all the years since 1905.[28] Summing up the prevailing opinion of western Americanists, Henry Raup Wagner recently observed, "It is a most amazing fact that the University has paid so little attention to this magnificent library."[29]

There are other respects in which the University, though frugal, has been a good steward. Through gifts, exchanges, and purchases it has added to the resources of the library until books and manuscripts now amount to three times the number originally held. Accessions of Spanish American materials have been particularly stressed and the tendency has been to add the South American continent, at least for its colonial

[28] According to figures supplied in a letter from President Robert G. Sproul to the writer, Berkeley, September 16, 1943.

[29] Henry Raup Wagner, *Bullion to Books* (Los Angeles, 1942), 252.

period, to the field of Bancroft collecting. Largely through the instrumentality of the Native Sons fellows, the library has acquired transcripts and photocopies of more than 200,000 pages of manuscript materials from foreign archives. The library fell heir to the entire archives of the Panama-Pacific International Exposition of 1915, to the papers of the California Food Administration in World War I, and to various other bodies of significant materials. Recently President Sproul, evincing an acute awareness of the problems confronting the libraries of the University, appointed Mr. Lindley Bynum as consultant in such matters and as field representative for these several libraries. The appointment presages a coördination of library policies and revives Bancroft's old custom as a collector of "lying in wait" for opportunities.

Perhaps more important than this expansion of holdings has been the transformation of the collection into a working library and its maintenance as such. The first step in this process was to sort and catalogue the contents. Books and pamphlets now respond to their call numbers. A considerable fraction of the manuscripts has also been systematized, though there are other groups—for example, those pertaining to the writing of Bancroft's *Works*—not yet lifted out of chaos. Maintenance and operation also involve housing and staffing, safeguarding the materials, and making them available to qualified researchers. Here the University has rendered a great service to western historical scholarship.

Here, also, it has been called upon to foot substantial bills. The $75-a-month honeymoon of 1906 did not last long, and in the first thirty-eight years of sponsorship the University expended some $310,913.20 for operation and maintenance. This sum, it will be noted, is more than twice the cash outlay involved in the original purchase. For purchases of additional materials, mostly books, the University in this same period expended $51,007, which averages about $1,350 a year.[30]

[30] According to figures supplied in a letter from President Robert G. Sproul to the writer, Berkeley, September 16, 1943.

In addition to these outright advances, the University has several other items to its credit. There has been, of course, no charge listed for the upbuilding and maintenance of the main library hard by, though without its facilities the Bancroft would have required much more in the way of reference materials. In accordance with general University practice, no charge appears for rent, light, heat, or janitor service. Since 1916, furthermore, the salaries of Bolton as Director and of Priestley as Librarian and Director have been charged entirely to the Department of History. Both officers carried normal teaching loads and were in no way drones upon the instructional staff. The Bancroft Library, in more than a bookkeeping sense, got their services gratis. All told, therefore, the University's contribution to the upkeep of the library has been considerably in excess of the amount that shows on the books.

On behalf of the library, the University has also been the recipient of numerous gifts. Chief of these, both in amount and in significance, has been the more than $50,000 with which the Native Sons of the Golden West have supported the fellowships. No fraternal order in the country has surpassed this freehanded and effective patronage of local or regional history. Numerous gifts of materials have been received, and on other occasions the library has been enabled to acquire rare books or manuscripts by donations ranging from $200 or $300 to $3,500. These gifts were usually "for specific purposes of interest to the donor," yet advantageous to the library. Casting no aspersions upon the individual donors, whose generosity deserves high praise, it may still be remarked that Bancroft's initial gift far exceeds the grand total of all subsequent monetary contributions.[31]

---

[31] *Ibid.* I exclude from the reckoning some $30,000 advanced by Regent Sidney M. Ehrman for the publication of the documentary history of early California, nearly all of which has been repaid through sales of the publications, and some $6,000, advanced by him on the same basis to finance the editing of the Carondelet and other Louisiana papers in the library. The

Most of these gifts were solicited; most of them answered recognized needs in the library which the University would have striven somehow to meet. It is appropriate, therefore, to consider them, along with the moneys directly appropriated and the heavy costs indirectly absorbed, as elements in the University's support. Its administration has been economical, certainly a desirable feature in a state institution, but it can be defended against accusations of parsimony.

As suggested above, the University has altered the definition of the Bancroft field. Negatively, it has shorn off most of the northern and eastern parts of the half-continent area on which he collected. Perhaps this was inevitable—it may even have been wise. The pulsations of development in western North America have proceeded so rapidly in recent decades that comprehensive coverage of the entire area would have required a larger budget and more commodious quarters than have been available. On the positive side, the University has extended the field of collecting to colonial South America and has intensified it with regard to Mexico, both colonial and national. This has been the program most actively pushed, and it has given rise to the impression that the Bancroft Library is essentially Latin American. Actually, the Library has a long way to go before it can lay claim to adequacy on the southern continent. As to Mexico, the situation is more favorable; but the real strength of the collection—its central core now, as in Bancroft's day—is on California. Certainly that is where the Library's resources are the richest, and, in the light of California's continued preëminence in the West, it appears that locally centered regional history is still the Bancroft Library's best opportunity.

In the selection of men to take charge the University has

---

loan feature does not impugn these advances as benefactions, but the books carry no indication of Bancroft Library issuance or sponsorship and must be assumed to be publications of the University of California Press and the Regents.

been uncommonly wise. As first custodian Teggart was the logical choice and served the library well. Stephens, as has been indicated, followed with a dynamic contribution. Then, for a quarter century which constituted its Golden Age, the library was headed by Bolton as Director and Priestley as Librarian. Bolton was most effective in stimulating the prosecution of research and in representing the library to the public. Priestley contributed in these two functions and also assumed responsibility for the detailed management of the library's operations. Each was a man of eminence and strongly individualized, yet for the needs of the library the talents of each ideally supplemented the other's, and they got on together remarkably well. The spirit of camaraderie was admirably illustrated at the time of Bolton's retirement from the directorship in 1940. Priestley, returning from a journey by rail, bribed the porter to let him have a plaque to hang on Bolton's door, "Quiet is requested for those who have retired."[32]

Priestley, who succeeded to the directorship for a prospective five-year term, was soon struck down by illness which forced him to take leave of absence, and, early in 1944, resulted in his death. In the emergency Bolton was called back to resume the directorship, ably assisted by Mrs. Eleanor Bancroft, who through long experience has come to know the intricacies of the collection better than anyone else. The high esteem in which Priestley was held by all who had made use of the Bancroft Library was quickly manifested in the establishment of a memorial to him, an endowment fund for the purchase of significant books and manuscripts. Soon after the opening of the lists, more than a hundred friends of the library and its librarian had entered their names and contributed several thousand dollars. The ultimate benefits of this gesture are incalculable.

A fundamental feature of the University's policy with re-

[32] As related by Priestley in conversation with the writer.

gard to the Bancroft has been to commit it to historians, specialists in research and in the training of researchers in the field of western America, rather than to experts in library method. Observe, by way of illustration, Priestley somewhat facetiously greeting Archibald Macleish of the Library of Congress: "We should know each other. We are heads of the two greatest libraries in the country, and neither of us is a trained librarian."[33] In the Bancroft this policy certainly has borne rich fruit, for the library has flourished and has become a center of scholarly investigation.

In the course of the decades at Berkeley, furthermore, the library has undergone a remarkable appreciation in value. A dealer is reputed to have appraised it at $3,000,000; and Director Bolton has said that with $10,000,000 and twenty years in which to spend it the collection could not be duplicated or satisfactorily replaced.[34] These figures are not to be taken literally, but as symbolizing a substantial rise in value. Whatever the actual increase, only a small fraction is attributable to accessions. Nor is it all owing to the rising market in Californiana. For the most part it is due to the improved integration of the collection and more especially to the use of the materials in scholarly research. A research library is one of the few things in the world that is enhanced in value by use. Its materials are used without being consumed, and they emerge better known and more highly esteemed. Paradoxically, therefore, the University has been recompensed fabulously for all that it has spent to operate and maintain the Bancroft as a working library.

Astute businessman that he was, Hubert Howe Bancroft would certainly have taken great pleasure in this outcome. Doubtless he would have liked it still better if the University had managed to provide the library with more conspicuous housing, ample in space and planned for efficient operations. Steps in this direction are in prospect as part of the postwar

[33] *Ibid.* [34] In conversation with the writer.

building program. Certainly he would have been appreciative if the Regents had set up a history professorship in the Bancroft field. In the fullness of time that also may come to pass. Meanwhile, Bancroft would have taken greater satisfaction, I am confident, in the vindication of his collecting for content and of his pioneering in the field of the Pacific states in their entirety. He would have been particularly gratified that his collecting and writing had set in motion a long train of scholarly investigations, expanding and improving upon his preliminary findings. So far as it has been informal and unpretentious, unhackneyed, zealous in the pursuit of factual information, and, above all, productive, the library has been a prolongation of Bancroft's own career and the most suitable monument that could be erected in his honor.

Index

Academy of Pacific Coast History, 396–398
Acapulco, 26
Adams, Charles Francis, 149
Adams, Henry, 150
Alaska: Indians, 126–128; history, 201–204, 228–230
Alemany, Archbishop, 88
Andrade, José María, library of, 74–77, 90, 169
Antiquities, Indian, 134–135
Appleton, D., and Company, 147, 280–281
Archives, Spanish and Mexican, Bancroft's neglect of, 73–74, 84–85, 169, 199–200
Ashburner, William, 355
Aspinwall (Colón), 22
Astor, John Jacob, 316, 322
Avery, Benjamin P., 142
Ayer, Dr. Washington, resolution of, 344

Bachman, Charles, 62
Baker, E. D., 222, 390
Baker, R. S., 320
Balboa, Vasco Nuñez de, 161
Baldwin, E. J., 316, 321–322
Bancroft, Albert L.: ability, 46–47, 66, 388; mentioned, 301
Bancroft, Mrs. Albert L., 117
Bancroft, A. L., and Company, stationers, 46–47; successor to H. H. Bancroft and Company, 51–55; business of, 57–66; letter from, 294–295; reorganization of, 311–312. *See also* Bancroft, H. H., and Company
Bancroft, Azariah, 4
Bancroft, Azariah Ashley: in Ohio, 5–6; goes to California, 6, 16; in the mines, 33–36; at Fort Simcoe, 49; invited to San Francisco, 49
Bancroft Brothers, 311–312
Bancroft Building (721 Market Street): erection of, 51–53; described, 58–65; fire in, 78–79; accident in, 299; fire destroys, 301–312, 351; rebuilt, 310–312
Bancroft, Charles E., 60

Bancroft Company. *See* Bancroft, H. H., and Company
Bancroft, Curtis, 33, 36
Bancroft, Mrs. Eleanor, 405
Bancroft, Mrs. Emily Ketchum: marriage, 44–45; travels, 47–48, 71–74; death, 52
Bancroft, George, 281
Bancroft, Griffing, 383
Bancroft, Harlow P., 61
Bancroft, Hubert Howe: interest of, in books, 1; identified with the West, 1–2; ancestry, 3–6; birth, 6; Puritan upbringing, 7–11; schooling, 12; employed in bookstore, 13–16; goes to California, 17–29; in San Francisco, 32–33, 36; in the mines, 33–36; at Crescent City, 37–39; visits States, 39–40; opens bookstore, 41–44; first marriage, 44–45, 52; travels, 47–48, 55, 71–74; considers retiring, 48, 54, 56; erects building, 51–53; business house of, 57–66; collector, 67–85, 146–147; undertakes history writing, 86–98; uses assistants, 91, 99–114, 119, 127, 131, 253–277, 331–337; descriptions of, 114–116, 330, 378–379; second marriage, 116–117; studies Indians, 118–139; gets publicity, 140–144; eastern tour, 144–152; engages publisher, 147–148; arranges reviews, 152–156; historian of Spanish America, 157–181; trip to Mexico, 173; historian of California, 182–200; bibliographer, 190–191, 248–250; historian of neighboring states, 201–230; essayist, 231–252, 367–376; theory of history, 248; autobiography, 250–252; writing habits, 251–252; process of authorship, 253–277, 331–337; others' criticisms of, 268, 273–277, 325, 330–348, 380–381; as an employer, 273–275; marketing the *Works*, 278–300; fire loss of, 301–312; subscription publisher, 313–329; libel suit against, 337–340, 348; sale of library, 349–365; retirement, 366–381; later writings, 367–376; scrapbook for Philip, 375–376; anecdotes about, 376–379; president of Pacific Coast Branch, 380; death, 382–383; eulogies of, 382–385; later appraisals of, 385–390; compliments Priestley, 398; library a monument to, 406–407
Bancroft, H. H., and Company: establishment, 42–44; growth, 45–55; installed in Bancroft Building, 51–54; renamed A. L. Bancroft and Company, 54; departments, 57–66; book publishing, 59, 63–64, 157–252; sales program, 278–300; disastrous fire, 301–312; tributes to, 307–308; reorganized, 311–312
Bancroft, John, 3
Bancroft, Kate, 52, 117, 144, 383
Bancroft Library: beginnings, 67–68; growth, 69–78, 80–85; installed on fifth floor, 78; endangered by fire, 78–79, 392–393; moved to Valencia Street, 79–80; newspaper holdings, 80; manuscript holdings, 80–81, 188–190; described, 81–82; indexing materials of, 91–98; a working library, 104; wealth of materials in, 185–190, 351–355, 358–363; Royce in, 272;

sale of, 349–365; appraisals of, 355–356, 360–363, 406; later development, 391–407; gifts to, 403–405; a monument to Bancroft, 406–407
Bancroft, Lucy, daughter, 383
Bancroft, Lucy, granddaughter, 377–378
Bancroft, Lucy Howe, 5–6, 8, 49
Bancroft, Mary, 49
Bancroft, Mrs. Matilda Coley Griffing, marriage of, 116–117, 263
Bancroft, Paul, 377, 383
Bancroft, Philip, 375–376, 383
Bancroft, Samuel, 3
Bancroft, Tabitha, 4
Bancroft, Will B.: employed, 63; printer, 311–312; libel suit of, 337–340, 348
Bancroft-Whitney Company, establishment of, 311–312
Baranof, Alexander, 229
Barber, John B., 354
Barker, Eugene C.: book by, 177; quoted, 386–387
Barnes, John C., 41–42
Barry, T. A., book by, 64
Barton, John, 317
Bates, Alfred, writings of, 262–263, 320
Bear Flag episode, 184, 340–342; resolution on, 345
Beatty, Patrick, killed in fire, 303, 306
Bell, Horace, quoted, 320–321, 325
Bibliography, Bancroft's contribution to, 190–191, 234
Bierce, Ambrose: excoriates Bancroft, 268, 299, 328, 330, 332–333; quoted, 340; eclipsed, 390
Billings, Frederick, 316
Biographies: in Pioneer Register, 195–198; in *Chronicles,* 313–329
Blake, Isaac Elder, 317
Bliss, Porter C.: assists Bancroft, 145–148; promises review, 149–150
Boalt, John A., 355
Bolton, Herbert Eugene: book on Kino by, 177; request to Bancroft Library for material, 394; work of, 399–400, 403, 405; quoted, 406
Book of the Fair, The, 326–329
Book of Wealth, The, 326, 329
Bowman, A., 262–263
Brannan, James, killed in fire, 303, 306
Brannan, Sam, 31
Brasseur de Bourbourg, 136–137
Brewer, William H., book by, 145
British Columbia, history of, 201–204, 217–220, 226–228, 230

Brown, Edwin, 62
Browne, J. Ross: visits library, 142; review by, 154–155, 332
Bryant, William Cullen, 150; quoted, 151
Buffalo, New York, Bancroft at, 13–16
Bynum, Lindley, 402

California: Panama route to, 17–29; coast described, 27–29; Bancroft's career in, 32–39, 41–66, and *passim;* Indians, 129–130; history, 180–200, 231–252; materials on, 185–190, 249–250
California Hall: described, 392; library in, 393, 397–398
California Inter Pocula, 197–198, 234–237, 386
California Pastoral, 197–198, 231–234, 386
California Pioneers, Society of: charges by, 340–348; ridiculed, 374
Calvary Presbyterian Church, 45
Carlyle, Thomas, quoted, 151
Carondelet papers, 394
Caughey, John Walton, writings of, 194, 200
Central America: history, 119–120, 159–168; Indians, 130–133, 137–138; *History of,* reviewed, 139; materials on, 248–249
Cerruti, Enrique, 110–112; articles by, 143; collector, 251
Chagres, 22
Channing, Edward, 281
Chapman, Charles Edward: book by, 193–194; quoted, 386; to Berkeley, 399
Chávez, Ezequiel A., 393
Chittenden, Hiram M., book by, 219
Chronicles of the Builders, subscriptions to, 296–298; analysis of, 313–325
Church, Moses J., 317
Civil War, effects of, 47, 65
Cleland, Robert Glass, book by, 193–194
Coblentz, Stanton A., book by, 246
Coleman, H. R., 58
Coleman, William T., 88; book dedicated to, 239; heads vigilantes, 243–245; biography of, 316, 321–322
Collecting: Bancroft's work in, 67–85; Bancroft's theory of, 83
Colley, F. A., 58
Colorado, history of, 201–204, 212–213, 230
Columbian Exposition, Chicago, 326–329
Comstock Lode, 206–207
Cooke, George W., 63
Cooke, William B., 36, 39, 53
Cooney, Joseph T., reporter, 339

Coöperative writing of history, 269–273
Cortés, Hernán, characterized, 170–171
Cowan, Robert Ernest, collection of, 67, 401
Craig, D. W., 83–84
Crescent City, Bancroft at, 37–39
Crocker, Charles, 2, 316
Cronise, Titus Fey, book by, 64, 250
Crowell and Fairfield, 38–39
Culture-area concept, Bancroft's use of, 125–126

Dana, Richard Henry, Jr., book by, 27, 186
Darwin, Charles, 150; quoted, 151
Davidson, George, 142, 355
Davis, Washington, 319
Davis, W. W. H., book by, 179
Deady, Matthew P., 321
Derby, George H.: employs Bancroft, 13–16, 33, 187; death, 36
Derby, Mrs. George H., 39, 41
De Voto, Bernard, quoted, 275, 387
Díaz, Porfirio, 173–174
Dorland, T. A. C., cashier, 62, 388; missing in fire, 306; testimony of, 339
Downey, John G., biography of, 320–321
Doyle, John S., 355
Draper, John W., 149; quoted, 151, 157
Dulles, Foster Rhea, 370
Dunne, Peter M., books by, 177
Dwinelle, John W., 88

Easton, Wendell, 317
Eldorado, Taylor's, 27–28, 186
Eldredge, Zoeth Skinner, 193, 199
Emerson, Ralph Waldo, visited, 146, 148
Encyclopedia, Pacific states, 87–90, 142, 254
Evans, A. S., book by, 64

Failing, Joseph, 322
Fair, Pacific states, Bancroft urges, 327–328
Farwell, J. D., letter of, 310
Farwell, W. B., charges by, 340–348
Faulkner, R. D., agent, 293–294
Field, Stephen J., 316, 321
Fischer collection, 76

Fisher, Walter M., 112; arranges review, 153–155; writings of, 257, 262–263
Fleisher, Robert, 306
Footnotes, Bancroft's use of, 161, 209
Fort Simcoe, Bancroft's father at, 6, 50
Fowler, Edwin W., agent, 320–321
Freeman, Daniel C., 317, 322
Frémont, John C., 2, 184, 354; *Report* of, 186; Bancroft's treatment of, 340–346
Fur trade, Bancroft's history of, 219–220

Galán, Carlos F., 102–103
García Icazbalceta, Joaquín, 88
Garnett, W. H., 397
Gayley, Charles Mills, praises library, 357
George, Henry, 390
"Georgia," steamship, 21–22
Gilly, F. A., agent, 290–291
Gilman, Daniel Coit: visits library, 142; review by, 153–155, 332, 350
Gilpin, William, 322
Gird, Richard, 321
Goddard, P. E., 394
Godkin, E. L., 149
Goldschmidt, Albert, 113; assists reviewers, 153; writings of, 257, 262–263
Gorgona, 23
Graff, R. W., 62
Grant, U. S., 343
Granville, Ohio: Bancroft's boyhood at, 6–11, 12; notes on, 375–376
Gray, Asa, 145
Gray, Nathaniel, 317
Griffin, G. B., writings of, 262–263
Gunnison, Lieut. J. W., 210
Guthrie, the Rev. W. K., 383

Hale, Edward Everett, 150
Hall, Frederick, book by, 64
Hambly, H. B., memorandum of, 321–322
Hamilton, Edward H., 383
Hanna, Phil Townsend, quoted, 197–198, 386
Haraszthy, Agoston, 343, 347
Harcourt, T. Arundel, 103, 112–113; arranges review, 153–155; writings of, 257, 262–264, 275
Harrison, Ralph C., 355

Hart, Albert Bushnell, editor, 271; quoted, 391–392
Harte, Francis Bret: story by, 187; eclipsed, 390
Hatch, Augustus T., 317
Havana, Cuba, described, 21–22
Hayes, Benjamin, collection of, 80
Helps, Sir Arthur, 150, 159
Higginson, Thomas Wentworth, 149; quoted, 152
Hilgard, E. W., 354
Hillyer, Edgar, 12
History Building, construction of, 310–312
Hittell, John S., 88, 113
Hittell, Theodore H., book by, 193, 199, 250, 333
Hoffman, Ogden, 88, 355
Hofmann, J. A., 59
Holden, Edward S., 352
Holmes, Oliver Wendell, 150; quoted, 151
Hopkins, Moses, 322
Horton, Alonzo Erasmus, 322
Houghton, H. O., and Company, 147, 280
Howe, Curtis, 5
Howe, Ephraim, 5
Howe, John, 4–5
Howells, William Dean, 149–150
Howison, George H., 354
Hudson's Bay Company, 216, 219, 224, 227
Humboldt, Alexander von: collection of, 76; mentioned, 132
Hunt, George W., 321
Hunt, Jonathan, 42, 44, 46
Hunt, Rockwell D.: quoted, 276; paper by, 380–381
Huntington, Collis P., biography of, 316, 324–325
Huntington, Dr. T. W., 383

Idaho, history of, 201–204, 215–217, 230
In These Latter Days, 367, 371, 373–375
Index of Bancroft's materials: devising of, 91–98, 100; use of, in writing of the *Works*, 255
Indians: written up in *Native Races*, 118–139; relations of whites with, 214–215, 221–223, 236–237

Jackson, Helen Hunt, 266
James, George Wharton, 394
Jones, Charles C., review by, 149

Jones, William Carey, 341, 354
Juárez, Benito, 172–173, 316, 321

Kearney, Dennis, 245
Kelsey, Rayner W., 395
Kenny, George L.: accompanies Bancroft, 17; in the mines, 35; salesman, 36, 39, 42, 43, 46, 60, 279, 388
King, Clarence, 144; review by, 150
King, James, of William, 242–246
King, Thomas Starr, 390
Kip, William Ingraham, 354
Knight, William H.: book by, 64, 67; and the beginning of the library, 67, 78, 86
Kroeber, A. L., 125–126

Lane, Joseph, 222
Languages, Indian, 133–134
Latham, R. G., 150
Lecky, W. E. H., 150
Lick, James, 390
Lincoln-Roosevelt League, 9, 325, 372
Linn, W. A., book by, 211
List and Francke, auction, 74–76
Little, the Rev. Jacob, 375
Locke, Dean J., 321
London, bookstores of, 69–72, 74
Long Bar, 33–36
Longfellow, Henry Wadsworth, 148–149, 150; quoted, 151
Lowell, James Russell: visited, 148; quoted, 151

McAllister, Hall, 355
McKinley, William, praise of, 368
McLoughlin, John, 219, 221
McMaster, John Bach, 80, 281
Macleish, Archibald, 406
Maloney, J. J., losses of, in fire, 305–306
Manuscript materials: Bancroft's collection of, 80–81; Bancroft's use of, 188–190
Marsh, John, 2, 343, 347
Mayer, Brantz, 142
Mecham, J. Lloyd, book by, 177
Medina, José Toribio, 278

Merrill, Annis, 321
Mexico: Indians, 130–138; history, 168–177, 367–368; materials on, 249; sales campaign in, 299–300
Mid-Winter Exposition, San Francisco, 327–328
Miller, Henry, 316
Miller, Joaquin, 390
Modern Fallacies, 372
Modoc War, 223, 236–237
Montana: history, 201–204, 215–217, 230; Bancroft criticized in, 293–295
Monterey, described, 28
Montgomery, John B., 31
Morgan, John S., 317
Morgan, Lewis H., Bancroft's disagreement with, 139, 246
Mormon War, 210
Mormons: in Nevada, 205; in Utah, 208–212
Morrill, W. P., 53, 63
Morris, William A., article by, 266–267, 380–381
Moses, Bernard, 159, 354
Mythology, Indian, 133

Native Races: plan and execution, 118–139; launching, 140–156; reviews, 150–156; authorship, 257, 262–263; promotion, 282–283
Native Sons of the Golden West, fellowships, 399–400, 402, 403
Nemos, William, 103, 105–107; assists reviewers, 153–154; directs indexers, 253; work of, 257, 259–265, 320
Nevada, history of, 201–208, 230
Nevins, Allan, 346
New Mexico: Indians, 130; history, 177–180
New Pacific, The, 367–370
Newark, Ohio, 9
Newkirk, John, sketch of, 113
Newspapers: Bancroft's collection of, 80; Bancroft's use of, 167; Bancroft's opinion of, 243–244
Nordhoff, Charles, 149
Northwest Coast: Indians, 127–129; history, 180, 201–204, 217–220, 230
Nugent, John, 243

Oak, Henry L., librarian, 91–92, 255, 257; trains indexers, 95; sketch of, 103–105; articles by, 143; assists reviewers, 153–155; writings of, 257, 261–265, 345; claims authorship, 266; reports censorship, 296; discusses sales methods, 296–298; cuts salary, 311; on the *Chronicles,* 325; threats by, 331–337, 348

"Ohio," steamship, 19–21
Old age, Bancroft's comment on, 374–375
Oregon, history of, 201–204, 217–224, 230
Osmurt, H. C., agent, 290
Overland Monthly, 112, 142–143; Oak's articles in, 143; review in, 153–155, 332; editorship of, 259; Farwell's article in, 341

Pacific Coast Branch, American Historical Association: Bancroft elected president of, 380–381; obituary notice by, 384–385
Pacific Mail Steamship Company, 19, 23–29
Pacific Ocean in History, The, 370
Palfrey, J. G., 146, 148
Palmer, Harlow, death of, 36
Palmer, Mrs. Harlow, 44
Palóu, Francisco de, book by, 186, 249
Panama, described, 23–24
"Panama," steamship, 24–29
Panama route, to California, 18–29
Paris, book buying in, 72, 74
Parkman, Francis, 149, 281; review by, 150
Patten, B. A., book by, 64
Peatfield, J. J., 113; writings of, 262–264, 296
Pedrarias Dávila, 161
Person, F., 60
Petroff, Ivan, 113–114; writings of, 262–263
Phelps, Alonzo, book by, 64, 250, 314
Phillips, Wendell: visited, 148; quoted, 151
Pierre and His Family, 2
Pioneer Register and Index, 195–198, 202, 313
Pirates, Bancroft's accounts of, 163–165
Plymouth Company, 34–36
Pomeroy, Theodore S., 39
Popular Tribunals, 237–246; changes in, 347
Porter, Benjamin K., 317
Pratt, Gerard, 4
Pratt, Judge O. C.: account of, in *History of Oregon,* revised, 296–297, 343, 347; life of, 323–324
Prescott, William H., 118, 132, 159, 170, 174
Priestley, Herbert Ingram: books by, 177, 398; work of, 399, 403–405; memorial fund, 405; quoted, 406
Primitive history, 135–137
Prince, L. Bradford, book by, 179

Publishing, Bancroft's activity in, 59, 63–64, and *passim*
Pullman, George M., 319

Railroad, transcontinental, effect of, 54
Ralston, William C., 390
Ramírez, José Fernando, collection of, 76–77, 80, 169
Ream, Daniel, 321
Resurgam, 370
Retrospection, 371–373
Reviews: of *Central America,* 139, 166; of *Native Races,* 150–156
Rich Bar, 33, 35–36
Richards, Franklin D., 265
Riesenberg, Felix, 370
Riordan, Bishop P. W., 354
Ripley, George, 149
Robertson, James R., 394, 395
Robinson, Alfred, 187, 249
Rowell, J. C., 354; library appraised by, 355–356, 360; on commission, 396
Royce, Josiah, 270; in Bancroft Library, 272

Sacramento, Bancroft at, 33
San Diego: visited by Bancroft in 1852, 27; again visited, 308; his property in, 310
San Francisco: Bancroft's arrival at, 28–29; described, 30–33; Bancroft's bookstore in, 41–66, and *passim;* founding of, 233–234; vigilance committees of, 237–246; problems of, 370–374
Sanborn, F. G., 61
Sargent, A. A., 355
Savage, Thomas, 107–108; work of, 261–263, 264, 320
Sawyer, Lorenzo, 321, 355
Scannell, Chief, San Francisco Fire Department, 303–307
Scherer, James A. B.: on the vigilantes, 246; on Frémont, 346
Scott, Irving M., 316–317, 321
Scott, the Rev. W. A.: books by, 63; hanged in effigy, 245
Serra, Fray Junípero, 316, 321
Seville, archives in, 73–74
Shuck, Oscar, book by, 64
Simonton, James W., 88
Simpson, Asa Mead, 317
Simpson, Dr. William S., 344
Sisson, George H., 316, 322
Smith, Don: translator, 361; teaching fellow, 395

Smith, James H., 53, 63
Smith, Justin S., book by, 177
Smithsonian Institution, 77
Some Cities and San Francisco, 370–371
Spain, book buying in, 73
Spanish America, history of, 157–181
Spanish borderlands, history of, 180–181
Spence, E. F., 321
Spencer, Herbert, 150; quoted, 151
Sperry, Austin, 317
Spofford, A. R., quoted, 151
Squier, E. G.: collection of, 76; promises aid, 88
Squire, Watson C., 321
Stanford, Leland, 2; order for Bancroft's *Works* cancelled by, 297–298; biography of, 323; university endowed by, 390
Stebbins, Horatio, 354–355
Stephens, Henry Morse: urges purchase of library, 358–365; pallbearer, 383; eulogy by, 383–384; library praised by, 393–394; named director, 394–395; on commission, 396; founds Academy, 396, 398; death, 398; work of, 398–399
Stevens, Henry, bookdealer, 77, 279
Stevens, Isaac Ingalls, 225
Stockton, Robert C., 342, 346
Stone, F. P., 59
Stone, Nathan Jonas, sales manager, 284–300, 311; telegram from, 308
Sullivan, Jeremiah F., 321
Sutro, Adolph, 390
Sutter, Johann A., 342, 346
Swett, John R., 103, 355

Tabor, H. A. W., 316
Taussig, Rudolph J.: interested in library, 359–360; pallbearer, 383; on commission, 396
Taylor, Bayard, book by, 27–28, 186
Taylor, George, 370
Teaching fellows: introduction of, 395; work of, 397
Teggart, Frederick J.: library purchase urged by, 357–365; work of, 393–397
Terry, David S.: arrest of, 244; Bancroft's criticisms of, 343, 347–348
Texas, history of, 172, 174–177
Thwaites, Reuben Gold, editor, 278, 282; library appraised by, 360–363; Stephens nominated by, 395

Towne, Alban N., 322
Turnbull, Walter, 53, 63
Turnbull and Smith, printers, 53, 62
Tuthill, Franklin, book by, 64, 141, 250
Twain, Mark, 150–151, 187
Twitchell, Ralph Emerson, book by, 179
Tylor, E. B., 150

Underground Railroad, 8
University of California: offers to house library, 79; purchases library, 350–365; Bancroft's prediction for, 373; library policy of, 391–407
Utah, history of, 201–204, 208–212, 230

Vallejo, Mariano Guadalupe, 31, 79, 81; Bancroft aided by, 111, 251
Vanderbilt, Cornelius, 316, 321
Van Loon, Willem, 370
Victor, Mrs. Frances Fuller, 108–110; writings of, 261–266, 274, 324, 385; claims authorship, 266; suggests biographies, 295; information from, 380
Villagrá, Gaspar de, book by, 177, 179

Wagner, Henry Raup: book by, 218; quoted, 401
Walden, Joseph, 72
Walker, Franklin, quoted, 387
Walker, William, 165–166
Warner, Charles Dudley, 149–151
Warner, J. J., 88
Warren, Frances Emory, 322
Washington, history of, 201–204, 217–220, 224–226, 230
Waterman, Robert Whitney, 321
Wheeler, Benjamin Ide: interested in library, 357–365; aids library, 391; chooses Stephens, 394–395; on commission, 396
Wheeler, Charles S., 383
Whitaker, J., bookdealer, 72, 75–76, 279
Whitney, Sumner, 311–312
Whittier, John Greenleaf, visited, 148–149
Why a World Centre, 371
Whymper, Frederick, 142
Williams, Mary, book by, 246
Winsor, Justin, and coöperative writing, 269–270
Wissler, Clark, 125–126
Works, Bancroft's: beginnings, 86–98; plan, 157–159, 201–204; process of authorship, 91, 99–114, 119, 127, 131, 253–277; description and analysis

Works, Bancroft's (*Continued*)–
of, 118–139, 157–252; reviews of, 140–156, 166; marketing of, 278–300; Oak's estimate of, 331–334; criticism of, 331–348, 380–381; measure of, 346–348
Wyoming, history of, 201–204, 214–215, 230

Yale University, 379
Young, Brigham, 88–89, 210–211